Praise for *Cosmic Scholar*

"Szwed has ably shaped [Smith's] chaos . . . A mammoth recording of Smith's movements."
—Sasha Frere-Jones, *Bookforum*

"This biography argues persuasively that Smith's contributions to art, anthropology, avant-garde film, and, most of all, popular music were profound."
—*The New Yorker*

"[A] masterful feat . . . of reconstruction, and long overdue."
—Michael Casper, *The Baffler*

"[Szwed] assiduously and passionately constructed this engrossing, re-velatory, often beyond-belief portrait of a reckless, maddening, cosmic, and transformational genius."
—Donna Seaman, *Booklist* (starred review)

"Szwed, as lively a writer as he is scrupulous, has produced an excellent and engaging biography, the story of an elusive but important and ut-terly fascinating figure."
—David Keymer, *Library Journal* (starred review)

"In this vividly detailed biography, music scholar Szwed brilliantly cap-tures the life and legacy of the enigmatic . . . Harry Smith."
—*Publishers Weekly* (starred review)

"Szwed, piece by obscure piece, masterfully puts [Harry Smith's] puzzle of a life together . . . A revelatory portrait of a unique pop-culture figure."
—*Kirkus Reviews*

"Harry Smith did more than compile the world's most influential mixtape; he was a polymath . . . This biography transforms facts into magic-laced storytelling—which is what Smith was all about."
—Will Hermes, author of *Lou Reed: The King of New York*

courtesy of the author

JOHN SZWED

COSMIC SCHOLAR

John Szwed is the author or editor of nineteen books, including biographies of Billie Holiday, Miles Davis, Sun Ra, and Alan Lomax. He has received fellowships from the Guggenheim Foundation and the Rockefeller Foundation, and in 2005 he was awarded a Grammy for *Doctor Jazz*, a book included with the album *Jelly Roll Morton: The Complete Library of Congress Recordings by Alan Lomax*. A former professor of anthropology, African American studies, and film studies for twenty-six years at Yale University, he was also a professor of music and jazz studies at Columbia University and served as the chair of the Department of Folklore and Folklife at the University of Pennsylvania.

COSMIC SCHOLAR

COSMIC SCHOLAR

THE LIFE AND TIMES OF
HARRY SMITH

John Szwed

PICADOR

FARRAR, STRAUS AND GIROUX

New York

Picador
120 Broadway, New York 10271

Grateful acknowledgment is made for permission to reprint the lyrics from
"His Tapes Roll On," reprinted with the permission of Peter Stampfel.

The Library of Congress has cataloged the Farrar, Straus and Giroux
hardcover edition as follows:
Names: Szwed, John F., 1936– author.
Title: Cosmic scholar : the life and times of Harry Smith / John Szwed.
Description: First edition. | New York : Farrar, Straus and Giroux, 2023.
   Includes bibliographical references and index.
Identifiers: LCCN 2023008707 | ISBN 9780374282240 (hardcover)
Subjects: LCSH: Smith, Harry Everett, 1923–1991. | Artists—United
   States—Biography. | Beats (Persons)—Biography. | Motion picture
   producers and directors—United States—Biography. | Anthropologists—
   United States—Biography. | Anthology of American folk music.
Classification: LCC CT275.S5429 S97 2023 | DDC 791.4302/33092—
   dc23/eng/20230331
LC record available at https://lccn.loc.gov/2023008707

Paperback ISBN: 978-1-250-33810-5

1   3   5   7   9   10   8   6   4   2

Frontispiece: Film frame from *Film No. 1: A Strange Dream*
(courtesy of and copyright Anthology Film Archives) and Harry Smith, circa
1965 (photograph by John Palmer, courtesy of the Harry Smith Archives)

For Raymond Foye and Rani Singh

CONTENTS

COSMIC SCHOLAR

Harry Smith: An Introduction

You don't know what you're up against.

—Harry Smith, to a student asking for help in writing a paper about him

I'm standing in the ruined shell of a nineteenth-century glass factory in Red Hook, the far fringes of Brooklyn, shards of glass crunching underfoot. Stacks of more than 120 shipping boxes surround me, enough to fill a small New York apartment, floor to ceiling. They contain the books and records of Harry Everett Smith, at least those that survived his life on the streets, in other people's homes, in rooms paid for by someone else. This building will soon be converted to artists' studios—ateliers, workshops where things are created, thoughts made visible: spaces that Smith never had in his life. But for now, it's a warehouse of Smithiana.

The first boxes I open are filled with what must be thousands of long-playing records: Library of Congress folk song albums, music of all the countries of the world. There are stacks of discs by Charlie Parker, Pink Floyd, Shel Silverstein, Thelonious Monk, Cajun singers and musicians, the Chieftains; there's Grand Ole Opry, church sermons, raunchy proto rap and comedy skits, New Orleans parades, bootleg Bob Dylan, square dance music, Alan Lomax's field recordings, bird songs, blues, and American Indian chants. In other boxes lie journals and magazines: runs of the *American Anthropologist*, *African Arts*, *American Bee Journal*, *Journal of the American Society for Psychical*

Research, Bio/Technology, Oral History, Blake Studies, Ancient Indian Tradition and Mythology, Nature, Howard the Duck, and dozens more.

The books are next, thousands of them, on folklore, linguistics, and ethnography, lots of Yates and Yeats, books on board and table games, Native Americans, dreaming, divination, apocrypha and pseudepigrapha, the Dogon, Santeria, beaches, spiders, Yoruba headgear, and histories of rain; children's books, Lewis Carroll, Leonardo da Vinci, cosmic plasma, effects of low-frequency magnetic and electric fields, Claude Lévi-Strauss's *The Origin of Table Manners: Mythologiques, Vol. 3*, a book on table setting for all occasions, concordances to Shakespeare and Faulkner . . . I have to stop opening these boxes. I feel as if I am entering Jorge Luis Borges's Library of Babel, a universe of books and records, or maybe a labyrinth of paper and vinyl, as there is no order, and the content is random and seemingly meaningless. The temptation is to read and listen to every one of them in hopes of at least finding the meaning behind Harry Smith the reader and listener. But then I might never be able to write my book. Or worse—maybe my book is in there, already written.

How did I get here? Who is Harry Smith? Why am I writing this book?

In the middle of my youth, I found myself straying from the true path. I'd just begun my first year of graduate study in anthropology, but I had somehow also wandered into an assistantship in English, another one at the same time in film studies, and at night I was playing jazz gigs. It seemed like a great idea, broadening my horizon, making money instead of going into debt, having fun; I wanted something more than classes in anthropology and I needed to explore those other worlds. Someone suggested I speak to Roy Harvey Pearce, a distinguished professor of English poetry at The Ohio State University, admired by students for his interests, which went well beyond those expected of a professor. He listened to my discontents, to my new-found enthusiasms for film and folk music, my fear of having to leave jazz behind, and when I finished, he bluntly suggested I forget about graduate school, move to Greenwich Village, and study with Harry Smith. Thing is, I'd never heard of Smith, but rather than admit it, I told the professor it was something I'd think about.

Even though I fancied myself as knowing the off-off-Broadway and music scenes in the Village, I'd never heard anyone mention Smith, nor had I run across his name in the *Village Voice*. When I asked around, the only person I found who knew of him was a folknik who told me that Harry Smith was a pseudonym for Alan Lomax, who'd produced some bootleg records of old country and blues songs.

Time passed, and I forgot all about whoever Smith was, completed a PhD in anthropology, and began teaching, until one day in 1965 I read in the *Voice* a piece that opened, "Does Harry Smith really exist?" It was Jonas Mekas, the godfather of American avant-garde cinema, introducing him to New York readers: "For years Harry Smith has been a black and ominous legend and a source of strange rumors. Some even said that he had left this planet long ago—the last alchemist of the Western world, the last magician." My curiosity fired up, I started looking for Smith. I was told that it wasn't Lomax who had produced those records, it was Harry Smith—a folklorist. No, he's a painter, said another. Harry could be found nightly among the artists at Stanley's or the Cedar Tavern, and currently at the Five Spot jazz bar, where Thelonious Monk had been playing for weeks. Someone said she'd heard that Smith had studied anthropology with Melville Jacobs at the University of Washington.

Now I was interested. Filmmaker, folklorist, painter, jazz aficionado, anthropologist . . . and I had also studied with Jacobs! Was this what Professor Pearce was trying to tell me? I'd even been at the Five Spot a few nights while Monk was playing, and now I was thinking I might even have seen Smith. He'd been described to me as a small, scraggly, old-before-his-time, ghostly presence and an alchemist (Rumpelstiltskin, someone called him), but also a panhandling drunk, a frequently homeless polymath of the streets and the flophouses who could discourse sagely on any subject, dropping names like Franz Boas, Alice Roosevelt Longworth, Dizzy Gillespie, Berenice Abbott, and Giordano Bruno. He always dressed in coat and tie (as did men among the Beats before Jack Kerouac brought lumberjack chic to the Village), but Harry's clothes were shabby, and the patches that covered holes in his coat were made of duct tape that had been inked and colored to match the pattern of the fabric. You couldn't miss him, they said. But I did.

And I wasn't the only one. When the man named Harry Everett Smith died in 1991, a memorial service was held at St. Mark's Church on the Bowery. On the program was a wild mix of speakers, performers, music, and film: a Gnostic Mass of the OTO (Ordo Templi Orientis), a spiritual order closely related to Aleister Crowley's religion of Thelema; music by the Fugs and the punk band False Prophets; a demonstration of the art of string figures; several of Smith's films, along with films about him made by Jonas Mekas and Robert Frank. Slides of Smith's paintings were projected, accompanied by some of his field recordings of Kiowa peyote songs. The speakers included Allen Ginsberg, Patti Smith, Dave Van Ronk, and a long string of mystics, film scholars, apocalyptic poets, Beat chroniclers, art gallery owners, a Smithsonian archivist, and a psychiatrist. Impressive it was, but almost no one there knew who all these other people were, or why they were there, just as they were unaware of all of Smith's activities and interests. Most people knew him as the creator of that anthology of old recordings, because it had already changed the trajectory of folk and rock. A few thought he was just a colorful if irascible Village art moocher or drunk, and they'd come that night out of curiosity. As the evening progressed and it became clear that he was an anthropologist, a pioneering filmmaker and multimedia artist, a painter, folklorist, poet, jazz scholar, collector, archivist, record producer, magician, translator, and hermetic alchemist, there was confusion: Could he be the same person they knew?

There is a belief among biographers that the bigger the name, the more versions of the person there are. Shakespeare, for example. As I've searched for Harry Smith among those who knew him, each has described a different person, depending on where and when they first met him, the interests they shared, or what they expected from him. Who he was often depended on the medium he was working in. Young filmmakers and animators offered to assist him in his work for nothing if he would teach them. Those who were more established, or at least infamous—like Andy Warhol, Terry Gilliam, Robert Frank, Kenneth Anger, and Jack Smith—were fascinated by what Smith was doing with animation, his painting on film, his innovative soundtracks, and his use of multiscreen imagery. Henry Geldzahler, the curator at the Metropolitan Museum of Art and the New York City commissioner of cultural affairs, who had helped push Andy Warhol to the front of the art world, had come to view Harry as a more serious filmmaker than Andy and helped fund Smith's opus, *Mahagonny*. Musicians such as Bob Dylan, Philip Glass, Leonard Cohen, Patti Smith, Percy Heath, the Fugs, Jefferson Airplane, and the Grateful Dead all sought his company.

His work as an anthologist of recordings is still his greatest claim to public recognition. The *Anthology of American Folk Music*, his six-LP collection of lost commercial recordings of American folk music, was essential to the folk music revival, and even to the shape of American music in the decades to come. It was the Rosetta stone of music for the writers who were reinventing popular music criticism. Lucy Sante, Amanda Petrusich, Robert Christgau, Sean Wilentz, John Jeremiah Sullivan, and Greil Marcus all found in these recordings and

Smith's notes to them a new way to think about the history of American music. The voices and lyrics of Smith's *Anthology* are for Marcus a point of entry into an alternate, darker, and more complex history of the country, the "old, weird America." But few of his admirers knew that he had done field and studio recordings of an enormous range of music and sound, including shape-note singers, folk ballads from Oklahoma, blues, street singers, Jewish songs in Hebrew, Yiddish, and Arabic, avant-garde music and punk bands, and some of the earliest recordings of acoustic environments; or that he had recorded Beat poets like Gregory Corso and Allen Ginsberg. Harry was also a student and collector of the oldest and most widely practiced folk arts, such as string figures, and some of the newer, like paper airplanes. He is said to have been the first to create light shows with music in nightclubs and dance halls.

As a painter, Smith brought elements of the Kabbalah and Northwest Coast Native American aesthetics to his work, and contributed new materials to surrealism (though unlike other surrealists who were enamored with Northwest Coast art, Harry had an intimate understanding of that tradition, and had not merely seen it in museums). He even created paintings that visually transcribed recordings of jazz, with each brushstroke representing a note or chord, something so unique (and difficult) that it has never been tried again. When he later produced a painted rendering of the language of angels that had been revealed to the Elizabethan mystics John Dee and Edward Kelley, it was hard to believe that this was the same artist. It was for these works and his nonobjective paintings on film that Harry was given financial support from the Guggenheim Memorial Foundation.

Smith's least-known accomplishments are his studies of Native American culture and philosophy, and of the occult. His knowledge of magic and mysticism, ancient and worldwide, was substantial enough that he served as an adviser to a number of the famous, including Tennessee Williams, Jackie Gleason, and a co-inventor of the helicopter, Arthur M. Young. His anthropological research among

Native Americans began when he was a teenager, when he traveled alone to the reservations of the Lummi and the Swinomish in Washington and was permitted to photograph, sketch, paint, and record their language, songs, dances, and rituals, something no non-Native had ever been allowed to do. Soon he was communicating with anthropologists at several universities and was the subject of local and national newspaper and magazine accounts that applauded his phonetic renderings of Native American languages, his musical transcriptions, and his development of his own methods of describing dances. Before he finished high school, he had excavated mounds, salvaged carved and painted longhouse poles, and begun compiling a dictionary of Puget Sound Native American languages. His work was donated to museums, but lack of proper preservation and documentation has sometimes resulted in scholars and the public alike not knowing it was Smith who did the work.

Though Harry Smith remains largely unknown, his existing work is not hard to find. His films were first shown more than sixty years ago at the San Francisco Museum of Art (now the San Francisco Museum of Modern Art) and are now in the collections of the Museum of Modern Art, the British Film Institute, the Cinémathèque Française, and the Getty, as well as other museum and university collections across the world. They've been shown at the Whitney, the Kennedy Center, the Louvre, the Pompidou, and the Venice Biennale, as well as in folk and jazz clubs.

Smith's murals once adorned the walls of San Francisco jazz clubs, and what's left of his other paintings are now in the collections of a number of museums and the Anthology Film Archives, in New York; his art could be seen on 1950s "underground" greeting cards, lobby tiles in buildings, and cover designs for books by Aleister Crowley and Allen Ginsberg. The impact of his animations was evident in Terry Gilliam's work for TV and film. The *Anthology of American Folk Music* is still available seventy years later, and concerts based on its songs have been performed by some of the best-known musicians in the United

States and Europe. His Native American recordings, ethnographic, and archeological works are housed in museums across the country. Smith's name echoes throughout the history of the Beats and the hippies, and his face was seen by thousands every night for a month on electronic Times Square billboards along with those of Bob Dylan, Lou Reed, and Edie Sedgwick as samples of Andy Warhol's screen tests. He is the only person whose works are in both the United States National Recording Registry and the National Film Registry.

Who was this man, this omnipresent and impactful but shadowy Village figure? How did he survive when he diligently avoided any kind of work for pay? He had cut himself off from his family after his midtwenties, was never forthcoming about his past, and even his later life was hard to fathom. Was Harry gay, straight, or what? (He boasted that he might be the only person on earth who had never had sex, but he also said he had a son by a torch singer in San Francisco.) You could never tell with Harry, everyone said.

How are we to understand the paradox of an artist whose life was almost completely outside the public's view, who was always on the edge of calamity—if not death—and yet was so influential in so many ways? Such puzzles and ironies made this book a challenge, but they also raised the narrative stakes of discovering the long-overdue story of this strange and singular character, an outsider who found his way into nearly every form of art, low and high.

The state of his health, what he was working on, his addictions— all might present a radically different person. Harry was wary of having his picture taken, and when you see him in one of his rare photos, he's often behind someone, at the edge of the shot, surprised or angry. Even those who knew him well said that he could disappear for a month or so, and then turn out to have been somewhere nearby all along. Still, Harry could be seen in public at Studio 54 in its heyday, shuffling past the sullen-faced guardians of the velvet rope despite being ill-suited (and ill-tempered) for the carefully curated crowd. Or found in the Columbia University bookstore on the opening days of a semester, noting what books professors in a dozen fields were requiring on their syllabi.

He could be mean, impatient, and insulting, yet also helpful and quotably insightful and funny. He could intrigue by the attention he paid, the efforts he made to ferret out guarded secrets, or he might dazzle with the sheer range of his knowledge. Harry made a practice of inflating the importance of those nobodies he liked and puncturing the famous. His encyclopedic monologues might be mesmerizing in their detail and arcana, in the swerves and careens his narratives could take; or he could be a crushing bore, a Professor Irwin Corey–like pedant with a dry northwestern drawl, who warned his listeners that he left his sentences unfinished, only to return to finish what he was saying in the middle of the next day's perorations. At times he played the fabulist, constructing and deconstructing himself. One of his admirers, the filmmaker Andrew Noren, recalled one of Harry's discourses upon his first meeting him:

> He told me about the relationship between the Elder Eddas and the ceremonial masks of the Bella Coola tribe on the coast of Washington State, and how these related to Seminole textiles and to the music of Heinrich Biber and the partitas of J. S. Bach and the poetry of Robert Desnos. It was an amazing performance . . . you could practically see the sparks flying upward from his brain. At first, I thought this was all brilliant but preposterous, in fact I had no idea what he was even talking about, but then I listened more closely and it began to seem plausible and even logical . . . he often had that effect on people. Needless to say, I was stunned and enchanted by him. Finally, he stopped abruptly, leaned forward and whispered, "Can you loan me 20 bucks?" The next week he was back, blasted again, and repaid the 20 and gave me a foot-long piece of film stock he'd hand painted, as "interest," as he called it.

Harry often, sometimes daily, walked to bookstores and libraries and appeared to memorize long passages of books while speed-reading them. His room was stacked with books organized by size, volumes of the *Oxford English Dictionary*, catalogs, rows of LPs, boxes of cassettes and reel-to-reel tapes, a closet of Seminole dresses and cloth samples, string figures fastened to boards, rare children's books, preserved birds, Tarzan pop-up books, and a sign that said DO NOT TOUCH. It took his curatorial powers to unravel their placement and meaning and his explications of how they were related. His room—whether it be in the Hotel Chelsea, in Allen Ginsberg's apartment, his hut in Boulder at Naropa University, or a flophouse on the Bowery—was his cabinet of curiosities, his mystery theater, his mnemonic construction of ideas, the world he had built in miniature.

Art operated very differently before the 1950s and early 1960s, especially among the avant-garde. Audiences were smaller, more focused, and devoted. At the Anthology Film Archives, where Harry's films were often shown, audiences were largely the same from week to week. They knew who their stars were and they knew one another. It was much the same in jazz, folk music, dance, and art. An artist could be famous in one such group, and not be known at all by those in other arts. Without an agent or a publicist, a gallery or university art courses behind them, artists worked in a more folklike culture, where word of mouth and the relationships between individuals were most important. Influence, if not fame, could be considerable among artists in these smaller groups, especially among the young, who had themselves come to communities like Greenwich Village to learn from and be near those who would become their inspirations. It was why Harry came there in the first place. The way art circulated is one of the reasons so many artists of that era became well-known only after their death. It poses the question of who gets to have a biography written about them, and what a biography should look like for those whose influence spanned diverse and insular creative worlds.

Smith's life was so scattered, his work so widespread, that even when it caught the attention of writers or journalists he suffered from the artist-of-all-trades curse: those who continually shift from medium to medium, subject to subject (in his case, pre-electrically-made recordings, outré forms of filmmaking, Native American clothing, Ukrainian hand-painted Easter eggs, paper airplanes, and tarot cards) are difficult to follow, write about, and market. He arrived in New York at a time when an artist's painting was viewed as a position paper, and success depended upon an influential critic offering a theory that explained the artist's intention. An artist who lived in an alternate America and was operating in the occult (literally, knowledge that is hidden) was just out of luck.

Much of Harry's best work has disappeared, having been lost while he lived on the streets, often when he frequented different locations, sometimes every night. His paintings, films, books, and collections were sometimes forgotten, stolen, given away, left with others for safekeeping or in lieu of rent, and, when he neglected to pay his rent, thrown in the trash by his landlord. Some of Harry's works were thrown away by Harry himself, whether from his disgust or boredom with his creations. With Harry it was not always the product or its completion that was important but the doing, the making of the work, and once he knew that it could be done, he might move on to something else. At other times it was anger, at himself or others, or his frustration with a work that was humanly or financially impossible to complete that led him to destroy it, as he once did by rolling the original of a reel of film down Broadway, watching it unspool in traffic, or, another time, in a fit of pique tearing up an $8,000 limited-edition art portfolio that included one of his own works. Many of Smith's paintings are known today only because photographs of them still exist.

He also effaced, erased, or trashed most of the facts of his life, as he did his art. It was a form of self-editing and a renunciation of self. He was capable of "fabulation" or lying, but he considered this to be a kind of joking—though it was often not as funny as he seemed to think.

Harry was impoverished for most of his life. Early on he had worked briefly in the aircraft industry, done some office work, and done a bit of freelance photography. One of the mysteries of Smith is how he was able to live in New York for thirty-six years, never hold a job, and almost never pay rent, with no relatives to help him out. And yet he could buy an endless stream of records and books, art supplies and film stock, to say nothing of food, cigarettes, drink and drugs, and nightly trips to clubs and concerts. His real work was art, but he was averse to the commerce that drives the art world. He seldom tried to sell anything he had created, and even when he did, "sale" is not the appropriate term: any money he earned (or begged) was used to support his creations. Though he might ask for money for food, he would go hungry if art supplies or books were needed. Even before he became more dependent on drugs and alcohol, food and housing had to be dealt with through the begging and borrowing that consumed much of his life. He frequently asked new acquaintances on first meeting if they were wealthy, in hopes of finding potential Medici on the streets of Greenwich Village. On one occasion he offered several of his drawings of Native Americans as good faith for a loan of a few dollars to Izzy Young, the proprietor of the Folklore Center in the Village.

Getting money for a meal might require him to ask a number of people for some money until he had enough, being careful not to let his benefactors know that there were others helping him. Yet he could also ignore his mail, letting it pile up at one place or another, and then throw it all in the trash without opening it, letters and checks alike.

Why am I writing this book? There have been biographies of mysterious and reclusive figures, those on the margins of history whose lives nonetheless have influence from the shadows. Some of these biographies have chronicled the lives of fakes, failures, and others who perhaps seem unworthy of a book. The classic is A.J.A. Symons's 1934 *The Quest for Corvo: An Experiment in Biography*—a book about the difficulty of writing the book itself. The subject was Frederick Rolfe, a self-proclaimed priest and baron, a minor author, photographer, and painter who ended as a gondolier in Venice. Symons wrote it as something of a detective story, but one that reveals how a biographer works when a subject escapes him.

Thomas Carlyle's 1851 biography of his friend John Sterling (*The Life of John Sterling*) concerns an individual who would seem likewise destined for oblivion. Sterling was briefly and unhappily a priest who had to publish his own poems (which Carlyle called "crude"). Carlyle himself said that Sterling's life was "inconsiderable." But like Dr. Samuel Johnson, Carlyle believed that any person's life, even the "smallest," could be of interest. Sterling, he said, was in his own way representative of his time.

Writing a biography under even the best of circumstances is a humbling experience. The first life history I wrote was that of Sun Ra, a difficult choice for a beginning biographer. He denied being born, said he and dates didn't get along, disallowed any earthly origins, in fact rejected even being human. He was notorious for his evasiveness in interviews, dodging details and dates, turning them into biblical, even science fictional, jeremiads about the evils of humankind. His time line ran through Egypt, Alabama, Chicago, New York, Philadelphia, and Saturn. I wanted to avoid the conjectures of biographers who pretend to know what their subject was doing or thinking, covering their guesses with speculative and presumptive past tenses like "she must have thought" or "maybe he would have known."

I had access to Sun Ra's library and reading notes, and although the content of many of his books often seemed strange to me, I was able to read most of them, in effect reading over his shoulder. It was a revelation, a window into his ambitions, his seriousness, his way of reading books and understanding life. Harry Smith is something else again. He, too, was fascinated by ancient history and outer space, but also by dozens of other matters, and had gathered a large archive that tracked his interests. But if I attempted to read and listen to all of what was in those piles of boxes as if it were his entire existence, I'd never live long enough to get through them. Harry, like Sun Ra, frustrated those who wanted to know his life, or sought to understand it. Though I thought I'd never again encounter anyone as mysterious and undecipherable as Sun Ra, along came Harry. He once warned an interviewer:

> Now if you would like to ask any questions regarding specific points, regarding names, dates, places, events, lawsuits, attempted suicide, attempted suicides, attempting keeping other people from committing suicide, total lack of identification, the fact that I have not paid my taxes for forty years, I have never voted, I've never had a driver's license, I only wear clothing that people throw away, I've never been in the army, and I'm always behind on the rent.

Smith left no significant paper trail behind him. His autobiographical accounts are few, and sometimes unreliable. What remains are the anecdotes about him and the few surviving people whose memories of him are vivid and evocative. Their stories, along with a few letters, two volumes of interviews with Smith, a book of essays by scholars on his various interests, his films, art, recordings, and his "strange anthropology" lectures (as they came to be called at Naropa

University) were what I had to work with. From these I hoped to pull together some understanding of the relationship between the way he lived and his ideas, and how those ideas represented everything around him—how his work as an artist, anthropologist, anthologist, and collector is a form of autobiography.

The equation that audiences and critics see between the lives of artists and their art—the one as being shaped by or reflected in the other—becomes much more complex with Harry Smith. It's a simple but deceptive idea: a work of art will tell us something about a life, or a biography will tell us something about art. It's surprising, then, how little is known about the everyday lives of artists. Unless they cut an ear off, kill themselves or someone else, or maybe have a partner who's also an artist and willing to write about them, we're not likely to hear just how dull, slow, chaotic, or destitute some of their lives were. Harry Smith may have been an extreme case, plagued as he was in so many ways, but he found a way through life. Many artists and musicians who knew him say that Harry, more than anyone else, had devoted his life completely to art, in some ways turned his life *into* a work of art, his own personal surrealism. Put another way, he approached life in an artistic manner and, in doing so, weakened the distinctions between life and art. As a surrealist he collected and rearranged elements of the everyday world to show that another reality was already there, in plain view, and said that it was up to us to change our perception to see the world in a different way.

I finally came to terms with those boxes of Harry's books, magazines, and records—at least I saw the titles of everything in them, enough to confirm to me that it really was as confusing and seemingly random as the Library of Babel. I also bought a number of rare books that Harry owned at one time or another, and sought out others that I hoped might contain some small but revelatory mention of him. I knew I would never get through them, or have enough money to buy what I thought I needed. Was this what it was like to be Harry? Was his archive a kind of medicine cabinet containing what he felt he might need on some dark and stormy night of the soul when bookstores and drug dealers were closed? Or, like Dr. Faustus, did he really have the knowledge that the range and array of his collection implied?

When I first imagined a book about Harry Smith, what I had heard about him told me that the way to go was gonzo all the way. But I came to respect Harry and his projects too much to treat him as just another Village character, albeit an autodidactic, polymathic character. So, in the spirit of Carlyle, I chose to write a real biography, even as I understood the difficulties of that task; I knew that Harry could flicker and jitter, fade, and disappear from the screen like the circles and squares in one of his early abstract films, that his elusiveness might mean having to write more about his works than his life and locating those who were around him in order to hopefully find him.

1

A Boy's Life

1923–1945

I had a lonely childhood.

—Harry Smith

As Harry Everett Smith told it, he was born into a family of theosophists and Freemasons. Though his account of his family history was always sketchy, he did want it known that his was not your normal family, and that he attributed much of what he had become to their idiosyncrasies. His father, he said, was "deeply into Mohammedanism," his mother, Buddhism, and that his father was a descendant of important Masons. If it was true, "to a degree," as Harry once put it, it was perhaps not quite so exceptional. The early part of the twentieth century was an era when Freemasonry was widespread, theosophy was as trendy as other forms of esotericism and early New Age thinking, and they were both widely known in the same way that a somewhat exotic book like Kahlil Gibran's *The Prophet* could become a bestseller and be found in even the smallest of backwater communities. On Orcas Island, near where he was raised, on Puget Sound in Washington, the Theosophical Society had (and still has) a family summer camp named Indralaya.

On the other hand, Harry said that he had been sent to different Sunday schools and was exposed to a number of religions. One of his grandfathers was Catholic, and Harry said he was influenced by the beauty of the church's ceremonies. But then he also said his grandmother was a friend of the theosophists Annie Besant and Bishop Charles Webster Leadbeater. On yet another hand, he said that after lunch on Sundays the family would gather around the radio to listen to a pastor's sermon, after which his mother would question him on its meaning. Both of Harry's parents declared themselves to be Episcopalians, and were cremated as such.

Sometimes he pushed the family story over the edge, as when he said he might be the bastard son of Aleister Crowley, the English occultist and magician, and then spun out the scene on a beach in Washington where this coupling might have occurred. Or when he declared that his mother might be Anastasia Romanov because she had taught at an Indian school in Alaska funded by the czarina of Russia. He seemed to be joking, and on another occasion said it was a fantasy of his mother's. But a surprising number of people took his claims at least semiseriously. With a past as murky as Harry's, any background scenery he might provide helped prepare his various audiences for something special, even when they didn't always quite grasp what he was talking about. What little is known about his life between birth and his early teens is largely from a number of asides in school documents, brief local newspaper mentions, and comments he dropped in interviews or to a few friends who still recall them.

What is certain in Harry's family history, and something he was proud to tell, was that his father was descended from the distinguished family of John Corson Smith, a brigadier general in the Union Army, and later the treasurer and lieutenant governor of the state of Illinois. The general had also revived the rite of the Masonic Knights Templar in the United States after a split with the Scottish Rite Masons. His son, Harry's grandfather, Robert Ambrose Smith, was the assistant general manager of the Pacific American Fisheries, one of the largest canneries in the world, and later the president of the smaller Sehome

Cannery, where Harry's father, Robert James Smith, was an assistant foreman.

If Harry's mother's family was not as notable as his father's, it was nonetheless noteworthy. His mother, Mary Louise Hammond, was born in Sioux City, Iowa, and when the family moved westward to the San Juan Islands off the coast of Washington, Mary Louise's mother, Esther, became a teacher and a political radical, and ran for county school superintendent for the People's Party in 1900, a time when women were not allowed to vote. Mary Louise studied to be an artist and a teacher, and taught at schools near Bellingham, Washington, where she had gone to college. After a divorce, Esther moved to Alaska in 1907 to teach at the Native American school on Afognak Island, a few miles north of Kodiak. Afognak village was the third community founded in Russian America, and the school was attended by the Alutiiq (or Sugpiat), the Native people of the island. Over the next two years Harry's mother and her sister, Constance, joined Esther as teachers at the school. The U.S. government had taken over previously Russian-run schools, and as government employees, the Hammonds were relocated frequently. In 1910, Harry's mother was moved to the Inuit Native school in the tiny village of St. Michael south of Nome on the Norton Sound, and again in 1911 to an even smaller village, Eagle, on the Yukon River, where she taught Han Native American children. In 1912, she returned to the United States and married Robert James Smith, whom she had met on a boat between Orcas Island and Bellingham.

Harry's father began working as a marine engineer at various canneries and also worked in logging. He and Mary first lived on a farm on Orcas Island, and in 1921 he joined his brother in running a hardware store in Estacada, Oregon. Two years later, Harry Everett Smith was born on May 29, 1923, in Portland's Wilcox Hospital. The hardware business never prospered, and the Smiths returned to Washington in the fall of 1924, this time living with Robert's parents in Fairhaven, in South Bellingham, along Puget Sound near the Canadian border. Before Euro-Americans arrived in the mid-1800s, it was the home of tribes of Coast Salish–speaking peoples such as the Lummi, the Samish, and, nearby, the Swinomish.

In the second decade of the century the prosperity produced by salmon fishing and canning declined drastically from overfishing and environmental issues, and many businesses closed or downsized. Harry's father then began working for the Pacific American Fisheries, and the Smiths moved to a smaller house in Fairhaven, where their back porch overlooked Bellingham Bay and the company's cannery.

At an early age Harry suffered from rickets or some form of digestive disorder that resulted in spinal problems and left him a foot shorter than most of the boys in his class. He was never fit for the games and sports of other children, but he could say that he began to read when he was four by a method his mother and grandmother had developed to teach Native Alaskan students. The first thing he recalled reading on his own was Edgar Allan Poe's "The Gold-Bug," a short story that impressed him with its use of two forms of arcane language—cryptography and a text version of the speech of the Gullah people of the South Carolina Sea Islands. Harry was free to read anything in a house stocked with books on travel, music, alchemy, adventure, art, and esoterica—but not his grandfather's secret books on Freemasonry stored in the attic, which he was once caught reading. Throughout the house there were also a number of Asian relics, such as Tibetan prints and a Japanese wakizashi samurai sword. Harry recalled that he "insisted on dressing in Chinese style until I had to go to school. I can remember weeping and wailing. And I had all these Chinese things laid out." Harry was forbidden to play with guns, even a cap pistol on the Fourth of July.

In fall 1930, seven-year-old Harry entered first grade at the Campus School of Washington State Normal School at Bellingham (now Western Washington University), an elementary school within a teacher-training college noted for its commitment to progressive

education—a child-centered curriculum focused on creativity, exploration, and freedom of movement and thought. Students raised
vegetables and animals; wrote books; learned photography; built teepees, Greek temples, and model cities; and staged children's versions
of nearby Lummi Indian longhouse ceremonies. It was a curriculum
that shaped Harry's activities for the next ten years and beyond.

> I had built [the Emerald City] many times as a child. I had
> fairly severe hallucinations, and I had built something called
> my Fairy Garden for many years. I actually used to see lit-
> tle gnomes and fairies, and stuff until I was seven or eight.
> It's a typical psychic phenomenon, I mean, I wasn't nutty
> or anything. All children see that stuff. Up until I was 18
> or so, I worked hard on my Fairy Garden and then started
> building Oz.

As Harry finished the second grade, the Smith family moved
again in 1932, this time to Anacortes, a town on Fidalgo Island south
of Bellingham, still on Puget Sound, an area where the Swinomish,
the Lower Skagit, and the Samish were again the original inhabitants.
Euro-Americans were late settlers, and there was no town recognized
there until the late 1800s, when lumber, fishing, and canneries turned
it into a boomtown. But by the time the Smiths arrived, the depression of the 1930s and the decline in salmon had slowed the town's
progress, and Harry's father was a watchman of what was left of the
giant Apex Fish Company.

At age nine, Harry began third grade at the Whitney School but
was absent with bouts of illness for three different weeks out of eleven
in his first term, then missed almost half of his classes in the second term, and though he began to improve in the spring was still
absent many days in his third. Despite his missed classes, he kept up
with his work and, recognizing his interest in art, his mother and father joined with three other children's parents to find a teacher to give

their children art lessons. The teacher they found, Louise Williams, was a well-trained painter and poet who was part of an arts project for the Works Progress Administration. Harry first studied with her in her studio in a sailmaker's loft in one of the abandoned cannery buildings and later in the Anacortes Hotel. Williams encouraged her students not to copy things photographically but to create their own images. Her focus was on fundamentals such as color and structure, and she left it to the children to use their individuality on whatever they chose. Harry was serious about art and had saved all his work from his first drawings at age two. By the time he finished high school they amounted to thousands. As he grew older, he copied designs from theosophical tracts and the forbidden Freemason books, and his father taught him to draw a geometrical representation of the Tree of Life, a map of creation, the central mystical symbol used in Judaic Kabbalah, also known as 10 Sephirot. It was something he would repeat for years in various configurations.

On Harry's twelfth birthday, his father gave him a set of blacksmith tools that had been left behind at the cannery. "He had me build all these things like models of the first Bell telephone, the original light bulb, and perform all sorts of historical experiments," Smith recalled. He learned how to play the piano, explored classical music, and taught himself how to write down the music that he heard. By his early teens he knew how to record speech and music on a 78-rpm disc-cutting machine. The first recordings he made were of his mother singing Irish ballads, and his father, cowboy songs. Songbooks like Sigmund Spaeth's *Read 'Em and Weep: The Songs You Forgot to Remember*, and Carl Sandburg's *The American Songbag* were among his parents' favorites.

Over the next three years, Harry's health began to slowly improve, though he was still absent from many classes. Nonetheless, his grades were high, with the exception of mathematics and spelling, and by the time he was ready to enter the seventh grade, the junior high school newspaper, *Searchlight*, would single him out as a "scientific genius" and one of the two best artists in the incoming class. By the end of the eighth grade his achievement tests showed him to be years above his grade level. He was also on the staff of the *Searchlight*, and in a list of students' "Secret Ambitions" published by the paper, Harry said he would like to "break one of the fire alarms in the hall."

In the Smiths' neighborhood there was a wide view of the bay and the sea. The waters were filled with a large variety of marine life, and pods of orcas could be seen, their distinctive cries reaching the shore as if they were calling to earth dwellers. In stories told by the original peoples of the Northwest Coast, whales were rulers of the sea and lived in underwater cities. They embodied the souls of dead tribal leaders and had the ability to turn themselves back into humans when they surfaced. Harry grew up with such stories, both those of the Native peoples and others from the white settlers, as the mysteries of the sea were an ever-present thread in coastal life. When his father built a rowboat for him, he spent hours floating on waves deep with kelp, watching and calculating their rhythm and amplitude, seeing their undulation, how they grouped together—an odd project perhaps, especially for a young boy, but one with which Leonardo da Vinci also filled his notebooks and used to develop ideas for new forms of waterworks. Asked years later if the occult had been an influence on the films he made, Harry answered, "sort of, but mainly looking in the water, because I lived this kind of isolated childhood."

He could often be seen walking the beach below his house in Anacortes, collecting things cast up by the sea—bits of driftwood and shells—and the skeletons of birds and small animals. His father arranged for him to store his collection in an unused one-room house of the cannery company, not far from their home. Harry soon turned it into his own museum, with neatly organized birds' nests, seagull feathers, agates, sea creatures in formaldehyde, various other beach findings, and some unidentifiable objects—everything in it marked DO NOT TOUCH. He would conduct tours for the occasional child or adult who might wonder what a boy could be doing in there.

At one point his mother and father moved into two separate small houses, the only buildings left behind by the Apex cannery on a block of Sixth Street. They communicated by a system of bells, ate meals and played chess together. Harry would later say that his parents were not compatible—his father was gone much of the time, and he thought his mother may have had "boyfriends," because she would sometimes drop him at the movie theater for an hour or two. The Smiths remained for ten years in Anacortes, where Harry said they were considered a "low family" by their neighbors despite his grandfather and other well-respected relatives living nearby.

LIGHTING OUT FOR THE TERRITORY

Like other children of his era, Harry was fascinated by American Indians. But unlike those who read about them in comic books, went to Saturday matinee cowboy films, stuck feathers in their hair, and played with dime-store bows and arrows, Harry saw them as real people, living close by, and in his school. This was the beginning of what would become a long search to understand their lives, improbably crossing lines of race, age, and history. It was a quest worthy of an early twentieth-century boys' adventure novel.

The indigenous people of the Northwest Coast had lived for thousands of years in parts of Alaska, British Columbia, Washington, Oregon, and Northern California on a coastal stretch broken by inlets and bays, separated in part from the rest of North America by mountains. Trees a hundred feet high once lined that misty coast and kept it in shadows. Those trees were sometimes carved and painted with faces of animals and humans, and in some places the dead were suspended high in them. As one scholar put it, "It looked like a place that could keep a secret." It was so secret that the coast was missing from European maps of North America for years, left blank, a cipher that tantalized geographers, sailors, and those who dreamed of salmon, furs, and even gold, as if it were the true location of El Dorado.

It was also home to a culture far different from that of most of North America's Native peoples. In a region whose climate was moderated and warmed by the Pacific Ocean current, and with vast aquatic resources and forests rich with wildlife and cedar, fir, spruce, and redwood, lives were sustained by fishing, hunting, and gathering, but as part of a more complex social order than those subsistence terms would suggest. The distinct geography allowed for far-reaching travel by water, for large wooden houses, for stability of settlements, and for the development of social classes (including slaves)—trade, division of labor, production lines and schedules—a form of early indigenous industrialization. When the smallpox plague of the late eighteenth century devastated the population and weakened social ties between local communities and more distant Native American groups, the traditional practice of gift exchange called potlatch was elaborated on and extended. The cultures of the Northwest Coast were so complex that much was misunderstood by missionaries, government officials, and anthropologists alike, resulting in laws that were illogical and repressive.

One element of the cultures of this area that survived devastation and occupation, and even flourished, was their art. The two-dimensional carvings on boxes, masks, canoes, memorial markers, and funerary containers, their unique flowing line figures spreading over the surfaces, forming eyes, faces, and mouths, and depicting bears, ravens, whales, eagles, humans, legendary creatures, and nonrepresentational images, captivated and puzzled non-Indians. Most famous are the totem poles and interior house posts depicting sacred beings, family legends, revered animals, and historical events. It's hard to resist describing Indigenous peoples' works using terms like "abstractions" or "visual puns," but that is what outsiders see when a fish has the face of a human on its tail, or a mask of a bear opens to reveal a raven behind it.

There was no part of the Northwest Coast without an Indian community or reservation nearby, and between 1938 and 1944 Harry visited as many as he could, certainly as far north as Vancouver Island. Those seven years among the Indians had enormous influence on him, and in spite of his later works in film, painting, and folk music, and his study of the occult, he would always identify himself as an anthropologist, and over the years continued his studies of Indian life in Northern California, Colorado, Florida, and Oklahoma.

The Smiths kept alive family stories of contacts with Native peoples, as Harry's mother had taught their children in Alaska and his father had worked with them in the canneries and logging. Harry's grandfather Robert A. Smith had given the Smithsonian Institution a pictographic autobiography of Sitting Bull that he had received from his father, General Smith. Harry remembered the moment at which he first became fascinated by Native American culture: "When I was a child, somebody came around to school one day and said they'd been to an Indian dance, and they saw somebody swinging a skull on the end of a string, so that I thought, 'Hmm, I have to see this.'" What he had seen was a bull-roarer—an animal skull that was spun around to make a whirring sound, an instrument widely used in curing and religious rituals. It was the beginning of a lifelong adventure of immersion in other cultures that would give a sickly, undersized, severely nearsighted, and, by his own accounts, lonely boy with social problems a sense of purpose that would lead him far beyond anyone's expectations.

When he was a teenager and in the eighth grade, Harry began bicycling, or remaining on the bus with Native children, to visit the Swinomish reservation near Anacortes. Soon he was spending days there on weekends and during summer vacations. There is no record of what the elders thought of this young white boy when he first appeared, or why they allowed, and even encouraged, him to use a notebook, sketch pad, camera, and recording machine. They clearly saw him as something more than a curious child, perhaps even as another means of preserving their culture against all odds: compulsory public education, the intervention of missionaries and the police (some of the rituals Harry witnessed were banned at the time by U.S. law), and the seductiveness of radio, phonographs, and movies were reducing the number of young people interested in preserving tradition. Harry's seriousness, persistence, and humility gained him the respect of tribal leaders, who allowed him to use technology they might otherwise have had good reason to fear to document their songs, narratives, customs, language, and games. Over the next five years he would pursue this work, year-round, and would later continue it on the Lummi reservation near Bellingham.

A few anthropologists had made recordings of Native peoples of the coastal area as early as the 1920s, but Harry was the first to record the Lummi, and to record them with a disc-cutting machine that produced higher-quality sound than the then popular wire recorders. After the mid-1940s such recordings were forbidden by the Indians, and today people of the Northwest Coast find it difficult to understand why he was given such freedom.

Harry also made watercolor paintings of these events, and even painted dances and rituals that were no longer practiced. In the only painting that survives, the dance is as Harry saw it, but the clothing is from an earlier era and based on what the elders had told him.

To record and document what he saw, Harry had learned how to photograph with minimal lighting, to use a recording machine, and to translate the words of songs. Because he had no way to film dancers, accurately describing the dances was a problem. Dance notation is notoriously complex and difficult, and usually applicable to only a few specific forms of dance (such as ballet). No method existed for writing Native American dances, and anthropologists showed little interest in it. Even sketches of the movement of body parts would require a large series of frames that would take many viewings to do and at best would end up as a flip-book. But Harry thought it was important, maybe more important than the music, since dance was also a cultural universal, but one that was less abstract, perhaps more primal, and was connected to everyday bodily movement in social and work activities. He had to invent his own system:

> I got interested in the designs in relation to music . . . It was an attempt to write down the unknown Indian life. I made a large number of recordings of that, which are also unfortunately lost. I took portable equipment all over the place long before anyone else did and recorded whole long ceremonies sometimes lasting several days. Diagraming the pictures was so interesting that I started to be interested in music in relation to stuff.

ANTHROPOLOGY AND THE NORTHWEST COAST IN THE 1930S

There would seem to be very little for a boy to find in his local library about anthropology, a field of study that had existed in university departments for scarcely twenty years. Yet that was where Harry discovered the writings of Franz Boas, the founder of American anthropology, whose research work was done largely in Alaska and British Columbia. His accounts of the people who lived just up the coast resonated with Harry, opening a door into the lives and history of people who were often thought of as living outside of history. They offered Harry a model for his research well before he ever met an anthropologist.

Though Boas was trained as a physicist, he first came to North America as a geographer on Baffin Island in the 1880s, and he traveled across Canada to continue research on the upper Northwest Coast. As a scientist he was concerned with facts more than theory, and his reports, articles, and monographs were filled with what he had observed as he moved among different groups of people with different cultures—housing, language, means of subsistence, children's games, folk art, eating habits, kinship terms, tools, clothing—all of which Boas thought should be documented before they disappeared. As these lists and descriptions piled up, their variations and similarities noted, he began to see them all as fundamental to understanding what it means to be human.

To begin with: Was there anything that could be called human nature? Was anything innate? Was it possible that one people's way of life was better than another's? Did "race" as it was understood in the West even exist? Were there any cultural universals, and if there were, were they independently invented or the result of diffusion across the globe? How did cultures come into being? What roles did environment and biology play? What could we learn about ourselves by learning about others? None of these questions were rhetorical. These were issues that the United States and Canada were facing as a world war began. Race, eugenics, and immigration were politically and ethically divisive, and Boas addressed them both academically and personally in his writings, public lectures, and testimony to Congress. The local libraries of Washington had diverse books by Boas, such as *The Mind of Primitive Man* (1911), *Primitive Art* (1927), and *Anthropology and Modern Life* (1928). For Harry, Boas's vision of anthropology was something more exciting, more real than anything he had been taught, and something that might offer an alternative to the solitary life he faced.

After Boas immigrated to the United States in 1887, he eventually became a curator at the American Museum of Natural History in New York and then formed the first American anthropology department to train PhDs, at Columbia University. His students were the founders of the first anthropology departments on the West Coast. One of these doctoral students, Alfred Kroeber, the head of the new Department of Anthropology at Berkeley, wrote the first introduction to the subject, his 1923 *Anthropology*, a book that Harry read. Under the word "Anthropology" on the cover was printed: "Race, language, culture, psychology, prehistory." What might seem like a carnival tent show poster was a serious statement, a declaration that a new field of knowledge, a new human science, had been established. Kroeber had first studied literature and drama, and this textbook contained a staggering breadth of knowledge: the fossil record and its meaning for evolution, ecology, the concept of race and the problems it caused, language, the processes of culture, the story of the alphabet's creation, prehistory, the origins of civilization, and a discussion of psychoanalysis and its implications for culture (Kroeber was himself a lay analyst, one of the first in the San Francisco Bay Area). He had no doubts that it was possible for a single field of study to analyze and understand almost every aspect of human behavior, and his book and other publications were evidence of what one person could accomplish. (He had even written a comparative study of the rise of the novel in Europe and Japan.) The book was a challenge to beginners, but it could also incite them to do whatever interested them. Anthropology at that moment was something of a calling, a mission, and to a young person like Harry, living in the West among some of the oldest cultures of the world, it could seem an imperative on which one could make a life.

Ethnography was not listed on the cover of Kroeber's book, but a large part of the text was about just that—the close study and documentation of a human culture from the point of view of its members. Anthropologists who do ethnographic research often note the irony that underlies their task: no matter how well educated they may be in the ways of life of many cultures, ethnography requires asking people for their help in understanding how they organize their lives. Such researchers are likely to know less than the younger children of the people they are studying. This has sometimes been called the role of the cultural dope, one whose naïveté and ignorance is on display every day. How could a child such as Harry Smith successfully undertake such an adult outsider's role? His was not a child's excitement over newly discovered interests, picking up new ones along the way and then dropping them when they found there was hard work ahead. Harry's childhood was one of boundless curiosity, intense focus, and self-discipline.

There is little record of Harry in junior high school other than his work with Indians, and whether it was the time spent on the reservation, illness, or some other matter that distracted him, his grades fell, with the exception of art and social science. His years in Anacortes High School are also largely a blank. His health was better and his attendance improved, his work on the reservations continued, and his grades rose dramatically in 1938–1939, his freshman year. At the age of sixteen, tests showed him to have the mental age of nineteen. But in the second year his grades fell again, as he failed Latin and dropped algebra. In the fall term of 1940, what should have been his junior year, Harry was seventeen and in serious academic trouble, failing and dropping courses, and not yet listed as a junior. Having failed to complete algebra the year before, he was taking it once again, but was signed up for only two other classes, English and Latin. And yet he was doing good work in those courses and involved in school activities: he was in charge of lighting for the school play *Young April*, an essay he wrote on "Learning the Ways of Democratic Institutions" was printed in the *Anacortes American* in November 1941, he was a member of the debate team, and a report he did for his English class on the characters in the Chinese alphabet would be singled out in the school newspaper. He also entered one of his projects in a school-sponsored hobby show. There, among the collections of salt and pepper shakers, was Harry's miniature house, "completely furnished, even to pictures, mirrors, and chandeliers. The furniture was of a size in proportion to a one-half inch square piano." In the spring of 1941, Harry finally passed algebra with a B, but dropped the only two other courses he was taking. In March of 1942, he stopped going to classes and disappeared from the school's records. His work among the Indians was now a full-time activity.

Years later, his classmates in Anacortes said they scarcely knew him and were surprised to hear what had become of him. He was remembered as a thin, bent, and rather fragile boy, but noted for his classroom reports on "deep subjects." A few said that his interest in Native Americans left him with no time to be one of them, and it's true that other than Native American adults, Harry had few friends. One person in his high school he might have then called a friend was Jack Wells, a boy who, like Harry, had medical problems and sat out most of the physical education classes. Wells had an interest in electronics, helped Harry with recording equipment, and accompanied him on several trips to the Swinomish reservation near La Conner, a few miles south of Anacortes, where they recorded music with a portable disc recorder and battery. Wells's mother was a music teacher and composer who had visited the same reservation to hear music, but what Jack and Harry really shared in common was classical music. The two of them bought and swapped records, listening to them together. In a few years, Harry's taste in music would move far beyond the classical, but as late as his senior year in high school he could still declare in the yearbook that his ambition was to write a symphony.

One weekend in late January 1940, Harry was on one of his many visits to the Swinomish, this time to see a winter dance on Treaty Day, a celebration of the 1855 agreement between Indians and settlers. He was surprised to see another high school student there, fifteen-year-old Bill Holm, who had been invited to join some anthropology students from the University of Washington on a visit to the reservation with their professor, Erna Gunther. Holm and Smith, unknown to each other, had both been studying the cultures of the Coastal Salish-language-speaking people. After that weekend, they began visiting each other at their homes, and sharing what they had learned. It was an extraordinary pairing: Holm had already been allowed access to Indian art in the storerooms of the Washington State Museum in Seattle (later renamed the Burke Museum of Natural History and Culture), and Harry had read deeply into Northwest Coast anthropological literature. Their friendship was based entirely on their research into Native life; for fun, they painted red pictographs of whales on rocks along Chuckanut Bay or searched for soapberries to make frothy "Indian ice cream."

For several years, Harry took Holm along with him in the winter to visit his friends among the Lummi, some ten miles northwest of Bellingham. Together, they also traveled to see the winter spirit dances held in what the Lummi called in their language a smokehouse—a long building with four fires blazing along the length of the structure and smoke holes in the roof. Harry sometimes asked Holm to help carry and run the recording machine since he was trying to photograph the ceremonies in long exposures with only the light of the fires and a few lanterns, record some of the music, and transcribe the rest on paper.

Spirit dances were deeply sacred events at which supernatural helpers, who in the past had aided the Lummi in war, now guided them in hunting and survival through the winter. The dancers painted their faces, some still wearing black for war, others red. They wore knickers with knitted stockings and hats with beaver or human hair and eagle feathers on top that spun with the wind or their movement. Their clothing was heavily beaded and covered with rows of small wooden paddles that in the past were seen as war clubs. "Spirits," Holm said, "powerful, unseen beings, circle the earth and came around across this part of the country in the winter time and they might become available for help by individuals . . . And when the spirit came to a person . . . that individual has to express this power in a dance. The song he sings either in dreams or during these dances, and when a spirit appeared to one of them in the smokehouse, they were possessed and had to express what they had been told by the helpers through dancing, moaning, and singing. The song he sings is one that comes to him from this power."

Others gather around the person who had been spiritually contacted and sang along, jumped, ran, danced, and gestured with his or her hands. If the spirit song was an older one and already known, they sang along; if the song was new, they had to learn it on the spot. One after another experienced these visitations. The smokehouse shuddered as the Lummi drummers played without stopping through the long winter night. Their volume made it impossible for Harry and Bill to hear what had been successfully recorded, and they hung a blanket over the machine and put their heads underneath. Sometimes during playback those nearby could hear the recording and became possessed by it. Holm recalled:

> Toward the end of one of these experiences a man came to Harry and he said, "did you record that woman's song?" And Harry said no. He said he didn't have permission to record it. We always had permission from the people to record their songs, because they were personal and powerful things. He said, "well she wants you to record it." So he said OK. We got the machine all ready, and she began to have this possession experience, and then pretty soon she got up and began to dance. She was a red paint dancer, so she had the red marks on her face. And she had a cedar bark head ring.

With more than two hundred people gathered, the fires blazing, the smoke, the hours of steady drum rhythm, the swirling dancers, the singing never ceasing all night long, Harry and Bill themselves slipped toward trance.

The sight of these white boys climbing into a bus with a fifty-pound Presto disc recording machine, along with an auto battery and transformer that Harry had adapted, blank record discs, cameras, and notebooks, and then carrying it all onto the reservation would have surprised the white community. A very few might have attended if invited, but no one but the Lummi and other Indian guests from different tribes were allowed to attend the whole ritual because of its importance and secret nature. "Harry made all the contacts with the people and arranged to do the recording," according to Holm. "He and I never discussed the purpose of the recordings and the things we collected, except that we thought they would not always be there."

Professor Erna Gunther, the director of the Washington State Museum, came to Anacortes to see Harry's collection in February 1941 and to borrow some of it for the museum. Harry gave them much of his collection of material culture. Among it was a Tlingit carved pipe, a bear's head, a wooden canoe bailer, and carved wooden grave markers in the forms of frogs, bears, and birds. From the Samish, there were two longhouse posts. There were photos and paintings of formal events at various reservations; recordings of speech in the Lummi, Swinomish, and Samish languages; recordings of Lummi and Swinomish myths and folktales (with Harry's written English translations); children's games with directions for playing them and detailed drawings of objects used in the games; and fishermen's chants and prayers for beginning canoe trips.

Some of what he gave to the museum seems to have been lost, or given to other institutions. In 2016 a notice of inventory completion in the *Federal Register* from the Department of Anthropology at Indiana University in Bloomington said that human remains found in a Lummi refuse heap by Harry had somehow migrated from the Burke Museum in Seattle to the University of Chicago and on to Indiana, and were only recently identified as coming from Harry. (The *Federal Register* noted that curators had thought there were two Harry Smiths, and now realized there was only one.) "He was way ahead of many trained anthropologists," according to Holm, "and the loss of his notes and probably most of his pictures is tragic."

THE SURREAL AND THE ETHNOGRAPHIC

Harry and Bill carried out their field studies unaware that the art of the original inhabitants of the Northwest Coast had become a passion of European surrealists, despite none of them ever having visited the area. If the boys even knew the word "surreal," they'd see no connection to the people they knew. It was a word perhaps first used by the French poet Apollinaire in 1917 to replace "supernatural" (though both words literally mean "above" or "over" reality or the natural). Its meaning was rather unclear and still evolving among surrealists: it could indicate the discovery of alternative reality, the search for the hidden or repressed self, surrender to a state of mind where there are no constraints, or the unconscious as a territory to be explored to create a synthesis of outward and inward unconscious. The surrealists were interested in what Indian spiritual life and art could mean for them, how Euro-American art could be reshaped by what they imagined Native art meant. To Harry and Bill, what mattered was understanding and preserving the art of their neighboring people, which most whites misunderstood or ignored.

The line between surrealists and anthropologists has not always been easy to see. In France, there's a long history of controversy over the difference between an ethnographic object and a fine art object, and separate museums were built in Paris to house the different items. (The French anthropologist Claude Lévi-Strauss once quipped that when an object whose code is not known arrives in Paris it's sent to the Musée de l'Homme; when its code is known it's sent to the Louvre.) In New York, the disputes that erupted over the exhibition *"Primitivism" in 20th Century Art: Affinity of the Tribal and the Modern* at the Museum of Modern Art in 1984 were a sign that things had not been settled in North America, either. Who decides if an object is useful, or beautiful, or a work of art, or even what it is?

In the 1940s and 1950s, a time when anthropologists were expected to publish in conventional academic journals, in prose that read like a lab report, there were anthropology professors on the West Coast who also wrote for avant-garde and surrealist magazines like *Dyn, View, VVV,* and *Tomorrow: Quarterly Review of Psychical Research.* Faced with subjects like art, dreams, spirit possession, witchcraft, shamans, and drugs, the usual anthropological methods and theory were of limited use.

In the first quarter of the twentieth century, there were far more non-Western cultures and languages, many of them endangered, and the anthropologist's task was to find and document them. In some ways anthropology has overlapped with other disciplines, but what sets it apart is its long and deep immersion in vastly different ways of life. Anthropologists talked about culture shock—the confusion, disorientation, and psychological stress that came with assuming a life far different from their own—but they thought of it not as a risk to avoid, but as a necessary step toward serious understanding. The rules for success in such work were far from clear. Early anthropology was more experimental and performative than any modern social science. There was not yet a canon of works, no clear boundaries around the subject, and methodology was often borrowed from other fields. Sketching was common, photography went beyond the scientific to the artistic, some wrote short stories about their fieldwork, others poetry (sometimes even in the languages of the people they studied), biographies were written, autobiographies recorded and edited. Boas made films of himself doing Indian dances from memory, and academically trained anthropologists like Katherine Dunham and Zora Neale Hurston choreographed dances they had seen in their fieldwork and had them performed by their own dance companies.

Surrealists were also drawn to cultures beyond that of the West, especially the arts of Oceania, Africa, Mexico, and the Indians of the Southwest and the Northwest Coast. A witty surrealist map drawn in 1929 pictured the areas of the world that interested them swallowing up major countries. It was part of what was to be a long history of Europe and North America having its engines of creativity restarted by what it considered the primitive, the alien, the bizarre, or the mad. André Breton, the godfather of surrealism, thought of these exotic arts as offering new ways of thinking about redirecting the contemporary world, a view also shared by some anthropologists. But part of the surrealists' attraction to cultures such as those of the Northwest Coast, with their striking carvings and paintings, was that they had little idea of what the art meant to the people who created it, and so surrealists were left to their own interpretation. Attending an exhibit, Breton spoke of a lingering aura of the masks he saw, that "Even removed from the atmosphere of worship from which it originates and displaced to a degree among us, the hold it has on our being can only depend to a small degree on the 'plastic' quality that we ascribe to it." Claude Lévi-Strauss said that Breton "didn't like scholarly matters getting between him and the object." On the other hand, Lévi-Strauss said that the abrupt and unexpected comparisons of the surrealists, especially those of Max Ernst, influenced his own anthropological writing. The first two books on Northwest Coast art appeared in early 1929, and were written by authors who knew only what they'd seen in European ethnographic museums. Boas's 1927 book *Primitive Art* drew on works he had seen in Alaska and British Columbia, but did not discuss the use of art in ceremonies and rituals, as he had in his academic articles.

In June of 1938, the year that Harry began to seriously study and document Native American culture, Kurt Seligmann, the Swiss surrealist painter and author of the widely read *The Mirror of Magic*, was sent by the Musée de l'Homme in Paris to northern British Columbia to collect Native art, and left Canada with a fifty-four-foot-high totem pole that for years stood in front of the Musée de l'Homme. Following Seligmann's trip, the Austrian painter Wolfgang Paalen, having just come from organizing the *International Exhibition of Surrealism* in Paris with Man Ray, Marcel Duchamp, and Salvador Dalí, also turned up in British Columbia, on another buying mission from the Musée de l'Homme. Like Seligmann, he had seen some pieces of Northwest art in a few books and in ethnographic museums in Germany and the United Kingdom. Paalen would later create the arts magazine *Dyn*, which would focus on the links between what was being called primitive art and high art. His 1943 essay "Totem Art" in *Dyn* drew on his readings in anthropology to argue for the creation of a new form of art and laid out ideas that lit up the imaginations of Martha Graham, Isamu Noguchi, Jackson Pollock, Robert Motherwell, Mark Rothko, and Barnett Newman.

It would be twenty years before Harry Smith would discover the writings of Lévi-Strauss, but once he did, he was excited by everything he read, and mentioned him repeatedly over the years. Boas and Lévi-Strauss were the two most eminent anthropologists of Europe and North America, and were Harry's chief anthropological influences.

Lévi-Strauss escaped the Nazi occupation of France in 1941 by boat from Marseille to New York City. On the way he met André Breton in Casablanca, and the two of them spent the voyage discussing the nature and sources of art. Once he arrived, Lévi-Strauss chose not to move into an apartment near Columbia University suggested to him by Boas, but into Greenwich Village, downtown, in a neighborhood of artists' studios, jazz clubs, bookstores, sailors, prostitutes, and his émigré friends Max Ernst, Marcel Duchamp, and Yves Tanguy. He quickly joined a circle that roamed New York's art galleries and ethnic neighborhoods, had cocktails at Peggy Guggenheim's, and joined in surrealist activities like tarot cards and the chance-based drawing game exquisite corpse. He treated the city like a series of ethnographic sites, visiting Chinese restaurants and an opera house, making regular trips uptown to Harlem to buy Puerto Rican tobacco and visit the Savoy Ballroom to see swing dancing (which he compared to Brazilian carnival dance). He also discovered what he called a "magic place," the American Museum of Natural History, where in 1899 Boas had installed the Northwest Coast Hall, the oldest and one of the museum's most revered galleries. It was a long, dark, earth-toned place with alcoves of carved and painted masks, boxes, paddles, tools, cooking utensils, and clothing, with a sixty-three-foot canoe hanging overhead and totem poles rising up from the shadowed floor toward a ceiling darkened by blacked-out windows.

These carved, painted, and woven works struck Lévi-Strauss as something more than an ethnographic find, or a museum's idea of vestiges of another era of art. Despite a relatively small number of people on the Pacific Northwest Coast—"a rosary of villages . . . strewn along the coast and the islands"—they had produced an astonishingly rich and varied number of art forms, and continually renewed them. To Lévi-Strauss, the art he encountered was the equal of or better than the greatest works of art from Egypt, Persia, or medieval Europe. He was overwhelmed by "dance masks that opened suddenly like two shutters to reveal a second face, and sometimes a third one behind the second, each one imbued with mystery and austerity." To describe the painted and sculptured posts that had once supported house beams, he quoted Charles Baudelaire's poem "Correspondances" on nature's being a temple with "living pillars" and "forests of symbols." Baudelaire was an apt source, as he, too, celebrated the arts of Native Americans, whom he envisioned as classic dandies in their ritual dress: "Dandyism is the last flicker of heroism in decadent ages; and the sort of dandy discovered by the traveler in Northern America in no sense invalidates this idea; for there is no valid reason why we should not believe that the tribes we call savage are not the remnants of great civilizations of the past."

Europeans brought a different perspective to the art of Native Americans, though only Seligmann and Paalen had ever visited the Northwest Coast or seen its arts as they were made, viewed, and understood by its artists and their communities. Even Lévi-Strauss, who made them the subject of much of his work, would not visit them until thirty-two years later.

In New York, Max Ernst discovered a small antiques store on Third Avenue owned by a German refugee, Julius Carlebach, that had a number of curious objects. Soon Ernst, Bréton, André Masson,

Seligmann, Georges Duthuit (Henri Matisse's son-in-law), and others were haunting the shop, which they called Ali-Baba's Cave. It was the sort of store that sold glass beads and dyed feathers to Boy Scouts who turned themselves into summer camp Indians, but it also had an odd mix of stone masks from Teotihuacán, Mexico; Hopi kachina dolls; and Northwest Coast carvings. That shop led Lévi-Strauss up to the Bronx to one of Carlebach's sources, a warehouse that was George Gustav Heye's Museum of the American Indian, a surrealist's Macy's, containing the largest such collection in the world. He arrived just as Heye, in need of cash, was selling some things.

Though Harry may have been one of the very few non-Indians who had witnessed the secret ceremonies that used the sacred objects that so interested the surrealists, he rarely mentioned them, and never seemed comfortable when he did. A lecture he called "Native American Cosmos" that he would give at Naropa University in Boulder on July 8, 1990, was an occasion that called for a recollection of his own experiences, and he began to speak about the Lummi spirit dances but then suddenly stopped, saying that he wanted to give detailed descriptions of those events but had decided that wasn't "a good idea." Instead, Harry went into more detail about a trip he took in the early 1940s to Vancouver, where he rode to the end of the streetcar line to witness a four-day Coast Salish winter ritual. These were people he didn't know, and he had no invitation to attend. As he came close to the four longhouses on the edge of the city, a woman warned him that he might be killed if he went on. When he nonetheless entered a longhouse, four hundred people were already there to be part of a ritual of the Dog Howlers, one of two secret societies. He recounted, "I really can't describe it because in a way I feel I'm desecrating the trust that was placed in me. The organization supposedly having been stamped totally, thoroughly, completely, and forever, out in something like 1843. [Laughs.] Something that hasn't been seen for a hundred years is suddenly seen."

> All I can give is a description of what happened, like for example all of the motions of people going around crawling on the floor . . . They were naked except for a wolf mask and this of course as I said happened after you'd been up for something like 48 hours listening to incessant drumming that increased the adrenochrome in the blood to such a point that everything glistened, sort of. And just as the sun came down through the smoke (because the entire house of course was full of smoke from the fires), it made beams that shot down onto one of the actual fires that was there and very old women came in. Everybody that comes into this type of house comes in backwards. This is explained in several ways: to avoid stepping on your shadow, to go into a form of reversal . . . They had very old women with [skulls—I mean, rattles shaped] like skulls, but with the mouth very stylized [twisted]. Anyway, they sang some song while the whistles blew on the roof, then while all this was going on there was a certain hanging made of mountain goat wool . . . dropped, and there was a person there . . . with their tongue sort of down over the front of their mouth, and a string with knots in it run through the tongue, blood had run down over the blanket he was wearing . . . he had a cedar bark headdress on. There was a certain type of totem-pole that's set in the wall: a house-post . . . and a man on the platform, he stood there for the entire (I presume) four days. I don't know, he didn't move.

He broke off his narrative at that point. Clearly, Harry had been frightened by what he saw, and feared being struck by lightning; he took no pictures and made no sketches, and he asked only one question and was given a "secret answer." "They give the impression that Hieronymus Bosch is alive and well in the woods."

Most of Harry's early photographs and ethnographic research notes have been lost. They included such things as the genealogy of the leaders of the Lummi told to him by the chief, which took Harry hours to write down since they went back hundreds of years. It was a feat of memory that astonished him. But some of Harry's work in the archeology and linguistics of Native peoples did survive. Archeology has a much longer history than modern anthropology, several centuries longer, and it had become popular enough that it would not be surprising to see a young person hunting for arrowheads in a farm field anywhere in the country. But Harry's search for artifacts was not that of an amateur; it was the product of knowledge of the history of coastal-area peoples and the techniques of contemporary archeology.

American anthropology had developed alongside the study of linguistics and had contributed much to the serious study of language. The International Phonetic Alphabet had only recently been standardized to allow any spoken language to be made visible through writing, and the phonograph had made it possible to record and then slow down speech to hear it in greater detail, no matter how strange it seemed. As a result, anthropologists on the West Coast of the United States were discovering the existence of hundreds of Native American languages, many of which were rapidly disappearing. Boas had organized an American Council of Learned Societies Committee on Native American Languages in 1927, and he called on his students, especially those on the West Coast, to find the last speakers of such languages before they disappeared. In Berkeley, at the university and in the community, there were anthropologists and poets and novelists who joined in this campaign, and the salvaging of languages became something of a modernist project that paralleled the recovery of languages and dialects in the works of Ezra Pound, James Joyce, and T. S. Eliot.

This was critical business to those who understood that language is one of the few cultural universals and a key to understanding all of culture. A lost language meant a lost way of thinking, the vanishing of a way of life and whatever secrets it might hold. But even learning to use the phonetic alphabet itself could be exciting. Once a language, even one's own, was transcribed into universal symbols that represented the sounds of speech more accurately than the traditional alphabet, it could reveal things that the alphabet concealed, and show similarities and differences between words that were not apparent when they were conventionally written. Much of language operates outside of conscious awareness, and as with the transcription of music onto paper, phonetic transcription could change how things were heard, or reveal that they had never been heard at all. Suddenly questions about language were springing up everywhere: If there was no such thing as a universal language, was there at least a universal grammar? Does language determine thought? Do different languages produce different kinds of thought? And what *is* a language, anyway?

Harry made long trips to Seattle, to the Department of Anthropology at the University of Washington, to talk with Professors Erna Gunther and Melville Jacobs, both former students of Boas, to learn how to preserve an unwritten language. Jacobs had spent years finding the last speakers of at least five Native languages, translating them, and studying their structure. In 1941, at the age of eighteen, Harry began to work on making a list of nouns in the Samish and Swinomish languages, and the next year he started to collect verbs. This meant sitting with a speaker of a language, asking about words and their meanings, sometimes making recordings of them, and writing down the words with the phonetic alphabet that Professor Jacobs had shown him how to use. It was a slow process that required the patience of both speaker and researcher. Harry had to learn the etiquette of speaking with an elder, to know the importance of close listening and when it was acceptable to interrupt to ask questions. Nothing

could be assumed when asking a question in one language and getting the answer in another. Some of the sounds in Native American
languages were not found in European languages. Harry's goal was
to make a dictionary of the words and then to compare the different
languages, a huge undertaking made more difficult because he was
in many cases the first to attempt it. Only scraps of his work on this
project survive.

Once, on a visit to his cousins in Southern California, Harry saw a
book about string figures—Kathleen Haddon's 1934 *String Games for
Beginners*—that told how to weave, twist, and knot a loop of string into
geometric shapes or patterns that suggest objects, people, animals, or
places. When he read that these figures could be found everywhere
in the world, he asked Native American children on his school bus if
they or their parents knew how to make them. On his visits to reservations, he asked to see the figures made and to have them explained
to him. What he found was that they were of far greater significance
than he'd thought, and it set him on a lifelong quest to find as many
of them as he could.

Most people in North America know of similar string sculptures
as a children's game called Cat's Cradle, in which the players compete to see who can turn the other players' figures into the greatest
number of new forms. But Harry learned that in most of the world
string figures are an adult art or story form, sometimes elevated by
shamans for use as part of curing rituals. Some societies used them
as a map of the earth, the ocean, or the sky, sometimes to illustrate
tales or myths. Native American figures were found everywhere on
the Northwest Coast, and were elaborate and complex, some with
multiple moving parts, some accompanied by music that itself could
be quite complex, in cycles with small variations in each version. He

thought they looked like patterns for a quilt, or that they could be thought of as a widespread form of pre-film animation. String figures are a performative art, an animated art, but one hard to describe and difficult to display. They are usually mounted on a two-dimensional surface like a picture on a wall, and thus lose their motion and grace.

Harry taught himself to make many of these figures, practiced them daily, and photographed others forming them. His library research revealed that ever since Franz Boas's 1888 article on Inuit string figures, many, if not most, of the early anthropologists had collected and studied these forms across the globe. It was the sort of thing that early anthropologists found challenging and intriguing.

When Smith was asked years later in an interview with John Cohen about what it was that so captivated him, he replied:

> My interest in [string figures] was merely as something that a lot of people did who are usually lumped together as being primitive. The distribution of anything else isn't the same— the bow and arrow, pottery, basketry, or clothing—any kind of conceptions. As far as I know, the string figures are the only universal thing other than singing. But singing may exist universally for the same reason: that a lot of experiences are lumped together as songs which probably aren't.

Harry made extensive notes and diagrams, developing a system for cataloging the variations in methods and results, and wrote a lengthy discourse, all of it part of a project that would take years to complete: a comparative study of an art-game-map-religious-healing practiced by all the people of the world for as far back as we know.

He taught others how to create some of the most complex forms, and years later some were featured in two of Smith's movies: *Film No. 18: Mahagonny*, and *Film No. 23*. In the latter film, the figures were performed by Kathy Elbaum, a graduate student in anthropology and Timothy Leary's secretary, whom Harry encouraged to study figures among the Inuit of Rankin Inlet, Nunavut, Canada, as part of her doctoral research.

Collecting and annotating string figures was only one of many of Harry's projects in his teen years. He continued to study music, delving into the world of symphonic works and buying the large twelve-inch RCA Red Seal records that were regarded as the sonic equivalent of finely bound classic books. He was painting and drawing, copying images from other cultures, and learning about the mandala in Carl Jung's books. His reading took him into works on the occult and books of contemporary cultural and aesthetic analysis like Wassily Kandinsky's 1914 *The Art of Spiritual Harmony* (later retitled *Concerning the Spiritual in Art*), Jung's *Modern Man in Search of a Soul* (1933) and *Psychology and Alchemy* (1944), and Annie Besant and C. W. Leadbeater's *Thought Forms* (1905).

At the center of Harry's childhood was his complete engagement with the lives of adults of a different culture. Yet he would never "go native" like a Natty Bumppo or Deerslayer of James Fenimore Cooper's fiction. Nor would he fall into what Leslie Fiedler once called "this pattern, individual biography recapitulating cultural history. Born theoretically white, we are permitted to pass our childhood as imaginary Indians, our adolescence as imaginary Negroes, and only then are expected to settle down to being what we are told we really are: white once more." Years later, when hippies retreating from urban modernity by turning themselves into faux–Native Americans sought out Harry as a spiritual ancestor, he viewed them with curiosity, as something worthy of study. He said of such cosmetic identity-changing that he was "pretty sure there have always been things like people dressing up in Indian clothes."

> It's a romanticism of a sort to be followed by something else when this dies down. I would say it hasn't much association with the Indians, other than that everybody is now more sympathetic to the Indians. After all, their grandparents were murdering millions of them. I suppose that children dressed up like Saracens during the crusades, and when Genghis Kahn was coming they all dressed up in Genghis suits. It's all the same: Marie Antoinette was sitting around in a stable built out of solid gold. It's the same as they do now. It's a way of evading the catastrophe that overtook the Indians, and an attempt to irritate parents, relieve guilt, and other things all at once.

In the summer of 1942, when Harry was nineteen, the Smiths moved back to Bellingham again when the property of the Apex cannery was sold to be turned into a shipyard for naval vessels—a difficult relocation at a critical time in any student's life, but given Harry's academic problems at Anacortes High School, it was far worse. Those of his classmates who remembered him at all knew him only as a short boy with a stooped posture, thick glasses, and a thin, nasal voice, often seen with a large four-by-five camera. Some of his classmates recalled years later that he had a sense of humor and talked with adults about topics they knew little about. He was not one to hang out, or turn up at athletic events, and he was never at dances. Yet there he is in the *Shuksan*, the Bellingham High School yearbook, his picture among those on the yearbook photography staff, as a member of the Art Club and as an actor in the senior play, *You Can't Take It with You*, George S. Kaufman and Moss Hart's comedy about a family of spiritualists, eccentrics, musicians, and painters.

It seems odd that the students knew so little about him, since

Harry had given talks about Indian culture with his mother and by himself for adult and children's groups, and articles about his work with Native Americans appeared in the high school newspaper, the *Bellingham Herald*, and the *Anacortes American*. He also was acknowledged nationally in 1943 in *American Magazine* with a feature titled "Injuneer" (unsigned, but written by Vance Packard, later famous for his 1957 book on subliminal advertising, *The Hidden Persuaders*), with a color photo of Harry recording Lummi tribal leaders. Despite the leaders' ritual dress and the article's claim that he was recording the Lummi winter festival, the photo was taken in Harry's parents' home in South Bellingham. Much to Harry's distress, Packard emphasized that he knew more about these Native American groups than any other white person.

There was also some confusion in the article. The photo of Harry was taken when he was about to turn twenty, much later than the article suggests. Before Packard began to write the article, he contacted Professor Jacobs to verify that Harry had really done legitimate research. Jacobs's reply was positive, although he seemed to think that the magazine was asking if they should publish something written by Smith:

> He is undoubtedly a lad of most remarkable high serious-ness, intelligence, and potentiality. My impression of his anthropological interest is that it amounts to reading and work which goes far beyond the level of a mere youthful hobby. He has an excellent nose for the best scientific literature in the field, and has read a lot of it with rare discrimination and insight. It is almost absurd to regard him as a boy of high school age. He is of outstanding college caliber, and if he were here in college I don't doubt that he would be getting high A's in his college courses, and certainly so in anthropology. He is years ahead of his chronological age, in mental attainment. He did very impressive work, all by himself, in

attempting to record the sounds and words of the difficult native Indian language (Salish) spoken near his home . . . I have no doubt that he knows enough of the proper scientific methods that should he publish such data [on Indian customs] it would be of fine quality and constitute a contribution to our knowledge of local Indian life.

In all the years I have been here (fifteen) I have not run across a more promising lad, or one more deserving of aid and encouragement in whatever he may choose to interest himself. If he should write for your publication I think that what he has done should be trusted with utmost seriousness and respect. He is a grand fellow.

Harry was still making records of language, myths, and songs during the school year, and now alternating between the Lummi, the Samish, and the Swinomish. Few people, if any, other than Bill Holm, knew then that Harry was also doing some kind of film and animation, but without the use of a camera. (He would later say that it was years before he had access to a projector to see what he had done.) The first movies he had seen as a child were those made when the silent era was coming to an end. Walt Disney's 1928 *Steamboat Willie* was the film that Harry remembered impressing him, as it did audiences and critics, being the first cartoon to synchronize voices, music, and sounds. He begged his parents to take him, and when he saw it, he realized the music was being played in the wrong order and had to tell the projectionist, who then played it in the right order. He also favored serials or cliffhangers with sudden, unresolved endings that were carried over to the next week's showing. Particularly memorable to him were orientalist serials like *The Return of Chandu*, a 1934 twelve-part thriller with Bela Lugosi as a magician who learned his skills in the

Orient but now was in love with Princess Nadji of Egypt, who is hiding in Chandu's home in Beverly Hills yet is still being menaced by magic-wielding evil forces in Egypt; or *Shadow of Chinatown*, a 1936 fifteen-part serial with Lugosi now as a crazed mixed-race scientist who disrupts business in San Francisco's Chinese community; or the 1936–1940 Flash Gordon films, in which the wealthy polo player and Yale graduate Gordon attempts to save the world from the evils of the planets Mongo and Mars. It was *Drums of Fu Manchu* that influenced Harry the most, a fifteen-part 1940 film about the mastermind Manchu attempting to take over the world. These films may have been thought of by some adults as trash of a genre fiction type and not suitable for children. But to children of a certain age, like Harry, they were their unfiltered myths and fairy tales, populated by magicians, superheroes, and exotic wielders of power and vengeance. They were the means by which children could escape what Breton called pedagogical practices built on a hatred of the marvelous.

Harry had been experimenting with various techniques of image projection as early as a grade-school class project he called a "Jesus box"—a shoebox with a hole cut in the lid and spools on each end so that a paper strip with hand drawings of a Bible story could be cranked past the hole. He went on to use a flashlight to project on the wall his parents' photo negatives from Alaska: "I had thousands of those, enormous masses of this stuff. I can remember the amazement that I felt when I took the lens of the flashlight and was able to see one of the snow scenes on the walls of the hall." Later he made camera obscuras and pinhole cameras. It was as if he had read the history of photography and cinematography and was recapitulating the past until he was stopped by the costs involved with modern motion picture cameras, film, and processing. "I went to cowboy movies when I was a child, but I looked at the stills of movies . . . [I]t is more interesting being alive and observing the perfect 3-D widescreen effect produced by the central nervous system than sitting in a theater watching some kind of myth."

Harry's sense of what anthropological research should include continued to expand. His interest in music and phonograph records had shifted and intensified after he began to make his own recordings and became aware that major recording companies had issued records of American Indian music. He found that recorded music could be a means of understanding other peoples and cultures, and that there were other ways in which he might devote himself to anthropological fieldwork, not always in the traditional sense of living among a group of people, but by searching through art galleries, libraries, bookshops, concerts, flea markets, record stores, even dumpsters.

Buying and listening to commercial recordings of music in the 1940s was usually the business of fans. Harry, however, approached the collecting of records with a sense of discovery, looking for what he and others of his age didn't know and hadn't heard: strange music that might appear to have no useful function, sung in a manner that might seem humanly impossible. This, too, was a form of culture shock. But records could also be a kind of aural notebook for research, played over and over for close listening.

Not that Harry was unfamiliar with the popular music of his time. He'd heard it in movies and on the radio, and even knew the dances that accompanied it, having seen his babysitters demonstrate them. But in his last year of high school his interest was in salvaging folk music that might be disappearing. Folk songs were familiar from his parents' singing and their books, but he had also seen John Jacob Niles perform them. Niles sang folk songs as if they were art songs, as lieder, for which he had been trained. His music was something of a guilty pleasure for Harry, as it later was for Bob Dylan and Joan Baez, who were struck by Niles's intensely dramatic, high-pitched performances.

The day that Harry stumbled onto his first blues recording was a moment of shock. It was a single record that somehow got into a store in Bellingham: "New Highway No. 51" by Tommy McClennan, a raw-edged Mississippi singer and guitarist who recorded forty songs between 1939 and 1942. Recording companies had recognized as early as the 1920s the extraordinary diversity of people in the nation, whether they were in regional enclaves, new immigrant communities, or racially isolated neighborhoods. Even before folk song collectors had begun trekking down the back roads of the country, record company scouts were already in search of local performers to be recorded, especially in the Southeast. Soon the companies' catalogs were including African American, Irish, Albanian, West Indian, Greek, Irish, Jewish (in Hebrew and Yiddish), German, and Italian music. Since such records were categorized and sold by region and ethnicity, it was hard to find such things as blues or white country music in a store anywhere except in the South, some rural towns, or Black neighborhoods. This was music that could unsettle listeners with the starkness of its production, the alien sound of the voices, the vernacular lyrics, and the undisguised emotion.

Harry was moved by the power and sheer strangeness of that McClennan recording, just as Bob Dylan would be when he recorded a version of McClennan's song as "Highway 51" years later. To find more like it, Smith went searching in other towns in Washington, where he found copies of recordings by Memphis Minnie, Rev. F. W. McGee, Yank Rachell, and the Carter Family. Sometimes the performer's name was the only clue that he needed to hear a piece of music, like the Uncle Dave Macon record he found in the basement of a Salvation Army store. Once he began visiting thrift stores, there were discoveries everywhere. He found Japanese recordings, something completely unknown to most Americans, that had recently surfaced when Japanese Americans were sent off to internment camps and forced to sell or dispose of most of their property. Knowing that such music existed, Harry began looking for Chinese recordings next.

His discovery of the blues would take him to Black communities and warehouse districts and lead him to advertise in collectors' magazines and ask other collectors in other states to find things for him. It was a musical journey also being made by a small number of record collectors across the country, many of whom would come to know one another. It's easy to think of hunters and gatherers of old recordings as geeks or loners living in a past not their own. But these were the people who wrote or enabled the first histories of jazz, blues, and country music. Harry's fellow collectors included the Ertegun brothers, Ahmet and Neshui, the Turkish ambassador's sons in Washington, DC, both of whom would become founders of Atlantic Records; Griffith Borgeson, then a leading writer on high performance cars and elite automobiles, and an editor of *Motor Trend*; Marshall Stearns, professor of English literature at Hunter College, the first major writer on jazz and the founder of the Institute of Jazz Studies at Rutgers University–Newark; George Avakian, an Armenian immigrant who later became the recording executive who made Columbia Records the powerhouse of pop and jazz in the middle of the last century; and John Hammond II, one of the Vanderbilts, whose family income allowed him to seek out the people he heard on those records and introduce them to the public at Carnegie Hall concerts and recording sessions that he himself produced.

One of the most fervent collectors was Alan Lomax, who from his teen years had haunted Black record stores in Austin, Texas. But Lomax had an advantage over other collectors by becoming the head of the one-person Archive of American Folk Song at the Library of Congress when he was twenty-one. Despite the common view that Lomax's life as the preeminent folk song collector meant that he viewed commercial recordings as somehow inferior, he began his career in the library by producing recording sessions for folk and jazz musicians with major companies. But he also set out to make the library the site of the largest collection of commercial folk recordings in the world, by not only asking record companies to send their current recordings but also gathering lists and catalogs from the companies and searching through warehouses and shops for older records. When he was warned that it would be impossible for the library to handle the massive number of records that had begun to pile up on the loading dock, and, next, that the companies themselves were scrapping their stock to save space, what would have been the world's largest collection was put on hold. Instead, Lomax hired a young Pete Seeger to join him and his sister Bess in listening to as many records as they could and saving the best. A year later Alan put together a mimeographed "List of American Folk Songs on Commercial Records" that he distributed free from the Library of Congress. Of the 3,000 records they heard, 350 were selected, which he then classified by style, social function, and importance. From that group, he created a short list of what he considered "the most remarkable" recordings.

When World War II began, Harry heard that records were also being collected by the U.S. government, not for Americans to hear but for the shellac that was used in their making, which was scarce and needed for the war effort. If he could find them before they wound up in scrap piles, he would be able to buy them for almost nothing. Harry acquired some twenty thousand, and then began advertising for the rarest records, trading and selling what he had to get them. He was learning more about America's vernacular music, and he, like Lomax, was winnowing his collection to find the best.

Harry's enthusiasm for the blues was followed by a passion for Irish music, and that led him deeper into white country recordings (what the companies then were labeling "hillbilly" music). Later, he became excited about Hungarian bagpipe recordings. Fellow collector and future anthropologist Luis Kemnitzer met Harry in Berkeley in the 1950s, and described him as still in constant search for more records, begging and borrowing and then keeping the records he borrowed because he felt his collection was made up of only the best and would one day be given to some institution. He considered himself as the custodian rather than the owner of these records. Otherwise, Harry could be generous: "He would lend out books that he thought you might want, gave away paintings and collages, but once a record came into his room it never left." The two of them brought the zeal of the ethnographer to their collecting. "We shared a love for the records themselves as well as the music that was encoded in them," Kemnitzer said. "The labels, the record jackets, the catalogs, and the announcements from the early thirties and before were sensual tokens of the eras, and we felt, and smelled what the music was expressing."

After graduating from high school in the spring of 1943, just as he turned twenty, Harry was given a medical exemption from military duty, though he said he had already planned to register as a conscientious objector. In the fall, he entered the University of Washington as an anthropology major. Very little is known about Harry's college days. Bill Holm predicted that the other students in anthropology would be far behind Harry because his knowledge was so advanced. But that led to problems: "In college I was sort of a smartass type," Harry said, "thinking that I knew more about the Indians than anyone else, even the teachers, and that led to a bad feeling." Harry's grades were mostly Cs, with a few Bs and several withdrawals and incompletes. Six of the Cs (including one on American Indians) and two Bs were in courses in anthropology, classes taught by Professors Gunther and Jacobs, who both had seen him as so promising only two years earlier. He believed his trouble in classes was caused by never having learned to write prose. (He failed the entrance examination in English.) His studies lasted for five semesters, from 1943 to 1945, when he withdrew from the university. Yet while there he had done some research work for his professors and given talks for them in classes, and they expected him to continue.

Holm and Harry lost touch with each other when Holm was drafted into the army. Years later, in 1965, Holm would write *Northwest Coast Indian Art: An Analysis of Form*, a book that made him the leading authority on Northwest Coast art, a professor of art history, and a curator at the Burke Museum. He was honored by both Native Americans and academics, and by the creation of the Bill Holm Center for the Study of Northwest Native Art at the Burke Museum. Another student of anthropology at the University of Washington, Wayne Suttles, later acknowledged as the dean of Northwest Coast Native American anthropology, followed in Harry's footsteps when he did research with Julius Charles, Harry's best friend among the Lummi. (When Suttles first approached the Lummi, some confused him with Harry and asked if he was "boy," using the Lummi word they used for Harry.) Harry's name has never appeared in any anthropological works on Washington State's coastal Native Americans.

During his years at college, the war affected the university in ways that led students such as Harry to become involved in campus and off-campus political activities. The state of Washington had been the center of heated politics for years, with the Communist Party USA and unions such as the Industrial Workers of the World, the Congress of Industrial Organizations, and Harry Bridges's International Longshoremen's Association being the foci of opposition. As the war was ending the fear of communism swept the state. At the university, Melville Jacobs was one of a half-dozen professors charged with being members of the Communist Party. Jacobs had just written an anthropology textbook with Bernhard J. Stern, a leading Marxist anthropologist, who had also written about Lummi culture and who was called before Senator Joseph McCarthy's committee on Government Operations. Jacobs and Stern had also given public lectures against racism for years. Though Jacobs survived the threat of being fired, along with several other faculty, he was disciplined and put on probation.

No longer the solitary outsider, Harry became involved with the work of the American Friends Service Committee and the Fellowship of Reconciliation, as well as with students and faculty at the university, in their efforts to aid Jews who had escaped from the Nazis to the United States, and in efforts to resettle more than seven thousand

Japanese and Japanese Americans back to their homes in Seattle and western Washington when they were released from an internment camp in Minidoka, Idaho. Japanese resettlement was opposed by the governor of Washington, the mayor of Seattle, several Washington members of Congress, and some of the largest unions and newspapers. Though he later made light of it, Harry might easily have been swept up in the search for communists in Seattle. But, as was so often the case, he was on the margins, and the FBI never found him of interest, nor kept a file on him. Though little more is known about Harry's other activities in Seattle, he said he had sometimes preached in the Church of God in Christ, a Black Pentecostal Holiness group that welcomed white pilgrims.

To support himself he worked nights as an engine degreaser operator at a Boeing aircraft factory that was making bombers for the air force. He worked there from March 19 until August 29, 1945, when the war ended and most wartime employees suddenly lost their jobs.

But despite dropping out of college, Harry had not given up his plan to study anthropology. He contacted Professor Paul Radin at the University of California about taking classes there, and after an encouraging response took a train to Berkeley. There was reasoning and planning behind this decision, but somehow a different and condensed version of this move became the standard story on Harry. By the 1970s, those who wrote about him said that he had traveled to Berkeley in 1945, gone to a party given for Woody Guthrie, and been introduced to marijuana, and his life was never the same again. It was a way of explaining Harry's break with Washington and academia, and some found it all the more amusing to assume that Woody was his drug connection. But what Harry originally said was that while visiting Berkeley in 1942 he was taken to a International Longshoremen's Association union strike committee meeting when its leader, Harry Bridges, was being threatened with deportation. "Someone had taken me to see [Woody] . . . The person who invited me was connected to Harry Bridges. In the hall I suddenly met a lot of people who had interest in records and stuff." (The date was more likely July 1941, as Woody Guthrie was then in the Bay Area with the Almanac Singers—Millard Lampell, Guthrie, Pete Seeger, and Lee Hays— for the Harry Bridges gathering.) It was there that Smith first heard folk singing used for contemporary political causes. "But I didn't like [Guthrie's] singing. It was too sophisticated and too involved with social problems . . . It wasn't the sort of stuff I was interested in." Harry then returned to Washington, finished high school, and entered college. He was not introduced to marijuana until some five years later, and not by Woody, but by Griff Borgeson.

2

Dark They Were, with Golden Eyes
Harry Smith in California, 1945–1947

In 1945 the Bay Area seemed to be the point where all lines met. Soldiers were mustering out from the Pacific front, and conscientious objectors turned up on weekend passes from their work camps in Oregon. The population had recently swelled with the arrival of African Americans recruited from the South by the federal War Manpower Commission to work on the naval docks, and Mexicans invited by the government's Bracero Program for farmwork. Japanese Americans were beginning to return from internment camps. There were anarchists, theosophists, spiritualists, self-declared futurists, ex-Wobblies, jackleg astrologers, Reichian analysts, American Buddhists, Eurosurrealists, and nonobservant Kabbalists. UFO sightings and the Kinsey Report were hot topics. Peyote and Benzedrine were legal.

Harry arrived in Berkeley just as Kenneth Rexroth was declaring the existence of a San Francisco Renaissance in poetry (even as the poets Robert Duncan and Jack Spicer were threatening a response from a Berkeley Renaissance). Most people in the arts on the East Coast may have thought of San Francisco as a nineteenth-century town, part of the old Wild West, a cultural wilderness. But in the Bay Area, artists there saw it as a place for experimentation free of tradition and old European culture. California was not yet the site of the cool, chromatic lifestyle that in the sixties would be promoted by Hollywood movies and land developers, and the Bay Area's bohemians were not quite, yet were almost, a mirror image of New York's Beats.

Things were changing fast. Too fast for some. In 1947, *Harper's Magazine* published "The New Cult of Sex and Anarchy," a purple-tinted portrait of the new bohemians of the Bay Area that cast them as "sentimental mystics," "sexual anarchists," "deviants," and "Neo-Nazis."

For Harry, the main event was the Department of Anthropology at the University of California at Berkeley, and namely two members of its faculty, Jaime de Angulo and Paul Radin. De Angulo was a Spaniard raised in Paris who had been a cowboy in Colorado, mined silver in Honduras, received a medical degree from Johns Hopkins, worked as a genetics researcher at Stanford, run a cattle ranch in California, homesteaded in Big Sur, and done research among several California Indian groups. He'd written books and articles of poetry, fiction, language, and ethnography, and worked out the grammars of a number of Native languages, all without training in anthropology or linguistics. But he also could test the limits of a university department, even Berkeley's, as he was sometimes suicidal, a "cross-dresser," a drug user, and, more intolerable to academics, the kind of teacher who canceled classes to travel to reservations to make sure that what he was teaching was correct.

Paul Radin had been one of Boas's students, but unlike others of the first American anthropologists, he failed to gain Boas's trust and was never recommended for a teaching job. He could be annoyingly contentious when he disagreed with his teacher or his colleagues, was accused of being reckless, and held strong political views that resulted in his being trailed by the FBI for much of his life, though without ever having any charges brought against him. On the other hand, his research and publications on the Winnebago Indians of Wisconsin were considered among the best work done by any anthropologist or linguist. Few were aware that he had also collected narratives of God's calls to African Americans to become preachers, and had written a study of Italian American dockworkers in San Francisco. Recommendations or not, he managed to teach at Mills College, Fisk University, Black Mountain College, Kenyon College, the University of

Chicago, Berkeley (three times), and Brandeis University, and worked for the Bureau of Indian Affairs, the Works Progress Administration, the C. G. Jung Institute, and the Bollingen Foundation.

Though Radin and de Angulo both were on the margins of the department's teaching staff—de Angulo taught in the summer school for only one year, and Radin was relegated to the university extension—their research was admired and financially supported. Both had friends in and out of anthropology. De Angulo's associates included D. H. Lawrence, Carl Jung, Henry Miller, Ezra Pound, Robinson Jeffers, Henry Cowell, Harry Partch, Robert Duncan, and Jack Spicer. Radin was close to his students, freely sharing his research notes with them and inviting them to his parties, along with poets, artists, and intellectuals. These were occasions where Harry later met people like the poet Josephine Miles, the collagist Jean Varda, and the anthropologist and poet Robert Barlow. Radin introduced finger painting (then not widely known) as a kind of adult party game and Rorschach test. Guests took turns painting on sheets of newspaper, and then putting them up on the wall to be discussed.

Even the most respected and orthodox members of the Berkeley department could cross into areas that modern anthropology would consider frivolous at best. Alfred Kroeber, the chair of the department, still maintained his interest in the arts and literature, and was translating A. E. Housman's poetry into German. The other major figure in the department was Robert Lowie, whose wide concerns included Native American dance, art, and myth, but even he published some of his work in nonprofessional magazines like *Tomorrow*.

At that time, anthropologists were finally abandoning the concept of the "primitive" in favor of what they began calling "traditional," "preliterate," or "non-Western" peoples. Boas and other anthropologists had cast aside the widespread belief in a hierarchy of social evolution with the "primitives" at the bottom and Euro-Americans at the top. Their deep interest in languages gave them a way of making their point: There were no primitive languages, no underdeveloped or inferior languages. All were complex. A people who may not have invented the wheel or agriculture nonetheless invented complex grammar and vocabulary that gave them the means necessary for their own understanding of the world and survival. At the same time there were others, like Radin, de Angulo, and Lévi-Strauss, who were forcefully arguing that there were still reasons to rethink and learn from people who had been called "primitive." Perhaps advances in technology and "reason" had resulted in modern peoples losing other forms of knowledge and reasoning. Was that not why anthropologists distanced themselves from their own culture to join other peoples to learn different ways of being human? De Angulo saw the Achumawi Indians of Northern California as not having exchanged their culture for that of white Americans, but only added it to their own. Radin thought that the "Negro was not converted to the white Christian God. He converted God to himself." These were and still are radical ideas to many.

Berkeley was open to having nonstudents serve as assistants to professors, and it was not unusual that a number of poets were hired to help with research for the faculty: Robert Duncan typed de Angulo's manuscript for *What Is Language?*, and Jack Spicer worked with Professor David Reed on the use of quantitative methods with American Indian languages. When Radin agreed to hire Harry as his assistant, he returned to Seattle, gave some of his recordings and ethnographic notes and documents to Professor Jacobs, sold some of his commercial folk recordings, shipped the rest to Berkeley, and headed south again. Harry sat in on some classes in anthropology at Berkeley, but never registered. His work for Radin was done while the professor was writing what would become *The Culture of the Winnebago: As Described by Themselves* (1947) and *Winnebago Hero Cycles: A Study in Aboriginal*

Literature (1948). Though Harry claimed that he made mistakes in his work (he typically denounced any work he did for hire as flawed), he was close enough to Radin to walk to work with him and be invited to his parties.

When he first arrived in Berkeley, Harry moved into a 490-square-foot, three-room apartment (the bathroom was also the kitchen) at 5½ Panoramic Way. The owner of the house, Mrs. Stern, let him live there in exchange for yard work and ivy trimming, though Harry said that he made a wreck of the yard. His apartment was in a building also occupied by the folk music scholar Bertrand H. Bronson, a professor of English at Berkeley who was then finding and analyzing tunes that matched the texts of Francis James Child's classic *The English and Scottish Popular Ballads*. The result would be Bronson's four volumes of *The Traditional Tunes of the Child Ballads*, one of the most important works in American folk song scholarship. Unlike other scholars, Bronson used commercial recordings as part of his sources, which strengthened Harry's belief in the importance of his own collection. Soon he was borrowing from the professor's library and recordings, and talking with him about folk songs. Harry later regretted not spending more time learning from Bronson, though he did manage to trick Bronson's wife into trading him some of the professor's records while he was out of town.

One of the first people Harry met in Berkeley was the painter Jordan Belson, a senior at the university. Belson and a few other art students were walking past Harry's apartment when they stopped, peered through the window, and saw what looked like a tiny museum gallery with dramatically lit artwork, books, a cot, a kachina doll, and a large desk, all very tidy. Harry noticed their interest and invited them in for peppermint tea. "He was so odd and strange," Belson recalled, "[such a] gnome-like, intense creature, that I didn't think any of us knew quite what to make of him . . . He was extremely ingratiating, charming and dressed in a sort of shabby, professorial manner with a tie and a dress shirt and a regular jacket—none of us were like that. We were all very sloppy, paint-smeared art students." Harry had begun what would be a lifelong practice of radically narrowed food preferences, at that time eating only a mixture of sugar and butter, which left him weak and bedridden.

Strange or not, Harry and that apartment with its odd books, music, and paintings became an attraction for other art students, musicians, and poets. Some of his paintings were in the style of Paul Klee—human figures made out of geometric forms, with strong colors and weaving lines that might suggest the polyphony of music. (Belson recalled seeing a Klee-like figure made up of triangles with the letters *s-s-s-s* coming out of his mouth, "smoking dope illustrated.") On one wall there were carefully executed collages similar to those of Max Ernst—cutout antique steel engravings with texts from various sources now placed in new contexts. This surrealist technique is what Ernst once described as "the systematic exploitation of the accidentally or artificially provoked encounter of two or more foreign realities on a seemingly incongruous level—and the spark of poetry that leaps across the gap as these two realities are brought together." Throughout most of Harry's life he worked somewhere close to such breaks, whether with collage, montage, musical intervals, or in the natural or forced cracks in cultures. In a lecture he gave at Naropa University some forty years later, he referred to surrealism as "a specialized way of bringing people into unity with one another through the medium of insults and arbitrary interactions between them."

When he had visitors, Harry played old jazz and country music records that none of them had ever heard, showed them strange collages, and introduced them to the exquisite corpse game. When he was with those he knew well, he'd spring tricks on them (Dadaist, or sophomoric, depending on their tolerance): spreading mustard on a friend's finger and pretending to eat it like a hot dog, or licking a slug from the garden. He also served joints along with the tea. "Harry Smith was the first person who turned me on," Belson said:

I had never heard of grass. We puffed on it and we had all kinds of unusual perceptions of time and space. Everything slowed down. Music really slowed down enormously, so that you could really *hear* it, you could hear in between the notes. Harry showed me some non-objective paintings he had, reproductions of Kandinsky, and they no longer looked flat and printed on a piece of paper. They were like looking into a box of some sort: Everything was floating in space, which is probably the way Kandinsky had hoped they would look.

Philip Lamantia, another of Harry's new friends, was, by his own words, a prodigy, first publishing his poetry at fifteen and sixteen in the surrealist journals *View* and *VVV*, and then a book of poems at seventeen. He first met Harry in 1946 at the San Francisco Museum of Art at an exhibit of the work of André Masson, the surrealist painter whose belief in automatic writing had led him to experiment with sleep deprivation and drugs to heighten his subconscious. Lamantia had already met Masson, as well as Duchamp, Ernst, Rexroth, Lévi-Strauss, Seligmann, Paul Bowles, and André Breton, whom he called his mentor. He came to know them, and other surrealists and artists, when he spent a year in New York after dropping out of high school at sixteen and becoming an assistant editor at *View*. He understood how Harry could see the connection between art and anthropology, and introduced him to the writings of Lévi-Strauss and Seligmann, as well as to de Angulo and poets like Duncan and Spicer. Harry, in turn, shared with him old books on alchemy that he had been rounding up from local bookstores.

They were both serious devotees of jazz and spent long nights together in local jazz clubs, and Lamantia was said to be one of the first to read poetry to live jazz accompaniment. Both had studied and come to know Native American people and their cultures, Lamantia's focus being the Amerindian peoples of California and their differences from Indians elsewhere: they lived in smaller-sized groups, and had a far greater number of languages. Along with some of the anthropology students, Lamantia had found his way to the rituals of the Washoe people near Lake Tahoe and used their peyote for his own spiritual ends. This led him to Jaime de Angulo, who he thought was similar to Harry in many ways. "Harry was passionate about Indians," Lamantia said. "He knew the Salish best, the Lummi next. He felt the Salish culture was still intact and had kept their language, rituals, and taught them to their youth, and they thought Harry was doing the same thing. Harry had a manuscript he was working on, transcribing the language, songs, and conversations of the Salish. But he never intended it to be published." That passion continued for the rest of Harry's life, and he was known to break into tears at learning of injustices afflicting some of America's first inhabitants.

When they met at the museum and saw Masson's work, Harry told Lamantia that he thought his own paintings were closer to Miró's and Dalí's, but he was beginning to disagree with the surrealists—he would soon be drawing and painting works derived not from the physical world, but from what he heard on jazz records. He was interested in the occult in only the literal sense of the word—something that was hidden—but less concerned with the esoteric, the cryptic, or the enigmatic.

It's hard to fathom how Harry navigated his way through the arts communities of the Bay so quickly and seemingly found a place in all of them. He entered an ever-widening series of circles—folk music fans, musicians, painters, filmmakers, anthropologists, students, surrealists, occultists, and poets. "He was surprisingly social," Belson said. "There were always a bunch of people around him. He seemed to know everybody. He *lived* with everybody!"

Many of his friends and allies are known only through vague

memories of his contemporaries, but the range of them is extraordinary: the painter, occultist, and art house film actress Marjorie Cameron, who was married to the rocket scientist Jack Parsons, a follower of Aleister Crowley and business partner of L. Ron Hubbard; Bern Porter, poet, physicist, and publisher of *Circle* magazine and books; Charles Stansfeld Jones, an occultist and close associate of Aleister Crowley; and Wallace Berman, the filmmaker, collagist, creator of the very influential mail art folio *Semina*, who, despite not being widely known, found himself on the cover of the Beatles' *Sgt. Pepper's Lonely Hearts Club Band* and in a role in *Easy Rider*. Many of Harry's friends were avid record collectors, people like Bob Waller, whose taste also ran to Arab, flamenco, African, jazz, blues, and country records, or Peter Tamony, who was an internationally known and published authority on the etymology of slang words such as "hip" and "funky."

One group that Harry discovered in California was the small number of urban, well-educated record collectors who were devoted to early country music. Griff and Lil Borgeson were two of the most enthusiastic and knowledgeable of them all. Once, when driving through a storm, they stopped at a trailer park in Altaville, part of the gold rush city of Angels Camp, California, where they discovered their next-door neighbor was Sara Carter of the Carter Family, one of the best-known commercially recorded country music groups. Following the breakup of her marriage and the family singing group, she was escaping her ex-husband, A. P. Carter; the Carter Family's fans; and country music itself. But Lil managed to record some interviews with Sara and tried to convince her that, with the help of some of their Hollywood friends, she could return to performing. The Borgesons had some fun teasing Harry by making him guess where she was, and when he finally guessed right, he set out to find her.

Just as he was arriving at her trailer in a thunderstorm, he tried peyote for the first time ("I wasn't sure if the top of my head wasn't going to fly off"). Since she had retired from singing Sara had devoted herself to raising peacocks and making patchwork quilts. She allowed Harry to photograph the quilts, and answered his questions about the name of each quilt's patterns. If she didn't have a name, he asked her to make one up. He wanted to see if there were any connections between the names of patterns of quilts and the names of songs that were sung by the Carter Family.

> She didn't understand me or what I was trying to say. It was some kind of Rorschach response like thing. She'd say, "Well that one is called 'Field of Diamonds,' I guess that's like 'Diamonds in the Rough.'" That was about as close as she came . . .
>
> It was like a way of investigating something. It was just what I might have been doing with the Indians at the same time . . . The problems that I'd set myself on have to do with correlating music into some kind of a visual thing, into some kind of diagram . . . I'm sure that if you could collect sufficient patchwork quilts from the same people who made the records, like Uncle Dave Macon or Sara Carter's houses, you could figure out just about anything you can from the music. Everything could be figured out regarding their judgment in relation to certain intellectual processes . . . One thing is to try and compress data, whatever it happens to be, into a small area and study that thing, for the same reason an archaeologist studies pot shards, because you can sit down in trenches and determine stylistic trends. At the end of gathering all this data, whether it's music or whatever, it has to be correlated with other fields of knowledge.

Smith's interest in the connection between quilt pattern names and song titles anticipated later approaches to studies of tradition. In one of the first articles written about Harry, John Cohen noted that the Carter Family created many of their songs from older songs, and borrowed older songs' titles as well. Harry returned to see Sara Carter several times, and wanted to talk to her about the career she had put behind her and replaced with a commitment to a Christian life (she wouldn't allow records or even a guitar in her house). She gave him pictures of herself, including some from the period in which she had performed solo on the Mexican border radio station owned by the millionaire quack doctor John R. Brinkley, who claimed that goat glands could cure male impotency. When Harry asked her why she had recorded and claimed songs such as Ma Rainey's "Jealous Hearted Blues" and retitled it "Jealous Hearted Me," but only slightly changed the original's bawdy words ("Got a stove in the kitchen / And it bakes nice and brown / But I need a papa / To turn the damper down"), Sara "said something about 'dirty old ugly talk.'"

JAZZ AND ART: NON-OBJECTIVE ANIMATED FILM AND VISUAL MUSIC

Though Harry's range of interests was unusually wide, much of the time he was looking backward to the antique, or away to what some would call the exotic. Even his interests in painting and jazz were originally limited to the pre-1940s. But at age twenty-seven, he stepped into the modern.

Jazz, motion pictures, modern dance, and modern art all developed together and shared a number of characteristics and aims. The American affinity for jazz and painting was apparent shortly after the Armory Show of 1913, when painters like Arthur Dove and Stuart Davis attempted by various means to paint this new music, and made a point of explaining how the music inspired a new approach to art. For some artists there was the appeal of crossing class and racial lines in their practice, and if their intention was to break the European hold on art in order to create a truly American aesthetic, jazz, like African sculpture, was an ideal model. It had already spread around the world and was widely understood to be at the heart of modernism. When the subconscious sources of surrealism were discussed, the improvisations of jazz musicians were sometimes mentioned as a form of spirit possession. It was noticed that the use of multiple perspectives could be found in both cubism and jazz, since jazz musicians had already weakened the distinction between accompaniment and soloist, background and foreground, by putting them all on the same sonic plane.

The Museum of Modern Art in New York City and the San Francisco Museum of Art both began presenting concerts of jazz in the early 1940s, though the San Francisco Museum committed itself more fully to recognizing the music as another form of modern art, and in 1943 began regular jazz concerts and sponsored the first series of lectures on jazz in the United States, given by Rudi Blesh, an interior designer and music journalist. His talks launched his career as a gallery owner, a record producer, and an art critic who published books on jazz, modern art, and collage. (It was his friend Marcel Duchamp who suggested that he name his record company Circle.)

Although the link between jazz and modern art was not always obvious in painting (especially since critics and art historians largely ignored it), when abstract-art filmmakers in Europe and North America began using jazz soundtracks there was no avoiding the influence. Rhythm in sound and images were threaded together. While Clement Greenberg was holding forth on kitsch vs. the avant-garde on the East Coast, the West Coast avant-garde filmmakers were inserting jazz into their artworks, not because they considered them as low art disrupting modern art but because they thought jazz *was* high art.

Harry Smith's paintings are not as widely known as his music and film work, although he thought his painting was his most important contribution: "The films are minor accessories to my painting. It just happened that I had the films with me when everything else was destroyed. My paintings were infinitely better than my films, because much more time was spent on them." But Harry was nevertheless ambivalent, according to Belson:

> He always had a rather scornful attitude towards artists. He didn't like to be thought of as one. He thought of himself as some sort of anthropologist or something of that sort. I can understand why he didn't want to be identified with artists, from his point of view they were just pathetic misfits. Intellectually they didn't interest him at all. But he did produce extraordinary works of art. In fact, I think his painting, his drawings, and other graphic work is where his genius shows through.

Only a few of the paintings and thousands of sketches that Harry said he did before he moved to California still exist. His Samish dance painting done in Washington at age seventeen is enough to show that he had broken with the tradition of paintings of Native Americans by Europeans and Euro-Americans, and that he had a modernist vision in the point of view and the positioning of the dancers and their stylized faces. It would be important to know what his other early works were like, to see to what degree Northwest Coast Indian art had influenced him as it had some American abstract painters and what he had gathered from the spiritual and theosophical illustrations he had dutifully copied from his father's and the library's books, and how much he had learned from the nineteenth-century botanical and zoological illustrations of Karl Blossfeldt and Ernst Haeckel that also helped shape his abstract painting.

A few photographs of his paintings from his time in California exist, though most of the originals were given away, lost, or destroyed by him. Several of those missing have brief cameo appearances in a few of his films. The loss of his paintings or films was sometimes devastating to him, but at other times he seemed not to care, claiming the loss forced him to find a fresh perspective. Once, in a burst of profanity, he denounced the preservation of films as a waste of money, since it could have been spent on a time machine that could retrieve them from the past.

> Indeed the more the arts develop the more they depend on
> each other for definition. We will borrow from painting first
> and call it pattern. Later we will borrow from music
> and call it rhythm.
>
> —E. M. Forster, *Aspects of the Novel*

When Wassily Kandinsky's 1926 book on non-objective painting, *Point and Line to Plane*, was translated into English in 1947, Harry was excited by the language it offered him for relating abstract art and jazz, and the way it tied painting to geometry and other subjects. It was at once a new kind of art theory and a how-to guide for artists. He was especially impressed by Kandinsky's example of how geometric forms could be used to paint a visual representation of Beethoven's *Fifth Symphony*. Harry had also read Annie Besant and C. W. Leadbeater's *Thought Forms*, one of the basic books of Victorian theosophy, in which the authors proposed that words, colors, and sounds are all related and can emerge from thoughts and spiritual states in a form of synesthesia. Harry saw its illustrations as the first non-objective art. These two books led Harry to try to create far more complex paintings of jazz recordings. Painters like Arthur Dove and Stuart Davis had used jazz recordings as subjects, but their works were abstractions or abstract visual translations of what was on the records. What Harry wanted was as literal a visualization of a record as possible, what he called a "transcription," in which every note and chord would be represented by dots, strokes, and other actions on the canvas. Philip Lamantia remembered some of Harry's paintings as being based on the same Dizzy Gillespie Latin jazz works he later used on his first four films—*Manteca, Algo Bueno, Guarachi Guaro*, and *Manteca* again. Following Smith, Jordan Belson's first films, *Caravan* and *Mambo*, also used Latin jazz recordings as soundtracks.

Harry first worked out his record paintings with sketches in notebooks and on barroom napkins, and they were among what he and Belson called "brain drawings," depictions of pure consciousness as glyphic mind maps. Harry sketched everywhere he went, especially at jazz clubs, or when he visited Belson's studio in North Beach. (They often worked in each other's spaces.) Lamantia recalled that "Harry would set the painting, approximately 3 feet by 4 feet, on an easel, and put a Dizzy Gillespie or Pérez Prado record on the phonograph. He would then stand to one side of the painting, long pointer in hand, slightly huddled over, and formally point to one small area after another in succession as the music progressed." Anthropology student Luis Kemnitzer had seen the same thing: "Time and events were in a linear progression and happening all at once at the same time." Harry declared it a new art form, a type of painting that was at once a performance and a form of instruction. But it was also a type of animation-in-painting, in which a form underwent metamorphosis.

Jordan Belson once diagrammed how Harry demonstrated the way to read his painting of Dizzy Gillespie's 1948 recording "Lover, Come Back to Me." His sketch was made from memory; Harry's demonstration would have been fuller and more complex. But it does show how he distributed the sections of the recording in the formation of a mandala—a word that in Sanskrit means "circle," though it's usually drawn as a square with four gates that contain a circle. In Hinduism or Buddhism, Mandalas are representations of the universe. To Harry, these jazz records were universes in themselves. But his performance of the music and the painting together was also a form of mutual collage, one that would resurface in his 1948 painting of Dizzy Gillespie's "Manteca" and his 1949–1950 *Film No. 4*, which alludes to the same recording. "Each stroke in that painting represents a different note on the recording," he told the film scholar P. Adams Sitney. "If I had the record, I could project the painting as a slide and point to a certain thing. This is the main theme in there, which is a doot-doot-doot, doot-doot-doottadootdoot—those curved lines up here. See, ta-doot-doot-doot-dootaloot-dootaloot, and so forth. Each note is on there . . . There's a dot for each note and the phrases that the notes consist of are colored in a certain way or made in a certain path."

He told Sitney that "the most complex one of these is . . . one of Charlie Parker's records . . . ["Koko"]. That's a really complex painting. That took five years. Just like I gave up making films after that last hand-drawn one took a number of years; I gave up painting after that took a number of years to make. It was just too exhausting." Harry's other known paintings of records were Dizzy Gillespie's 1948 "Algo Bueno" and "Ool-Ya-Koo."

Could these painting-transcriptions be read by musicians and played as if they were music scores? Assuming that Smith's methods are consistent, and could be explained to musicians, there's no reason why they couldn't be read and played. How accurate they would sound is a question, but it's also a question for traditional music transcription, which is often inadequate for transcribing improvised jazz from recordings. In any case, this was not his intention in making these visual transcriptions. He wanted to animate painting, and to see how improvised music would look, a practice somewhat similar to that of jazz musicians, who commonly transcribe solos from recordings to see how they work. Harry's paintings also anticipated the first modern graphic scores of composers like John Cage and Morton Feldman, though Smith's would be better described as graphic transcriptions.

OLD WEIRD CINEMA

The San Francisco Museum of Art began screening films in 1937 and introduced the Art in Cinema program in 1946. This new film initiative first rented from the Museum of Modern Art in New York City films by Buñuel, Dalí, Cocteau, Duchamp, and Man Ray, but as they had done with jazz, they emphatically declared (against some angry objections) that avant-garde film was an art equal to other arts. Art in Cinema's founder, Frank Stauffacher, stated their goals in the program for their first series:

> We hope that this series will . . . show the relation between the film and the other art media—sculpture, painting, poetry: that it will stimulate interest in the film as a creative art medium in itself, requiring more of an effort of participation on the part of the audience than the Hollywood fantasies, before which an audience sits passively and uncreatively, and that it will give assistance to those contemporary artists who labor in obscurity in America with no distribution channels for their work.

To make their point, they began presenting a wider range of films, like those from younger, innovative filmmakers such as Maya Deren and James and John Whitney. Next was the program "Non-Objective Form Synchronized with Music," with films by Oskar Fischinger and Mary Ellen Bute, and "The Animated Film as an Art Form," with Hans Richter, Viking Eggeling, and Walt Disney (featuring his *Steamboat Willie*). Harry and Jordan Belson were at those first programs in the fall of 1946, and were so excited by Fischinger's films that they both began making their own. They saw film as a means of using their mutual interests in mystical experience and experiments with drugs in ways that were not possible with painting. Harry volunteered to work for Art in Cinema in exchange for free admission, and he saw every one of their screenings over the next five years, even when they repeated showings in Berkeley. Within a year, Stauffacher replaced his principal collaborator with Harry, who took over handling correspondence, working on film rentals, setting up showings, and traveling to meet filmmakers to invite them to show their films. He was not paid for his work, but in the beginning no one at Art in Cinema was making any money except the filmmakers, who were paid for rentals of their films.

There were special problems connected to running a film program, especially in a museum not designed for film projection. Most of the films they presented were not distributed commercially and had to be searched for. The filmmakers sometimes had to be convinced to ship their only copy to San Francisco, and music often had to be provided because many of the filmmakers did not yet have the means to add sound. Some of the films, like those of the Whitney brothers, were advertised as "experimental"—that is, not yet complete. Others were in rough condition, giving them a homemade, uncertain feel, as if they were not made for public viewing. With Hollywood just to the south, some of these films could seem bizarre to many, but feature films had already begun to embrace surrealism for special effects in dream sequences. Disney's cartoons were filled with abstract images, and Busby Berkeley's dance choreography to jazz music showed moving geometric figures of lines of dancers filmed through holes in the ceiling.

The audiences for Art in Cinema were usually larger than those for any of the other special programs at the San Francisco museum. They were recognized as serious art events, and drew in viewers from various fields, gathering a much more diverse group than the typical crowd at the museum. Barbara Stauffacher Solomon, no fan of the films her husband programmed, said, "The audience was the best part of the performance."

> Berkeley professors with tweed jackets and frumpy wives . . . arrived early to get good seats. Architects and their dates, high-styled with expensive haircuts, dressed in black-and-white, or grey, or black-and-grey, looked for seats near each other or rich looking potential clients. Young lawyers arrived in three-piece suits with ladies in pearls and little black

dresses. The Woman's Board of the Museum, socialites, and rich blondes devoted to the arts . . . wore cashmere sweaters, Pre-Columbian jewelry, and pageboys, and walked as if they owned the place and their gay escorts. Pretty young women, recently graduated from Art Appreciation 101, who had practiced how to eat hamburgers without smudging their lipstick, looked for sensitive young men. Artists on the GI Bill, recently attacking the Axis, instead of big canvasses, jazz musicians, and poets arrived late, wore black turtlenecks and Levi's, and slinked into the remaining seats or slumped against the walls . . . It was a pity to turn the lights off.

Harry had never encountered the kind of films that the museum was showing. There were no museum or gallery displays or books about them, and if there were any screenshots in print media, they looked like paintings. In the early 1900s painters in Europe such as Kandinsky and Rudolf Bauer had begun making what were called non-objective paintings. The artist and curator Baroness Hilla von Rebay described them as something different from abstract films, because abstract art can reveal its natural or biomorphic sources, while non-objective art refers to no subject at all. Such art was often geometric, or aimed at some forms of spirituality. (Jordan Belson, however, said that it wasn't really non-objective: "People just didn't yet know what the subject was.") From their beginning, non-objective films were viewed skeptically by galleries, museums, and many artists who thought they were not art. It was not clear to everyone that they were handmade, that they were the products of inspired individuals working alone. Viewings needed more time and space than paintings or even photographs, which ruled out their being shown in most galleries and many museums. Films couldn't be framed and hung on the wall. They were likely to be damaged after a number of showings and were not the kind of art that would be collected and then donated to a museum.

Since many of these pioneering experimental films were very brief, hand-drawn, and without sound, they were often understood to be a form of animation, but were puzzling, since they had no story line or actors. Within a few years the development of sound on film would make the distinction between art and mainstream film even more pronounced. Films without sound began to look both weird *and* old. When music was added, they were usually mistaken as art illustrating music. Audiences attuned to the Hollywood style of production, in which story, pictures, and sound seamlessly worked together, were made uneasy by the brevity and lack of context of these films. Some of these art films were so private, so different from the world of commercial film, that the first viewings of them were provocative and disturbing, as if they were secretly coded messages, or films made by the insane. It didn't help that when art films *were* actually shown in theaters, they were placed before or between full-length films, in the slots in which cartoons usually appeared. In an effort to get their work into movie theaters, some tried adding written prefaces to their films to explain that they were experiments in art and music, but it was not successful.

Inevitably, some art filmmakers did want to draw attention to the music, by making it visible in ways other than transcribing it onto scores to be read by musicians. It was an old idea, beginning at least as early as the eighteenth century, when organs that might play colors as well as musical notes were conceived. The early twentieth-century dream of animating the invisible flow of musical notes through space would seem to undercut the whole point of non-objective art. But to some, music was already surreal, with no subject, and sound on film was a temptation that some painters could not resist, especially when they had seen Hollywood use visual abstractions with music for special effects, or when Disney used abstractions in the full-length musical *Fantasia* in 1940. When the German engineer-turned-filmmaker-and-painter Oskar Fischinger arrived in the United States in 1936, his animated art film *Allegretto* got the attention of Hollywood with his use of a Gershwin-like jazz soundtrack. Projected on a big theater screen, his films took on a spectacular look, like fireworks and falling stars. Fischinger was successful at bringing painting, drawing, and music together in his films as a new form of art, which got him work at MGM, Paramount, and Disney. But he had doubts about art films aimed at popular audiences, and quit Disney during the production of *Fantasia* in protest over what he thought was a dilution of his work. Still, he was admired by painters and the more adventurous filmmakers like Orson Welles, who put him on salary for "The Story of Jazz," one part of his never-completed anthology movie *It's All True*.

Smith and Belson were deeply influenced by Fischinger. In a letter to Fischinger in July 1947, Richard Foster, cofounder of Art in Cinema, praised his work and introduced him to Harry in a letter:

> Your films have excited many people here, and one of them, Harry Smith, 5 ½ Panoramic Street, Berkeley—has begun an abstract film to music. Harry is an artist with a background in New Orleans jazz and anthropology, and his work is very exciting. He is using the animation technique that you and Ruttmann first used—that of drawing directly on the film. He is using various dies [*sic*] instead of oils, and is making about 1000 feet in 35 millimeter. His first experimental 100 feet we showed at a private showing, and the colors were excellent. He didn't have the music ready for the film, but his idea of the music seems a good one, a combination of certain New Orleans jazz and some percussion instrumentation he recorded himself. He is very interested in drawing the sound track directly on the film and when I told him you had done it already, he wanted to see you right away.

Harry did see him right away, and when he returned from Los Angeles he wrote: "I am writing you, first of all, to thank you for the time you gave to me when I was in Los Angeles a few weeks ago. It was a very great pleasure to be able to talk to you, as there are so few people who know anything about the abstract film, and there are certainly none, other than yourself, who have more than just scratched the surface of the medium." Harry later said that the trip was also memorable since they were kicked out of a restaurant because "[I] looked like some homosexual off the streets."

He returned to Los Angeles several times, hitchhiking rides, sometimes staying with the Whitney brothers and visiting Fischinger again, once when John Cage and Merce Cunningham were there (Cage said they liked Harry very much). In a testimonial about Fischinger that he wrote years later for the film scholar William Moritz, Harry said:

> I learned concentration from him—visiting his home and seeing how he could sit serenely in that small house, crawling with children, and still painting those stunning pictures. That great film *Motion Painting* makes the process seem deceptively simple—and it was simple for him: the images really did just flow from his brush, never a ruler or a compass, all free-hand—but you can't see all the obstacles he had to overcome in order to work at all. Something so wonderful happened in that film, and in those paintings, something so much better than all the Pollocks and other stuff that the museums fight to get hold of.

On these same trips, Harry visited the Whitney brothers and Kenneth Anger, all of whom were taking film in remarkably new directions. John and James Whitney brought advanced animation, technology, and contemporary classical music composition skills to their films, and set out to rethink how visual images and sound could be produced. They were the only filmmakers other than Fischinger that Harry acknowledged as an influence. Kenneth Anger was then a twenty-year-old filmmaker who, like Harry, had been working alone, exploring drugs, music, and finding new possibilities in film. He had just made *Fireworks*, a film that brought homoerotic desire and sexuality into American cinema in a dreamlike form based in World War II–era Los Angeles gay history. It was a film that stunned everyone, even Harry, who said, "Everybody was very embarrassed by his films at that point . . . He was embarrassed . . . I didn't recognize the artistic quality."

Harry's deepening interest in filmmaking after he moved to California might seem surprising since he had never operated a motion-picture camera. He said that between 1939 and 1942 he made his first film ("or part of that") by painting on film, though some have doubted him, believing that he was attempting to claim that he was the first. But he did think that he had been the first, and said he was shocked when he learned that the New Zealander Len Lye was more than a decade ahead of him with his 1935 *A Colour Box*, a direct drawing on film mixed with documentary footage that also used soundtracks of jazz, Latin, and Caribbean music. And just as shocking, he learned that Lye painted on the much smaller 16-millimeter film stock. But even if Harry was not the first, what he created in California with the same techniques was totally original.

Although neither Smith nor Belson knew anything about motion-picture cameras, they had met Hy Hirsh, a cinematographer and still photographer who had worked for Columbia Pictures. He taught both of them camera technique and loaned them equipment they couldn't afford. "Occasionally we [three] would go to a downtown theater that showed nothing but cartoons," Belson said. "I think we were looking for anything that was visually dynamic and animated. In those days animated cartoons were about the only creative things going in the commercial film world. (Harry identified with Tweety Bird, Hy Hirsh was Sylvester [and I was] Daffy Duck.)" Hirsh was impressed by Harry's personal involvement and creativity in how he projected his own films, re-edited them, and changed their color by using spotlights, literally performing the films. Hirsh then began to perform his own films by re-editing and changing the music, usually jazz, for different performances. Both Harry and Hirsh viewed jazz musicians' improvisations and their in-the-moment editing of their solos as the model for their performed films.

In Harry's earliest film work, he looked backward to the beginnings of film history, well before the invention of sound on film had generated a whole new era. As a child he had first seen motion pictures just at the point where they were changing from silent to sound, and he was inspired by some of the possibilities of silent film. In the early days of motion pictures there was a sense that anything seemed possible. Animation had developed at the same time as motion pictures, and it was the freer and more daring form from the beginning. Time and space could be altered, stopped and started, reversed, sped up and slowed down; objects came alive; animals turned into humans; anything could be made to disappear and then reappear, and nothing could be turned into something. Animated figures could step out (or fall out) of the film, then peek back in to read the credits or see what was happening without them. Methods and processes of production seemed limitless: images could be scratched, painted, photographed, drawn, or etched on film. Silhouettes, cutouts, and photos might be attached, and fluids, gels, smoke, and gas could be used in the process. The real and the surreal, the earth and the heavens could all be put into play without the use of special effects.

This excitement over the potential for animation was evident when in his 1941 writings on Walt Disney the filmmaker and theorist Sergei Eisenstein linked animation to the oldest forms of artistic expression, using words like "animism" and "totemism" when speaking of the synesthetic effects of sound, color, and visual rhythm in Disney's *Steamboat Willie*. Eisenstein and other Soviet filmmakers who feared that soundtracks for feature films with speech and synchronous sound could doom cinema as art were excited by the wacky noises and un-synchronized sounds of cartoons.

The downside of animation was that it was difficult. Why would anyone, much less a young beginner like Harry, want to undertake the discipline and commitment that animation demanded? Before video and digital technology, it could be hellishly slow. In order for a traditional animated film to be viewed, it is necessary to first draw pictures on paper, and each picture must be slightly different from the last one to create a sense of movement. The drawings are then traced or photocopied onto transparent acetate sheets and filled in by painting in color on the other side of the sheet, then photographed one at a time as frames onto a motion-picture film. Harry, lacking a camera or money for film processing, hand-drew images onto film, at 24 exposures per second, 1,440 a minute, to be visible when shown through a projector. His early films of five to ten minutes in length could easily take over to a year to complete. The process was tedious, as well as laborious. Belson described batiking, one of Harry's methods:

> He would have the clear film, with a thin coat of emulsion on it so that it would hold the dye, and a lot of colored inks, and a mouth atomizer—artists use [them] for spraying fixative on their drawings. He used it for painting, which was a good trick . . . He would block out certain areas of the frame with pressure-sensitive tape, gummed labels that were cut in circles or squares and things of that sort, and stick them onto the film. And then he would spray the ink on it, the parts that were not covered, so it would soak up the color and texture. And then he would spread petroleum jelly all over the film. Then remove the tape and that would allow him to spray another color all over the film. Then remove the tape and that would allow him to spray another color there, inside the areas that had been previously covered, without affecting the areas that had the jelly on [them].

The pressure-sensitive labels that he used were precut into dots and circles for office filing systems, and Harry went to the manufacturer of Come-Clean gum dots in Los Angeles to buy every size they made.

If those who see abstract paintings as lacking an artist's intention—as only the thoughtless result of chance and spills—could see the labor and care that went into Smith's films and paintings, they would never dare claim it was something any child could do.

Though Harry's work on the film was meticulously clean, according to Belson, the floor and rug were spoiled from spraying and dripping:

> He got paint all over this nice room that he had. He did it on the floor so that the floor was sprayed these different colors, and generally made a mess of this room, which was previously remarkably neat—neater than [he'd] ever be again, I suspect. I know from that point on, various places where he lived were always tiny little rooms, no bigger than a large closet usually, and he'd throw everything that he owned into it. So he had things hanging from the ceiling and things hanging from the bed—there was no room to move around at all—he just moved from furniture to furniture without ever touching the floor.

Other visitors' descriptions were much the same, with only his work projects changing: painted canvases on the floor, recording equipment and books scattered about, and any number of collections that currently occupied him. Harry's museum/apartment in Berkeley had become a workshop/studio. The complexity (or disorder) of his rooms fascinated all of his visitors. Philip Lamantia said that throughout Harry's life his rooms all looked the same. But to Belson, he was a chameleon—it was Smith who had changed, not his apartments: "The New York Smith, the Berkeley Smith, and the San Francisco Smith were different people . . . different in intensity."

Those who wanted to animate abstraction or make non-objective film art believed that it could link together modern art and cinema and even jazz and other music. They saw it was possible to change the way space was used in painting, and to add and expand the way time and rhythm worked. Animated abstraction on film allowed for radical means of crossing or ignoring borders and boundaries, of introducing a moving polyphony of changing colors and shapes, light shimmers and pulses, and new ways of using perspective. Viewers of filmed abstractions would have to change the way they looked at paintings.

Hand-drawn or -painted film animation was a cheaper method of filmmaking, but also a different way of thinking about not just painting but film as well. The individual film frame was a still image, like a painting. Filmmakers who worked by hand didn't see things in motion through a viewfinder that shows the boundaries that will appear in the film. As Belson put it, with animation you think of one frame at a time, and you don't have to think about linking shots by fades or resolves. Harry once advised a group of young film viewers watching a realist film that "you shouldn't be looking at this as a continuity. Film frames are hieroglyphs, even when they look like actuality. You should think of the individual film frame, always, as a glyph, and then you'll understand what film is about." Some filmmakers who used handmade techniques seem to have thought of their films in almost spiritual terms. Len Lye, for example, saw his films as a means of communicating his DNA directly to an audience. Harry thought of it as less hands-on: he said he was merely a conduit for some greater force, like God. He rejected many of the newer developments in film technology, even those invented by Fischinger, devices that he could have borrowed, as he did the cameras.

His early films were numbered and unnamed. "The titles . . . were added for the museum audience. Originally they were not titled," he said, "and I still feel that giving them specific titles is destructive because it tensions them to specific emotions, and for these particular films are as out of place as a chemist naming his experiments according to the color they produce, rather than the purpose." Harry allowed Art in Cinema, and years later Jonas Mekas and the Anthology Film Archives, to give them names. He did number them, though, and by numbering his films created a sequence, an order, as they moved from hand-drawn to filmed with a camera, and from geometric to animated cutout figures and collage. Years after their creation, seven of the early films—*1, 2, 3, 4, 5, 7,* and *10*—were grouped together under the general title *Early Abstractions. Nos. 6* and *8* survive in fragments or poor condition, and *No. 9* is lost, as were the screens he had made for different films: "All those so-called abstract films had special screens for them. They were made of dots and lines. All these things disappeared."

Some twenty years later Harry wrote notes for his films when they became available for rental in the *Film-Makers' Cooperative Catalogue No. 3*:

> My cinematic excreta is of four varieties—batiked abstractions made directly on film between 1939 and 1946; optically printed non-objective studies composed around 1950; semi-realistic animated collages made as part of my alchemical labors of 1957 to 1962; and chronologically superimposed photographs of actualities formed since the latter year. All these works have been organized in specific patterns derived from the interlocking beats of the respiration, the heart and the EEG alpha component and should be observed together in order, or not at all, for they are valuable works, works that will live forever—they made me gray.

"They were first meant to be silent," Harry said, "married to two rhythms, one for the heart, and one for the respiration, so the rhythms would lock in . . . it's thirteen and seventy-two [average per minutes], and those are both very important occult numbers"—a gematria for loving kindness that bridges heaven and earth, or Psalm 72, number 13 ("He shall have pity on the weak and needy / And the souls of the needy shall he save").

Harry wrote in the catalog that *Film No. 1* (1946–1948) was "Hand-drawn animation of dirty shapes—the history of the geologic period reduced to orgasm length. (Approx. 5 min.)" It was hand-painted on both sides of clear 35-millimeter film stock and then photographed in 16-millimeter color. The film was silent, until he later used Dizzy Gillespie's Latin jazz recording of "Manteca" ("lard" in Spanish, "marijuana" in Afro-Cuban slang) as a soundtrack. It was the first of three Dizzy Gillespie Latin jazz works that added to the soundtrack an extra layer of Cuban rhythmic complexity on top of jazz's already dense rhythms. It was later retitled *A Strange Dream*. Harry's description of the film is rather cryptic, even for him. P. Adams Sitney, in *Visionary Film*, understood him as pointing to a short moment of vaguely phallic and triangular shapes interacting in the middle of the film. Harry seemed to confirm that reading when he said that "orgasm length" was the photographer Robert Frank's idea, what Frank called "every man's experience." But sometimes "dirty" can just mean "dirty," and in this case, the rough qualities and fuzzy edges of the figures in a hand-painted film.

Film No. 1 can still be something of a shock after seventy-five years. With no characters, no narrative, no title, and nothing filmed with a camera, it's not an easy film to grasp. And yet its lightning-fast animation of squares and triangles on a flat surface is fascinating. Throughout, there is always the sense that this is a painterly film. Non-objective films defy description. With no "reality," what's left is background and foreground, depth, shapes in motion, colors, lines, and the like. It's very hard to avoid using the vocabularies of traditional art, narrative, or choreography, and those who try invariably wind up retreating into the language of representational art. (No wonder Hilla von Rebay said, "You don't understand art, you feel it.") Everything in *Film No. 1* is in motion, even the background and foreground, but with no apparent pattern or synchrony. Squares, rectangles, circles, triangles, and blobs of paint are racing across the screen, bouncing, dancing, morphing, with fuzzy edges and occasional vibrations. Even though the first audiences to see this film might not have known it was handmade, they would have realized it was like nothing they had ever seen projected on a screen.

Harry's films *No. 2* and *No. 3* were made between 1946 and 1949, and were again hand-painted batiked animation. There was no soundtrack to either, but he later synchronized *No. 2* to Dizzy Gillespie's recording of "Algo Bueno" (the film was later retitled by others *Message from the Sun*) and *No. 3* (retitled *Interwoven*) to Gillespie's recording of "Guarachi Guaro." New to the latter film are bars, grids, diamonds, and superimposed shapes, and the background to the end title of Harry's painting of Charlie Parker's recording of "Koko" was changed.

In a letter to the Guggenheim Foundation, Harry offered further comment on these films and others:

> Please remember that these films were not made for entertainment but for exploration and instruction. All the motions across the screen in this second one are unfortunate, but make the clearest two-dimensional diagram of what is happening. In a three-dimensional film on this same subject I will make someday, the forms will move out of infinity toward the spectator. Also remember that these films are made up of visual percussions in strict time like music, and must be thought of by the mental sequence that integrates strongly rhythmic auditory sensations, for example, and not the ones used for stationary art. Some people who see my movies for the first time say that they move too fast, but this is because they are using the wrong parts of their brain.

Film No. 4 (1949–1950) was "Black and white abstractions of dots and grillworks made in a single night. (Approx. 6 min.)" It was in 16-millimeter, black and white, and color, and silent, though intended to be again used with Dizzy Gillespie's "Manteca," and in fact the film opens with a brief camera scan of some details of Smith's 1949–1950 painting in color of the music of the Gillespie recording before turning to black and white. Someone later titled it *Fast Track*. For this, Harry used a camera for the first time, with the help of Hy Hirsh. It was handheld, and he used it to "paint" the surface of the film with short camera strokes, moving in and out, changing speeds, giving the impression that the still forms and white lights are in motion. He credited the Whitney brothers for helping him learn photographic animation and develop a theoretical view of film.

Harry was doubtlessly asked many times about these first four films, but there is little record of his comments. Questioned if the colors of the films were symbolic of spiritual states, he replied that "The colors were based on colors that were available. They're not necessarily 'occult' colors, they're just the basic colors." He also said that these four films should be shown at silent speed (sixteen frames a second) and projected on as large a screen as possible. *Film No. 4* was one of several made with a borrowed camera and a homemade light box. According to Belson:

> [He] put cutout forms on the lightbox so that everything was blacked out except perhaps a circle with the light behind it, and at night with the lights out, playing a phonograph record, he would dance around his room and film the lightbox from various angles. Then he'd wind the film back, put the record on again, and film another cutout, say a triangle. And so on. The record would give him cues as to when to bring things in, when to take things out. He improvised a couple of little films in that way. In one night he could do a whole abstract film and have a synchronized soundtrack as well.

Film No. 5 (1949–1950), "'Color abstraction. Homage to Oskar Fischinger'—a sequel to *No. 4*. (Approx. 6 min.)," is a 16-millimeter, silent, color film. It was later retitled by Art in Cinema as *Circular*

Tensions. The camera again is used to animate still forms. Circles dominate the second half of the film, bouncing about, jostling one another, and forming concentric patterns.

Film No. 6 (1950–1951) Harry described as a "Three-dimensional, optically printed, abstraction using glasses the color of Heaven & Earth. (Approx. 20 min.)" It was silent, in red-green anaglyph 3-D, in a one-and-a-half-minute version.

Harry added a note to the *Film-Makers' Cooperative Catalogue* on what drugs he used in the making of various films. "For those who are interested in such things: Nos. 1 to 5 were made under pot; No. 6 with 'schmeck' [the Yiddish word for 'smack,' the slang word in English for heroin] (it made the sun shine) and ups ['uppers,' slang for amphetamine-based drugs]." But shortly after the catalog appeared, Harry admitted that his notes were "slightly inaccurate. I've never experienced the real heroin addiction thing." He had seen several people die from overdoses of heroin, and was aware of the risks in using it. Inaccurate or not, Harry's inclusion of the list of drugs was serious: he thought it important to know the sources and means of his inspiration. He had not been the first to paint on film as he thought, but he had gone well beyond those who were the first, and even beyond his contemporaries, the Whitneys and Belson. The painting and batiking of the films' surfaces were done with an intricacy not seen before, the colors were opulent, the animation unpredictable and visually engaging.

EVERYTHING GOES WITH EVERYTHING: FILM AND UNIVERSAL RHYTHM

Harry was keenly attuned to questions about soundtracks for films: What films should be seen silent? What was a soundtrack supposed to accomplish? What kind of music should be used? Belson remembered that Art in Cinema once called Harry to ask what should be played with Luis Buñuel and Salvador Dalí's 1929 silent film *Un Chien Andalou*. He immediately replied with Richard Wagner's "Liebestod" from *Tristan und Isolde*, music that Buñuel himself had played on a phonograph behind the screen during the original showings. Harry's own first films were silent, he said, because he couldn't afford to pay for the transfer of music to optical soundtracks or for producing sound prints for commercial distribution.

His experience with different forms of music often led him to choose soundtracks by means of chance, well before John Cage's *Music of Changes* or William S. Burroughs's cut-ups made chance a byword in the arts. Call it alchemy, or just a product of his encyclopedic knowledge of recorded music: Harry settled on what he called "automatic synchronization"—the use of any form of music with any of his films. But then Harry's "automatic" also recalls the surrealists' quest to surrender control to "automation." Jean Cocteau had gotten there before him, in 1930, by moving parts of a music score by Georges Auric around when he thought it followed the film too closely, or, more radically, in his 1946 ballet *Le jeune homme et le mort*, when at the last minute before a performance he switched the music from jazz to a Bach passacaglia. Cocteau called this "accidental synchronization," a means of awakening the imagination of an audience. In Harry's view there were no accidents—everything could go with everything. When he first considered using sound with his early films, he thought of Bach, but then he heard jazz while stoned and began using Dizzy Gillespie's records:

After I met Griff B[orgeson] . . . and started smoking marijuana, naturally little colored balls appeared whenever we played Bessie Smith and so forth—whatever it was I was listening to at that time. I had a really great illumination the first time I heard Dizzy Gillespie play. I had gone there very high, and I literally saw all kinds of colored flashes. It was at that point that I realized music could be put to my films. My films had been made before then, but I had always shown them silently.

Years later, he updated the music by using a Fugs record, and once asked if the punk band False Prophets would record a soundtrack for him. But he settled on the Beatles, as he was a serious fan, and used songs such as "Please Please Me" and "I Want to Hold Your Hand." (Harry told his friend Rani Singh that he wanted his films to be at the same commercial and popular level as the Beatles; to the writer and publisher Raymond Foye he said that it was the newest and most commercially offensive soundtrack that would offend art audiences that he could find.) The choice of the Beatles may seem a bit jarring today, and many viewers turn off the soundtrack when they watch Harry's films. But Beatlemania was a huge phenomenon in the 1960s, drawing together people who otherwise might never have shared musical tastes. Allen Ginsberg said that the Beatles were played nightly at the Dom, the old Polish hall on St. Mark's, in the Village, and he and many of the Beats and hippies were all dancing for the first time.

Harry's intention was to never try to make the film completely sync up with the music rhythmically. Len Lye and Norman McLaren had scrupulously matched their animations to jazz rhythms (a practice that when done poorly would be called "Mickey Mouse synchronization"). Though Harry did sometimes adjust the speed of the projector to match the tempo of some music, he still insisted that automatic synchronization was real, and implied that there was a rhythmic universal.

Jonas Mekas was one of those who encouraged Harry to change his soundtracks with the times, but by 1967 Mekas was beginning to worry about the use of pop music with art films after Harry's films with Beatles soundtracks were being appreciated for the wrong reasons: "They were, really, listening to the music." Teenagers at film festivals were singing along with the Beatles songs during the films, and becoming bored and objecting to silent films or films with music they didn't know. Because Harry hadn't synced the songs to the films, and one film came after the other, when they were transferred to videotape or DVD, the films sometimes end before the music, and the Beatles record runs over into the next film, or is cut off abruptly when the film ends.

The *Early Abstractions* films that are on YouTube have various soundtracks added by different people. One of the more interesting has tracks or excerpts from Don Cherry's *Symphony for Improvisers / Nu Creative Love*, Tod Dockstader's "Traveling Music," Edith Frost's "Telescopic," Supersilent's "6.6," and Sun Ra's "Tiny Pyramids."

At Naropa University in 1989, students tried different types of music with Harry's *Early Abstractions* films, including Enrico Caruso, the Butthole Surfers, Thelonious Monk, Charles Mingus, and tracks from his *Anthology of American Folk Music*, and all seemed to work with them. If anything could work with anything, why not several anythings? Stan Brakhage recalled a mind-boggling experience of attending one of Harry's film showings in New York, and Kurt Weill and Bertolt Brecht's opera *Rise and Fall of the City of Mahagonny* was playing on one side of the screen and a jazz record on the other.

The artist and writer Fred Camper once attended a 1972 seminar with Harry Smith in the Chelsea Hotel, and "[he] started by passing out joints, suggesting a toke was necessary to get in the proper mood."

> He also kept interrupting himself to ask Jonas Mekas, who had invited him, "Can I just get my $100 and leave now?" . . . At one point he explained automatic synchronization, and preparing to show one of his films to demonstrate it, pointed at me, as I was sitting on the floor near a stack of records, and said, "Hey, you, pick a record, any record." Without looking . . . I passed the first record on the stack up to him. He looked at it and said, "You idiot, not *that* record."

I handed another record up to him, and he looked at it, and said, "You moron, not *that* record!" Finally the third record was acceptable, and he played it while showing a film he was working on.

In 1963 Ernest Pintoff created *The Critic*, a short comedy film that was a series of moving geometric figures modeled on a film by Norman McLaren (but close enough to Harry's). The soundtrack had Mel Brooks speaking in a faux-Yiddish-English accent, puzzling over whether it was trash or a dirty movie. It won an Oscar in 1963, and Harry said it was one of his favorite films.

3

Harry the Hipster
1948–1951

Harry's interest in jazz, like that of his taste for folk music, was at first limited to recordings made before 1932. He believed that when recording technology was still new, the performers had a spontaneity focused on that moment—they were not creating something for listeners in the future. Later recordings had the weight of history behind them, he thought, and their performances were more cautious and generic. His defense of early jazz was rather unique, but there were a fair number of others also drawing a line against swing, the newer form of jazz that was then the popular music of the country. For these rearguardists (who were often dismissed as "moldy figs"), swing was an invention of media moguls, a dilution of true jazz, an introduction into Black music of unwelcome European musical elements like large orchestras, written arrangements, choral harmony, and excessive technique. For the traditionalists jazz was a folk art, and they sometimes included in their pantheon of Louis Armstrong and Sidney Bechet rural blues singers and folk performers such as Lead Belly. Their dismissal of newer music was sometimes strongly voiced in the language of antifascists and Marxists.

A somewhat simplified version of early jazz was being played by some older New Orleans musicians who were discovered and recorded in the early 1940s by a few amateur researchers and record collectors. It was their music that Harry used in some of his lectures on jazz that he was asked to give at UC Berkeley: recordings made for Bill

Russell's American Music Records by the likes of Bunk Johnson, George Lewis, Wooden Joe Nicholas, Johnny St. Cyr, Kid Thomas Valentine, and other, lesser-known figures. In later years Harry had little to say about the music he played in those lectures, but he did remark, rather uncharacteristically, on what he wore when he gave them:

> I habitually wore, for example, corduroy or velvet knickers and ruffled shirts and things. Until one day came, because I'd been hanging out with a lot of what used to be called *pachucos*, who were like Puerto Rican juvenile delinquents, connecting their folklore and life histories for analysis— they were all wearing Levis which have to be prepared in a certain way. Like the little red tag has to be ripped off in a certain way and blah blah. So I wore Levis, and Do-funnies and the University had a fit because it had been a thing that was not allowed, although when it was finally thrashed out, I got to wear them, and from then on anybody else at the University of California in 1947 or 1948, whatever this was, could wear them. Now everybody wears them, and I don't wear them, because nobody has given me a pair for years . . .

San Francisco in the early 1940s was a site of considerable re-sistance to swing and popular music, and had developed its own revivalist New Orleans–like bands, like Lu Watters and the Yerba Buena Jazz Band or Turk Murphy's Jazz Band. These groups were attempting to catch the spirit of the earliest jazz they had heard on recordings. Harry knew some of these musicians, and briefly Jerry and P. T. Stanton, brothers who were part of the revivalist movement, shared his crowded apartment. He even managed to record some of this music in that small space.

BEBOP: THE ATOMIC AGE OF JAZZ

> We were dropping bombs on Japan, and Max Roach was
> dropping musical bombs from his drum kit.
>
> —Raymond Orr

> Nietzsche's *Beyond Good and Evil* is the best book
> ever written about bebop.
>
> —Bernard Wolfe

Bebop was the first new form of jazz in over a decade, and Harry, along with some other younger San Francisco–area visual artists, was swept up by its audacity. "It was simply the most radical thing at the time," Jordan Belson said. "Dissonance, a curious take on pop music." Rhythm and blues was at its apex by the 1940s, and was reaching an audience larger than the Black community. Yet despite Harry's commitment to African American music, he paid little attention to R & B, or to swing, and turned to bop, a music so shocking and modern that he could not ignore it.

Compared to the song-based music of swing, bebop was musical abstract expressionism slightly avant la lettre: it was non-objective, almost entirely without lyrics, rhythmically off-center, harmonically unpredictable, and called for audiences' close attention. Bebop compositions typically put a newly minted melody over an existing pop song's chord structure and left it up to the individual to hear or not hear what lay behind it, much as a viewer of Robert Ryman's "all white" paintings with jazz titles might or might not notice the colors under the overpainted white surface, or maybe think those flecks of color that were peeking out from the edges of the canvas were just mistakes. For bebop musicians, the doubleness of these compositions set up a tension that opened up new possibilities for invention. Like action painting, then also on the horizon, bebop was often performed as fast as a human could think and move: Charlie Parker's improvised solo on "Koko" was played at thirteen notes a second.

To most dancers and music fans, bebop seemed a musical affront, a derailment of swing. To them, bebop musicians were amateurish, hitting wrong notes, or deliberately using weird chords and broken rhythms. The music was heard as aggressive and undanceable, and in a sense it was true: bebop broke many of the rules of swing, abandoning its steady, even rhythms, its smoothly modulated passages, assuredly resolved harmonics, and the repetition of musical lines called riffs that helped make the music's structure clear to its listeners. Even when a bop composition was based on the blues, the oldest and simplest form used in jazz, it, too, could now be packed with complex chords and rapid harmonic movement.

The young bebop musicians of the 1940s took pride in their ability to thread their way through the chordal and rhythmic minefields their compositions demanded. Their idea of improvisation was based on mastering the new rules and constraints that they accepted as part of their aesthetic. They sometimes dressed as artistes or bohemians, with berets, goatees, horn-rimmed dark glasses, and Pre-Raphaelite hipster oversized bow ties. They had their own argot, naming their tunes with arcane titles like "Epistrophy" or "Ornithology." It was music made by ex-soldiers or those who flew beneath the draft, and it mimed their experience of wartime, strikes, discrimination, and dislocation. And to the cognoscenti, it was a music that had all the signs of high art. The young painters on the West and East Coasts got it, but art historians and critics failed to see the parallels between abstraction in painting and music.

From the beginning, Harry was drawn to Dizzy Gillespie, whose fast and bravura trumpet playing often obscured just how innovative and finely drawn his ideas and compositions were. Gillespie's 1946 "Anthropology," for example, was based on the harmonic structure of George Gershwin's "I Got Rhythm," but was made up of five musical phrases, each different in length and each beginning on a different beat of the measure. Though it was within the conventional pop song form of swing, instead of flowing ever forward, its phrases now sounded irregular, and the melody had a jagged, start-and-stop angularity. The rhythmic complexity of Gillespie's recordings put Harry's asynchronous matching of images to sound to the test.

Despite his fascination with this new music, recordings of old and exotic music were still important to Harry, and he was advertising to find more. He had a routine for checking what was new in the various record stores each week, especially the Yerba Buena Music Shop in North Oakland. It was there that Phil Elwood, who later became San Francisco's leading jazz and nightlife writer, first ran into Harry. "Smith looked like most of the record collectors I knew . . . He was sloppy, unmannered, always hungry, and not terribly pleasant. He was very sharp, and he knew his records, knew what he wanted, and had the knack of finding rare items in places none of us Natives thought to look." Harry and Luis Kemnitzer took hour-long bus trips to a shop in Richmond, California, that was a veritable museum of 78-rpm records of every type of music from the early years of recording. The two of them dreamed of finding the money to buy the whole shop. By then Harry had gone from searching for the exotic and the exceptional in American folk music to trying to hear everything that had ever been recorded. Among his purchases was Torkel Scholander, a Swedish tenor and lute player who was popular among Swedish Americans and had made a few recordings in the United States; Yvette Guilbert, the French singer, actress, and novelist, who was a master of the speech-song style of cabaret chanteuses; and Mexican police bands, Italian bagpipes, Asturian bagpipes, and street organs. His hunger to discover new forms of music matched the early recording companies' quest to record everything, everywhere. Those pioneer record producers were the anthropologists of recorded music. Ralph Peer, most known for his omnivorous recording of white country music, also recorded jazz, blues, Mexican and Cuban pop songs, Hawaiian music, and crossover recordings such as Louis Armstrong and the country music star Jimmie Rodgers's 1930 duo of "Blue Yodel No. 9."

Harry's search for records was never distinct from his filmmaking, as his need for soundtracks was largely enabled by finding recordings. On September 24, 1948, Art in Cinema included in their early fall program a previously unannounced film by Smith, *Primitive Visual Rhythm*, which he had been working on for the last year. In his program notes, Smith wrote:

> The forms used in this film have been limited to two classifications: a circle (or circles) moving across the field of vision, and a stationary circle segmenting itself on its own axis. These two simple actions are arranged in a slowly accelerating rhythmic series, with angular movements and highly saturated colors in the body of the film, replacing and being replaced by oblique movement and a grayed spectrum at the beginning and end of the work.

In the fall of 1948, Harry left Berkeley's art and academic community and moved to the Fillmore District of San Francisco, a Black neighborhood. It was a move that his friends never quite understood. San Francisco was a city of segregated neighborhoods, and before World War II the Fillmore had been an area with a number of Japanese businesses and residences. With the forced relocation of Japanese and Japanese Americans to government camps, it had been emptied. At the same moment, there was a rising demand for wartime labor, and large numbers of African Americans arrived in the district, soon making it the center of Black commerce and entertainment in the Bay Area. In years past, it was the Barbary Coast near North Beach that had been the site of African American nightlife, where most of the music was rhythm and blues or older styles of jazz. But within a short time, dozens of new bars and nightclubs were crowding together down the streets of the Fillmore, with bop musicians and fans moving from one to the other every night. The Texas Playhouse, Club Alabam, the Long Bar, the Plantation Club, the Blue Mirror, and others formed the new center of Black entertainment.

It was a place of which Philip Lamantia would say that whites and Blacks who had "gone underground" could meet in jazz clubs, and he was one who continued to visit with Harry in the Fillmore. In Lamantia's papers there is a note headed "1948," in which he reflects on his visits to Harry that year: "Important contacts with genius Harry Smith, painter & ethnomusicologist—a very important exchange between us re magic, gnosis, & music—Nights of Jackson's Nook & Jimbo's Bop City within Fillmore, & Post & Buchanan."

But a single white man who actually lived in a Black neighborhood in the 1940s was, to say the least, highly unusual, and surely made his motives suspect to both Blacks and whites. To call it "ethnographic fieldwork" would not explain it. "Participant observation" might be closer to the truth. It was a life he wanted to experience, in a community that gave rise to such a great musical art. He kept no notebooks, made no recordings, took no photographs. Most white people knew very little of the music of African Americans beyond nationally known artists like Louis Armstrong or Duke Ellington. For Harry, the music was a gateway to a new civilization hidden from white society in plain view.

He found a room above Jackson's Nook, a Creole restaurant at 1638 Buchanan Street. It had a large backroom with a piano where musicians working at clubs in the area ate breakfast and lunch and often jammed. For two years Harry lived there, paying little if any rent, as Mrs. Jackson and her family were fond of him.

Bebop inspired new ways of thinking in several arts. Kenneth Patchen read his poetry at the Blackhawk jazz club. The poet Robert Creeley talked about the inspiration he derived from patterns of jazz rhythms. The jazz vocalist King Pleasure put syllables to notes of well-known bop instrumental solos and turned them into sonic poetry. Jack Kerouac wrote about what he called spontaneous prose and bop prosody, using the breathing patterns of bebop horn players as models for poetic phrasing and energy. In explaining Kerouac's method, Allen Ginsberg used as an example Dizzy Gillespie's recording of "Salt Peanuts," in which the horns imitated the pitch and rhythm of those words: "Black musicians were imitating speech cadences and Kerouac was imitating the black musicians' breath cadences on their horns and brought it back to speech." Kerouac went even further in oral performances of his prose poems: he also tried to make his lines speak musically. In the recording of his prose poem "The History of Bop," he said Charlie Parker "puts his alto to his mouth and says, 'Didn't I tell you?'"—a phrase with a rhythm and rising pitch that mimes a standard bebop musical figure.

Shortly after Harry arrived in Berkeley in 1945, he discovered daliel's Gallery and Bookstore (they insisted on the small "d") on Telegraph Avenue, which had just opened. It was started by George Leite, a twenty-four-year-old college dropout, yacht hand, taxi driver, and physical therapist with a taste for the arts, anarchism, surrealism, peyote, UFOs, "free sex," and life in Big Sur. Within two years, daliel's art gallery had shown the works of painters like Marc Chagall, Man Ray, and Jean Varda and presented poetry readings and concerts by Harry Partch and the then unknown Dave Brubeck. Leite created *Circle*, a magazine that featured E. E. Cummings, Robert Duncan, Anaïs Nin, Kenneth Patchen, Darius Milhaud, Lawrence Durrell, and William Everson; he also established Circle Editions, a press that published books by Henry Miller and Kenneth Rexroth, and opened the Cobra Club bar in Oakland.

In late 1947, Leite began a new project called Circle Extension that would repeat some of the Art in Cinema presentations on the university campus, and offered a series of lectures on graphic aesthetics, sexual adjustments, experimental writing, and creative anthropology. The first three of the series were Robert Duncan's "James Joyce: A Survey," Lawrence Hart's "Ideas of Order in Experimental Poetry," and Harry Smith's "Afro-American Music," a five-week course described as "A series of five lectures with phonographic illustrations of American Negro music. This course will survey the field on a regional basis, with particular emphasis on New Orleans, Memphis, and Texas vocal and instrumental performances including jazz." It was likely that no one else in the United States at the time had the knowledge to offer such a course.

Among Harry's new literary friends one of the most interesting was Jack Spicer—another member of a generation of poets who found in jazz a secret language. Spicer was a theorist of language and moved in both academic and underground circles. He was among the first to read poetry to jazz, with a group led by Ron Crotty, Dave Brubeck's first bass player. Spicer roomed in the same building as Philip K. Dick (who was then working in a used record store) and Robert Duncan. He befriended the jazz musician Chet Baker and Helen Adams, a poet who worked folk ballads into her poems, which she read, sang, and danced to. During his graduate studies, Spicer took classes with Paul Radin and Roy Harvey Pearce, and he and the poet Robin Blaser helped with research for Pearce's *Savagism and Civilization*, a book of cultural criticism that so radically exposed the view of Indians in early American literature that it might have come from the Department of Anthropology rather than the Department of English.

How could Harry not be drawn to a poet who had drafted a study of tarot cards by means of personal experience mixed with statistical rigor? Spicer also valued the power of tradition in folk song and used elements of these songs in his poetry. Spicer had a weekly radio show on KPFA in Berkeley in 1949, which he introduced on air as the "most educational folk song program west of the Pecos." And that it surely was, though it often veered away from folk music, maybe tracing a single word or a phrase into contemporary poetry, or looking backward in time to some archaic source. Spicer's own poetry could edge into Bible stories, nursery rhymes, *The Odyssey*, or *The Wizard of Oz*. His 1962 book *The Holy Grail* tells the story of Galahad in part through Woody Guthrie's song "Ranger's Command." Berkeley was then a center of folk song well ahead of the folk revival of the 1950s. But Spicer brought on guests such as Harry, encouraging them to join him in drinking wine before the show, and then, while drunk and singing badly, make up bawdy and profane versions of well-known folk songs, which he would introduce as if learned from an old bus driver fishing off Santa Monica Pier. He might have been forgiven such liberties by those who knew him as the poet who in his book *After Lorca* had included his letters to and from the poet Federico García Lorca, all written after Lorca had been dead for twenty years, or who could include the Virgin Mary in a poem about Buster Keaton. But the folk show was canceled after forty weeks, when listeners objected to some of the lewd material that appeared in his remaking of children's songs like "Skip to My Lou, You Bastard!" How much Harry joined in on such merriment during his appearances is not clear, but he did later tape himself singing parodies of folk songs.

It was never clear to anyone who knew Harry in California how he survived without a job. After his assistantship with Paul Radin ended, he briefly had an office job on the afternoon shift at Aramco, the

Arabian American Oil Company, but one that he didn't keep for long. Knowing that the unemployment office was required to find a person a job in their established field, Harry said he filed for unemployment compensation listing his occupation as the most obscure field he could think of—duck decoy painter—so as to stay out of work as long as possible. "I think he really believed that," Kemnitzer said, "or at least he expected us to believe it." In 1950, he did some freelance photography for the *San Francisco Examiner*, or at least had a press pass from the *Examiner* and carried a Speed Graphic four-by-five press camera. The rest of the time he asked for handouts, stayed with friends, sold some records, occasionally received small amounts of money from a fund set up by Art in Cinema for local filmmakers, and made a little more from the rental of his films or giving talks on jazz at the university. None of this amounted to enough to live on, but Harry was never on welfare. Philip Lamantia said he never saw Harry pay for anything.

He had not been back to Washington for four years. His mother and father had separated, and his mother had moved into a cabin built for her by Henrietta Blaisdell on a beach she owned on Guemes Island, near Anacortes. Blaisdell (who preferred to be known as "One Bubble") was what the town called their free spirit—an artist, photographer, exotic dancer, magician's assistant, hunter, fisherwoman, and collector of Native American artifacts. She'd been a close friend of the Smiths for years. When Harry learned in October 1949 that his mother was dying of cancer, he returned and stayed with her through her illness. He said he was using heroin, and that at his mother's bedside he read the psychiatrist Karen Horney's writings on the sadistic side of love.

When his mother died later that month, Harry gave the Whatcom Museum the last of his Native American artifacts and left for San

Francisco. Blaisdell wrote in her scrapbook that "Harry walked out greatly relieved he could now go live his own life and we never heard from him again." Harry's father moved into the cabin. He'd been trying to find Harry, and had written him when he learned about the Art in Cinema programs. Harry answered by sending him one of his Tree of Life drawings, but said he never heard back from him.

A waffle shop just down the way from Harry's place turned its back room into Jimbo's Bop City in the spring of 1949, and quickly became the city's quintessential after-hours jazz club. From 2:00 until 6:00 a.m. it drew visiting stars like Duke Ellington, Billie Holiday, Charlie Parker, Miles Davis, and Count Basie, and Hollywood nobility like Sammy Davis Jr. and Kim Novak, and even an unknown sixteen-year-old saxophonist named Clint Eastwood. The regulars included local musicians and radio DJs, hipsters such as Lenny Bruce, and Willie Brown, the future mayor of San Francisco. Musicians who had finished their nightly gigs came by to sit in with the house band, a small group that worked for chili, rice, and beverages. (Despite a sign that said NO LIQUOR SOLD OR SERVED ON PREMISES, it managed to find its way in.) Musicians and Harry were admitted free, everyone else paid $1. Though open to anyone, it had the feel of both a master class and a social club for musicians and their friends.

Harry was at Bop City every night, taking notes, making sketches of the music. Lamantia said that Harry considered owner John "Jimbo" Edwards his patron. "He was kept in food by him, though sometimes it was the only thing he was eating at the time, like casaba melons, and the restaurant was always stocked with them." In 1950 and 1951 he painted a series of large murals on the club's wall during the day, listening to records while he worked, painting what he heard fueled by marijuana and Benzedrine. The saxophonist Dexter

Gordon sometimes sat listening with Harry while he was painting. This was not the usual nightclub Afro-Deco exoticism, or a gallery of caricatures of favorite musicians on the wall. He escaped the frame and canvas, the film, the projector, and the screen, filling the room where jazz was performed with his visual perceptions of the music. In his most noted mural, large discs hang like planets with smaller discs within, giving off solar flares or starbursts (or photographers' flashbulbs) that mime the colored balls, flashes, and illuminations that Harry described from his first encounters with Dizzy Gillespie while on peyote. Running beneath the mural is what looks like a hand-scratched film soundtrack. He sometimes signed his paintings "delt," short for the Latin "delineavit," "one who drew this," but without his name along with it, as was normal in older printing or painting.

Percy Heath, jazz bassist and one of the founders of the Modern Jazz Quartet, first met Harry at Jimbo's in 1950 when he was in town with the Dizzy Gillespie band. "Since he was there every night and went to breakfast with the musicians at Jackson's Nook in the morning," Heath said, "they all knew him, and called him 'Smith.' He called everyone 'Man,' as in 'Man Heath' or 'Man Chase.' We knew him as a bebop fan who was what he called a non-objective painter who had a following of people like Patricia Marx and Jordan Belson. He was a mystical person, and had a demeanor about him so that nobody would approach except with awe and fascination . . . I used to ask him about so-and-so, and he'd say, 'You don't need to know about that, you've been through that in other lives. This is all an illusion except in your mind.'"

Harry could drop names and let them bounce through his comments, but he was not so quick to bring up the names of famous people he knew. Harry knew and was known by a number of jazz musicians—Dizzy Gillespie, Ornette Coleman, John Lewis, Thelonious Monk, Charles Mingus, and others—but he mentioned them only as reference points in autobiographical tales. In one, an interview in which he was discussing several occasions on which he came close to death, he described a party at Jackson's Nook after a performance of the Lionel Hampton Orchestra in 1950, where he had drunk a quart of gin, sampled some heroin and marijuana, and was seated next to Betty Carter, Hampton's singer. Later that night he was in an automobile crash in which he was thrown through the windshield.

The poet and multimedia artist Gerd Stern encountered Harry in the early 1950s:

> I first met Harry—I think the first time I came to San Francisco he was working as a photographer for the *Examiner*, and he was living in a black hotel. Philip Lamantia introduced me to Harry, and we sat there [in Jimbo's] eating Harry's favorite food . . . Then he took us to see some of his visuals at his hotel. But when we reached the lobby, we had to take our shoes off, and we had to not say a word between the time we got in and the time we left. We then crept up the stairs, and he whispered that there was a whore living in the next room, and she was in the pay of the FBI or some government agency to keep an eye on him . . . He took us into his room, and it was totally dark. He turned on a flashlight which had a cardboard tube attached to it. He put these works on the floor, and he illuminated them slowly so that we could see them, and in total silence we crept out holding our shoes and went down the steps and put our shoes on.

In New York City the Solomon R. Guggenheim Museum of Non-Objective Painting first opened on East Fifty-Fourth Street in Manhattan in 1939, in a building previously occupied by an automobile showroom. Hilla Rebay was the first director of the museum. She had convinced Solomon Guggenheim to begin collecting modern art and to create a museum to house it. It was designed as what she called a "museum-temple" for "the religion of the future," reflecting her theosophist belief that non-objective art was a window into another, greater reality. The floors were carpeted and paintings were hung in a decidedly nontraditional pattern, close to the floor, to awaken and shape visitors' responses. Incense and recorded music by Chopin, Bach, and Beethoven flowed through the rooms. (Though non-objectivity would seem to rule out music as something that would shape or distract a viewer's response, once Rebay saw Fischinger's films with music she decided that the future of art needed to be open to interactions of all the arts.)

She was moved by Fischinger's work to the point that she believed that film had a place in modern art and that he should be financially supported, but she fretted over the problems film posed for a museum: "The film has always, as has music, one handicap, which is that it has to be produced or it is not there . . . the painting . . . once created [is] not dependent on performance." But her bigger issue was convincing Solomon Guggenheim and others in the world of art that film was not simply a form of entertainment. Guggenheim had no interest, and wouldn't come to the museum when there were screenings. To keep within budget, she paid very little for the films she bought for the museum or to the filmmakers she was supporting.

Once Belson and Harry learned that Oskar Fischinger was being underwritten by Guggenheim funds, both wrote Rebay asking for support, and sent her samples of their paintings and films. When she visited San Francisco in 1948, they picked her up at the Oakland airport in Belson's Ford Model T and drove to his studio in North Beach, and then to what Jordan called Harry's "wretched little room" in the Fillmore, where Harry projected his work for her. They knew that Rebay was a force in the art world and that she had aided the careers of Fischinger, László Moholy-Nagy, and Alexander Calder, but they were not prepared for her imperiousness, or her insistence on setting the standards for modern art. When they entered Belson's studio and began to set up the projector to show her one of the first two short films he had made, "she grabbed the reel and started unwinding it onto the floor," he said, "looking at it with her naked eye. She told me that this was not advanced filmmaking, compared to Oskar Fischinger." Nonetheless, Fischinger recommended them both, and she came to see something in the two young men's efforts and promised them money.

Harry proposed to make three-dimensional films, and sent her some slides of his paintings he made for viewing with a stereoscope, an old-fashioned device in which two photographs of the same objects or pictures, taken from slightly different angles, are simultaneously shown, one to each eye. Belson said that Harry "had worked out the stereoscopic principles of what made things look in front of or behind other things," and Harry assured her that he could now draw freehand in 3-D almost as easily as he did in two-dimensional sketches, so that he could finish within a month. "It will have no forms within it, just carefully composed rhythmic and spectral sequence for the musicians to improvise on." It was a daring proposal in every respect, something no one else was attempting. He was asking for enough money to continue developing new ways to work in 3-D, the first being a series of three hundred or so double 35mm slides that could be projected at a much slower rate than a motion picture, but rapidly enough to give the impression of motion. He had already modified a slide projector for this, and thought it would provide a much less complicated and expensive means than standard motion-picture films. Harry had told Baroness Rebay that he had wanted to come to New York in early 1950 to show her his work, but now he had to delay his trip because Dizzy Gillespie was coming to San Francisco and he wanted to show him the paintings and films he had made using his recordings. A month later Rebay wrote that she would give him $50 a month [$528 in current money] for the next six months, and would try to get him $150 more to continue his work.

Harry had been projecting *Film No. 3* on the wall of Jimbo's with jazz musicians improvising a soundtrack live, and using a variable speed projector borrowed from Hy Hirsh that allowed him to slow down or speed up the images to match the music. He was turning a nightclub into a theater. *Film No. 3* was something of a visual solo with instruments, and it could claim to be the first light show of the type that would later shape psychedelic rock bands on the West Coast in the 1960s. Jordan Belson and Henry Jacobs followed Harry with increasingly complex light shows for the Vortex Concerts series at the Morrison Planetarium in the 1950s, in which they projected color, line patterns, and film on the planetarium's ceiling and set it to music. Once Harry's pulsing and flying geometrics were seen in rock clubs and art school classes, they helped shape music videos, TV advertising, early video games like *Tempest* and *Space Invaders*, and films like *Tron*.

When the spring series of Art in Cinema opened in May of 1950, it presented a program featuring a number of innovations in sound and film, including Norman McLaren's *Loops*, which introduced a method of drawing directly on a film's soundtrack to create music to accompany the animated drawing, and Dick Ham's *Fantasy for Girl and Orchestra*, which set a spoken narrative to a preconceived orchestra track. But the audience's favorite was Harry's *Five Instruments with Optical Solo*, which was shown before Fritz Lang's *Destiny* on May 12, 1950. The evening's program notes described it as a film "that will serve as the sixth instrument in a be-bop jam session to consist of an expert group in person, on the piano, cornet, valve-trombone, bass, and drums. This is the first presentation of a performance, anywhere, in which the optical images will be tried, not as visualization of the music, but as a basis for its departure." The program was not strictly accurate, as he had already performed a film with improvised music at

Jimbo's. He had also used recordings of jazz and African music with silent films he screened at previous Art in Cinema events, but having jazz musicians improvise live to a film was something new to a film audience. Silent films for many years had often been accompanied by live music to cue the audience to the mood, even the meaning of a scene, but Harry's films had no subject or narrative for the music to match, and the musicians collectively improvised on compositions they thought were suitable. The films shown were Smith's *Nos. 1–4*, and the compositions they chose for improvising on included "Boplicity" and "Move," by Miles Davis, recorded a year earlier as part of his *Birth of the Cool* period, and Duke Ellington's "Cotton Tail," a composition noted for its early use of bebop elements. *DownBeat* magazine described the event:

> SAN FRANCISCO—Atlee Chapman's band, rehearsing for their recent appearance at the San Francisco Museum of Art to accompany Harry Smith's non-objective films seemed to take their peculiar assignment right in stride. Smith, an artist who has received a Guggenheim grant to further his work, draws designs on film which bear the same relation to music as dance would. The shape and color of the designs suggest all the harmonic possibilities and the progression of the music. Chapman's band, which played such numbers as *Cottontail, Move* and *Boplicity*, is composed of . . . drummer Warren Thompson, bassist Robert Warren, pianist Stanley Willis, trumpeter Henry Noyd, tenorist Kermit Scott, and the leader on bass trumpet and valve trombone. Scott and Willis gave short talks on bop before the program, sixth in the museum's "Art in Cinema" series.

A different version of that evening's printed program suggested that the musicians were to interpret "measured rhythmic designs" that

Harry had "composed": "Each frame itself is considered as a separate composition, altering gradually from frame to frame."

In retrospect, the selection of these two Miles Davis recordings might seem to be an obvious choice. But Davis was then known only for his work with Charlie Parker, and these compositions had just been recorded. It would be at least seven more years before there was much interest in them. Jazz of World War II was typically played by large bands and was loud. This Miles Davis group was half the size of others at the time; played quiet, even delicate, understated jazz; and if its music was known at all, was thought to be closer to chamber music. To use it as a score for an abstract film made it doubly challenging to viewers.

Yet jazz soundtracks would quickly become an expected part of non-objective films. Norman McLaren, Hy Hirsh, Shirley Clarke, Len Lye, and Charles Eames all used some form of jazz. Patricia Marx, a successful landscape painter from Australia, had her career turned around by seeing Harry's films, and her 1953 *Things to Come* made with a track off Dizzy Gillespie's record of the same name was presented by Art in Cinema on the same night as Leni Riefenstahl's *Olympia*.

Five years later, Len Lye did live jazz and film collaborations in New York at the Five Spot, a favorite dive among artists and poets at the north end of the Bowery. He also created a light show for the Count Basie Orchestra and projected his painted films behind the music of Henry Brant at Carnegie Hall. Lye may have made painted films before Smith, but when Harry was in New York in 1955, he had the pleasure of knowing that he had influenced Lye.

Harry knew of Hilla Rebay's own early work in collage, and his letters to her suggest that he also knew of her watercolors, sketches, and cut-paper images of African American dancers and jazz musicians in Harlem, and Black farmworkers in South Carolina. Though he was asking for money for his films and paintings, he also saw an opportunity to persuade Rebay that bebop musicians possessed a special form of genius and were deserving of attention and support. On June 17, 1950, he wrote:

> Since I showed my films at the museum here using live musicians improvising from the images rather than from a score, the musicians who gather nightly in the back room of a café near here, to play for their own amusement, after they have their regular jobs, have asked me to bring my projector to the "jam sessions" several times, because everyone now wants to try playing while looking at the film. I am sending you some photographs taken at the museum of the musicians who played there, and who are the most advanced here. These people now are intuitively creating a new kind of music that will not be accepted by the public probably for 50 years. They are all really poor, sometimes hungry, because they would rather express what they call soul in their playing than hurt themselves by changing it to fit the backward standards of today's listeners . . .
>
> . . . Stanley Willis, a piano player . . . saw my diagrams about a year and a half ago, and told other musicians about them. Those in the photo group all got interested in my work at that time and most of them had played with the films long before the museum showing. Hardly any of these people can read music and many have trouble reading and writing English, but for these very reasons they are often in very unknowing contact with the true sources of creativity. None of them had ever heard of modern painting but they all appreciated it at once. The trombone player . . . for example, pointed

out many remarkable things in your "Royally" the first time I showed it to them. Last month I luckily borrowed a tape recorder and made records of about thirty different performances of musicians following the films. By comparing these tapes with each other and with the film it has been possible to make a start toward an investigation of intuitive creation. By observing these observable forces which affect man, but which are scorned by pedantic science, it will be possible for us to soon realize the final stages of man's development.

He asked Rebay to send him several copies of "New Age," a very short essay she had written that he wanted to distribute among the artists he knew. The new age of art she envisioned "appeals to the degree that the onlooker himself is developed and progressed in the evolution of his soul's spiritual advance." The "paintings of earthly make-believe and faked pretense have never represented truth on which the universal law is based, their material adoration brought no usefulness. The creative non-objective painting, however, develops the spiritual evolution of man based on truth and the lawful beautification of space, which brings useful order and increasing joy." It was a language that Harry picked up quickly and used in his letters to her seeking more funding, though at times he might be seen as gently mocking her. Much the same could be said for Fischinger's letters to Rebay, whose demands on him had grown to the point that virtually nothing he did would satisfy her. In Harry's first year of support from the Guggenheim Foundation he had received six months of fellowship payments of $50 a month and nine checks for supplies that totaled $150. It amounts to $4,631 in today's currency.

Harry wrote Rebay again on January 26, 1951, apologizing for taking so long to finish the films he had promised when she first began funding his work. He was still working on a two-dimensional color film and two 3-D black-and-white films to be in finished in April. He hadn't finished them all, he said, because they cost more than she had given him, and he reminded her that she had said she might be able to get him $150 more. He also asked permission to show the films he had completed at Art in Cinema so that "they can give me a very liberal rental in advance, and I need the money to finish the films." To show that he had been at work, he sent her some 35mm slides of the paintings that had gone into the making of the film he was trying to finish. The baroness granted him permission to show the film, but declined to give him more money because the museum was moving to a new building and expenses were mounting. What she didn't mention was that since Solomon Guggenheim had died two years earlier, with the lack of his support her control over the museum had been weakened. But once she saw Harry's slides, she did promise to send him $15 for supplies "from time to time."

The Art in Cinema program announced in its fifth year a program titled Two Events of Tremendous Interest for April 27, 1951: an evening of films by Harry Smith and Maya Deren.

Three Dimensional Films by Harry Smith. The premier public showing of the first three-dimensional non-objective films to be made. There will be four short subjects. They will be projected both with synchronized sound track(s) of Balinese, Hopi, and Yorouba music, and also accompanied by modern instrumentalists and a vocalist improvising directly from the visual stimuli. (By permission of The Solomon R. Guggenheim Foundation).

Maya Deren, this country's most eminent individual film maker, will be present to show her films and to deliver a lively lecture on them. Miss Deren needs no introduction to the followers of Art in Cinema. Her films were the first to be shown here and it is due to her energy and talent that the experimental cinema in this country has been established.

Deren was something of a superstar in what would soon be called underground film, or the New American Cinema: a director, producer, writer, film theorist, dancer, and anthropologist who succeeded at virtually everything she tried and had worked with performers and artists like Katherine Dunham, Anaïs Nin, and Marcel Duchamp. Her films were deeply personal and developed a new film language that drew on dreams and myth. She was accustomed to being given long evenings in which she talked and showed her films, so she responded tartly to the invitation Frank Stauffacher, Art in Cinema's founder, had sent her, saying,

> The activities which you describe seem extremely lively, and what with bop musicians, "live ones at that," etc., etc., I am afraid that I will seem a bit anti-climactic. Maybe I can dream up a leopard or two to work into my act. Or maybe the special thing that I should work on would be the fourth dimensional movie which would involve the appropriate perfume being squirted at the appropriate moment. In any case I shall do my best to live up to the glamorous standards which are being set.

Just as he was becoming known in the California art world Harry was planning a move to New York City. He wrote Rebay that he had sold almost everything he had to finish the films he'd promised, and he planned to be in New York in June and would bring her the films. When the director of the San Francisco Museum of Art heard about Harry's plans, he scheduled a special seminar in early November at which Harry could show his recent films and discuss them. Seventy people came, and Harry was given the money from the ticket sales plus some additional funds for the trip. He quickly gathered some things together, shipped several thousand records—collect—to Pete Kaufman, a record aficionado in New York he knew from his mail-order sales, and boarded an eastbound train.

4

Harry Smith in New York
1951–1954

On the way to New York, Harry made a stop to visit George C. Andrews, a farmer in the tiny town of Drury, Missouri. How Harry had heard of him is hard to imagine; Andrews's biography is even sketchier than Harry's. But they connected by some means through their common interests in drugs, UFOs, jazz, and the occult. Andrews was then twenty-five years old, and it would be years before he became known as the author of *The Book of Grass*, an anthology of writings on hemp; his LSD-inspired poetry in *Burning Joy*; anthologies on sex, drugs, and magic; and *Extra-Terrestrials Among Us*, a book that went beyond the usual UFO accounts to conspiracy theories of space aliens secretly in league with governments of nations on Earth. Andrews would move to London in the 1960s and become part of the legendary LSD gatherings at Syd Barrett's 101 Cromwell Road building, then move on to Tangier—the interzone of spies, eccentric millionaires, and drug-seeking writers. He was in and out of jail in London and Morocco for drug-related charges, all the while mixing with sixties sages such as R. D. Laing and Timothy Leary.

How Harry paid for his move to New York is another mystery. Jordan Belson thought Baroness Rebay had covered his expenses and provided him with a small studio in the Museum of Non-Objective Painting where he could live and work—an artist's dream. But by the time Harry reached Penn Station in New York he was penniless, and he set out walking in a pair of shoes that Andrews had given him that belonged to the head of the Rosicrucians in Belgium. Those shoes, Harry said, led him fifty-four blocks north to a seventh-story walk-up in a Puerto Rican neighborhood on West Eighty-Eighth Street near the Hudson River, the apartment of Lionel Ziprin, a poet, artist, and scholar of Jewish Kabbalah, soon to be almost famous in the underground of the Lower East Side. George Andrews had urged Harry to contact his friend Lionel, who, he assured him, could help him learn about Kabbalah and Tibetan Buddhism, broaden his knowledge of mysticism, and maybe update him about the Grays, those small, spindly space aliens that some said they had encountered. Harry wrote to Ziprin before he left San Francisco, asking if he could stay with him, filling the bottom of his letter with a series of complex drawings as a goodwill offering.

He arrived the morning after Lionel's wedding to Joanne Eashe, a dancer, model, illustrator, and clothing designer who once worked with Edmund Kara on Lena Horne's wardrobe. Lionel affectionately called her a Beatnik, since she had introduced him to a number of downtown New York artists and musicians. (Charlie Parker was the godfather of their first son.) A knock on the door, and . . . "There is this creature. He looked forty times older than when he died—with black eyes . . . black rings under each eye, carrying a bunch of Indian feathers, a staff and a seal"—an Inuit sculpture that punned on a seal carved in white marble breaking a circular magical seal. This was the first of many of Harry's shock entrées in New York. Like those dandies that Baudelaire described, Harry lived to surprise and never himself be surprised.

Lionel was annoyed by Harry's untimely arrival, thinking it was a bad omen: "He drops in the day after we were married and doesn't leave for 10 or 12 years." But he, and especially Joanne, were nonetheless fascinated by his strange demeanor and his seemingly limitless knowledge of art and everything else. As Harry rummaged around their apartment the morning of his arrival, he found two books in the unpacked piles on the floor that excited him: *The Tibetan Book of the Dead* and *The Great Beast*, a recently published biography of Aleister Crowley. Crowley declared that "magick" was "the science and art of causing change to occur in conformity with will." From that book Harry learned more about the Rosicrucians, the Hermetic Order of the Golden Dawn (a British secret society focused on occult rituals and spiritual development), and what lay behind the strange career of Crowley. Seeing Harry's interests, Joanne introduced him to Tibetan mysticism.

A few days after arriving, Harry contacted Baroness Rebay's office to announce that he was finally in town, but he was put off by her assistant, who, instead of welcoming him, abruptly asked who owned the films he had sent Rebay. Writing back with a return address of General Delivery, he answered that the films "made at your inspiration" had cost him much more than he had been given by the museum, and "the films were made with the Guggenheim Foundation in mind because you are the ones who know the power of rhythm." The question of ownership, he said, should wait until Rebay had a chance to see them, for "if you don't like them then they are valueless." He concluded, "I made two ten-minute reels for you. They are the first non-objective films made. Looking at them makes people strong."

Harry stopped by the museum almost daily, studying the paintings and hoping to find a place for himself in the baroness's temple of art. One day he was handed an envelope with $10 as a Thanksgiving present from Rebay, along with a verbal message relayed from the baroness, questioning his claim to having produced the first non-objective film when "Fischinger's films were completely non-objective." Harry replied with a letter that effusively praised her paintings, thanked her for her financial support, but at the same time defended his claim to being the first non-objective filmmaker:

> I didn't mean to indicate in my last letter that they were not, as he is certainly the best filmmaker so far (especially *Study in*

Blue), but to me he is handicapped in trying to follow music. In the true non-objective films of the future, non-objectivity of motion, trajectory, and rhythm will be just as important as non-objectivity of form-relation, and this is impossible if the film composer has music in mind rather than his own soul which is nourished by silence and light.

It was not a terribly convincing response from an artist best known for using music as a source for paintings and film soundtracks.

Rebay told her assistant that as he was "probably very poor," to have him stop by the museum on Thanksgiving Day, where there would be an additional $15 for paint and a turkey dinner. But by late December it became clear that he was not going to receive any further funds from the Guggenheim or handouts from Rebay. His last effort was a letter asking her to return the stereoscopic drawings he had made, and to give him an accounting of all the monies he had received. Since he was leaving town and hadn't completed all the work he had promised, he thought he should pay back all the money. An office note at the museum said that "Mr. Smith thinks it best since he hadn't been able to deliver the films to Miss Rebay in the last two months, to recover all his property & destroy it & return the money to Miss R." Whether he was serious or bluffing, Harry neither left nor paid back the money.

LIFE WITH THE POET MAGUS OF THE LOWER EAST SIDE

Harry had hoped to be able to continue his stay with the Ziprins. Lionel's mix of old-world mysticism and New York street sagacity was nothing like what he had witnessed among his Bay Area companions. Some said Lionel reminded them of Lenny Bruce—a New York Jewish hipster with talent to spare, a storyteller who mixed Yiddish and Black American humor, and an outsider to the jazz world who had its respect. Though Lenny was no Yeshiva boy, much less an Orthodox Jew, he could make a joke sting like a moral tale told by an old-school rabbi. In fact, Lionel was raised by just such a rabbi, his grandfather, Nuftali Zvi Margolies Abulafia, an immigrant from Safed in Galilee, along with his grandmother and his mother, in his grandparents' home on East Broadway in the Lower East Side of Manhattan. Safed was populated half by Muslim Arabs and half by Sephardic and Ashke-nazi Jews. Arabic was taught in Jewish schools and was spoken by everyone in public. His grandparents, Lionel said, "walked barefoot in the house, the whole place was like a tent. They spoke Arabic when they wanted privacy, so I wouldn't understand. They ate with their fin-gers, like Arabs, but if guests came they brought out a spoon and a fork." As a sickly child, he'd look out the window and see horse-drawn carts, men with beards, women in long dresses, angels in trees. "I felt I was living in the Bible." He was left to wonder why automobiles were not mentioned in the Bible. His mother, Sheba, was more worldly, active in Lower East Side social causes and politics, work that often took her away from home. But she was protective of young Lionel, and warned him to stay close to home, never to cross Delancey Street to the non-Jewish Lower East Side until he was twenty-one.

Lionel spoke Yiddish through the sixth grade in a traditional Jew-ish school, then moved to public schools and studied art at the Henry Street Settlement House. He entered Columbia University, earning a scholarship, but later transferred to Brooklyn College and then to the New School. Holding down a job was a problem for him: he made no effort for acclaim and prided himself on being unknown. Yet there seemed no limit to his ingenuity and curiosity: he wrote story lines for Dell Comics, scripted TV shows, was a news editor and a film re-viewer, painted, and wrote poetry, much of which is more interesting than that of some well-known Beat poets. But as was said of Thomas Hardy, a poet who writes too many poems is asking to be ignored . . . or in Lionel's case, poems that were largely unpublished and too long: his *Sentential Metaphrastic* was 703 pages ("the longest," he declared, "and most boring poem in the English language since Milton's *Paradise Lost*"), though in 1970 some of it appeared in the "Psychedelic Issue" of *Aspen*, the first multimedia magazine.

Harry stayed with the Ziprins as long as he could, by day visiting rare bookshops or libraries, where he copied magical engravings onto parchment paper, translating their texts from Latin, Hebrew, German, or medieval French, languages he had been learning on his own. Lionel recalled that "At night he would bring them to the house and the whole night goes":

> So finally there were 2,000, 3,000 pages fantastic ink drawings . . . And every night he would come and bring all the work and lay it out to me and give me all these lectures. Now this is the European Cabalistic traditions—it was a tremendous education. I was interested in magic—not in that kind of detail—but then Harry went and did everything with European magic. There is what you call Christian Cabalism.

He continued to return to the Ziprins for dinner, to read their books, to show them his films and those of Hy Hirsh, perform his paintings of jazz recordings ("Harry would stand there like a schoolteacher—with a pointer—pointing at each note as the music played."), and lecture them on whatever he had been reading or copying that day. "Any damn subject you talked to him—Harry is like tuned into a computer memory bank on Pluto that has every subject in the world and he can talk about it . . . anthropology, science, grammar, medieval logic, modern scientific electronics; also he knows how to work a camera; use any measuring tools . . . then there's the Tibetan thing too." When it became too much for Lionel to bear and he tried to stop him, Harry would further annoy him by flamboyantly kissing his feet and declaring him "my master."

Lionel resented Harry's freedom to explore any interests he

wished, while he had to work to support his family and Harry, so he warned him that this was not Berkeley, that he and Joanne would not continue to feed and house him, and he wasn't going to survive in New York without money. To speed the departure of his guest, Lionel found him a job working for the Montag Brothers Stationery Company, but he quit the first day and warned Lionel to never find another job for him. It was the last occupation that Harry would ever have with fixed hours and steady pay, and the beginning of a long and uneasy ambivalence between Lionel and Harry.

Harry soon found a tiny basement apartment in the Bronx. When Lionel visited him, he saw that he had turned it into an atelier with Day-Glo paint and black lights, "alchemical" substances bubbling on the stove, paintings on the floor, walls covered with collages, and a box with cutouts in the sides that he'd light from inside to project on the wall. "Harry was always interested in everything that could be made geometric, diagrammatic. Whatever you couldn't put in a diagram didn't interest him."

Once away from the Ziprins, Harry expanded his exploration of the city, wandering through the subcommunities of Harlem—Irish, West Indian, Puerto Rican, and African American; through neighborhoods like Little Germany, Little Italy, and Chinatown on the Lower East Side; and making weekly trips to the Museum of Natural History, doing fieldwork on roughly the same trail of discovery Claude Lévi-Strauss had blazed a decade before him. (Harry, like Holden Caulfield, fell under the spell of that giant canoe in the Hall of the Northwest, and also found his way to Heye's Museum of the American Indian in the Bronx.) Those Rosicrucian shoes, he said, had led him to some curio and book shops like the Warlock in Brooklyn, which later turned into the Magickal Childe in Chelsea, the Manhattan center for magic, exotic spiritual goods, and witches' gear. He was particularly drawn to Mary and Billy Gordon's Gateway Bookshop on East Sixteenth, which specialized in writings on the occult. There, Harry could sit and read, or listen to the owners' stories about their friendships with Aleister Crowley and W. Somerset Maugham. Soon they were paying him for occasionally helping out in the store, and continued giving him small sums of money for a few years.

The shoes next pointed him toward Count Stefan Colonna Walewski, a former member of the Polish delegation to the United States, now the owner of Esoterica, a shop near the fashionable Sutton Place, that overflowed with Tibetan objects of questionable origin, Egyptian "rods of power," good-luck charms of every denomination, and what the count said was the world's largest library of demonology. "It is pure escapism," according to the count. "People who don't have a happy life, who feel they are misunderstood or surrounded by problems too heavy for them, turn to occultism and mysticism . . . you cannot say they actually work magic—it's against the law . . . it's all—how do you say it?—it is all alleged." The count put Harry to work designing occult jewelry, briefly let him stay in his artifact- and book-filled apartment, and gave him some Tibetan *thangkas* (Buddhist paintings of deities or mandalas) and what was claimed to be Aleister Crowley's own typescript of an initiation ritual.

While working in the count's shop, Harry met Gerrit Lansing, a poet recently arrived in the city along with his Harvard classmates John Ashbery, Frank O'Hara, and Edward Gorey, who was employed at Columbia University Press while studying for an MA in English. Harry and Lansing were both visiting the rare book room in the New York Public Library, where Harry was working through *Das Kloster: Weltlich und geistlich*, a nineteenth-century German collection of spells, charms, and divinations. They were also spending nights together at Birdland, the "Jazz Corner of the World," the epicenter of bebop, where it was possible to stay the whole night for a small entrance fee and a single glass of beer (or in Harry's case, a glass of milk, as he had been avoiding alcohol). "I smoked a lot of weed with him," Lansing said, "on the streets even . . . he was fearless. One of his characteristics at all times." Lansing had recently discovered Crowley's writings, and together they sought out his followers in New York in the Metaphysical Institute and the Parapsychology Foundation. In Jersey City, Harry met Albert Handel, another student of Charles Stansfeld Jones with whom he thought he could study, but he broke with Handel when he made racist remarks about some of his Black tenants.

In his early years in New York City, there appeared a number of Harry Smiths. A census of his personae would show a varied and disparate array of often contradictory characters: a painter and a filmmaker seeking financial support; a collector and a curator; a flaneur; a professor of anthropology, folklore, and ethnomusicology; an occultist and magician. Dr. Joe Gross, a psychiatrist with whom Harry had an uneasy medical and nonmedical relationship, described him as "a stoned, drunken, hunched-over demonically creative gnome. Raw spirit, an intense beacon of truth, blinding in his rages, capable of unexpected, touching moments of ultracool charm, his head emblazoned with streaky wild Einsteinian hair, wielding a sly, cutting W. C. Fieldsish sense of sarcastic wit."

Herbert Huncke, a writer and hustler, recalled his first encounter with Harry:

> If my memory serves me in good stead . . . he was noticeably small of stature, with sharply defined, small facial features. A small sharp nose, which came almost to a point. His eyes, I think, were gray or green and twinkled sometimes and became piercing at other occasions, behind small,

plain, perhaps metal-framed glasses that fit in the center of his nose, held in place with thin metal bands which extended to his rather faun-shaped little ears, projecting a trifle obviously from both sides of his small face that ended below his mouth, thin and somewhat colorless, with his sharp, pointed chin. I seem to recall his hair as being a little curly or wavy, with a somewhat high forehead, light brown in color and neither sparse or very abundant. The neck was thin, centered between narrow, fragile-appearing shoulders with thin arms, ending with small hands. He wasn't what could be referred to as tiny, yet he was short and small, giving off an attitude I thought resembling a little fox, although not as appealing as a fox might appear.

The musician Peter Stampfel knew Harry by repute and held him in high esteem, so he was embarrassed that when he first met him he was "disillusioned by seeing this legendary genius as a disheveled bum—loud, drunk, and obnoxious. People were already fearing for what would happen to his films and art." Izzy Young, a folknik and early promoter of a young Bob Dylan, said, "I met the real Harry Smith at a party in my apartment where he vomited on the ample bosom of a famed folksinger, to everyone's horror or delight. Harry could insult anyone he met and did. He once made fun of my father's Polish background and I immediately threw Harry out of the store, which my father always thankfully remembered. From time-to-time Harry left films, recordings, and manuscripts in my store and I reproach myself to this day for returning them at his demand—to be dropped in a sewer, or its equivalent, five minutes later."

Jonas Mekas encountered him during the premiere of Andy Warhol's *Sleep*, when Harry greeted him with "I'm Harry Smith and I hate you," turned, and walked away. A week later he came back to Mekas with cans of films and said, "Can you take care . . . can you show my films, here they are, you can have them, do what you want with them," and walked out. Describing her first contact with Harry, the poet Diane di Prima said:

> Harry came for a visit unannounced. He came storming in, demanding to know how dare I reveal Kabalistic secrets. Well, since I really, at that point—I was in my twenties—had no idea what a Kabalistic secret was, I was quite awed by the fact that I'd revealed them. He was very, very angry. He had been at this reading I'd just given, or had heard something about it (I was never sure), and said that I was telling things that should never be told.

Joanne Ziprin, like Harry and Lionel, found no appeal in employment just to make a living, and proposed to Lionel that they should both be doing something creative, maybe designing a new kind of greeting card, one that could challenge Hallmark's lifeless verse and stock artwork. They would return to the Victorian origins of cards—handmade cutouts, eye-fooling collages, and trompe l'oeil. They'd update that early experimental spirit with 1950s hipster understatement, "sick humor," and a modern made-by-hand concept. The company would be called Inkweed Studios, and they would produce "greeting cards we believe in . . . having to do with imagination, bits of black magic and shoe strings, which all too few people accept in lieu of cold, hard cash."

Joanne and Harry were the only artists at the beginning. His designs were innovative, but expensive to produce, and too far-out to ever sell, whether it was his self-portrait as a devil, his hand-colored, three-panel foldouts, or the three-dimensional Christmas cards that came with special viewing glasses. 3-D might have been a big seller, since the early 1950s were the golden age of three-dimensional movies produced by major film companies, like *House of Wax* or *Inferno*. But when Inkweed's green-and-red cards arrived from the printers and were viewed through the 3-D glasses, they were out of focus. They were sent back to the factory for another print run, but when they arrived, they were still blurry. Since Harry had worked on the cards alone to avoid intrusions, he was blamed for not taking account of his astigmatism, a failure that had cost them a lot of money. But years later it was discovered that the problem was not in the cards, but in the 3-D glasses that were much too blue, and the cards would have worked if the correct glasses had been used. The other cards they produced did reach some department stores and college campuses, but by 1954, Inkweed's management and financial troubles forced them to sell the concept and their remaining stock to another company.

A year later, they were back with an idea for a new business, the Haunted Inkbottle, producing cards and artfully designed books with the help of new artists like Bruce Conner, who brought a touch of the occult and magic to the company's products, and Barbara Remington, later known for her Tolkien book cover illustrations. In 1958, Lionel started yet another company, the Qor Corporation, to take advantage of the recent invention of Mylar, the thin, polyester film that he saw as potentially a great medium for adding print and images to tile, wood, fabric, paper, and aluminum. Harry played a bigger role in this venture, with sketches, doodles, and esoteric designs, but despite some attention from the building and design worlds, the business never developed.

With Lionel's support, Harry set to work in 1954 painting *The Tree of Life in the Four Worlds*, his own interpretation of an archetype found in the philosophies, myths, and religions of the world. All have arboreal forms that may represent creation, heaven and hell, the mapping of a spiritual universe, a means of organizing ideas, tarot cards, letters of the Hebrew alphabet, deities, and the four elements. It was an expensive project. Using the older collotype printing process rather than cheaper and simpler offset lithography allowed them to produce an image with much finer detail. Jordan Belson was then in New York, and Harry brought him in to engrave the collotype plates and got him a place to live upstairs. Though they were intended for sale, Lionel ended up giving away most of the copies.

After several brief moves between apartments downtown, the Ziprins settled into a brownstone house on Seventh Street between Avenues C and D, a traditionally Jewish neighborhood (although the Mamas and the Papas, still in their folk song manifestation, were their next-door neighbors). There was a backyard with room enough for Lionel to realize his UFO dreams by building a spaceship landing site (subsequently destroyed by unidentified men in black). Aliens and angels figured in his private universe. He had seen angels since childhood. "It's no big thing; it's only another species." Once, while waiting to learn the results of some medical tests at Bellevue Hospital and wondering if he'd be able to get a cab home, he saw the Angel of Death coming toward him, old, multiracial, in dirty clothes . . . Lionel turned away as it got closer so as not to have to face it. "So it passes about six inches from me, it doesn't stop, and as it passes it says 'Zay gesunt' (stay healthy)."

Joanne introduced Lionel to bebop and Birdland, and they attended performances so many nights that their table became a gathering point for musicians looking for something to do during breaks. Charlie "Yardbird" Parker was a regular tablemate until his no-shows got him barred from the club named after him. (Parker and Lionel spent one break drawing cartoons of birds on napkins.) Miles Davis and Lionel got into it once over Joanne when Miles didn't seem to know (or care) that she was married to Lionel. One night Lionel had what he said was a perfectly normal conversation with Bud Powell, while the preeminent pianist of bebop lay in the gutter in front of the club.

Now, at a bigger house, people began to gather there late at night, drawn by the Ziprin's interest in painting and poetry, Lionel's Kabbalistic knowledge, his stories of encounters with visitors from the heavens, and his generous supply of peyote (then still available in large quantities by mail order). Joanne's friends came by, people like Rosemary Woodruff (later the wife of Timothy Leary), Allen Ginsberg, and the musicians Junior Collins, Stanley Turrentine, and Bob Dylan. Joanne's reputation as a skilled cook was a late-night draw. In no time, their house became a salon, an art scene, frequented by painters and dancers, geniuses and freeloaders, saints, unidentified weirdos, and jazz musicians like Bill Heine, a sometime drummer with Charlie Parker and a genuinely scary magician; or Thelonious Monk, who visited between sets at the Five Spot, and often sat in a rocker singing wordlessly to the Ziprin children on his lap. Harry was there, too, but he frightened the children, and their daughter Zia said she and her sister Dana hid in a closet whenever Harry appeared.

The move to New York had not been easy for Harry. His mother had recently died, he avoided talking about his family, said he had no friends, and had left most of his belongings behind in Bellingham and Berkeley. Lionel tried to get Harry to contact his father and was appalled when he resisted. He saw Harry as playing the role of a child who splits up married couples and makes trouble. "But children do that . . . classic Freudian stuff. He'd make fights between Joanne and me. First he'd side with her, and then he'd side with me." Lionel assumed it was what he had done to his own parents, ultimately driving them apart.

THE RABBI'S BASEMENT TAPES

When Harry was still new to the city, Lionel and Joanne invited him to the Lag b'Omer celebration in the spring of 1952, an annual party thrown by Lionel's rabbi grandfather to honor Rabbi Shimon bar

Yochai, a fabled second-century Kabbalist from Safed, the heart of mystical messianic Judaism and the city where Rabbi Abulafia was born when it was still part of Ottoman Syria. People from Galilee living in New York were invited to Clinton Hall, an old opera house, to join the rabbi, dressed in a Turkish fez and white robe, who sang while others danced. Lionel said:

> I said, "Listen Harry, I'm going to go with Joanne. You wanna go?" Yes, he would like to do that. I said "[You] gotta wear a yarmulke. It's a religious thing. You wear the hat." Fine. He already looked like a little Rabbi, with beard, oh God, everybody thought he was Jewish.
>
> So he came. And the dancing is going on, we're sitting, and Harry says, "What's the music?" He's never heard anything like it. And he's recording everything. Hours and hours on tape. That's Harry. He was never without a tape recorder . . . At the end, everybody's going home. So Harry shows my grandfather the tape. My grandfather looks at me and says "What is that?" Harry says, "Listen." He plays him a tape. Well, my grandfather's astonished to hear his voice on the tape there. Magic, right? That did it—so Harry says to him—I'm the interpreter but they got along somehow— would he like to make some songs and he will tape them.

The rabbi's house on East Broadway was next door to the Home of the Sages of Israel, a building the rabbi bought and dedicated as a place for retired rabbis and scholars, and where he had a small room off the library for study and napping. It was that room Harry turned into a recording studio with professional recording equipment the rabbi bought for him. Once a week for two years he recorded the rabbi's songs and tales. Though they had no common spoken language, Harry had picked up enough Hebrew to read it and could even make corrections to old manuscripts. They developed a close relationship:

Harry showed him all of his films, gave him books in Hebrew, and the rabbi performed string figures for him.

The recordings piled up, hundreds of hours of them, with stories told in Yiddish, and a rich mix of music from Safed: Arab songs, Ashkenazi songs set to Arab melodies, Arab Jewish songs in Hebrew, improvised songs sung in non-metered Arabic style, and Hebrew poems set to Greek or Turkish melodies such as "Misirlou," a song so popular and widespread that it turned up as Jewish wedding music, Middle Eastern belly dancing music, Greek rebetiko, American surf music (as recorded by Dick Dale, a Lebanese American), and in the Quentin Tarantino film *Pulp Fiction*. The music from Galilee fascinated Harry not so much because of its authenticity as folk song but because it lacked clear identity or origin—there were examples of what might today be called heterogeneity, transnationalism, deterritorialism, or creolization. He heard it as similar to what he had heard on some of the blues and jazz records he had collected, like "Palesteena," a 1920 instrumental recording by the Original Dixieland Jazz Band from New Orleans, the first recorded jazz band, and well-known by Harry and every other collector of early jazz. First titled "Lena from Palesteena," when sung it has the feel of Klezmer music, and a key part of it was borrowed from the Yiddish song "Nokh a Bisl."

Lionel grew unhappy with Harry's attachment to the rabbi. First his wife, and now his grandfather—Harry had insinuated himself into the family and engaged them in his interests, all in the name of anthropology. To Lionel it was just another exercise in Anglo-Saxon privilege:

> You see anthropologists are whites, super-racists . . . Looking at specimens . . . And Harry had a streak of it, I am sorry

to say. Whether it was the Cabala, my grandfather, the Indians on the reservation. He was somewhat saved because of his Marxist understanding. But you know the attitude. He's Anglo-Saxon . . . And they're looking at bebop and Bird's blowing his brains out on there . . . and you know it's being classified, right.

When he had had enough of Harry, he told his grandfather that he had to put him out of the house for making anti-Semitic comments. The rabbi was shocked: "But the man's a Jew!" When Lionel explained that he was just a goy from out West, the rabbi objected, "Then he's from outer space." Later, he decided that Harry must have been a Jew in a previous life. The matter was seemingly settled years later, on Harry's death, when Lionel had a brass plaque added to the wall of his grandfather's synagogue with Harry listed as a Jew so Kaddish could be said for him on his yahrzeit (the anniversary of his death) every year.

Harry's tapes of the rabbi were mastered, and one thousand copies of fifteen LPs were pressed and packaged for sale in 1955, paid for by the rabbi just before his passing. But the record notes had not yet been written, and there were religious issues among the family over how, where, and when these sacred recordings would be sold. They ended up stored in the basement of a Bronx public housing building that Lionel's mother administered, and there they sat for years until the basement was flooded. A few sets were salvaged and still await issue. Only one disc, a sampler from the larger project, was ever produced for sale, *Prayers and Chants by Rabbi Naftuli Zvi Margolies*, Special Record Q1 on Folkways Records in 1954, and it, too, was withdrawn over religious concerns.

The presence of Judeo-Arabic music from the late Ottoman Empire on the Lower East Side of Manhattan in the middle of the twentieth century had been documented.

5

The Anthologist
1952–1953

The *Anthology of American Folk Music* is perhaps the most
influential set of records in the history of recorded sound.

—Back cover of the Smithsonian Folkways release of Harry Smith's
Anthology of American Folk Music

I heard [the *Anthology*] early on when it was very difficult to
find these kind of songs . . . For me, on hearing it, was all these
songs to learn. It was the language, the poetic language—it's
all poetry, every single one of those songs, without a doubt, and
the language is different than current popular language, and
that's what attracted me to it in the first place.

—Bob Dylan, *Mojo*, February 1998

If God was a DJ, he'd be Harry Smith.

—Peter Stampfel

During the holiday season of 1952 I played two hours' worth
of tracks from the [*Anthology*] on KPFA-FM [San Francisco].
I received phone calls and letters from my jazz-fan audience
asking, not pleasantly, "What the hell are you playing?" I
explained, "This is the album of music that Harry Smith was
putting together a few years ago." "Oh, him," was a
typical response, "that explains it."

—Phil Elwood, *SF Gate*, November 12, 1997

Harry grudgingly realized that Lionel might be right: there was only so long that he could get by sleeping on people's sofas, cadging meals, and stashing his records, books, films, and paintings wherever he could. The records he shipped from California were his only liquid asset, something he was sure he could sell, but selling them was a slow process, and he hated the idea of his most prized records being scattered among collectors who would hoard them for themselves. He had justified his own collecting as creating a carefully curated selection of the best of American folk recordings, which he hoped would one day be placed in a library or museum, but who would pay for that?

Pete Kaufman suggested that he might be able to sell them in bulk to Folkways Records, a small new company at the center of what was becoming a folk music revival that was beginning to reissue old recordings. Harry had no idea that his records had any monetary value beyond a few collectors, though he thought that if they could somehow reach a larger audience, they might alter the way people thought about music. He was fond of quoting Plato on music having the power to change society.

The owner of Folkways was Moses Asch, a pioneer in boutique recordings of jazz and folk artists with his Disc and Asch record labels, and now with his new Folkways project he was on a mission to record, issue, and reissue seemingly everything—Pete Seeger, Dave Van Ronk, and other folk singers, but also poetry readings, the sounds of junkyards, instructions on how to learn Morse code, cantorial chants, the drumming and singing of boys' gangs, political speeches, and avant-garde, ethnic, and old-time music. Knowing there was no way for him to compete with the established recording companies, Asch's plan was to do what they wouldn't: record what they didn't record, aim at sales to libraries and schools, and keep everything available for sale forever. It was this openness to all forms of music and his promise to keep all the records in his catalog that quickly gained him respect among musicians and singers.

Moe Asch was the son of Sholem Asch, then the leading Yiddish novelist and playwright. Though Moe was born in Poland and had lived in Paris, studied engineering in Berlin, and grown up among theater people and Jewish intellectuals (it was Albert Einstein who encouraged him to record folk music), Asch said he had never met anyone like Harry—the closest was Woody Guthrie, that self-made, organic intellectual who arrived in New York disguised as a hick. "Woody would come to the studio or fall down on the floor . . . wild hair and everything . . . and pull off jokes . . . Get him in front of a microphone he'd croon and he'd cry . . . but his presentation was formal. You knew that the man had a statement to make and he made it."

Moe was one of the few people in New York who knew something of the full range of Harry's work in the arts, yet even he was astonished to find out how large Smith's collection of commercially recorded country, blues, and religious records was, and how much he knew about them. "He understood the content of the records. He knew their relationship to folk music, their relationship to English literature, and their relationship to the world," he said.

Harry offered to sell some of his collection to Folkways when Asch began putting together a five-volume set titled *Music of the World's Peoples*, selected by the composer Henry Cowell, and an eleven-volume set of long-playing, 33⅓-rpm records on the history of jazz made up of older, hard-to-find 78-rpm records selected by Frederic Ramsey, Asch, and Harry. The new long-playing format seemed perfect for anthologies. For the first time it was possible to listen to one song after another without changing the record or turning it over. Six or seven pieces of music could be put on each side of an LP, and the music could be sequenced creatively. Moe bought some of Harry's 78-rpm records for anywhere from 35 cents to $2 each, and used a few of them as part of several of his reissue projects. "I began selling off Bukka White, Champion Jack Dupree, and other stuff that I considered to be of a sort of second rate," Harry said, "and anyhow easily replaceable. [Asch] was astounded by the stuff!" Moe then proposed that they both could make more money if Harry put together a collection of these old records for reissue, something the big recording companies were slow to do. The idea of treating it as an anthology with extensive notes on the performers and the background of the music was Harry's idea, and it made the record sets appear as serious as books. If Cleanth Brooks and Robert Penn Warren's widely used 1938 textbook *Understanding Poetry: An Anthology for College Students* could contain the texts of songs like "The Daemon Lover" or "Frankie and Johnnie" and declare them literature, then Harry could include commercial recordings of the same songs in his record anthology and claim their equal importance.

On May 15, 1952, Harry signed an agreement with Folkways Records for a $200 advance ($1,900 today) with royalties of 20 cents ($1.87) per record sold. They also agreed that Asch could create new albums by using any recordings Harry had, but Harry would be allowed to sell them to collectors before Folkways reissued them.

Moe was excited by the idea despite some initial doubts about Harry's reliability, but he found him easy to work with, and often pointed to his anthology as an example of how record reissues should be done:

> Harry Smith is an authority. He not only is the collector, he knows the record, he knows what he wants to say in what form he wants to do it and he has a concept of the complete package. He comes to me and we discuss it. And I say, "Harry, I love it. You just give me the finished manuscripts and give me the form that you want it and I'll issue it exactly the way you want it." . . . Everything is Harry Smith.

Asch told the folk music collector and musician Ralph Rinzler that he had provided Harry with a room in which to work, a typewriter, the books he needed, and every so often he'd give him a button of peyote. Rinzler doubted that Asch was serious about the drug, but admitted that there was a "dreamlike, visionary quality" to Harry's album notes.

The transfer of the 78-rpm records to the 33⅓-rpm long-playing format was done by Peter Bartók, who was familiar with folk music and the problems of recording it, having already remastered the field recordings of his father, the Hungarian composer Béla Bartók, for Folkways.

In 1952 *The Anthology of American Folk Music* was released, a set of six LP records divided into three sets of two LPs, titled "Ballads," "Social Music" (both sacred and secular), and "Songs," each accompanied by an elaborately conceived booklet of notes. The music was a selection of white country music ("hillbilly") and African American ("race") records that were made between 1927, when, Harry said, "electronic recording made possible accurate music reproduction, and 1932, when the Depression halted folk music sales. During this five-year period, American music still retained some of the regional qualities evident in the days before phonograph, radio, and talking pictures had tended to integrate local types." Harry's record notes indicated that he had plans to do three more sets of records and that they would be "devoted to examples of rhythm changes between 1890 and 1950."

The models for this project were several compilations of previously issued commercial folk recordings that Alan Lomax produced in the 1940s: *Smoky Mountain Ballads* for RCA in 1941, and *Mountain Frolic* and *Listen to Our Story—A Panorama of American Balladry* for Brunswick Records, both of which first appeared in 1947 as 78-rpm recordings and were later reissued in 1950 among the first recordings produced on long-playing records. Another of Harry's sources was Lomax's "List of American Folk Songs on Commercial Records" that was put together in 1940 for the Library of Congress and made available to the public. After listening to some 3,000 recordings, Lomax had chosen 350 as especially important, and 60 of these as the best. Twelve of those 60 were included in Harry's *Anthology*, and many of the others were by performers who were also on Lomax's list. Smith urged other collectors he knew to write to the Library of Congress for a copy of the list.

Because Harry was unknown to most folk music enthusiasts, many assumed that the *Anthology* had been compiled by Lomax under a pseudonym to avoid legal problems. But Lomax's self-exile to Europe in the face of a congressional hunt for leftist folklorists and singers rendered his work largely forgotten by the public.

Smith said he had chosen the records for the *Anthology* not because they were the best he could find, but rather because they were "odd," or "exotic in relation to what was considered to be the world culture of high-class music." They were "selected to be ones that would be popular among musicologists or possibly with people who would want to sing them and maybe would improve the version."

> Intuition is employed in determining, in what category, information can be got out of. I intuitively decided I wanted to collect records. After that had been determined, what was then decided to be good or bad was based on a comparison of that record to other records. Or the perfection of the performance. To a great degree, it seems like a conditioned reflex. What is considered good? Practically anything can be good. Consciousness can only take in so much. You can only think of something as *so* good. When you get up among, say, top musicians or top painters—which one is the best? Either things are enjoyable or they are unenjoyable. I determined what the norms were. You can tell if you hear a few fiddle records, when one is the most removed [exceptional] violin playing of the Metropolitan Opera Orchestra. If that seemed to be consistent within itself, that would be the good record; if it was a good performance of what it was. Now, it was merely my interest in looking for exotic music. The things that were most exotic—whether it happened to be the

words or melodies or timbre of the instruments—that really
was what selected those things.

Yet he also said that some of them, like "Brilliancy Medley" by
Eck Robertson, were picked simply because he liked them or because
they were important versions of a well-known song. His criteria for
choosing commercial recordings were not far from what Lomax said
was behind his selections for his Library of Congress list:

> The choices have been personal and have been made for all
> sorts of reasons. Some of the records are interesting for their
> complete authenticity of performance; some for the melodies;
> some because they included texts of important or representa-
> tive songs; some because they represented typical contempo-
> rary deviations from rural singing and playing styles of fifty
> years ago; some to make the list as nearly as possible typical
> of the material examined.

The order in which Smith placed the records was apparently carefully thought out. His categories of "Ballads," "Social Music," and
"Songs" follow the groupings of songs from Francis James Child's
English and Scottish Popular Ballads, Cecil Sharp's *English Folk Songs
from the Southern Appalachians*, and Lomax's songbooks. "Henry Lee"
by Dick Justice was the first track on the "Ballad" set of records be-
cause it was the lowest number of the five ballads in his set that were
also in Child's classic collection of ballads in the English language.
But his reasoning was not always obvious, most notably with "The
Moonshiner's Dance, Part 1" by Frank Cloutier and the Victoria Café
Orchestra, a medley of songs, most of which would never be called a
folk song: "When You and I Were Young, Maggie," "How Dry I Am,"
"Turkey in the Straw," "At the Cross," "Jenny Lind Polka," and "When
You Wore a Tulip." This was the only recording from the Northern
states in the *Anthology*, and it appears to be part of a stage review set

in the Victoria Café in St. Paul, Minnesota, with a list of vaudevillian jokes and Prohibition humor tossed in between songs.

Though it would still be a few years before economic inequality and the civil rights movement became dominant topics of American life, poverty and race had long been subjects of American conversation. But when Smith's recordings from out of the past appeared, with their messages from people whose voices had not been heard so directly, so vividly, or at all, it was shocking. These songs were evidence of ways of living and performing not found in history books or even among the urban folk revivalist singers themselves: "You didn't see at the time how preachy the mainstream Folk Movement was," John Cohen said,

> because everybody was becoming a preacher. It was more like a pyramid club; every folk singer became his own preacher. People had this attitude of "I will now speak for Black People." Rather than listening to what blacks in this country might have to say for themselves. The voices on the *Anthology* are of complaint and suffering and humor and caustic comments on the world. And documentary depictions rather than moralistic statements . . . And in a strange way, the *Anthology* was also a tremendous foundation for the counter-culture.

Even though the songs had been recorded only some twenty years earlier, technology and tastes in music had changed so radically by 1952 that the recordings chosen by Smith were often referred to as if they were archeological finds, the sonic equivalent of the Dead Sea Scrolls or the Rosetta stone. That year the pop hits were the usual mix of love songs of longing and emotional insecurity ("Cry," "Auf Wiederseh'n Sweetheart," "Half as Much," "Wish You Were Here," "I'll Walk Alone"). But faux versions of songs from outside the mainstream of pop were also finding their way onto the hit lists: Latin ("Kiss of Fire," "Blue Tango," "Delicado"), the American West ("High Noon"), Cajun ("Jambalaya"), and blues ("Blacksmith Blues"). Before the *Anthology*, most people in urban areas thought folk songs were the Weavers' spirited, jukebox-aimed tunes with Gordon Jenkins's pop arrangements; the earnest, uplifting, and mildly political messages of Pete Seeger; or Burl Ives's easy-listening Americana. Folk singers and scholars of folk song alike were suspicious of what was then being called country and western music. Neither they nor the public were aware there were other kinds of working-class commercial recordings. The *Anthology* made it possible for anyone to hear a stunning variety of musical genres, content, singing styles, and emotions montaged together as old-time music: ballads, work songs, blues, parlor tunes, raw banjo pieces by Dock Boggs, the dark jeremiads of Blind Willie Johnson, hymns from the Alabama Sacred Harp Singers calling from the deep past. For the first time Cajun songs in French could be heard outside their territories. ("Pete Seeger couldn't understand why I was issuing those things, 'cause he felt they were out of tune," Harry said. "But once he went to Louisiana, he got back here, rushed up and said, 'Hey, Harry, you were right! They do sing like that!'") Dave Van Ronk said that the *Anthology* was a response to those who sang folk songs as if they were art songs, as a kind of classical music from the lower end of society. Though few noticed it then (or now, for that matter), the performers were not what people would have thought of as folk: Smith's choices included a Hollywood movie cowboy, an Appalachian lawyer, and city factory workers.

There was also something of a perverse authenticity in knowing that the songs in Harry's *Anthology* were *not* recorded by a folklorist for historical or academic reasons, but by record companies who intended to please diverse buying publics out in the hinterlands of America. In a time in which high-fidelity recordings had just appeared, promising "living sound," the scratchy thinness of these old records seemed like the sound of history, the voices of the dead. But at the same time, their sonic crudeness was a reminder of how challenging they were to record and thus brought with them an aura similar to early photographs of Abraham Lincoln or Civil War soldiers.

The reissue of this music may have come as a shock to the companies whose recordings were made for profit alone, not for presenting it seriously as music. In 1952, they would have been reminded of a part of their own forgotten corporate history as they remade their image, broadening sales by merging country and western music with pop trends like crooners, the use of professional songwriters, and the development of high-fidelity recording.

It seems odd that most folk song scholars and collectors were not more deeply interested in the content of songs, and would let pass without comment lyrics such as those about the stalking and murder of women. Folk song collections in print or on record left a song's story and meaning up to the reader or listener, but Harry's headline-like summaries of the songs' texts in his notes made them seem like the news of the day (though with the modernist edge and wit in the use of headlines in James Joyce's *Ulysses* or William Carlos Williams's *Paterson*).

Words of a song that might have been only half heard as they drifted past on a recording now had their message posted in bold type: the words of the 1927 recording of "Willie More" by Burnett and Rutherford are condensed to ANNIE UNDER GRASSY MOUND AFTER PARENTS NIX MARRIAGE TO KING, DEATH PROBABLY SELF-INFLICTED; Nelstone's Hawaiians' 1930 "Fatal Flower Garden":

GAUDY WOMAN LURES CHILD FROM PLAYFELLOWS; STABS HIM AS VICTIM DICTATES MESSAGE TO PARENTS; Chubby Parker's 1928 "King Kong Kitchie Kitchi Ki-Me-O": ZOOLOGIC MISCEGENY ACHIEVED IN MOUSE FROG NUPTUALS, RELATIVES APPROVE. Sometimes Smith seems to be suggesting thematic connections between the songs. For records (19) "Stackalee" by Frank Hutchison, (20) "White House Blues" by Charlie Poole and the North Carolina Ramblers, (21) "Frankie" by Mississippi John Hurt, (22) "When That Great Ship Went Down" by William and Versey Smith, (23) "Engine One-Forty-Three" by the Carter Family, and (24) "Kassie Jones" by Furry Lewis, Harry's headlines read: (19) THEFT OF STETSON HAT CAUSES DEADLY DISPUTE, VICTIM IDENTIFIES SELF AS FAMILY MAN; (20) MCKINLEY SWEARS, MOURNS, DIES, ROOSEVELT GETS WHITE HOUSE AND SILVER CUP; (21) ALBERT DIES PREFERRING ALICE FRY, BUT JUDGE FINDS FRANKIE CHARMING AT LATTER'S TRIAL; (22) MANUFACTURERS [*sic*] PROUD DREAM DESTROYED AT SHIPWRECK, SEGREGATED POOR DIE FIRST; (23) GEORGIE RUNS INTO ROCK AFTER MOTHER'S WARNING, DIES WITH THE ENGINE HE LOVES; (24) CRACK ENGINEER JONES IN FATAL COLLISION, KNEW ALICE FRY, WIFE RECALLS SYMBOLIC DREAM, LATER CONSOLES CHILDREN.

These tabloid news flashes remind that war, violence, hatred, the supernatural, imprisonment, jealousy, catastrophe, the vulnerability of laborers, death, civil rights, suicide, revenge, love, protest, the tensions of North and South, Europe and Africa, are all persistent throughout American history, part of a past that's not even past. They show that songs communicate by turning speech and writing into an intensely emotional form. Smith's notes convey how early recorded songs treated these messages, what they looked like, who communicated them, and how they were marketed, and hinted that there was a darker side of American history that only song (and Harry's stark headlines) could fully reveal.

Halfway through "Songs," the third set of the *Anthology*, Harry began to include words to the songs in his notes, even though they were not always complete, perhaps because he edited them to call attention to certain elements of the songs. His notes were quirky but at the same time scholarly: for each song he provided its origins, history, and importance; where it could be found in print; who had recorded it; and the record's master numbers, along with dates and places. There was a bibliography of books he used for research, and a scrupulous discography, with cross-references to singers and titles.

He went further into detail about the songs, if only briefly: the introduction of the banjo into white American music, then the guitar; the difference between rhythmic accompaniment in Texas and Louisiana; the role of pre-Columbian music in American music; the blurring of sacred and secular that appeared in blues, gospel, and jazz melodies; the country music roots of the popular musical comedian Spike Jones; and the use of similar melodies and words in different songs. No scholar or collector had ever provided this much information in a collection of folk music, especially folk music that was to be found on recordings.

Harry also added what he called "a few quotations from various authors that have been useful to the editor in preparing the notes for this handbook."

There were theosophical hints:

In elementary music the relation of earth to the sphere of water is 4 to 5, as there are in the earth four quarters of frigidity to three of water.

—Robert Fludd

Do as thou wilt shall be the whole of the law.

—Aleister Crowley

The in-breathing becomes thought, and the out-breathing becomes the will manifestation of thought.

—Rudolph Steiner

One early anthropologist's musings on the different functions of music and dance:

> Civilized man thinks out his difficulties, at least he thinks he does, primitive man dances out his difficulties.
>
> —R. R. Marett

Comments on the use of copyrighted recordings without permission:

> On plagiarism: "If by some magic a man who had never known it were to compose anew Keats's 'Ode on a Grecian Urn,' he would be an 'author,' and if he copyrighted it, others might not copy that poem, though they might of course copy Keats's."
>
> —Judge Learned Hand

> Really? Is it yours? I had supposed it was something old.
>
> —Unknown

These last two quotes and some other comments in his notes were boldly self-justifying, since the *Anthology* was a bootleg project: none of the companies that owned the rights to the records Harry selected had been paid. Moe Asch believed that it was wrong for recording companies to withdraw their records from circulation or destroy their original masters, and then forbid others to copy the recordings. "There is a provision in the copyright law," Moe wrote, "that says people have the right to know . . . Actually, it came out of the policy on automobiles . . . If a manufacturer stopped making a certain part of a car his whole factory could be thrown in public domain. Car owners had a right to those parts. We applied the same logic to these records that were no longer available."

Smith's essay at the beginning of the *Anthology*'s booklet of notes and another at the end by Asch tell the story of how such recordings had originally been niche-marketed to discrete groups of Americans in the early years of music recording. Since most people had never heard this music, Asch and Smith felt reissues were necessary. Similarly, Alan Lomax had published books, made field recordings sold by the Library of Congress, and developed his list of essential commercial recordings. The difference was that Lomax had the approval of the companies whose recordings he was using.

In Harry's essay he complained that the terms used by recording companies, like "hillbilly" and "race" records, were objectionable. By giving the albums the general title of "folk music" instead of "blues" or "country," Moe Asch had moved the music away from the sales managers' focus on regional and ethnic neighborhood record stores, giving it a broad American character suggesting something more appealing to everyone. But Harry had misgivings about Asch's using "folk music" to characterize the collection, which could also imply the imitative or polished versions of this music as performed by Richard Dyer-Bennet, Burl Ives, or the Weavers.

It's often said that because Harry didn't classify records by racial identification, he was the first to refuse to identify performers themselves by race. But the story is more complex. Recordings had been made by racially integrated bands without identifying them as such as early as the 1920s, and record companies occasionally violated their own racial marketing by issuing white musicians' records on race labels. The two 1947 Lomax-recorded folk song anthologies that Harry said shaped his own work included both Black and white performers, none of whom were identified by race, and many of them also appeared in Smith's *Anthology*. A Folkways recording issued a year before the *Anthology* had already dodged such classifications: the compiler Henry Cowell's notes for *Music of the World's Peoples* did not list the race or ethnicity of the performers, explaining that he wanted to draw attention to the influence of the different musics on one another. Nor were Harry's record notes entirely free of racial indicators, as he included pictures of some performers used in record advertisements.

What was interesting to Harry was that the musical styles of white and Black people had been reshaped and creolized by mutual influence, especially in the South, and, like Henry Cowell, he wanted to make that point through his selection. John Cohen said Smith was setting a trap:

> Harry talked in our interview about doing some things deliberately to fool the scholars . . . Before the *Anthology* there had been a tendency in which records were lumped into blues catalogs or hillbilly catalogs, and everybody was having blindfold tests to prove they could tell which was which. Harry said "I wanted to see how well certain jazz critics did on the blindfold test. They all did horribly. It took years before anybody discovered that Mississippi John Hurt wasn't a hillbilly . . ."

Early on, the blues scholar Paul Oliver understood Harry's intentions and pointed them out in what was the second review of the *Anthology*:

> This inspired collection . . . was surely the best pointer to the relationships as well as the differences between white and Negro music forms to have appeared in print or on record outside the more esoteric works which generally escape the jazz and blues collector's attention . . . No one has taken up the cudgels, no one has continued and extended the work that Harry Smith began.

The guitarist and composer John Fahey also saw this as a prime directive for the *Anthology*:

> Smith was acutely aware of a fairly simple truth . . . certain musicultural traditions were sympathetic to each other while

others were not . . . Smith had an encyclopedic knowledge of 78's and a preternatural feel for the connections between them—across race and ethnic boundaries—not only to codify them for us but to have this collection persist . . .

This shouldn't have been surprising, because Harry spelled out what he was trying to do in his brief essay prefacing the *Anthology*'s notes. At a time when academics who taught folk song disdained recordings and stuck to written texts, he was proposing a new kind of scholarship aided by existing technology:

> Only through recordings is it possible to learn of those developments that have been so characteristic of American music but which are unknowable through written transcriptions alone . . . records of the kind found in the present set played a large part in stimulating these historic changes by making easily available to each other the rhythmically and verbally specialized musics of groups living in mutual social and cultural isolation.

Smith understood that the recordings of white Appalachian music showed Black influence, and on the other hand that there were blues ballads like "Train 45" and "Frankie and Johnnie" sung by Black performers. He knew that string band music and early bluegrass had picked up characteristic ragtime rhythms and reused minstrel show tunes; zydeco music of Louisiana was the product of both white and Black musicians; and the banjo, the quintessential American folk instrument, was an African instrument also played by white musicians in a style far removed from European string music. European set dances like the quadrille changed into square dances when accompanied by Black musicians and danced by Blacks, and many dance calls—a kind of early rap—were the inventions of Blacks who called the steps for white and Black dancers. Many "hillbilly" and "race" songs were borrowed from minstrelsy or "coon" songs heard on the vaudeville stage. Western swing was a convergence of country string bands and big swing orchestras; these cross-genre, cross-racial efforts would help shape early rock 'n' roll: Chuck Berry's first recording, "Maybellene," is a 1955 reworked version of Bob Wills and His Texas Playboys' 1938 recording of "Ida Red."

Defending and celebrating the merger and creolization of Black and white music in America, Harry reflected Alan Lomax's thinking. But he differed with Lomax about his fear of the disappearance or "graying out" of cultural styles across the globe under the dominant influence of Euro-American mass media. In a conversation with the folklorist Nick Spitzer in 1987, Harry spoke of musical concrement— "a general feeling of unity among all mankind" and that "the new music should be a composite of all the musics of the world":

> The thing that amazed me was that everyone thought that would happen, of course, but they thought they'd be playing rock and roll in Bali. Nobody took into consideration the fact that enough rock musicians were going to be listening to Balinese music that they were going to [be infected] . . . and you hear more music from, at least to my jaded ears, sounds like Australian or Eskimo or any number of other places . . . I'm sure that Elvis Presley is just as big a star in Beijing as he is here, but nonetheless, Chinese music has been heard by a great number of people. The Central Broadcasting Folk Orchestra being my own favorite, and troupes of things that you'd never imagine. Like they've recently been here, Mongolian singers and stuff. All music is becoming united, but not in a form that had originally been imagined.

There is evidence that Harry thought his work in the *Anthology* was not being taken seriously by the public or Moe Asch. In an interview with Gary Kenton he said:

All the transcriptions have been made. The notes are elaborate, do you understand? They're philosophical statements regarding the science of musicology. I mean, it's not just a bunch of records, brought out to get some money. To produce a Folkways album—anybody that makes one spends thousands of dollars to make it and is given hundreds of dollars in exchange.

In its first year, only fifty sets of the *Anthology* were sold, forty-seven of them to schools or libraries, or at conventions, the places where Asch had aimed his sales from the beginning. Izzy Young, the owner of the Folklore Center, the Greenwich Village folk *bibliothèque* and hangout, said that he never sold more than five a year. The list price of the complete set was prohibitive—$25 for the set, or $244 in today's currency. Apart from a very favorable mention in the *Music Library Association Notes*, there were no reviews in academic publications such as the *Journal of American Folklore* or in folk music fan magazines like *Sing Out!* The next review would not appear until a decade later, and then only in the British *Jazz Monthly*. But near the end of 1953, RCA Victor Records noticed, and objected to the unauthorized use of some of their recordings, forcing Asch to withdraw the *Anthology* from sale and from the Folkways catalog until 1956, when it quietly returned, apparently unnoticed.

For years, sales never increased significantly, and averaged only thirty-seven sets annually. Foreign sales were roughly the same. The price dropped over time, but even in 1982, the cost of the three sets in today's currency was $140. Most were still being sold to libraries and book clubs (in 1962 the total sales of single discs were 504, for which Harry received $107.80). This pattern continued over the next twenty years. Yet the *Anthology* somehow reached the Kingston Trio,

Neil Young, Jerry Garcia, and others who later changed pop music by introducing elements of older song styles and folk songs to the public. Lomax himself strongly approved of Harry's work, and loaned a young Bob Dylan one of the recordings with the message that it was important. Dylan would later record at least fifteen of his own versions of the eighty-four records in Smith's collections.

The *Anthology* also motivated a new breed of record collectors to head south, looking not just for the original 78-rpm records, but for the original singers, many of whom they found and helped to restart their careers. Clarence Ashley was located by Ralph Rinzler, Mike Seeger found Dock Boggs, Mississippi John Hurt was rediscovered by Tom Hoskins, and Sleepy John Estes was found and recorded by Sam Charters and Bob Koester.

With so little money coming from the *Anthology*, John Hammond and Moe Asch suggested that Harry sell his remaining records to the New York Public Library. The chief of the Music Division, Carleton Sprague Smith, a major figure in expanding the music holdings of libraries, bought them for several thousand dollars after some quibbling over what was or wasn't a folk record. When word got out that Harry's collection was there, folkniks began asking for it, only to find that they weren't yet cataloged, and so were unavailable. Mike Seeger and Ralph Rinzler were two young musicians excited by the idea of access to Harry's collection, who couldn't wait to hear those records, and in 1956, they volunteered to catalog the collection for the library. But while Ralph spent months cataloging, Mike was tape recording the records. When they were told copying was forbidden, they began slipping the records out of the library at the end of each day, crossing the Hudson River to Ralph's parents' house in Passaic, copying them through the night, and returning them the next day. Eventually this resulted in Mike adding songs to the repertoire of the old-time music trio the New Lost City Ramblers, of which he was a member. Once Ralph became a producer of the Newport Folk Festival and the Smithsonian Folklife Festival, he encouraged the performance of songs drawn from Harry's records before large audiences.

Another outcome of their midnight rambles was the formation of the Friends of Old Time Music, by Rinzler, John Cohen, and Izzy Young. Between 1961 and 1965, the Friends discovered some of the performers in the *Anthology* were still alive, living mostly in the South, and they brought them to New York for concerts. The Great Depression and shifting musical tastes had ended the brief careers of most white country and blues musicians and singers, sending them back to work on farms and in factories and mines. Folk song fans in the 1960s had assumed that the singers on the *Anthology* were all dead, but suddenly they were back, playing and singing for new audiences. Some had been performing rockabilly music or working in vaudeville and minstrel shows down home and arrived in New York ready to appear in clownish hick clothes or in blackface and had to be persuaded to adopt Northern folk-revival correctness.

Such ironies were missed by Harry because he never attended any of these concerts. "He was not interested in the musicians themselves," Cohen said. "He was not a fan. It was the jazz clubs and their musicians that continued to fascinate him."

THE *ANTHOLOGY* AS ART

The *Anthology* was a continuation of Harry's childhood interests—the gathering of endangered songs and dance music of Native Americans, recording them, and placing them in a museum, as well as finding, buying, and researching other peoples' rare recordings. His approach to this new project was always scholarly and disciplined, though somewhat obscured by the outright strangeness of the booklet that came with the final product. The music Smith's *Anthology* contains may seem old and weird, as Greil Marcus put it, but the records were old and odd when they were first recorded as acts of revivalism by record companies. They illustrate an effort to preserve an authentic past more than they are an exercise in nostalgia, and are better understood as an act of American modernism. Harry offered up a collection of performances that tells us something of the power and utility of a broad collection, the ways in which it can realign perception, or shift historical perspective. The subjects of the songs, their sources and historical settings, their placement and montage in the albums, the cultural exchange among singers, and the album's notes' mix of traditional, scholarly, and proto-hippie imagery all contribute to a sense that cultural continuity was, and still is, being reimagined.

What was also striking about Harry's collection was the organization and graphics of the booklet of record notes included with the records. Far from a folklorist's or an ethnomusicologist's organization or classification of songs from diverse sources, Harry said, "The whole anthology was a collage. I thought of it as an art object," and he signed it with the signature he used for his paintings. (Moe Asch called it a mosaic.) The *Anthology*'s three double-LP albums were color-coded in blue, red, and green to correspond with water, fire, and air. Each of the three sets had the same cover art—a sixteenth-century etching of a stringed instrument by Theodor de Bry taken from a mystical treatise by the scientist/alchemist Robert Fludd: "like something or other tuning the Celestial Monochord. It's forming earth, air, fire, and water and the different astrological signs." Smith organized the music and the art to match his personal cosmology, with each color corresponding to an alchemical element—though earth was notably absent.

There was something both antique and modern in this kind of curatorial work. The cut-and-paste feel of the illustrations throughout the booklet echoed Smith's methods for creating painted collages and animated films: the white-on-black background printing of the information followed the design of older record labels; photos and illustrations were taken from record covers and musical instruments, Sears Roebuck and farm catalogs. There were disembodied hands pointing nowhere, and oversized numbers for each song from 1 to 84, all of it anticipating the homemade fanzines of the 1960s. At a time when compilations of country music might have had a cover photo of a sulky farmer's daughter lying in a hayloft, the *Anthology*'s cover *was* downright weird.

THE MYSTIQUE OF THE *ANTHOLOGY*

The improbabilities of the *Anthology* generated mythologies about its origin, organization, and meaning, which as a result has made it the subject of books and hundreds of articles, sometimes in quite moving and visionary prose. Greil Marcus, for one:

> This is Smithville. Here is a mystical body of the republic, a kind of public secret: a declaration of what sort of wishes and fears lie behind any public act, a declaration of a weird but clearly recognizable America within the America of the exercise of institutional majoritarian power.

Or Robert Cantwell:

> With its three volumes, its six discs, twelve sides and eighty-four bands the *Folkways Anthology* is indeed a kind of *Commedia* of folk music, and like Dante's poem, is suffused, initially at least, with strangeness. Entering the *Anthology*, we first meet a babble of voices—strange, even grotesque voices, everywhere unbeautiful. In some instances, they are comi-

cal, caricatures of voices—in others bathetic, in still others forbidding or unnatural. In this atmosphere of strangeness, a dialectical energy develops between the vocalities which lie reassuringly within the boundaries of familiar vocal traditions and those which transgress them . . . [The voices] accompany us like so many Virgils; they reveal, in the *Anthology*'s eerie environment of whines, cries, shouts, growls, and other weird vocal sounds, the path which our own traditions have taken, at the same time positioning our own voices in relation to sounds lost, abandoned, or forgotten.

John Fahey, perhaps eager to deflate such high-minded hearings (even while he himself drops names such as Charles Ives and G.W.F. Hegel), pointed out the bloodiness and nastiness of Harry's compilation:

Let us make a body count of all the people who get killed in this anthology of folk music. Twenty people are killed or commit suicide on the domestic scene, and 1,513 people died when the *Titanic* sank. If we add to that the 15 million killed in WW1, an event mentioned by Blind Lemon Jefferson and Cannon's Jug Stompers, we get a total 15,000,533 deceased. If we average this figure out among the 84 selections, we get 178,587.67 people killed per song in this collection!

Others saw the *Anthology* as a form of mixtape that one might give to friends, or a macro-sampling of Southeastern American music, or simply the whims of a quirky DJ. And perhaps "DJ"—in the fullest or most imaginary sense of the word—is closer to the truth: in Smith's version of DJing, a collector sifts through discs in search of something: Racial music parallels? Fortuitous hybridization? Creole discoveries?

Whatever the interpretations of what Harry was after, one recurrent misunderstanding in celebrating Harry's work is seeing he and

Lomax on opposite sides of the folk music trail: the collector of commercial recordings vs. the collector of field recordings, one of them wise to the market-tested product, the other a purist and romanticizer. Harry always credited Lomax as the inspiration for his own work and spoke of him with deep respect. And Harry, too, had made field recordings in Washington State, New York City, Oklahoma, and Boulder, and would follow Lomax's later theories of folk song and his computer-driven methods for understanding a culture through its music. After reading Lomax's 1969 *Folk Song Style and Culture*, Harry began to speak of recordings as one of the most convenient ways of gathering ethnographic information. The verbal content of songs and the styles in which they were sung was a means of grasping what he saw as the "cultural norms" of a society. The repeated listening that recordings allow makes it possible for performers and scholars of music to discover and focus on the most characteristic features of a culture's songs. With these elements singled out, it becomes possible to interpret musical performances or imitate them, even if one has never seen them performed live. Lomax had long acknowledged that the record companies had done a better job than the folk song scholars in reaching a larger audience, and he thought of Harry as continuing the good work: eight songs in Smith's *Anthology* are also in Lomax's 1960 songbook *The Folk Songs of North America*.

Smith and Lomax were both committed to using the latest technology to enhance recording and listening to music, and they saw the computer as the future of the work they were doing. If at first they appeared to be operating on different scales of analysis—Lomax the "distant reader" with his cantometric method of abstracting features of thousands of musical examples from hundreds of different cultures to do sophisticated statistical and computational comparative analysis, and Smith the "close reader" with only eighty-four songs offered for comparison by his private method of sequencing—it's sobering to discover that Harry admitted that his sample was too small for what he wanted to do, and talked of the possibility of using computers to properly complete his work.

Luis Kemnitzer spent more time than anyone else talking with Harry about the meaning of folk and ethnic recordings, and he remarked that "Harry's aesthetic was very complex . . . The formal attributes only had meaning or attraction or beauty as they accompanied and were accompanied by historical, cultural, psychological context. The possibility that contexts could be manufactured or manipulated only added spice to the aesthetic."

In an industry in which recordings typically disappeared from the market within a year or so of their first appearance, Moe Asch's practice of keeping everything he issued for sale allowed for twenty-some years to pass before the *Anthology*'s influence was widely acknowledged. Bob Dylan, the Byrds, Bruce Springsteen, Sonic Youth, Wilco, Nick Cave, Beck, and so many others would come to claim Harry's records as their Bible. And "Bible" was not an exaggeration: a collection of ancient texts that originated in diverse communities difficult to locate, texts made all the more sacred because their sources are mysterious and have to be decoded, and contain both high and low poetry. Dave Van Ronk, maybe the centermost figure of the Greenwich Village folk revival, spoke with reverence to David Hajdu about the Smith records:

> We learned everything we knew about old-time music from the *Anthology*. It was our Talmud. It was our Bible . . . We ate up the songs, even if we hated them. We thought they were all terribly exotic. We thought they were all antediluvian, and, you realize, quite a few of the singers were alive and well. It didn't quite sink in to us that everything on the

recording was a commercial recording. Some of them were quite popular in their day. We couldn't have fathomed such a thing.

John Sebastian, of the Lovin' Spoonful, saw these records as a mystery that led to an epiphany:

> Here's what it was about that music. First of all, it had an untamed quality. It also had mystery. The lyrics didn't necessarily follow each other, because very often it was the type of song that Harry Smith described as a kind of a laundry-list song that had accumulated verses from other songs that were similar to it so that it no longer necessarily made dead-on sense . . .
>
> These songs had this mystery to them—you know, "Featherbed," the Gus Cannon tune. What is that about? The "Prison Walls Blues" is a definite cousin of "Younger Girl." But part of my writing "Younger Girl" was because I had no idea what these guys were saying. So it was this untamed quality, un-produced quality, but it also had a joy and an unchained quality about it, that I really sensed and really gravitated towards . . .
>
> It sounded like a world of wooden floors and back porches, and you could tell that this was not urban music. For us in the late fifties and early sixties, it was a time when the first little ripple of really undomesticated music had already hit; we'd heard Elvis and we'd heard Jerry Lee and Little Richard, and now was the Pat Boone-ization of all the Fats Domino tunes and . . . this was a period where everything was very manufactured. So maybe it was that part of what attracted more than just me, was the fact that this music hadn't been run through a grinder—it hadn't been made to stand up and salute. It was unapologetically local in nature . . . it was

not trying to attract a mass audience, it was simply reacting to the needs, the musical needs of a town. And there was something about that.

Peter Stampfel of the Holy Modal Rounders first heard the *Anthology* when he came to New York in 1959: "It devastated me, it totally wiped me out. Hearing all this amazing stuff, enthralled and captivated me and I decided that I had to recreate this music because all of the people who did it were dead or dying. Once they were gone, by God if I didn't grab that torch, the flame would be extinguished forever! I needn't have bothered because thousands of other kids had the same identical response. So instead of it dying, there was a huge resurgence." He set out to write a series of songs that depicted Harry's life, to be called the "Harry Smith Anthology," but only completed one—"His Tapes Roll On."

Before Harry had completed the sale of his records to the library, Asch suggested that he create more anthologies. For a fourth volume to extend the original three, Harry selected at least twenty-eight recordings, all of which were made between 1928 and 1940; they included many of the performers he had used before, like the Carter Family ("Black Jack David," "Hello Stranger," and "No Depression in Heaven"), the Blue Sky Boys ("Down on the Banks of the Ohio"), and the Monroe Brothers ("Nine Pound Hammer Is Too Heavy"). There were other favorites he would have included, like Fiddlin' John Carson and Arizona Dranes, but the condition of many of his 78-rpm records was too poor to issue given the improved sound of LP recordings. But, as Asch put it, "we ran into the problem of everyone wanting to get into the act." Harry quarreled with Marian Distler, Moe's assistant, over her attempts to add a song on the reelection of

President Franklin Delano Roosevelt. The collector and writer Sam Charters made up his own list of what should be on the new record, but Harry rejected it. Ralph Rinzler, Mike Seeger, and Dick Spottswood wanted to make up a volume of music styles not in the original *Anthology* (such as Latin or Ukrainian immigrants' music) but it was never completed. An even bigger problem was locating some of the original records. Asch had made master tapes of them, enough for a fifth volume, but there was no information about them for use in the notes. Harry seemed to have disappeared, and there was no way to bring out a new set of recordings that failed to match the caliber of the work that had gone into the rest of the *Anthology*.

Harry's account of the absence of Volume 4 was that he had prepared headlines for the volume that told a story in a sequence he envisioned, but it had been changed by others who worked with Asch. Then, the tapes of the remastered 78-rpm recordings were lost in what he called the chaos of the Folkways' two-room office on Forty-Sixth Street. But regardless of what happened, Harry said he "didn't have sufficient interest in it," by which he meant he had moved on to thinking of more advanced ways to use old records:

> I wanted to make more of a content analysis. I made phonetic transcriptions of all the words in the songs, but those notebooks got lost. The content analysis was like how many times the word "railroad" was used during the Depression and how many times during the war. The proportions of different words that might have some significant meaning beyond their exterior. Certain ideas became popular, the word "food" was used increasingly in the record catalogs during the Depression.

A decade later, John Cohen found the tapes and Harry's notebook that contained the order in which he had planned to organize the records. It took yet another thirty-five years, but in 2000 the fourth volume of the *Anthology* was finally issued by Revenant Records with a large booklet with brown pages, presumably to represent the element earth. Once again, John Fahey had a cheerful summary of the contents of the songs:

> The evidence is in the shakedown. False hearts, the triumph of mechanization, cockeyed worlds, prostitution, TB, death, hunger, orphans, widows, tribulation, storm, fears, doom of millions, depression, fucked up highways, strangers, inflation, poverty, phony preachers, storms of life, failure, tribulation, persecution, battle, old and feeble, and chimleys, for God's sake. It's all in there.

If that's not a tribute to alienation, I don't know what is.

There was yet another anthology planned by Harry and Moe back in 1953, two or three LPs of commercially issued shape note (or sacred harp) records that Harry had collected in the early 1940s, recordings that very few people outside the singers' own communities were ever likely to know existed. Shape note is a method of writing music developed in New England in the late eighteenth century to make it quicker and easier to teach people to read and sing Protestant sacred music. Four different-shaped notes are used to represent the syllables of "fa," "sol," "la," and "mi," with three of them representing two different notes of the scale ("fa" is both C and F, for example). There are four vocal parts, but no key is indicated, and though the notes are placed on conventional printed musical staves, the lines of the staves can be ignored. A leader picks the songs and sets the key and the tempo. But this is also music that is highly participatory, with rotating leaders, without instrumental accompaniment, and open to amateurs. It's typically performed loudly, with a strong 4/4 rhythm and a distinctive harmonic feel, and often a fugal and multimelodic form. Those who hear it for the first time can be startled, especially when the choir begins by singing wordlessly to establish the voicings. The effect for the listener is otherworldly, as it is to many of its singers as well.

Though the melodies in shape note songbooks are signed with the names of composers, many of the same melodies existed as folk songs long before their publication and were used for dancing and as love songs and ballads, and even if they *were* original compositions, many were soon used to accompany nonsacred activities and treated as if they were folk songs from anonymous origins. It's a unique form of religious song in many ways, because the songs are sung not in church services but at singing conventions and song gatherings.

Harry had included three shape note recordings in his original *Anthology* (songs number forty-four to forty-six) and was drawn to this form of singing by its exotic sound. But he had long been interested in various methods for making music visible, an interest he developed during his efforts to find ways to document Native American speech, music, and dance. He studied a series of methods scarcely known even by music historians, such as sound spectrograms, phono-photography, and phonautograms, as well as the ninth-century Greek use of neumes, the earliest form of written music. He also planned to transcribe the words phonetically, as he had done with the Indian recordings he made when he was young.

Moe Asch was excited when he heard these little-known singers and their songs, and he remastered Harry's 78-rpm records himself. But, once again, the master tapes were lost in the Folkways office. Moe would find some of those lost tape reels twenty-seven years later and give Harry a $100 advance in 1980 ($302 today). Harry set about writing the notes for the recordings of the Alabama Sacred Harp Singers, the Denson Quartet, the Daniels-Deason Sacred Harp Sing-

ers, the Fa Sol La Singers, and others, including the only African
American shape note singers Harry was able to find on record, the
Middle Georgia Singing Convention No. 1. In his notes he states that
he made no attempt to organize these records by date because he was
"more concerned with showing the interrelations of singing styles."

Harry's first thought for a title of this new set of recordings was
Times Endless Moment, but he changed it to *Early Recordings of Shape
Note Singing*; a later title was *Looking Backward*, and perhaps, finally,
it was to be *A Grammar of Early Shape Note Recordings*. (He seemed
to be moving from eschatology to generic labeling, then gesturing
toward nostalgia or possibly utopia, and finally an academic's mono-
graph on the rules and methods of an art form.) In the rough draft for
the notes to the collection, he spelled out what interested him about
this music:

> This essay is an attempt to show that the sources from which
> the shape note songs or rather the melodies on which the
> shape note songs are based are more dependent on periods
> during which contact between music that is usually classi-
> fied as European and Afro-American came in contact with
> one another than is generally assumed. These periods were
> the "great awakening" (1820–1840) and the early days of the
> phonograph, roughly a hundred years later.

The Great Awakening that Harry points to was the second of a
series of religious revivals in the United States in which personal salvation increased at the cost of institutionalized religion. It was a time
in which slaves were actively being invited to convert to Christianity
(sometimes participating along with whites in large outdoor revival
meetings).

Harry also thought whites had claimed too much influence on
African American life and culture. His notes show that he was skeptical

of the biased and shallow conclusions of folk song scholars such as
George Pullen Jackson, who asserted that African Americans had
contributed nothing to the creation of Protestant hymns and church
songs. As Harry put it, "What shape note composer would credit a
melody to one he felt superior to, especially in the period of the Great
Awakening?"

Other than Lomax, there was likely no one at the time who had
more knowledge of the full range of America's vernacular music on
commercially issued recordings, and Smith was suspicious of a long
scholarly tradition asserting that Scots-Irish music was the basis of all
Black music in the United States, even spirituals and jazz (the all-too-
familiar "Ain't nobody here but us white folks" claim). It was a continuation of Harry's efforts in the 1952 *Anthology* to show that white and
Black music had mutually influenced each other far more than the
scholars and the public were willing to admit.

Smith had little recorded evidence with which to question shape
note singing's exclusive European pedigree, but he knew that there
were different songbooks in use by white singers (especially the 1844
Sacred Harp by B. F. White and E. J. King) and by African American
singers (J. Jackson's 1934 *The Colored Sacred Harp*). In one of the song
lists he made for the anthology of records he was preparing, he included several recordings from Africa: T. K. Browne with two Yoruba
songs sung by a chorus, Kwabima Mensa's two songs sung in the Twi
language with guitar accompaniment, and Kwasi Menu's "High Life."
He was calling attention to African choral similarities to shape note
singing.

Smith's projects often took years, and he was still working on the
shape note album notes in 1985, expanding the scope of what could
be learned from the songs. First, the words and music had to be accurately transcribed, including phonetic transcription with markings
where breaths were taken. He included a study of harmonic patterns and the differences from other folk songs, a formal analysis of

the songs' structures, and a study of verbal content by locating and counting recurring words and themes in songs. (Smith studied the occurrence of the word "travel," to and from home, from earth to heaven, and the possibility that some of the songs have the rhythm of a railroad train.) His work notes posed questions: Was there a parallel between weaving and polyphony, the lines stretching across one another? A similarity between the structure of myths and of songs? "Shape notes songs are a sort of work song?" "What was meant by phrases in songs such as 'I may be looking backwards but I'm going up the road'?" "Is it probable that an actual 'high' results from this type of singing, it having a steady beat known to increase adrenaline?" "Is the notion of travel to other states of existence possible borne out by the constant reference to travel in the singing texts themselves?"

Though it took forty-five years, the *Anthology* finally found a large audience at the turn of the twentieth century. Reissues, remakes, recordings by name artists, festivals, films, videos, books, conferences, concerts, and awards were spread across the United States and even Europe and the UK. But let Harry have the last word about what the *Anthology* meant to him. When he heard Bob Dylan on the radio, he was thrilled by the way Dylan had grasped his intentions. Harry told the guitarist-luthier Marc Silber, "When I first decided to compile the Folk Music Anthology much of my impetus was created by me noticing that the folk or ethnic music of America was not included in the 'popular' music of America. This is the sign of a very sick culture, perhaps unprecedented in history, for this was not the natural flow of development. So, I felt I might be able to adjust this somehow . . . But, well, I never thought it would turn out like this." "This" was the beginning of a long and obsessive admiration for what Dylan had done with the music. Though he was shocked by Dylan's turn to amplification and the trappings of rock, Harry stuck with him, and *Blonde on Blonde* became the soundtrack of his days and nights in 1966.

In a 1984 interview with the journalist Peter Goldsmith, Harry said of the *Anthology*, "At the present time I reject that entire approach to music. I can no longer be held responsible for having put that thing together in the way that it's put together." But then he added, "I would be lacking in self-respect if I said that the Anthology of American Folksong [*sic*] had anything less than a very powerful influence on what happened next."

6

The Parapsychologist
1954–1964

> I'm trying to found new sciences, to entirely overhaul
> anthropology and turn it into something else. I have to depend
> on psychopaths to pay for that kind of research.
>
> —Harry Smith

Those who knew Harry in the early years after his arrival in New York spoke of him as secretive, a recluse, more hermit than hermetic. But if he had a secret, it was his not disclosing just how far-ranging his activities were, and how a completely unknown young man from out of the west came to know so many people in the east with such divergent interests so quickly. Finding his way among musicians, artists, and the Village Beats was one thing; but his involvement with people such as Arthur M. Young, engineer, astrologer, and principal inventor of the Bell 47 helicopter; Andrija Puharich, physician, military parapsychological researcher, author of *Beyond Telepathy* and *The Sacred Mushroom*; and the millionairess Ava Alice Muriel Astor Bouverie (the only daughter of John Jacob Astor IV)—that is astonishing.

Following successes in the worlds of mathematics and engineering, Arthur Young traveled and read widely; discovered the works of Freud and the theosophist Madame Helena Blavatsky; became involved with Zen Buddhism and Hindu philosophy; studied dreams, mythology, and astrology; and devoted the rest of his life and considerable wealth to spiritual matters and phenomena that he felt science failed to comprehend. Just as Harry was arriving in New York in 1951, Young and his wife, Ruth Forbes, the wealthy great-granddaughter of Ralph Waldo Emerson, were establishing the Institute for the Study of Consciousness in Philadelphia with the goal of bringing scientific and esoteric knowledge together to better understand extrasensory perception and other forms of the paranormal.

Andrija Puharich was a physician, inventor, and researcher who worked in medical electronics and neurophysiology, and had the rare ability to attract money from the most unlikely and most legitimate sources for research projects. His work on extrasensory perception, consciousness-altering drugs, and mental telepathy was supported by a surprising group of extremely wealthy individuals—Joyce Borden of Borden milk products; Marcella du Pont; U.S. Vice President Henry Wallace; Ava Alice Muriel Astor Bouverie; Admiral John E. Gingrich, one of the heads of the Atomic Energy Commission; John Hays Hammond, Jr., inventor of radio-controlled devices; Congresswoman Frances Payne Bolton; Arthur and Ruth Young; and others committed to understanding paranormal phenomena. He created the Round Table Foundation of Electrobiology in Glen Cove, Maine, which Puharich's wife called a "scientific commune," and Aldous Huxley said was a "strange household." According to Huxley, Puharich's aim was to "reproduce by modern pharmacological, electronic and physical methods the conditions used by the shamans for getting into a state of traveling clairvoyance and then, if he succeeds, to send people to explore systematically 'the Other World.'" When Puharich was called by the army in 1953 to serve at the Aberdeen Proving Ground in Maryland, Arthur Young took over as director of research at the Round Table Foundation.

Harry never revealed how he became involved with these people, but Young and Puharich were sufficiently impressed by this impoverished young man with seemingly vast knowledge of books on ancient magic and alchemy that in late 1954 both hired Harry to do research for them. Before he received his first paycheck from Puharich, Harry's landlord evicted him for never having paid any rent. Ruth Young let him stay in a room in her New York house at 35 East Seventy-Fifth Street, but while he was moving, many of his things were thrown in the trash by his landlord. Harry wrote Arthur at his Philadelphia home that he was now safe in the New York house, and that he had managed to get the most valuable things moved in time.

The work he did for Young concerned esoteric symbolism. One of the projects was a study of George Wither's 1635 book, *A Collection of Emblems, Ancient and Moderne*. Harry said his interest in Wither was more "alchemical than Baconian," that is, more alchemical than scientific, but he was also alluding to Young's interest in a then current debate over whether Sir Francis Bacon was the real author of Shakespeare's plays, which resulted in Young's book *The Shakespeare/Bacon Controversy*.

Throughout the summer that Harry stayed at Ruth Young's, he came to know some of the people involved in the research directed by Puharich and Young who visited or were staying there. Among them were Frances Farrelly, who practiced radionics, using a machine that diagnosed health by measuring the radiation from a person's body, and then treated it; Harry Stump, a Dutch sculptor who, under trance, seated in a Faraday cage that blocked electromagnetic fields, could write scripts in Egyptian hieroglyphics; and Elinor Bond, who could read and see through a blindfold telepathically, and taught a class on ESP that Harry attended.

Harry was hoping to somehow stay within that circle, remain in a fine house, and do his own research as well as Young's. In a progress report to him, Harry described some devices he had been building:

> Francis [*sic*], Elinor, and the Stumps came down from the Round Table . . . we had several interesting meetings. I was very happy to learn that the harmonic cage I designed united

the best aspects of the toadstool and dodecahedron is in actual construction.

While you've been away I made a pendulum amplifier based on the correspondences between a plaster anatomical model and the subject, who holds the pendulum by an arm cut from the small figure. Touching various parts of the lay figure with the free hand while penduling, produces some curious rates. I am also planning another pendulum using partly incubated eggs for the bob to see if the Abrams reflex (the interior of the egg being wired to the subject's solar plexus) can motivate it.

Francis was kind enough to outline the Brunly [sic] method to me, so I'm making a scale similar to his, but using the rates of the thirty concentric aethers delivered to Dr. John Dee by the angel Uriel; they may form a convenient method for correlating the nodes to the alchemical principals [sic].

Although it's not clear what Harry was describing, he was creating some forms of radionic or electromagnetic devices, as his mentions of the early medical researchers Oscar Brunler and Albert Abrams indicate. While Harry was at work on these projects, Arthur had Frances Farrelly check on Harry's "financial situation," and asked Elinor Bond to work up Harry's astrology chart (though she got his birth date wrong twice).

Young, Puharich, and their backers were well aware that most radionic and psychic research had been heavily criticized or debunked by mainstream science, and the careers of once well-regarded physicians like Brunler and Abrams had been ruined by the negative publicity surrounding their work. But in the early 1950s, anthropologists were discovering mind-altering drugs that had been in use for years by shamans and healers among Native American peoples, all of which suggested that science had neglected ancient and non-Western evidence. It was also the early days of the Cold War, when the U.S.

government had become concerned with what they believed was psychological warfare research in Russia, and Puharich was part of the counter-research backed by the army and the CIA. When he left the military, his own research turned toward less scientific efforts: a Hindu medium who declared he had contacted ancient Egyptian mystics from outer space; the Israeli psychic Uri Geller, who claimed superhuman powers but ended as a popular TV entertainer; and a few other frauds and unsavory characters, such as Ira Einhorn.

Just how Harry related to these people of wealth is not known, though it's evident that he asked them for money. He said that when he met Alice Astor Bouverie and asked for her help, she replied that she didn't carry much money with her. Would $200 ($2,009 in today's currency) do?

He was still engaged with Young's research several years later, helping with the study of astrology, and working through the three volumes of Clarence Barnhart's *New Century Cyclopedia of Names* in search of twenty thousand names and brief biographies throughout history that could be used in Young's research. But at the finish of the project in 1957, Harry accused Young of forgetting what he said he agreed to pay him: he had received only $240 instead of $500, and that the distress of not receiving what was owed him had resulted in him losing thousands of dollars in spoiled alchemical experiments. He was so upset that he had been "forced to start making movies again. Entering the movie industry costs money, and as I am in it due to your mental condition, it is only fair that you should bear part of the cost. I have raised all that I can by selling my books, paintings, etc., but still need about 500 dollars to finish the film . . ."

It's not known whether his claim was successful, but Harry had already been quietly returning to filmmaking. *No. 7*, which he had begun in 1950, was what Harry called "Optically printed Pythagoreanism in four movements supported on squares, circles, grillworks and triangles with an interlude concerning an experiment," a fifteen-minute silent film he titled *Color Study*.

The film scholar P. Adams Sitney described Smith's homemade but innovative work on this film:

> To make this film, Smith set up a primitive, back-screen projection situation that worked with astonishing precision. One machine projected black-and-white images to a translucent screen. On the other side of the screen a 16mm camera rerecorded them. A wheel of color filters in front of the camera was used to determine the hue of a figure or a background. By keeping an accurate record of where any pattern was recorded on the film strip, the film-maker could make elaborate synchronous movements by means of several layers of superimposition. Most of the visual tropes of No. 7 derive from earlier animations of Smith's, but here they attain their apogee of intricacy and color control. No use is made of off-screen space.

Once again, audiences would not know how this film was made, nor would they know they were watching a movie of a movie, but they would have sensed that what William Moritz called "the soft luminescence of re-photographed images" was something new.

Harry finished three films in 1957, though they were not shown publicly, and apparently not seen by anyone. Films *No. 8* and *No. 9* were both lost early on, and all that remains are Harry's brief notes from some years later: *No. 8* was a "black and white collage made up of clippings from 19th Century ladies wear catalogues and elocution books." *No. 9* was a "color collage of biology books and 19th Century temperance posters. An attempt to reconstruct Capt. Cook's Tapa collection." (Tapa was a form of Pacific Island painted bark cloth clothing.) He added that *Nos. 8* and *9* (as well as *Nos. 10, 11*, and *12*) were made under the influence of "almost anything, but mainly deprivation."

No. 10, the first of what he called his "Mirror Animations," was a 16-millimeter, color, silent film: "An exposition of Buddhism and

A group of Lummi Indians
(Photograph by Harry Smith. Courtesy of the Harry Smith Archives)

ABOVE: A Coast Salish ceremonial dance, circa 1940, painted by Harry Smith (Courtesy of the Samish Indian Nation)

LEFT: Harry Smith recording a Lummi ceremony at the Lummi Indian Nation Reservation, Washington, circa 1942–1943 (Photograph by K. S. Brown. Courtesy of the Harry Smith Archives)

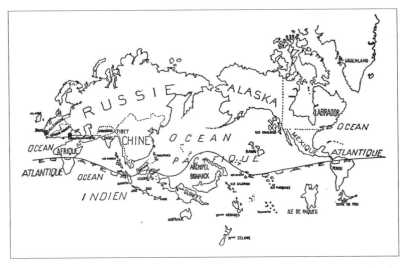

Le Monde au Temps des Surréalistes (The World at the Time of the Surrealists).
From a special issue, "Le Surréalisme en 1929," of *Variétés*, June 1929

Photograph of Harry
Smith for the 1943
Bellingham High
School yearbook,
Shuksan (Courtesy of the
Harry Smith Archives)

American Magazine photo of Harry Smith,
nineteen, at home with Lummi Indian Nation
guests, circa 1943 (Courtesy of the
Harry Smith Archives)

Harry Smith with his "brain drawings," circa 1950
(Photograph by Hy Hirsh. Courtesy of the Harry Smith Archives)

Harry Smith's painting of Dizzy
Gillespie's recording of "Lover,
Come Back to Me" (Courtesy of
the Estate of Jordan Belson)

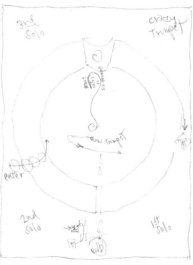

Jordan Belson's map of Harry Smith's
painting of "Lover, Come Back to
Me" (Courtesy of the Estate of
Jordan Belson)

Harry Smith's
painting of
Dizzy Gillespie's
recording of
"Manteca," 1948
(Courtesy of the
Harry Smith Archives)

Harry Smith's painting of Charlie Parker's recording of "Ko Ko,"
circa 1951 (Courtesy of the Harry Smith Archives)

Harry Smith's painting of Dizzy Gillespie's recording of "Algo Bueno," circa 1951 (Courtesy of the Harry Smith Archives)

Film frame from *Film No. 1: A Strange Dream* (Courtesy of and copyright Anthology Film Archives)

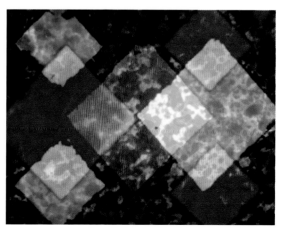

Film frame from *Film No. 3: Interwoven* (Courtesy of and copyright Anthology Film Archives)

From left, George Leite, Harry Smith, and Anaïs Nin in daliel's bookstore, Berkeley, 1946

Harry Smith with his jazz mural at Jimbo's Bop City, San Francisco, circa 1950 (Photograph by Hy Hirsh. Courtesy of the Harry Smith Archives)

Harry Smith's painting *First Notes, Fourth Chorus*, of Miles Davis's recording of "Boplicity," circa 1950 (Courtesy of the Harry Smith Archives)

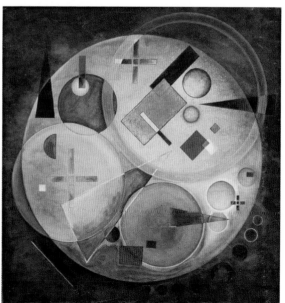

Early non-objective painting by Harry Smith, 1951 (Courtesy of the Harry Smith Archives)

Harry Smith, self-portrait as the devil,
circa 1953 (Courtesy of the Lionel Ziprin Archive)

Harry Smith (left), John Kraus (behind), and
Lionel Ziprin, New York City, 1952 (Courtesy of the
Lionel Ziprin Archive)

*The Tree of Life in
the Four Worlds*,
by Harry Smith,
1954 (Courtesy of the
Lionel Ziprin Archive)

Cover of the *Anthology of American Folk Music* booklet of liner notes

A page from the *Anthology of American Folk Music* booklet of liner notes

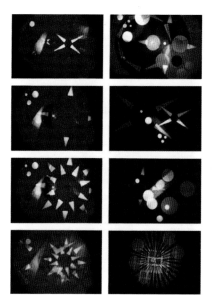

Film frames from *Film No. 7: Color Study*
(Courtesy of the Harry Smith Archives)

Dinner at the Heaths, unknown date
(Courtesy of the Harry Smith Archives)

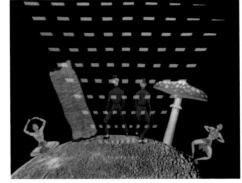

Film frame from *Film No. 10:*
Mirror Animations
(Courtesy of and copyright
Anthology Film Archives)

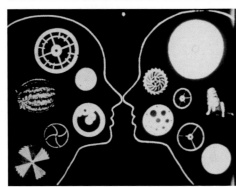

Film frame from *Film No. 12:*
Heaven and Earth Magic
(Courtesy of the
Harry Smith Archives)

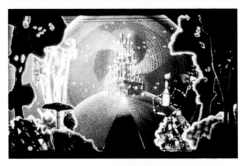

Film frame from *Oz*
(Courtesy of and copyright
Anthology Film Archives)

Film frame from *Film No. 14:*
Late Superimpositions
(Courtesy of and copyright
Anthology Film Archives)

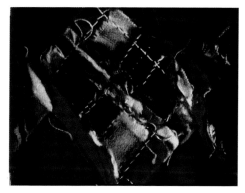

Film frame from *Film No. 15*, untitled animation of Seminole patchwork (Courtesy of the Harry Smith Archives)

Paper airplane (Photograph by Jason Fulford. Courtesy of and copyright Anthology Film Archives and J&L Books)

The Holy Books of Thelema, Harry Smith book cover design (Courtesy of the Harry Smith Archives)

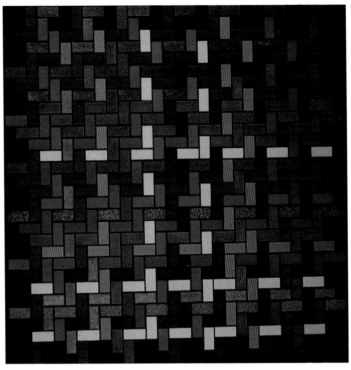

A Harry Smith painting with a design based on the Enochian
tablets, circa 1980–1981 (Courtesy of the Harry Smith Archives)

Bill Heine, Thom DeVita, and Lionel Ziprin (© Clayton Patterson
from the Elsa Rensaa and Clayton Patterson Archive)

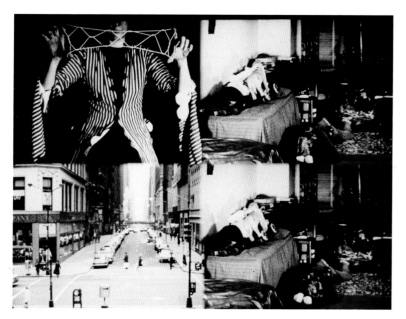

Film frame from *Film No. 18: Mahagonny* (Courtesy of and copyright
Anthology Film Archives and the Harry Smith Archives)

Film frame from *Film No. 18: Mahagonny* (Courtesy of and copyright
Anthology Film Archives and the Harry Smith Archives)

Untitled drawing, date unknown (Courtesy of the Harry Smith Archives)

Typewriter drawings, circa 1970–1972
(Courtesy of the Harry Smith Archives)

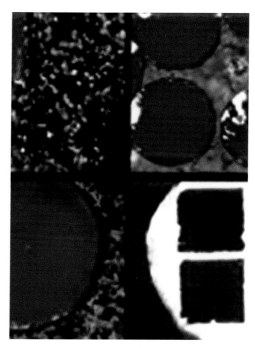

Untitled, 1980 (Courtesy of the Harry Smith Archives)

Southern Cult Composite—The Staten Island Massacre, 1984. Harry Smith's drawing for Allen Ginsberg's poem "Journal Night Thoughts" (Courtesy of the Harry Smith Archives)

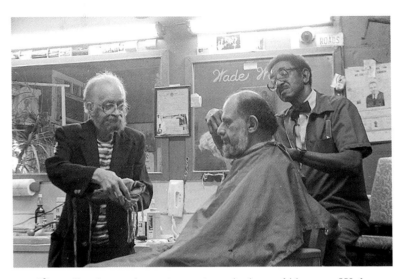

Harry Smith recording scissor snips as barber and bluesman Wade
Walton gives Allen Ginsberg a haircut in Clarksville, Mississippi,
in 1987 (Photograph by and courtesy of William Cochrane)

Harry Smith, 1987
(Photograph by William Ferris. Courtesy of William R. Ferris Collection,
Southern Folklife Collection, The Wilson Library,
University of North Carolina at Chapel Hill)

the Kabbalah in the form of a collage," cutouts of mystical elements, and an animated Tree of Life. He had been cutting up magazines, newspapers, and catalogs for twenty years, though when he left California, he gave the bulk of them to the poet and filmmaker James Broughton.

THE HIGH PRIEST OF BOP

When asked why he moved to New York, Harry would often say that it was to visit Baroness Rebay, meet Marcel Duchamp, and see Thelonious Monk perform. He had heard Duchamp speak and seen his films in San Francisco, and he may have met him in New York, possibly at one of the happenings where Duchamp often turned up. They shared a number of interests: alchemy (at least as a theory of creation), the importance of chance in artwork, the fourth dimension as an unseen shadow of the mysterious (Duchamp thought of *The Bride Stripped Bare by Her Bachelors, Even* as a fourth-dimensional projection), the belief that the artist was only a medium for an art object whose work is completed by an audience's reaction to the art, and the use of unusual techniques such as the stereoscope and putting paintings into motion on film. There is also the likely possibility, but no evidence, that Harry read Lamantia's writing on Duchamp in the March 1945 issue of *View*; or that he saw photos of Duchamp's experiments with string, such as the vision of him fumbling with a string figure in Maya Deren's partially completed *Witch's Cradle* (1944); or that he saw photos from Duchamp's act of ethnographic surrealism, the "16 miles of string" project for the 1942 *First Papers of Surrealism* show in Manhattan. At the front of the catalog for that show is the statement that "Surrealism is only trying to rejoin the most durable traditions of mankind. Among the primitive peoples art always goes beyond what is conventionally and arbitrarily called 'the real.' [These people make objects that] surrealists particularly appreciate." The list of peoples begins with "natives of the Northwest Pacific coast." Duchamp asked that the gallery be infused with the smell of cedarwood, the material used for totem poles and masks. The strings that crisscrossed the exhibit formed what might be seen as a huge string figure.

Harry's interest in Thelonious Monk was something else. He explained why he had become so involved in Monk's music, and why he was spending nights sitting close to his piano at the Five Spot Café on Cooper Square, where the Bowery begins: "I'd been able to hear Charlie Parker and Thelonious Monk, both of whom had come to San Francisco, but wanted to make one final thing, another painting of Thelonious."

Monk had first come to notice in the early 1940s as a house pianist in Minton's Playhouse, an after-hours club in Harlem that was frequented by musicians and artists, perhaps the most notable being the Dutch painter Piet Mondrian, who had just arrived from London. Mondrian was deeply involved with jazz, theorized its relationship to art, danced to it with Peggy Guggenheim and Lee Krasner, and made paintings such as *Broadway Boogie Woogie* under the influence of jazz recordings. It's said that Mondrian and Monk often talked, and that Monk had begun to describe his compositions in terms that Mondrian used for his paintings.

Thelonious Monk's music created a following among painters, musicians, and writers, and was especially popular among younger art film animators, who used his recordings as soundtracks. There was something wonderfully strange in his music that got the attention of musicians and nonmusicians alike: the intervals between his notes were unexpected—the chords he used may have been those that were commonly used, but the notes within them were so unusually placed that they became defamiliarized; and his shifting rhythms could create the feeling that the floor was moving beneath their feet. At this period in his career, Monk was playing mostly his own compositions written for instruments only, not pop tunes originally meant for singers. He was not setting a mood or portraying anything. His music was deceptively difficult for musicians to remember or write down correctly, and even when it seemed simple it could leave them wondering just what notes they were hearing.

During Monk's six-month stay at the Five Spot in 1957, the press depicted him as the weird and enigmatic genius of modern jazz. Lewis H. Lapham was often there and recalled the kind of response that saw Monk surfacing like the "Loch Ness monster from the sloughs of despond, 'the perfect hipster,' fond of wearing an Ottoman fez or a Chinese coolie hat, 'high priest of bop' playing 'zombie music' and given to whimsical and cryptic statement . . . An imposing figure elegantly dressed in a sharkskin suit, Monk carried himself with the dignity of a man who knows his own mind and doesn't countenance fools. He wore a goatee, a purple shirt, a dockworker's cap, and a diamond ring on the little finger of his right hand."

Monk had his own baroness, Pannonica Rothschild de Koenigswarter—his fan, patron, and sometimes driver and manager. Her Bentley parked in front of a Village nightclub was the sign that Monk was in the house. The filmmaker Andrew Noren once saw Harry outside the front door of the Five Spot "deep in conversation with Thelonious Monk. That was a sight . . . Monk of course was huge and bear-like, wearing his shades at midnight, and there was little Harry, eloquently gesticulating, intent on getting something or other across."

When Allen Ginsberg moved back to New York City from San Francisco in July 1958, he discovered that his new apartment was near the Five Spot, where the poets Frank O'Hara, Ted Joans, Kenneth Koch, and LeRoi Jones (Amiri Baraka) were regulars, and he talked about Monk's music in terms of prosody—its rhythm, phrasing, and consonance. Allen took to making nightly stops by the club, just as Monk was beginning an eight week run. One night in August, he gave Monk a copy of his poem *Howl*, which had been published the year before and had become something of a national scandal. A week later, Allen asked Monk what he thought of it. Allen was thrilled when Monk replied, "It makes sense." A few days after, a drunken

Ginsberg got onstage at the Five Spot late at night and read Gregory Corso's "BOMB," a poem written in the shape of a mushroom cloud. It was the night he met Harry Smith:

> I noticed an old guy, with a familiar face, someone I dimly recognized from a description, slightly hunchback, short, magical-looking, in a funny way gnomish or dwarfish, same time dignified. He was sitting at a table by the piano towards the kitchen making little marks on a piece of paper. I said to myself, "Is that Harry Smith?—I'll go over and ask him." And it turned out to be Harry Smith. He said he was calculating whether Thelonious Monk was hitting the piano before or after the beat—trying to notate the syncopation of Thelonious Monk's piano. But I asked him why he was keeping this track record of the syncopation or the retards that Monk was making, never coming quite on the beat but always aware of the beat. He said it was because he was calculating the variants. Then I asked him why he was interested in it, this is almost a Hermetic or magical study. I understood he was interested in Crowley, magic, in numbers, in esoteric systems, Theosophy, and he was a member of O.T.O. [Ordo Templi Orientis]. But he had practical use for it. He was making animated collages and he needed the exact tempo of Monk's changes and punctuations of time in order to synchronize collages and hand-drawn frame-by-frame abstractions with Monk's music. He was working frame-by-frame, so it was possible for him to do that, but he needed some kind of scheme.

The system that Ginsberg spoke of was Harry moving the frames of the film in relation to the music: "He had a theory that the time of the movement would be a crosscurrent of the alpha rhythm, certain kinds of brain waves, the average heartbeat pattern, certain biological rhythms and crosscurrents in the human body, and he was animating his collages and setting the time according to archetypal body rhythms." Harry had given up the idea of painting a Monk recording: "When I came to New York City I realized that it would be impossible to make it in the form of a painting, because his music was so complex, and it would be better to make a film."

Percy Heath saw Harry at Birdland one night, and when he learned that he had moved to New York, he and his wife welcomed him into their family. Harry stayed with them at times, even babysat their two children. "When we asked him if he had trouble getting the children to bed, he said 'I pushed their sleep button and they slept soundly.' He'd sit at the kitchen table and work on films, making cut-outs and using a camera held together by rubber bands and chewing gum, listening to Thelonious Monk's *Misterioso* over and over again."

> We went to see some cat name Harry Smith's house, who's making flip films that cut most of the famous flip/collage . . . shifting speed image cats. Cat uses Monk &c. as background. Also, weird natural sounds, wind, storms, &c. very spooky effect.
>
> —Amiri Baraka

What Baraka saw Harry working on was *Film No. 11*, another of his "Mirror Animations," a 16-millimeter color film that he described as "A commentary on and exposition of *No. 10* synchronized to Thelonious Monk's recorded composition 'Misterioso,' Approx. 4 mins." He said *No. 10* was a study for *No. 11*, and was edited to make *No. 11* fit a soundtrack of Monk's recording. Monk's piece is a simple melody in a well-disguised twelve-bar blues form, made up of a single two-note figure with an interval of a sixth that walks up and down the stairstep of a musical scale. The phrasing of the melody against the rhythm section manages to suggest two different tempos running at once. When the vibraphonist Milt Jackson takes an improvised solo, Monk accompanies him by hammering a series of melodic sevenths behind him. Near the end, instead of repeating the melody like in nearly every other bebop recording, the same sevenths are scattered across several octaves unpredictably, as in a pointillist painting. By varying the melody and placing it over the original rhythmic and harmonic structure, Monk created something of a musical parallel to what Harry would later do in his *Film No. 14: Late Superimpositions*.

Films *No. 10* and *11* are extremely complex, though both are only three minutes and thirty-five seconds in length, shorter than the versions that Harry described. P. Adams Sitney rightly says that their complexity would require a book to describe them correctly. Various animated characters, skeletons, animals, birds, and astronomical and alchemical symbols appear and are transformed against changing depths and planes within the frames.

No. 12 was Harry's first long work, later titled by Jonas Mekas as *Heaven and Earth Magic*, one of the oldest clichés in the world, but a far cry from Ginsberg's suggested titles of *Eyeball Head Poem*, *Asshole Homunculus Eyeball*, *Mandala Watermelon*, *Hammer Dog*, *A Bee in an Egg*, *Reptile Consciousness of Machines*, *Eyeball Vomit*, and *The Vomiting Lesson*, although Izzy Young said that several people did become nauseous viewing the film.

A number of descriptions of *No. 12* have been published, though Harry's own is the most concise, if not especially helpful:

> A much expanded version of *No. 8*. The first part depicts the heroine's toothache consequent to the loss of a very valuable watermelon, her dentistry and transportation to heaven. Next follows an elaborate exposition of the heavenly land in terms of Israel, Montreal and the second part depicts the return to earth from being eaten by Max Müller on the day Edward the Seventh declared the Great Sewer of London.

Sitney saw Harry's description as making the film seem even more obscure. Israel, Sitney believed, referred to the Kabbalah; Montreal

pointed to the work of Dr. Wilder Penfield of the Montreal Neuro-
logical Institute on the brains of epileptics. It was also influenced by
Daniel Paul Schreber's *Memoirs of My Nervous Illness*, a nineteenth-
century German jurist's account of his two mental breakdowns, a
book that particularly interested Freud. When Harry showed the film
at Queens Museum in 1978, he read passages from Schreber's book
aloud while the film was running behind him.

Harry elaborated on his methods in his interview with Sitney:

> I must say that I'm amazed, after having seen the black-
> and-white (#12) last night, at the labor that went into it. It's
> incredible I had enough energy to do it. Most of my mind
> was pushed aside into some sort of theoretical sorting of the
> pieces, mainly on the basis that I have described: First, I col-
> lected the pieces out of old catalogues and books and what-
> ever; then made up file cards of all possible combinations of
> them; then, I spent maybe a few months trying to sort the
> cards into logical order. A script was made for that. All the
> script and the pieces were made for a film at least four times
> as long. There were wonderful masks and things cut out . . .
> There were beautiful scratchboard drawings, probably the
> finest drawings I ever made—really pretty. Maybe 200 were
> made for that one scene . . . The script was made up for the
> whole works on the basis of sorting pieces. It was exhaust-
> ingly long in its original form.

This makes it sound a bit more logical than the way he described
working on the film to a student who was asking for help on a paper
he was writing for a course taught by Sitney:

> What I want to do for the time being is point out this sor-
> tilege process by getting books, getting subjects, cutting
> subjects out, filing them in glassine envelopes according to

subjects . . . So, various combinations could be made. Then, I'd get up and animate what I'd had dreamt. Just dreamt, as closely as I could. As soon as I'd reached total exhaustion I would go back to bed again and dream some more. I didn't go out of the house for food, except maybe once a week. I had the windows sealed off so it would be dark.

A film of this complexity and abstraction could give rise to any number of interpretations, but it continues to resist agreement on its meaning: Annette Michelson's psychoanalytic study saw it as explaining the filmmaker's childhood development; Noël Carroll said it was structured on the processes of the mind; Sitney understood it as the product of Harry's understanding and appreciation of Georges Méliès's silent films.

Years after the film was finished, Professor Allen S. Weiss was part of a panel that would screen and discuss *No. 12* in a conference on Schreber's book. When he spoke to Harry about it, Harry insisted on coming with him. According to Weiss, "He acted like so many artists, taking umbrage about speaking of his own work. When a woman in the audience posed a question to him, he asked if she was rich, and when she said no, told her she should come back when she had some money." At another showing of the film years later during Surrealism Week at Naropa University in Boulder, Colorado, Harry introduced it by simply saying it was "extremely boring" and full of "more of that alchemical stuff."

The soundtrack to *No. 12* was the only one that Harry ever made himself, assembling it from stock sound effects records of birdsong, babies crying, wind, dripping water, breaking glass, dog barks, cat howls, train whistles, a tolling bell, faint human chattering. Some of these sounds are synchronized to the images, as when a salamander appears (a symbol of fire in magical tradition) and a fire engine is heard on the soundtrack. Others are randomly placed.

The film runs a little over an hour and was shot in black and white, though he built a special projector that would allow filters to change the color of the film. A series of slides of borders in several other projectors would make it possible to change the shape of the screen into that of a watermelon, an egg, or other objects. The screen itself had ornaments around it. It was shown only once with these devices, at a screening in Steinway Hall in New York set up for potential financial backers for Harry's next film. But with Harry, there was always something else. He had hoped to have theater seats made in the shape of some of the slide images (like watermelons or eggs) that would have triggered changes in the color of the film as members of the audience moved in their seats. It would have outdone *The Tingler*, a 1959 film shown with a device called "Percepto" that vibrated some of the theater seats when set off by the action on the screen. Lacking the money to create these mechanisms, Harry tried to manipulate the changes by hand.

He had built a special projector to use for that film. "So he screened from '62–'63 on that contraption," Mekas said. "He was very temperamental—he was in a very heavy drinking period and clashed with a number of people." During an argument, he threw the projector out the window into the street, destroying it. After that, all *Heaven and Earth Magic* screenings were of a simplified version.

When the poet Carol Bergé went to Le Metro Café in 1965 to see Harry screen the film for a group of poets, he was nervous, she said, his eyeglasses broken, and as he started the projector he mumbled to the audience, "[This] film isn't entertaining." She saw it again at the Film-Makers' Cinematheque. Harry was surprised by the size of the audience of three hundred. Near the end of the film's second section, some people began to leave, and Harry shouted, "Okay, you fuck-ups, you can go now . . . next time you see this, if you're lucky, it'll be in a museum." His projectionist then put the wrong music tape on for the film, and Harry threw the tape recorder into the audience. They scarcely noticed, as by then two-thirds of them had left.

Writing to Arthur Young in hope of getting money for his next film, Harry said:

> I have shown the film to quite a number of people since see-
> ing you. A complete description of their sometimes curiously
> hermetic reaction would require at least another seventeen
> pages, so for the present it will suffice to say that both one
> of the television networks and a fairly large independent dis-
> tributor here have evidenced real interest in capitalizing on
> my productions.

As unlikely as it sounds, Percy Heath said that Harry had a meeting with William Paley of CBS and showed him a film "in which a cat was running around the frame. He never heard anything from him, but that showed up on TV. He was exploited but he didn't care. He said he would be famous when he was dead."

When Ginsberg was living in California in the early 1950s, Jordan Belson had told him about Harry, and Allen had imagined him as an "alchemical magician painter-filmmaker." Now, night after night, they were sitting together, close to Monk's piano. Allen was sur-prised when Harry invited him to his second-story apartment on East Seventy-Fifth Street, since Harry seemed to be keeping to himself and hesitated to even tell people where he lived. Percy Heath visited him at that same address and said, "He was paranoid about some-thing: if you wanted to see him, you had to call and say exactly when, and he'd be at the window peeking out of the curtains checking that you were alone. On the floor of his room, he had painted with lumi-nous paint a Tibetan Wheel of Life, and the room was so small you had to step around it."

Ginsberg was also struck by Harry's paintings, those which Allen called "cosmic monsters":

> Sort of like the idea of a green city which looks like some kind of strange leviathan, but then within the city are all sorts of patterns, traffic patterns, eyes, and people walking round and automobiles or strange machines and flying saucers. But the whole thing, maybe four feet by three feet, [was] very freely done and painted or water colored like Blake, sort of. He made these huge anthropomorphic cities and many other things.

Once Allen learned that Harry had produced the *Anthology of American Folk Music*, had written a bit of poetry, and was something of an expert on occult practices around the world, he introduced him to a number of downtown New York arts people. Robert Frank was one of them, a photographer who had trained in Switzerland, come to New York in 1947, and found work doing fashion shoots for *Harper's Bazaar*. He was supported by the Guggenheim Foundation just four years after Harry, and used the fellowship to travel across the country taking hundreds of pictures, eighty-three of which he published in a book called *The Americans* with an introductory essay by Jack Kerouac—two outsiders to the art world, viewing the country from the bottom up in black and white. Frank greatly admired Harry's films and the *Anthology*, and became one of his greatest supporters: "The only person I met in my life that transcended everything." He admired Harry's judgmental, difficult manner, his distanced sense of himself as an artist: "He was open to how people could reveal something for other people . . . He lived uptown like a hermit, all alone with all his windows closed." Frank was just beginning to add motion pictures to his still photography, just as Harry had done. "Sometimes," he said, "it is more interesting to think of what's between the frames as a photographer."

❋

Desperately in need of money, Harry got Allen Ginsberg high while he visited Harry in his apartment to view *Heaven and Earth Magic*, and offered to sell it to him for $110. Allen had no need for the film, but gave Harry the money, and then passed the film on to Jonas Mekas, a defender of films who opposed the Hollywood aesthetic. He was the force behind the beginning of the new American Cinema, the poetic, the underground, the personal film. Mekas founded the journal *Film Culture* in 1954 and began a column in the new weekly newspaper *The Village Voice* in 1958. He wrote in defense of films that opposed the Hollywood aesthetic and had no interest in storytelling or filmed reality. But he had not yet heard of Harry Smith.

Ginsberg knew Mekas from having visited the Film-Makers' Co-operative in Mekas's loft on lower Park Avenue. The cooperative was a screening room, library, and distributor of avant-garde film with a policy of never turning down any film, a gathering place for art filmgoers like Salvador Dalí, Frank, Ginsberg, Jack Smith, Peter Duchin, LeRoi Jones, Andy Warhol, and Robert Rauschenberg. What Ginsberg saw there inspired him to set up the screening of *Heaven and Earth Magic* at Steinway Hall, inviting people with enough influence or money to get Harry started on a new project—a full-length animation of *The Wizard of Oz*.

Ginsberg made sure that Timothy Leary was at that showing, and when Leary was impressed by Harry's film, they both thought William Burroughs should meet him. Ginsberg wrote Burroughs about an "interesting fellow here Harry Smith a mad inventor I know lives in solitude in E 74st took Gas and Hash and Junk for years and peyote . . . the one person here in NY who is more or less up your alley scientifically." Describing *Heaven and Earth Magic*, he wrote, "One and a half hours of jerky cartoon dream imagery all connected with

Mandalas and Kabbalahs and Tree of Life designs and weird cows wandering in and out of the screen—all done in collage."

Leary wrote Burroughs to tell him that he had "spent some time with Harry Smith the alchemist friend of Allen Ginsberg. He has set out to do the impossible: to put 'out there,' on film, the visual experiences that come in dream, hallucination, or drug vision . . . Modern technology allows Harry Smith to come closer to the vision—because the dream moves and the hallucination is in color. Harry's films come at you just like visions—the wave after wave of color and changing symbol, inundating you, orgiastic bangs, one after another in series. Harry has wrenched the vision off the retina and put it out there. I'd like to have you see them to get your reaction." Burroughs was impressed by Smith's animations, and may have been influenced by his cut-up technique, but once he met him in New York and again in Leary's apartment in Newton, Massachusetts, he thought he was creepy and a mooch.

In the summer of 1960, Harry was again doing research for Arthur Young, this time on ancient astrology, and, as had become his practice, always producing more than what had been requested. He sent Young eighteen pages that included Hebrew letters in black on shimmering gold paper that listed the twelve permutations of the names of God, the Tetragrammaton, "that high and holy name" forbidden in the third commandment in part for magical purposes, something done nevertheless for more than two thousand years by Jewish magicians. He told Young that he was aware that he was not to go beyond the names themselves and their connections to the twelve signs of the zodiac, but he had nonetheless gone on to connect the names to the letters of the Hebrew alphabet, the months of the year, the Twelve

Tribes and the orders of the Angels. This research led him to rare books such as Athanasius Kircher's *Oedipus Aegyptiacus* (1652–54), Christian Knorr von Rosenroth's *Kabbala Denudata* (1677–84), and Heinrich Cornelius Agrippa's *De Occulta Philosophia* (1533). It was Christian Cabala, rooted in Jewish Kabbalah, but developed in the Renaissance by those who thought that Jewish mystics had preserved ancient knowledge and were attempting to show how it could be fitted to Christian thought.

> Lucien and Harry Smith called me high on phone.
>
> —Jack Kerouac

Harry was only a fringe figure among the Beats, disliked by Burroughs and Herbert Huncke and slighted by Kerouac, but embraced by Ginsberg and the musician and composer David Amram. One of the strangest and least documented of his Beat connections was Harry's friendship with Lucien Carr. Carr was a lifelong friend of Burroughs, a Columbia classmate of Ginsberg and Kerouac (what Ginsberg called "the Libertine Circle"), and a brilliant, flamboyant, and engaging figure whose fame emerged from the killing of an acquaintance that he justified in court as defense against stalking and sexual violence—an early example of the "gay panic" defense. He was sentenced for second-degree murder and released from prison after serving two years. It was a story that haunted the counterculture for years, fictionalized in Kerouac's *The Town and the City* and *Vanity of Duluoz*, by Burroughs and Kerouac in *And the Hippos Were Boiled in Their Tanks*, and later in the movie *Kill Your Darlings*.

Carr remained close to his Beat friends after prison, but chose a quieter life, asking Ginsberg to remove his name from the dedication to "Howl." He had worked his way up from copyboy with United

Press International to night editor when he and Harry became drinking and smoking friends, paying Harry's way, sending him news stories that he thought would interest him, joining him on nights for cultural adventures. (On one such occasion Carr, Harry, and Peter Fleishman, another student follower of Harry's, attended a lecture on Australian Aboriginal art sponsored by Qantas airlines. Harry and Peter took to heckling the speaker from the balcony for racist comments, and when two Australians came up to quiet them, Peter protected Harry by knocking out the first one to step out of the elevator and sending the other one back in the car.)

OZIANA

The MGM film *The Wizard of Oz* had a long run after its premiere in 1939. It had been revived in theaters several times and often shown on television. What had at first been seen as a children's movie, an updated fairy tale, had become a musical with mythic dimensions, a film with spiritual undertones. To some, it presented perhaps a "satiric and cynical" vision of utopia, as its composer, Yip Harburg, called it. For a few, like Harry, it was secretly an art film, flooded with yellow, green, gray, and red, and spiked with geometrics—a spiraling yellow road, a spherical carriage, an arching rainbow, rows of Munchkins, and lines that led straight through space to the Emerald City. As a child, Harry had read some of L. Frank Baum's Oz books, had seen a Cornish Puppeteers children's production of *The Wizard of Oz* in Anacortes in 1934, had made his own miniature models of Oz in several places, and had been thinking of how it could be animated ever since. Inspired by the surprising success of Warhol's movies, Harry imagined that his *Film No. 13: Oz*, or what he sometimes called *The Magic Mushroom People*, could be a commercial film, and a big one—feature-length, 35-millimeter, wide-screen, stereo sound, yet not just another Hollywood movie. Joanne Ziprin thought it was a brilliant idea, encouraged him to do it, and offered to be his co-animator. But neither of them had ever worked on a commercial film. They lacked the money, a studio, the equipment, and the number of animators required for a film that would be on the scale of a Disney production. Still, Ginsberg's touting of Harry's genius to the rich and famous made it seem possible, and a string of investors became interested. Harry was excited. He was being taken seriously; money and drugs were flowing:

> Number 13 had all the characters out of Oz in it. I naturally divided Oz up into four lands, because Oz consists of the Munchkins, the Quadlings, the Gillikins, and the Winkies, and the Emerald City is in the middle. That is where the wizard's balloon had landed . . . It was to be a commercial film. Very elaborate equipment was built. The animation stand was about the size of the floor and exactly fourteen feet high. Oz was laid out on it, then several levels built up. It was like the multiplane camera of Disney, except that I was using a Mitchell camera that moved around. That's how I got into so many difficulties. Van Wolf had not paid rent on the camera, which was a thousand dollars a week. He was the producer but he was taking far too many pills a week to do much but try to wiggle out of situations that developed. He got various people to pay for it. Huntington Hartford, Henry Phipps, Peggy Hitchcock (Mellon), Elizabeth Taylor and so forth, invested in the film.

Huntington Hartford was an heir to A&P, known for his philanthropy in the arts and his distaste for abstract expressionism; Peggy Hitchcock, a part of the Mellon empire, also spread money through the arts, especially jazz; Henry Ogden Phipps, the film's principal investor, was the son of Ogden Phipps, the famed horse breeder and tennis champion; the actress Elizabeth Taylor was drawn into the project by Van Wolf, who had worked as promotion director for her husband, Mike Todd, and seemed to know everyone in theater, film, and jazz. It was he who organized the film's backers and issued class A shares in 1962 for what would be called Van Wolf Harry Smith Production, Inc.

For over a year in 1961, Harry, Joanne, and a few others worked in secrecy in a studio they created in a rented town house on Seventy-Sixth Street between Madison and Park Avenues, where work went on at all hours. ("It was the only film studio with parqueted floors," exclaimed Harry.) The filmmaker Conrad Rooks, one of the few who did find his way into the *Oz* studio, was impressed by what he saw:

> It was a palace and he'd taken the ballroom and turned it into his workroom to build a three-dimensional camera which shot in 3-D. He did it by taking old RKO cameras from the late ['30s] and tearing them apart. Then rebuilding them on huge levered stairways that moved up and down and had to be operated by cranks. He invited me over to a couple of showings. It was just incredible stuff. Very unusual. Very few of the people he showed it to had any idea of what he was doing.
>
> He was issuing Owsley's finest grade-A acid to people as they came in. He had, for the first time, enormous money behind him. He needed three or four projectors to show his work. All of it was based on trances that he had learned from American Indians, mind patterns . . . He knew how to trigger these patterns . . . he knew what results would follow. Talk about magic!

Harry's imagination was in overdrive on this film, in not just rethinking the MGM production but completely reimagining and deconstructing L. Frank Baum's book *The Wonderful Wizard of Oz*. Since Baum was well-known among theosophists, Harry's affection for his work is no surprise, yet he saw this film reframed in Buddhism.

> What I was really trying to do was to convert Oz into a Buddhistic image like a mandala. I can't even remember what those lands were. One of them was "Hieronymus Bosch Land." All of Bosch's paintings were carefully dissected. Another one was "Microscopia," taken from the books of [Ernst] Haeckel, who was the Viennese biological artist and very wonderful. The things he made are just marvelous. He picked out every possible grotesque object that there was. There was another land that was entirely made out of flesh. Enormous vistas for miles were made out of naked people from dirty mags. That would have been a nice film! Most of my material was prepared for it, and over six hours of tests were shot to get the apparatus to operate correctly. Only the little piece in the drawer there was ever synchronized to the music. In this particular section, the ballet music from [Gounod's] *Faust*, the Tin Woodman performs magic before leaving for the Emerald City. The soundtrack was made up for the whole film.

Near the end of the first year of work things began to fall apart. The sheer scope of the film now looked impossible for the small crew, and Harry's work habits and demands were beginning to wear them down. Joanne was the only person Harry would allow to touch the film, but she quit when, in a fit of anger, he tore up her drawings. He begged her to come back, even picked up every piece of her drawings and put them back together again, but she was gone.

In the *Film-Makers' Catalogue*, Harry gave a brief account of the film's failure:

Fragments and tests of Shamanism in the guise of a children's story. This film, made with Van Wolf, is perhaps the most expensive animated film ever made—the cost running well over ten thousand dollars a minute—wide screen, stereophonic sound of the ballet music from *Faust*. Production was halted when a major investor (H.P.) was found dead under embarrassing conditions.

Drugs had been served up like party snacks in the studio. Harry noted that the film was produced under the influence of "green pills from Max Jacobson [the original Dr. Feelgood], pink pills from Tim Leary, and vodka." He did, in a sense, have his own doctor, Joe Gross, a practicing psychiatrist and researcher of drugs who enjoyed the company of artists and for years attempted to stay close to Harry and aid him, despite his resistance and mockery:

I was trying to help Harry in various ways. In those days I was much more wary of medication, and medication effects, and Harry would always tend to overdo things—whatever he had or did, he would overdo. He told me he had taken I don't know how much peyote and mescaline, not to mention any other drug he could get his hands on at various times. To accentuate images he would take peyote and then start rubbing his eyes to induce these things, so I was always wary about giving him various things. I'll never forget once . . . he was doing this animated film, *The Magic Mushroom People of Oz*. He had gotten financed by this Henry Phipps, among other people, who was this wealthy heir, who was a junky . . . [Harry was] filming this incredible film, one frame at a time, and on this occasion well financed, so his pockets literally were stuffed with money. We'd be running around, he'd be foaming at the mouth—whenever he took a lot of

Valium . . . He would just keep popping them and popping
them and bounce around throwing dollar bills at everybody
in sight. Cab drivers, he'd shove fistfuls of dollars.

During the filming, Henry Phipps died of an overdose, which resulted in police inquiries and reporters' questions, and without him,
the flow of cash slowed. When the other investors asked to see what
had been accomplished over the year, they were shown only nine
minutes of finished film. Harry said it drove him to drink, or, more
likely, to more drink.

Harry tried to resume work, but found the locks had been changed
in the studio, and later discovered that most of their work had been
destroyed. Three to six hours of camera tests are said to still exist, and
only fifteen minutes of noncorrected rushes survive. Some of this footage appeared in films *No. 16*, *19* (now lost), and *20*, *Fragments of a Faith
Forgotten*. What should have been *Film No. 13* ended up as *Film No.
16*, *The Tin Woodman's Dream* aka *The Approach to the Emerald City*,
and is less than five minutes long. *The Tinman's Dream* (available on
YouTube) is fourteen minutes and forty seconds long, but only four
minutes and thirty-one seconds of it is the Tinman's dance, with some
choreographic chopping, his grasp of a heart, and a trip with Toto to
the Emerald City. The rest is ten minutes and nine seconds of images
created later with his homemade teleidoscope, a kaleidoscope that
draws its images from outside the tube, rather than inside, and re-
arranges and projects them. They were filmed in 1968 and added to
the earlier Tinman footage.

No one knows what the complete film would've looked like, but
it appears that it might have been far more complex than Harry suggests. Philip Smith recalled the rare opportunity he had to see a reel
of some of the camera-test footage. Though it was a poor-quality
print, "with almost no color registration and an inky black appearance," what he was able to see seemed remarkable:

The Land of Oz in the form of a Tibetan mandala, a mammoth and exquisitely crafted diorama with green glass domes that the camera zooms through in turn, entering each region. One of these is indeed based on microscopic life forms as depicted in Haeckel's curious portfolio series . . . Another is a quite incongruous and extremely amusing translation of the central panel of Bosch's triptych *The Garden of Earthly Delights*. Into these alien landscapes are placed the familiar characters of the Oz story, faithfully rendered in the unmistakable style of W. W. Denslow's original illustrations. An added curiosity is that many scenes appear photographed through a wall of rectangular panes of colored glass, which may be set at variable distances from the camera. When the camera is near the panes, the entire image area may have the cast of a certain color, and camera movements may result in unexpected "wipes" of color across the frame. At other moments, the glass wall being positioned farther from the lens, the entire wide-screen image is broken up into fields of different color, producing an affect perverse in its novelty and formalism.

In spite of his notoriety as a filmmaker in California, his Guggenheim support in 1951, and the *Oz* debacle, very few people in New York knew Harry had been making films for well over a decade. The first public acknowledgment of his film work was in Jonas Mekas's weekly film column in the June 25, 1964, *Village Voice*, where he briefly mentioned Smith as one of a small number of filmmakers who were radically reconceiving motion pictures without an audience: "Those who have been especially lucky have even had a glimpse of the work of

Harry Smith, the greatest wizard working in animated cinema since
Méliès—his multiple images, slides and projectors, his magic, cabalistic space cinema." Seven months later in a review of independent
films he again pointed to Smith's furtive filmmaking: "Harry Smith's
films introduced to New York—another historic (and clandestine)
screening revealing him as the foremost animation artist working in
cinema today."

Come March 1965, Mekas fully unveiled Smith as a filmmaker in
a *Village Voice* column titled "The Magic Cinema of Harry Smith," in
which the lede was "Does Harry Smith really exist?" Maybe he was
a black and ominous legend, a secret alchemist, a magician, maybe
he was even dead. But, no, the real Harry had just appeared above
ground at the Cinematheque for a three-hour presentation of his
films. Mekas excitedly declared that Harry was a genius:

> For thirty years Harry Smith worked on these movies, se-
> cretly, like an alchemist, and he worked out his own formu-
> las and mixtures to produce these fantastic images. You can
> watch his films for pure color enjoyment; you can watch them
> for motion—Harry Smith's films never stop moving; or you
> can watch them for hidden and symbolic meanings, alchemic
> signs. There are more levels in Harry Smith's work than in
> any other film animator I know. All those Czechs, Poles, and
> Yugoslavs, and Pintoffs, Bosustovs, and Hubleys are nothing
> but makers of cute cartoons. Harry Smith is the only serious
> film animator working today. His untitled work on alchemy
> and the creation of the world will remain one of the master-
> pieces of the animated cinema. But even his smaller works
> are marked by the same masterful and never-failing sense of
> movement—the most magic quality of Harry Smith's work.

High praise indeed, yet Mekas added that Smith "was still full of
evil, hate, small curses, and sneers," then tempered himself by saying

that "behind the beard and the curses [is] a sweet, humorous, and completely harmless man. We found that his little curses were only a protective wall, not an attack on others. The black magic was suddenly gone. But not entirely."

As Mekas's uncertainty about Harry was beginning to appear publicly, privately he felt he was being tested. No question that he thought Harry was a genius and a major filmmaker. Yet he wrote in his diary that Harry "is crazy, evil, nasty, very brilliant, very learned in certain cabalistic and alchemical areas, like nobody else, and he has been insulting everybody, spitting around, I don't know how I managed to make him show his films here, but he moved in and he is going to stay here with his machines and films for some time now, he's OK despite all the strange things he does, one has to put up with him."

Regardless of his misgivings, Mekas was always willing to set aside his qualms for the art of film. One month after his 1965 *Village Voice* column, his new organization, the Film-Makers' Cinematheque, sponsored a fundraiser for Harry, screening his films at the City Hall Cinema. By July, he wrote that "no festival in 1965 can be taken seriously if it disregards two such towering contributions to cinema as [Stan Brakhage's] *The Art of Vision* or Smith's work." A year later he declared yet another dimension of the new cinema: the relationship between the filmmaker's body and the camera, their actions and reactions in multimedia performances, dancing as they were shooting a film, or shooting with an empty camera in front of an audience. "Really, what's happening is that some of the work of Harry Smith, of Jerry Jofen, or Robert Whitman or Andy Warhol cannot be shipped in a film can: their projections have become extension of their creative work, the film in the can isn't really the thing itself."

"Action" was the term the art critic Harold Rosenberg used in place of "abstract expression" to describe the relationship such painters had with the canvas and paint, asking the viewer to see the work not as a picture but as an event, to consider the activity that went into the work and the state of the artist's mind while working. It was an idea that could be extended beyond abstract expressionism back to those artists that left their brushstrokes visible or said their art came from some source beyond themselves. Once Harry had begun to insist on being part of the screening of his films, he was free to alter them at every performance. He could use slides and colored gels to change the shape of the screen or the tint of the film. He often talked over the sound, argued with the projectionist, used different soundtracks for the same film, reversed, slowed, or sped it up, once set fire to the film while it was in the projector, even threw a projector out a window. Every audience saw a different film when Harry was there to perform.

Not many knew about the failure of the *Oz* project and the loss of its financial support. Harry's *Heaven and Earth Magic* was still being discovered, and the mystery surrounding its making and Harry himself made him a quintessential underground filmmaker. Instead of despairing, Harry began planning another film, though once again he had no source of income. But then along came Conrad Rooks.

The son of the president of Avon Products, Rooks had moved from his hometown of Chappaqua, New York, to Greenwich Village in the late 1950s, drawn by sensationalized news stories of Beat life and a dream of making films. He studied TV and film production, cofounded Exploit Films, which produced a few movies, like *White Slavery* and *Girls Incorporated*, and sought out the likes of Ginsberg, Leary, and Burroughs. Philip Lamantia recommended Harry to him, and he became Rooks's tutor on American Indian lore and on filmmaking, and added peyote to Rooks's expanding list of habits. Said Rooks:

> When I met him he lived at 300½ East 85th Street. It
> was a house that belonged to one of the big houses. Harry

somehow had a room on the top floor. A poet friend took me over there and we started throwing rocks at the window. Finally, this weird looking thing that looked like he was the assistant to Frankenstein or something, a Quasimodo type, as he was hunchbacked too . . . He stuck his head out, looking absolutely mad. His beard hadn't been cut for years, and he wore really thick glasses. We went up there to find cans and cans of film and sculptures from American Indians and feathers. It looked like he had a part of the Museum of Natural History at home. He was making these films in his bathtub. He did everything himself, even the developing! I started going there and studying with him, I realized immediately that this was an incredible source of information.

After Rooks's father passed away in 1962, he gained a sizeable inheritance and set out on a five-month trip in the South and the Midwest, filming the front and back of American life—the Melungeons in Tennessee, Winthrop Rockefeller's campaign for governor of Arkansas, the peyote rituals of the Cheyenne in Lame Deer, Montana. Back in New York, he rented a studio in Carnegie Hall, stored his travel film footage, switched from 16-millimeter to 35-millimeter film, and got serious about making some kind of full-length film.

When Harry was asked if he would work with Rooks on film plans, he instead talked him into hiring Robert Frank, since Frank's cinematography on *Pull My Daisy*, a film inspired by Beat life in the Village, had made him a local celebrity, and there was a vague similarity between Rooks's cross-country filming and Frank's book *The Americans*. As Rooks was preparing to start his travels abroad for his new film, he asked Harry if he would edit some of the footage he had already shot and to help with research on Indians. He offered him the use of the Carnegie studio where Harry could also do some of his own work. Harry accepted, but never considered himself an employee. Robert Frank described one of the encounters he and Rooks had with Harry:

Rooks rented a studio in Carnegie Hall. So I watched him—he was building a little model of an Indian reservation and he was working on a film—Harry was. And Rooks helped him—Rooks was also very difficult, a very, very rich man, extremely rich man . . . He wanted to use Harry and Harry wouldn't work with him. So Rooks asked if I would work with him, and I said yes, we could try, and so one day, he said, let's go and pick up some film cans there at Harry's. So we drove there—Rooks had a chauffeur and a car—I think I went to ring for Harry and he came down with two film cans and he stood there—I think it was on 57th street and seventh avenue, where Carnegie Hall is, and he stood there with these two film cans, and Rooks sat in the car and I was outside the car, and then he looked at me, and then he looked at Rooks, and took the two cans and threw them under a cab and the cab drove over them.

After he returned from a trip to Europe, Rooks found that Harry had filled the studio with a giant sandpile and had run up bills for $5,000. "Sand was everywhere . . . The goddam pile was forty feet long with film strips poking out all over. Smith said he was setting up to film a peyote vision. I asked him what he had done on my film since I'd left and he said, 'Nothing.' 'What do you plan to do?' 'Nothing,' he said. 'All right,' I said, 'You're fired.'"

7

The Anthropologist
1964–1965

Anthropology for Harry was a license to exit his own life and seek entry into those of other people, while bracketing his own culture and suspending disbelief to understand theirs. But unlike with professional anthropologists, this was an undertaking without the necessity or even much opportunity to share what he learned with others. It was a lifetime commitment, and though he crossed into the worlds of Black Americans, jazz musicians, and Orthodox Jews, he never lost his interest in the Indians of North America. He wanted to learn as much as he could about the great variety of their many cultures, and regretted having never gone to the Southwest to visit Indians there when he had the chance while in California.

THE KIOWA

The Plains Indians were far from New York, but when Conrad Rooks forgave Harry's behavior and again asked him to help with research on Indians and peyote for his new film, Harry saw it as an opportunity to visit the Kiowa in Oklahoma. He knew they still spoke their own language and also used Plains Sign Talk, a widespread trade language that he had learned to "speak" as much of as he could from the publications of the Bureau of Indian Ethnology. But it was their spiritual, social, and artistic use of peyote that was his real interest.

When he first moved to Berkeley, peyote was just beginning to appear there, brought home by University of California anthropology faculty and students, artists, and poets, who had learned of the plant from Native peoples in Mexico and the Washoe, who lived on the border of California and Nevada near Lake Tahoe. Smith and Jordan Belson had tried peyote when they learned about it from Jaime de Angulo and Philip Lamantia.

Rooks had met Jean Cocteau while he was in Paris and read his *Opium: The Diary of a Cure*, which gave him the idea for a film with himself cast in the role of Russel Harwick, whose fictional life would be almost identical to his own. After thirteen years of addiction, Harwick submits to a treatment in a private hospital in Paris, and the film follows his hallucinations, flashback memories, and visual metaphors, aided by expressionist cinematography, random changes of black and white and sepia color, with layers of superimpositions of Native Americans, modeled on Harry's *Film No. 14*. It would be called *Chappaqua*, after his hometown's Algonquian name, which meant "place of rustling leaves."

He gathered members of his film crew and cast like he did exotic drugs and other souvenirs of his travels. How could he fail using actors like William Burroughs, Allen Ginsberg, Jean-Louis Barrault (most noted for his role in Marcel Carné's *Les Enfants du Paradis*), Ravi Shankar, Ornette Coleman, Swami Satchidananda, Moondog, and Hervé Villechaize; with Robert Frank as cinematographer; Philip Glass as music supervisor; music by Shankar and the Fugs; editing advice from Man Ray and Brion Gysin; and Harry as recordist and consultant on Native American culture, music, and peyote? (Ornette Coleman's *Chappaqua Suite* was to be the original score for the film, but was replaced with one by Shankar. The notes to Coleman's recording of the suite explain that it was too beautiful for the film to do it justice.)

So began a journey of filming in France, Mexico, India, England, Sri Lanka, Jamaica, and across the United States. Rooks considered himself an intuitive artist, and intuition would have him stop whatever they were filming, pack up, and head for the Taj Mahal, the Chateau Marmont in West Hollywood, or a bar in Spain. "A monumental waste of film," said Frank, who was fired from the movie and rehired several times, but these bits of film were strung together in the spirit of what Rooks thought of as American Indian mythology. Harry was to be his on-site guide and recordist in such matters, but when Rooks, Harry, and Sheldon Rochlin, an additional camera operator, met at LaGuardia Airport to fly to Oklahoma, Harry suddenly decided not to go. Rooks urged him by handing him $200, which Harry immediately tore up in the middle of the terminal. He finally agreed to leave with them, but after they arrived in Anadarko, he failed to show up for a meeting and disappeared for days. "[Harry] received around $5,000 to cover all his expenses—recording equipment, films, etc.," according to Rooks.

> He didn't show up in Anadarko at the agreed time, and when he did just as we were leaving to go back to a peyote ceremony in Lame Duck, Montana, he showed up totally pissed with a drunken Indian. No one was amused. He was sent to find a peyote ceremony, and we were all on a tight schedule as a lot of money was gone already, he wanted more money. He was told to fuck off.

Rooks failed to mention that when Harry did meet with him, he brought along a bushel of peyote, which Rooks kept.

An ad appeared in the *Daily Oklahoman* on February 16, 1964:

"WANTED sound man to operate Kudelski Nagra for film Co. Contact Conrad Rooks after five o'clock, at 89er Inn. Phone JA 5–5595. Must be familiar with Nagra."

Harry had read James Mooney's 1897 book, *The Kiowa Peyote Rite*, and saw that for seventy-five years peyote had served as a medicine and a means of teaching proper behavior. It was the center of Kiowa all-night sacred gatherings for the most critical moments of life—birth, baptism, healing, marriage, and funerals. Peyote, a cactus containing the mind-altering substance mescaline and other psychoactive alkaloids, was the first psychedelic encountered by Euro-Americans, and was largely condemned by them. Over time, its use had become part of a new pan-Indian identity and a form of resistance to the culture of white colonists, a parallel to the Ghost Dance religious movement. After the Native American Church was formed in the early twentieth century and the religious use of peyote was declared legal for use by the church, it gave birth to new forms of art, jewelry, music, and musical instruments. These artistic uses of the drug by Native peoples, and the power of peyote to enable altered visual and rhythmic sensory responses, was especially influential among non-Indian musicians, artists, and filmmakers.

The history of the Kiowa is very different from that of the Northwest Coast tribal people that Harry knew. In past years, Kiowa were hunters and gatherers who traveled by horse or dogsled and carried their lodges—the teepees—with them. They were known for their warriors and their skill in horse riding, but also for their artistry in painting, sculpting, and beadwork. The Kiowa migrated from Montana to the Rockies, and then to the Southern Plains early in the nineteenth century, then were forced to relocate to reservations in Oklahoma in the middle 1800s. "They differed from other Plains tribes," Harry wrote, "in that they possessed a social organization so diffuse that its outlines can be ascertained only by statistical methods. They had no moieties or clans—those things would have been inappropriate for a group that was constantly absorbing refugees and lovers from the far-flung tribes that the Kiowa came into contact with."

Rooks's idea was to film the peyote rituals of the Cheyenne in Montana. But Harry believed that since the Peyote Religion originated in the Oklahoma Territory at the end of the nineteenth century, the Kiowa were at the center of the diffusion of the religion to other Indian peoples, and learning about their rituals would show him what the ceremonies were like among other Native people on the American Plains. He came up with a plan whereby he could get money from Rooks, Moe Asch, and Arthur M. Young (for "mythological recordings") at the same time, without any of them knowing about the others, a method he used throughout his life, whether panhandling for a meal or applying for grants.

In February 1964, Harry wrote to Muriel Hazel Wright, the doyenne of Oklahoma history and member of a distinguished Choctaw family, asking for her advice in finding a place in her state where he could locate the Kiowa. She suggested Anadarko, a town of 5,600 people along the Washita River, sixty-six miles south of Oklahoma City. A self-proclaimed "Indian Capital of the Nation," it was close to reservations and land owned by the Kiowa, Caddo, Wichita, Delaware, Comanche, and Apache. The town itself was largely Indian and Black, with white people in the minority, though many of the non-Indians knew at least some basic words in several Indian languages.

Muriel Wright told him that if he wanted to see "a real Western town, go to Anadarko . . . It really turned out to be a Western town," Harry said. "Before I had been there half a day I was arrested and held for a week for 'investigation.' Two guns had been stolen from the Candy Kitchen the evening I got there. I had unknowingly gotten myself involved with some talkative but, according to the police, rather unsavory characters in one of the local bars that night."

> Except for the police, white people are unique in the Anadarko jail. This is not because whites are rare in Anadarko, far from it, but because, like the rest of that town, the jail is exploited by the owners of the land; and so, the police arrest few but Indians. Out of the thirty or so people that almost starved in that place during the week I was kept there, only three were white; and thus it was I met some Indians and a short visit to Anadarko expanded itself into four months.

Harry called John Cohen, Ed Sanders, and others collect from jail and was sent enough that he made bail. He used the article that Cohen had written about him in the *Little Sandy Review* to show a judge that he was "something more than an indigent." But it was in jail that he met some of the Kiowa and was introduced to their visual art and rituals:

> When I awoke, after my first uncomfortable night on the floor of the "walk-around" in the jail, I saw by the increasing light on the wall at my feet that most ancient and thoughtful of designs, the circular and interlocked rainbow. Next to it there is an amazingly stylized drawing of a deer by a tree—a type of art which A. S. later explained "came from Siberia." Further to the left there is a scissor-tail bird above an upturned moon lettered "Peyote Altar." As I stared in amazement at this, my first friend, D. W., came up and spontaneously gave a description of the Peyote Meeting which, despite the fact that I had read literature on the subject, and had eaten the herb frequently, for the first time made clear to me the purpose

and ritual of the Native American Church. He also sang a
song or two in a very low voice.

But, Harry added, "I would like to make it clear that of the people
I later worked with, none were met in the jail; the unfortunate victims
of that place only provided the contacts. Also, it would only be fair
to say that while I was in Anadarko I was drinking heavily and it
was only natural that some of the people I worked with also drank."
When he was released from jail, he settled into the Bryan Hotel, a
small three-story building in the oldest part of town, where he remained during his stay.

What he later described about his life in Oklahoma in interviews
might suggest that his research was chaotic, his documentation am-
ateurishly random. The recordings he made of Peyote Religion ceremonies were not done on the reservation or in a studio, but in his
hotel room, the singers' homes, a pawnshop, a bar, and the hotel lobby;
some of them were made when he and a singer may have been drunk
or on peyote; the songs lacked the usual accompaniment of drums;
there is no mention of filming, though that was supposed to be one
of his roles in the project; he lost the biographical notes he had written of his singers when the police gave him a few days to get out of
town. But there was logic behind his work: though he did film some
dances, his chief concern was the songs of the Peyote Religion, which
make up the largest part of an all-night ritual event. He chose not to
record at the actual services because he had learned from his Northwest Coast ritual recordings that the drums that accompanied singers
made it impossible to record both instruments and vocals with only a
single mic. He wanted the words and music to be clearly heard, and
also to record the singers explaining the songs and their place in the
services before or after they were sung. Some of the singers said that
this allowed them to feel freer to talk to him away from the full religious services. Once the records were issued for sale, some Kiowa said
they were a great aid in learning the songs.

He treated the Kiowa with respect and appreciation. In his record notes, he speaks of the singers he recorded as "composers," "music connoisseurs," and "song collectors." (The development of portable tape recorders had made it possible for Kiowa song composers to make tapes of their works and share them with others.) The cover of the record album lists the singers' names, something rare at the time on anthropologists' recordings, as performers were usually treated anonymously, implying that they were typical of an entire culture.

The result of his work, *The Kiowa Peyote Meeting: Songs and Narratives by Members of a Tribe That Was Fundamental in Popularizing the Native American Church*, a boxed set of three LPs on Folkways Records, was a serious anthropological contribution, something noted by enthusiastic reviewers of the records in *Ethnomusicology* and the *Journal of American Folklore*. Harry thought his Kiowa research was the most important work he had done, and his record notes are the longest piece of writing by him that still exists. The notes were not written in an academic style, as a field research report in the arcane language of the expert. There were no hypotheses being tested, or secrets being revealed, nor was there writing in the breathless prose of a discoverer. What he wrote was honest and transparent, explaining his limitations as a researcher, and claiming little beyond what was to be seen in the notes or found on the recordings. He clearly wanted the reader to understand what he had heard and seen and to appreciate it as he did. (In his notes, he recommended that those with the recordings "partake of the herb" while listening. One reviewer said it was unfortunate that none was provided in the boxed set.)

He recorded more than 1,200 songs from the Kiowa singers in Oklahoma. The fifty-two tracks on the Folkways album were talking and songs by six individuals. They included songs used at different points during the peyote ritual—the "Four Songs" ("Opening Song," "Midnight Water Song," "Morning Water Song," and "Quitting Song") necessary for every peyote ritual occasion, as well as the "Personal Songs," those composed by individual singers that might appear during the services. The album provided examples of how these newly composed songs were used, along with those required for the event (Harry called this practice the "intercalation" of songs.). Several versions of the same song are included to illustrate the differences between the singers. One-third of the album's tracks were several singers giving their own description of the rituals. There are also some examples of "forty-nine songs," a genre of music that had first appeared in the nineteenth century and were sung to accompany social dances at powwows and other social occasions. By the time Harry visited the Kiowa, the songs' contents had changed from traditional concerns with family and tribal authority to stories of the complexities of love and loss. The frankness of the modern lyrics and their solo, first-person presentation are sometimes compared to the blues, and are a sharp departure from the typical Southern Plains style of men and women singing in unison.

Harry estimated that a third of all Kiowa songs had words, and the rest were what they called "plain," made up entirely of nonverbal syllables such as "yo," "ha," or "hey." Outsiders might consider such songs nonsense, but Harry was careful to warn listeners:

> There is no doubt that these syllables have fairly definite sets of emotional connotations. They are symbols in the same way a white line means "feather" (and hence "sky" or "up" or "joy") or a red line "ground" (and hence "earth" or "down" or "sadness") in the Kiowa beadwork. From a linguistic standpoint the vowel series of the "plain" songs conform to phonetic patterns more or less coincident with Plains culture. There are extensions of the most common series down the Mississippi and into the Algonquin [sic] Northeast. More specifically, they are coincident with the distribution of the Plains vocabulary sign language of which the Kiowa were perhaps the greatest masters.

During his recording, Harry had followed a procedure he had wanted to use with the shape note and the *Anthology* recordings, in which each word of the songs was put on a card to create lists for later content analysis. In his album notes, there was also a brief but promising discussion of Kiowa art and its relations to the songs and rituals. He planned to assemble another three LPs that would be called *A History of Kiowa Love Songs*. There were at least two of those records completed with songs in both English and the Kiowa language, but Harry never finished the notes or the covers for the albums, and none were released.

Years later, when the Smithsonian Institution bought the Folkways catalog and was preparing its recordings for sale to the public, a spokesperson for the Washoe Indians was asked for permission to issue their Peyote Religion songs. The response was that they should not be made public because of their sacred content. The Smithsonian removed the Washoe records from distribution. This raised the question of the Smith recordings, and the Smithsonian sought advice from the Kiowa. The chief and the descendants of the singers on the album said, "A hundred years from now we want our children's children to be able to hear the voices of their ancestors." Smithsonian Folkways then issued them for sale and put Harry's notes on their website. Although the Smith peyote recordings were not yet available in 1965 during the first appearance of pop psychedelia (the Kinks, the Yardbirds, the Fugs, the Doors, the Beatles, the 13th Floor Elevators, Donovan, and the Byrds), when they were finally issued in 1973 they could be heard playing before coffee shop poetry readings in Greenwich Village.

By the first week of April 1965, Harry had shifted away from the peyote music to recording Kiowa bedtime stories and their narratives of the origins of their people and culture, and began gathering examples of Kiowa harmony to create a more detailed picture of their music.

Sometimes the sessions were devoted to a single singer; at other times he recorded several singers at one session, which allowed them to remind one another of songs they'd forgotten, or he would encourage them to sing different versions of the same song.

He then moved beyond the Kiowa songs after he ran into "this 79-year-old woman with a handmade sunbonnet [who] was standing [outside the bank]." As he learned later, this lady, Litha Chesney, had planned to ask him to record her ever since she saw his name in the newspaper. "But she did it legitimately, she knew what I was looking for, she didn't sing any old important old ballads, because she recognized them from the tunes, she said, 'Oh, those old love songs.' But she had many hundred songs written on sheets of paper in a box under her bed, her ballad box."

Chesney led him to Florabelle Harrington and other singers. Some sessions produced songs that were then popular country and western music, some were old ballads and hymns, or the "Morphine Blues" mixed in with nineteenth-century sentimental songs. Some of these recordings were done in Miss Tingley's Pawn Shop, where Harry bought Kiowa art objects and had sometimes pawned his recording machine. In good folklorist fashion, he asked singers to let him record their biographical information. He urged them to recall the oldest songs they'd ever heard, and to tell all they knew about a song—its meaning, its history, and where they learned it. Did they know any other versions of the same song? If they had trouble remembering all the words, he'd pause and encourage them to try to remember them before they went on to another song. He sometimes attempted to record a singer's entire repertoire. Whole conversations were recorded on the origins of Kiowa traditions and practices, stories of tornadoes in Oklahoma, their different religions, or their travels. Altogether, he made approximately three thousand recordings in Oklahoma in less than five months.

During that time, and over several years, Harry was hired, fired, and rehired from the *Chappaqua* project. Rooks liked him, and could afford to put up with him. He boasted that it was he and Harry who had introduced Richard Alpert (Ram Dass), Timothy Leary, and Philip Lamantia to "magic mushrooms," which Rooks had bought from María Sabina, the fabled curer or shaman of Huautla de Jiménez, Mexico, "who warned that she would drive all Leary's followers mad. The Zapotecs didn't take too kindly to 'Turn on, tune in and drop out.' One of the reasons I made this film was to show Leary where it's at! What right does he have talking about this?"

Though the film's reviews weren't kind, *Chappaqua*'s fragmented narrative, innovative cinematography, and musical mix appeared at the right time, a moment when drugs, Native Americans, and new film techniques, music, and subjects had reached Hollywood. It was nominated for a Golden Lion at the Venice Film Festival in 1966 and won a Special Jury Prize. William Burroughs contributed a short statement on the film that appeared in the Chappaqua pressbook:

> There is a hiatus between blocks of association, rents as it were in the fabric of reality through which we glimpse the old myths that were here before the white man came, and will be after he is gone, a brief inglorious actor washed off the stage in the waters of silence. Rooks has brought to the screen the immediate experience of silent beauty conveyed in the Peyote vision—older Gods waiting impassively at the end of the line.

The film was not released until 1967, and if it had been shown earlier it might have been the first "trip" movie of the sixties, instead of Arthur Dreifuss's *The Love-Ins* and Roger Corman's *The Trip*.

Although Harry never owned a new motion-picture camera, whenever he needed one, he either borrowed it or rebuilt an old one. For some of *Film No. 14 (Late Superimpositions)*, shot in Anadarko, he used Lionel Ziprin's mother's camera and then pawned it. "I've usually just borrowed [a camera] then pawned it. That's always an embarrassing scene, trying to explain to the person where his or her camera is. I can remember Frank Stauffacher saying to me, 'Now, you haven't pawned the camera, have you?' He said it jokingly, but it was pawned. Usually, people get their cameras back, eventually."

Though he never said much about his plans, especially as he was hiding them from his several underwriters, he intended to make some form of film in Oklahoma with ethnographic content. He told Arthur Young he was going to give most of his royalties from the film to the Kiowa. Whatever his intent, the footage he shot of dancers and rituals appears in *Film No. 14*, a thirty-one-minute movie in color that he completed in 1964. It was his first effort at photographing the "real world," but it was not filmed and screened as capturing reality. A series of one-hundred-foot reels were assembled unedited, the blank leaders and tails showing, with double, triple, and quadruple exposures. He described it as "Superimposed photography of Mr. Fleischman's butcher shop in New York, and the Kiowa around Anadarko, Oklahoma—with cognate material. The strip is dark at the beginning and end, light in the middle, and is structured 122333221. I honor it the most of my films, otherwise a not very popular one before 1972. If the exciter lamp blows, play Brecht's 'Mahagonny.'"

The cognate material includes store windows, rooms, animated objects, neon signs, the lobby of his hotel in Anadarko, a cattle show, feet, hands, Central Park, pages being turned of the Hermetic Order of the Alpha et Omega notebook with magical diagrams, and Harry discussing the Folkways recordings of the Kiowa with Moe Asch. The soundtrack was from a recording of Kurt Weill and Bertolt Brecht's opera *Rise and Fall of the City of Mahagonny*. Asked if the synchrony between visual layers of the film was there by surrealist chance, he said, "It is totally through chance. There was no attempt at all to synchronize."

Sitney thought this was Smith's "most subtle film and demands very serious attention":

> At the beginning, the movements and superimpositions are very controlled, almost as if the film-maker were animating real scenes like cutouts. Gradually the layers pull apart; the form loosens until the illusion of reality implicit in the cinema mechanism takes over. Then just as gradually as the control has disappeared, it returns. The real world becomes more and more subjected to abstract orders, and the film ends with the actual animation of physical objects.

It was the first of several of Harry's films that would include biographical allusions, merging images of his life in New York with his time in Anadarko.

Harry returned to New York in May 1964 and found that another landlord had once again evicted him and thrown everything he had—films, paintings, books, collections—into the trash for not paying his rent or telling him where he had gone. Harry was devastated: for weeks he plodded through the stench, feral animals, and rats of the 2,200 acres of Fresh Kills Landfill in Staten Island. He had a breakdown, according to Dr. Joe Gross, who gave Harry's landlord $200 in hopes that he might have kept Harry's belongings. "All of my paintings, all of my films, all of everything was destroyed, taken to the garbage dump. Thrown in the garbage dump by mistake. The paintings became—some of them having taken as much as six or seven years to make, very small paintings, and they were more valuable than the films, you see. I regret having lost the paintings more than the films . . ." He took what he had left, including his tape recordings from Oklahoma, and moved into the Earle, a hotel popular with musicians.

When he was still in Oklahoma, Harry had asked Moe Asch for an advance against royalties, and Asch wired him $100 to rent a Wollensak tape recorder and for other expenses. A month later he sent him $30 more for blank tapes. When he returned to New York, Harry wrote Moe to confirm that he had sent him ten audiotapes of Indian material that he had recorded for Folkways Records, and that they had been received. The tape recorder he had rented was still in his possession, he said, and he intended to edit the tapes and return them to Asch to issue ten more American Indian long-playing records. For "collateral," he wrote, "I owe Moses Asch two paintings of American Indians that I have at the Hotel Earle, NYC for him." In a few weeks, Harry forwarded Moe a bill for $331 from Vaseco Visual and Sound Equipment in Oklahoma City for the tape recorder that he had never returned. Three months later, Moe wrote to Vaseco that he was "stuck with the cost of the tape machine because I can't locate Harry Smith."

As Rooks was completing *Chappaqua* in 1966, he wrote Asch from Paris, asking for permission to use some of the Kiowa music Harry had recorded for Folkways: "As I financed Harry Smith's OKLA trip—plane tickets, expenses, and carried him 5 months last year, it would be polite for me to use with your O. K. for the sound track of my film a few 100 ft. of tape as it was ostensibly created for this purpose. Harry made me spend $6,000 last year on him." What he wanted was "the use of a short bit of singing Harry recorded outside of a ceremony."

SEMINOLE

Some said that the loss of Harry's paintings and films drove him deep into alcoholism. He was distraught by his loss, and his drinking was far more damaging to his body and his work than all his experiments with drugs. Still, he had been drinking heavily before this incident, and his Kiowa research was successful in spite of it. And only two months after returning from Oklahoma in 1964, he was already making plans for a trip to Florida to see some friends in Miami, visit the Seminole Indians, and maybe dry out by getting away from New York City.

He'd read the writings on Seminole music in Florida by Frances Densmore, a folklorist who had pioneered using photography and the earliest recording machines among Indians. What intrigued him about the Seminoles was their success in maintaining their traditions and resisting the control of the U.S. government. The Seminoles have one of the most complex and varied cultural histories of all North American Indians. They emerged as a distinct tribal group in Florida in the eighteenth century, with some of the Creek confederacy joining the tribe. By the nineteenth century, they had expanded further by adding members of various other Indian tribes, as well as escaped slaves. The renegade African Americans who settled nearby were known as Black Seminoles. The Seminole Indian nation had lived under the British and Spanish occupations of Florida, but beginning in the early 1800s, they fought a series of wars for independence against the United States that lasted forty years. Even before the United States acquired Florida from Spain in 1821, General Andrew Jackson had invaded Seminole villages to recapture escaped slaves. Once the United States controlled the state, and Jackson was named military governor of Florida, there were ten more years of war between the Indians and government troops. Though heavily outnumbered, the Seminoles were never defeated, and this made a huge impression on Harry. When they were offered land beyond the Mississippi, many Seminoles left, and today the largest number are in Oklahoma. Of those who remained in Florida, some were in the Everglades, where their guerrilla tactics enabled them to survive. When the U.S. troops finally withdrew, and treaties were made, many of the

Indians moved to reservations in various parts of the state. But hundreds of Seminoles stayed within or close to the Everglades, and never signed any peace treaties. Today, some say they are still technically at war with the United States. This resistance, their cultural traditions, and the environment they defended spawned a series of Hollywood films and TV shows from the late 1940s through the early 1960s. *Seminole*, *Distant Drums*, *Key Largo*, *Yellowneck*, *Wind Across the Everglades*, and *The Everglades* kept the Seminole story alive to the public.

Those who remained in Florida were divided by where they chose to live, their political views, and their language. The largest group now are known as the Seminoles, and live in a number of reservations and towns. One smaller group are the Miccosukee, who live on reservations in South Central Florida. Another, much smaller, group refused to accept any of the conditions that led to reservations, treaties, and relocations, and were located some thirty miles from Miami along the Tamiami Trail, U.S. Highway 41. Earlier they were known as the Traditional Seminoles, later as the Trail Seminoles. These are the people who interested Harry, those who proudly declared that they wouldn't accept the free license plates that the government offered them, and sometimes drove their pickup trucks without plates, or simply bought plates with their own money. When Harry asked their spiritual leader, Peter Osceola, about the Vietnam War and whether he listened to Lyndon Johnson, he laughingly replied, "He's your president, not ours."

Harry's first trip to Florida was to Miami Beach to see Peter Fleischman. Peter was a student at Goddard College who had invited Harry to visit him and his mother, Peri, the sister-in-law of Judy Garland. It was during this visit that Smith first encountered the Seminoles. In notes that he later used to write a proposal to the Newport Festivals

Foundation for financial support for his research, Harry reviewed his
first contacts:

> I went to Florida with the express purpose of recording mu-
> sic of the Seminole Indians. I selected the Seminoles as my
> field of research because they seemed likely, on the basis of
> published studies, to provide the contrasting material nec-
> essary to test certain theories of personality types developed
> during my field work among the Kiowa during the preceding
> summer, and particularly because of the lack of accurate re-
> cordings of any South-Eastern music . . . It became appar-
> ent that a similar collection from a contrasting people would
> clarify the apparent relations between personality structure,
> social history and music. The Seminoles seemed ideal for
> this purpose because, in the first place, very few Seminoles
> born before WW II speak English . . . Different groups of
> Seminoles speak different dialects of language. Some were
> in other states and had fled or been forced out of Florida.
>
> The conservatism of the Seminole [culture] is truly as-
> tounding. More than one-half of them have steadfastly
> refused to have any dealings whatsoever with white people.
> Within 30 miles of Miami are seven hundred people who
> prefer to live the precarious lives of self-worth rather than
> accept either the land or the rather lavish monies offered
> them by the United States government.

Harry raised the money for that first trip to Florida in 1964 from
an assortment of patrons—Dorethea Weisner, Panna Grady, Moses
Asch, Conrad Rooks, and Arthur Young—though each of them seem
to have thought they were supporting a different project. While Harry
was searching for more funds in New York, Izzy Young said Harry
asked him for a couple of dollars to get a cab to Allen Ginsberg's to get

$5 so that he could take a cab to Peggy Guggenheim's to ask her for $2,000 for his research.

As he was making plans, he met Marc Berger, a student just out of the University of California at Berkeley, who was drawn to him by their common interests in anthropology, film, and music. Seeing his ethnographic collections and having direct access to Harry's esoteric books, most of which concerned indigenous people and their pursuits, such as string figures, fascinated Marc, who with Harry's help became an expert in performing them. He also helped Harry in the almost impossible task of trying to make sense of some of the garbled written instructions found in Harry's books on performing the figures. Furthermore, Marc, whose ancestry was Ukrainian, bought many of the hand-painted eggs in Harry's collection for him from Ukrainian shops on the Lower East Side of New York City. Harry invited him to join him on his trip.

Like gentlemen scholars, Harry and Marc moved into the Atlantic Towers, a "Miami Modern" hotel on the water, with a swimming pool overlooking the ocean. Harry mixed with the locals, one of whom was on the staff of the actor-comedian Jackie Gleason, and Harry offered to advise Gleason on purchases of books on the paranormal, UFOs, and folklore; Gleason's collection is now housed at the University of Miami Libraries.

"There was great difficulty in doing anything with Harry," Berger said. "He could be extremely cantankerous, obstinate, obstructionist, mischievous, drunken, etc. A large part of my job—as I interpreted it—was to keep the shit from hitting the fan. But with the Seminoles, we just showed up and Harry was quite comfortable with these kinds of impromptu, spontaneous types of meetings." Despite the humidity, heat, and dark clouds of mosquitoes, he'd put on his wool suit, have a drink of wine away from the Indians, who were forbidden to drink, and then approach the village. "Harry was entertaining, knowledgeable, and not the type of white man they had grown used to having to put up with." The older Seminoles, such as Peter and Mary Osceola, received him very well, but the younger generation, who had long hair, wore Beatle boots, bought Bob Dylan's records, and played electric guitars through amplifiers in their chikees (huts with thatched roofs and open sides, raised up on posts above the swamp), showed no interest, and shunned them.

Though they started to Florida with enough money to cover the trip, it disappeared rapidly. Once when Harry had some money wired to them, he spotted a gypsy fortune-teller next door to Western Union and thought Marc should have his fortune told. He sent Marc in, but when he came out, they had only $20 left, and Harry thought that was hysterically funny. "If we got cash, it was invariably gone in two days," Marc said. "The first day we'd eat and then he would go on a buying spree. In Florida it would be off to the Everglades for more Seminole patchwork. When we went to Philadelphia on the way back home, it would be down to the antique stores to buy Mennonite tools and Pennsylvania Dutch coverlets and quilts," which Harry used to compare their patterns against Seminole and Anglo-American quilts.

Once Harry saw the unique Seminole patchwork clothing of the Seminole women, he immediately related it to his old hand-painted geometric 35-millimeter films and abandoned his goal of recording their music. Patchwork is a process of doubling, cutting, twisting, and sewing different pieces of colored cloth into bundles to create long rows, which are then sewn to other rows horizontally to create an item of clothing. (Harry noted that the twisted pieces could be "cut"—that is, ripped—like taffy.) Some elements of these designs have a long tradition, but it was the introduction of hand-operated sewing machines in the early 1900s that allowed the modern tradition to develop. Older designs used the shapes of fire, lightning, waves, trees, and mountains. Later, they incorporated letters of the alphabet formed right side up and upside down, and "good luck arrows" (crossed as to form the four points of the compass). These bundled designs appear in the form of single squares, checkerboard squares, in a diamond- or X-shaped pattern. Some see African influence in this clothing, since there were Gullah-speaking ex-slaves among and around the Seminole.

By the 1960s, when Harry arrived, the colors had become much brighter, the patterns more complex and geometric, and clothing incorporating them was sold to tourists along the Tamiami trail. The designs of individual dressmakers were distinctive enough that they could be identified, even when some of the elements had been traded or given to other dressmakers and added to their own designs. Harry thought those bundled patches of material were in some way a parallel to the Plains Indian medicine bundles that contain sacred objects and function as a means of curing, or a method of containing and protecting the heart of a people's culture.

He came to know all the women who made patchwork clothing in the community, and spent $3,000 buying finished dresses and samples of all their patterns and designs, and even bought the contents of the entire work bag of one of the best designers. He later regretted that he had failed to ask the names and the meanings of the designs, since he had also intended to study the linguistic patterns in relation to color patterns, and to connect their naming to their cosmography.

"When I was in Oklahoma," he said, "I realized that it was possible to perform some kind of saturated study of something . . . the type of thinking I applied to records, I still apply to other things, like Seminole patchwork or to Ukrainian Easter Eggs":

> The whole purpose is to have some kind of a series of things. Information as drawing and graphic designs can be located more quickly than it can be in books. The fact that I have all the Seminole designs permits anything that falls into the canon of that technological procedure to be found there. It's like flipping quickly through. It's a way of programming the mind, like a punch card of a sort.
>
> There are a limited number of Seminoles and a limited number of ways pieces of cloth can be ripped and put back

together, if it is ripped by Seminole measuring methods. Also, the sewing method can only produce certain angles. This type of design—turned at an angle and made of stripes—only developed around 1941, and being that everybody who made this stuff was saving samples in case they wanted to make the same one again—it was possible to do an archeology by going through a barrel of stuff one lady had. Without too much effort it was possible to collect all of the Seminole designs.

A classified ad appeared in the January 1965 issue of the *East Village Other*:

> HARRY SMITH, brilliant young filmmaker, is drying out in the Florida Everglades, filming and recording the Seminole Indians. He needs financial assistance. So send negotiable encouragement to Harry Smith, 4201 Collins Av., Miami Beach, Florida.

When Harry and Marc left Florida, they went to Philadelphia, where Harry was to spend two months completing some research for Arthur Young and working on a Seminole film. "Harry told me that he showed up in Philadelphia," said his friend Bill Breeze, "after his stay in Miami—wanting to stay at Arthur Young's house there. At the time Young's brother was staying at Arthur's house, and somehow became aware that Harry wanted to move in with a set of Aleister Crowley's journal *The Equinox*, and he refused to allow them in the house. It was some scene with Harry on the porch with boxes and boxes of books, and the Crowley content of the library became an issue for Young's brother, who was clearly superstitious." Harry and Marc then moved into the Adelphia, one of the best hotels in the city.

Marc recalled that once, "on a state holiday, all the liquor stores were closed, and we went to visit an acquaintance on Pine Street, in the antique district. He had a giant bottle of Old Grand-Dad whiskey and we drank way too much, way too fast . . ." Harry was vomiting and acting in a bizarre fashion, a crowd gathered, they both passed out, and the police arrived. "We woke up in jail," said Marc, "and I had a wound over my eye with blood on my shirt. We had to appear in court the next morning and were simply released."

Folk music took a sharp turn at the Newport Folk Festival in the summer of 1965. Only a few years earlier audiences had been made up of middle-class families, aging leftists in thrall to Pete Seeger, maybe some regional folklore society members, and Ivy League and Seven Sisters students at ease with the Kingston Trio's cruise clothes and genial hints at a folk-rock yet to come. But with the death of Malcolm X, the racial violence in Selma, and resistance to the war in Vietnam, new folk arrived dressed like hobos with sleeping bags and guitars. The concerts were laden with civil rights movement figures like Bernice Reagon and Fannie Lou Hamer. Merchandise booths now had tie-dyed shirts and psychedelic posters, and there was a booth belonging to the Lowndes County Freedom Organization of Alabama, whose slogan, "Move Over or We'll Move You Over," rankled the nonviolent activists among the crowd.

Bob Dylan, then the most popular singer working under the sign of folk, dared to perform a set with electrical instruments at high volume and was greeted with a chorus of boos. Harry didn't appreciate the fact that Dylan had gone electric, according to Marc Berger, "but he absolutely loved Dylan's music. When we were at Peter Fleischman's sister Jane's birthday party in Miami Beach, Harry sang Dylan's 'Queen Jane Approximately' from the *Highway 61 Revisited* album."

Dylan's turn toward rock underlined the recent success of a number of the regular performers at the festival who were pricing themselves out of the folk circuit. The old-guard members of the Newport Festivals Foundation, like Alan Lomax, Mike Seeger, and Charles Seeger, feared traditional music's being swamped by this new form of pop, and the board of directors proposed that the next year's edition of the event should protect older and lesser-known forms of music from being lost in the musical spectaculars. They thought the festival should widen the idea of tradition to include folk arts and crafts. Ralph Rinzler was hired to spend several months a year on the back roads of America in search of singers and artists not known by the public.

"We visited Ralph Rinzler in Philadelphia on the second trip back from Florida," Berger recalled. "Harry was quite sarcastic toward him and charming to his wife—par for the course for Mr. Smith. But Ralph still trusted Harry to know what was important, and he asked him for recommendations as to who might be invited to the festival in 1966. When Harry suggested the Seminole Indian crafts people, Ralph said he should apply for funds from the Newport [Festivals Foundation]."

In one of his letters to the Newport Festivals Foundation board, Harry spelled out where he was in his plans to collect and now film Seminole dressmakers' work:

> About 1300 examples of patchwork were collected with the specific purpose of making an abstract film that would appeal both to the Indians and to the larger audience already familiar with my work. I believe this is the first time that film has been made in cooperation with American Indians in which they appear as artists rather than convenient objects to study.

During the 4 weeks surrounding the spring equinox, the priest of this ceremony, Peter Osceola has asked me to come back at that time.

My general plan has been to prepare the film before the end of March, show it to the Seminoles during April and May and record the sound tracks at that time. Peter O, a former priest of the green corn dance, suggests that I put a sound track of the Beatles on the first version of the film "because that's what the women hear when they're sewing."

The proposal concluded with Harry explaining that things had not been completed at the pace promised, but that he was finishing it in Philadelphia using what he had collected the year before. Though he doesn't mention it, he had fallen on the street and broken his upper arm, and was forced to work with only one hand.

Between 1965 and 1966 in Philadelphia, Harry worked on the film that would show his ethnographic research findings in Florida. According to Berger, "Mr. Smith constructed the animation stand out of cardboard, which was one of the things that freaked-out a Temple University film student that Young had brought by on one of his visits." An animation stand is a device that allows frame-by-frame photography of drawings, or in this case Seminole patchwork. The stand lets a camera move up and down, and the graphic materials can be moved in several directions or enable superimposed shots to be taken of layers of materials. "I thought it was totally astonishing what Harry could do with simple materials and tools, such as a box cutter. He painted it all matte black and it functioned perfectly when we filmed."

Harry's proposal for the Folk Festival was accepted, and a section of the Folk Festival grounds for July 1966 was set aside for crafts, with weavers from Nova Scotia and Tennessee, Alaskan Ivory carvers, and Seminole patchwork makers.

While staying at the Walnut Hotel in Philadelphia for two months (this time paid for by Peggy Hitchcock), Harry wrote the Newport Festivals Foundation hoping for an extension on the grant. He said that the film on patchwork he promised had progressed further. He would take the film to the Everglades to show it to the dress designers he wanted to send to the festival. His friends in Miami had been visiting the designers, keeping him in touch, as they had no mailing addresses or telephones.

The completed film was *No. 15*, untitled, an eight-minute, fifty-eight-second animated color catalog of quilt details that displays the various sewn patterns as if they were in a geometric art film. Occasionally, the patterns are turned over to show they were stitched in a fashion quite different from those in most American quilting. He had planned a soundtrack that would use Frances Densmore's 1930s recordings of Seminole songs, hiding their clicks and defects with "gurgling water and what not," putting echo on them, and using bird sounds. He then tried several other forms of music, but finally left it silent. It was an unusual film for Harry, something more like a fabric sales show presentation without lush music. But Jonas Mekas saw it as an important film innovation: "What made the . . . Harry Smith fabric movie work was the rhythm in which the sheets [of fabric] were changed. Through this rhythm the piece gained a definite structure in time."

Harry was asked to write a short introduction to patchwork dresses for the printed program of the 1966 Newport Folk Festival. In his rough draft he began in the spirit of Franz Boas: "In all places the human mind functions alike. There are no savage modes of thought, no civilized ones." Though the notes that follow are largely scratched out, it's clear that he was attempting to show that the differences that are claimed to exist between these alleged two kinds of peoples are the result of assumptions of cultural superiority and of ignoring differences of environment and historical changes. He addressed the Newport audience directly and challenged them to consider works of art from American Indians and African Americans and their relationship to the environments in which they were created. "Meditate on experiencing darkness falling on some country road in Alabama," and then ask themselves if they really think they are "mere geometrical exercises or the byproduct of technical necessity. Do they really believe that Euro-American artists could render those more perfectly?" Some of his essay did not make it to print, whether edited for length or ideology. The final version that appeared in the Newport Folk Festival July 1966 program offered dressmaking among the Seminole as an example of art in its cultural and natural environment:

SEMINOLE PATCHWORK SEWING
Harry Smith

Of all the Seminole arts, sewing is perhaps the most interesting. Why are the Seminoles interested in sewing? Perhaps first of all because, like the Eskimo, they must protect them from a potentially destructive environment. Anyone who has travelled through the incredible swarms of insects in the Southern swamps will realize how perfectly the form and cut of Seminole clothing is adjusted to necessity.

The women, who sew all day long, have developed a form and technique that is highly complex. A great part of their work, usually of a lesser sort, is sold to tourists along the Tamiami Trail, but the interest in cloth does not end there. For example, a skirt is given in payment for recitation of the formula to ease childbirth. Skirts are used almost as frequently to form the walls of the palm-thatched shelters of the camp or to wrap valuables, as they are for clothing.

The Seminole styles have changed year by year. The general patchwork style of today came about with the introduction of the sewing machine to Florida in about 1900. The specific type of cloth mosaic most popular at the moment (in which strips of cloth are turned forty-five degrees) became popular just after the Second World War.

We hope that the visit of a few Seminole artists to Newport this year will stimulate interest in their "songs without words" which enter the mind through the eyes rather than the ears, yet still possess the same qualities of rhythm, variation and beauty.

Harry's patchwork pattern collection was donated to the Smithsonian Institution in 1974, and the occasion was filmed. He is shown carefully unwrapping the items from boxes as he comments on them and how the collection was gathered. He kept just a few of the dresses. Patti Smith said she was only person in the Chelsea small enough to fit into them.

8

Nights in Bohemia

1965–1967

Harry Smith—the magus of the Chelsea Hotel, a genuine
modern alchemist turning rich suckers' handouts into
deliriously Kabbalistic art.

—Ian Penman

Lower Manhattan had long been the city's financial and governmental
center, a cluster of ethnic neighborhoods, the Bowery, the meatpack-
ing district, sweatshops, seaports, the oldest part of New York, but
by the 1950s it was also "Downtown," a term that marked the shift
of the arts from "Uptown" to below Fourteenth Street. "Downtown
was where it was all happening," Jonas Mekas reflected. "The Uptown
however produced the audiences for it. Uptowners went Downtown
for excitement . . . It was where Duchamp lived, Fluxus, Happenings,
Judson Hall, the [Film-Makers'] Cinematheque, Charles Theater, Jack
Smith, Richard Foreman, Robert Wilson, Velvet Underground, John
Cage, Yvonne Rainer, Yoko Ono, the *Village Voice*, the *Village Other*,
LaMonte Young, Rauschenberg, The Living Theater . . . the Cedar
Bar, all the jazz places, Café Bizarre, and Ginsberg, and Bob Dylan,
and Barbara Rubin, and [Angus] McLise, and Phil Glass . . . Cole-
man, Coltrane, Miles . . . Harry Smith."

The focal point of Downtown art was Greenwich Village, the capital of bohemia for over a century, a home for those who left home and

were willing to erase their pasts; a place where they could find themselves, be somebody else, or just disappear. The romantic stories of bohemians in quest of fame and freedom are the folktales of movies and novels, but in the Village itself, there were stories of those who did not end so well. Two such characters were still in the Village when Harry arrived. Maxwell Bodenheim, for one, a mediocre novelist and poet who moved from Chicago to the Village, where his alcoholism, panhandling, and obnoxious behavior made him a well-known figure of the streets, selling his poems at 25 cents apiece, a drunken regular in the San Remo Café. Bodenheim's reputation as a writer was kept afloat by Ben Hecht and others who enjoyed retailing his ludicrous adventures until he was murdered by a deranged dishwasher near the Bowery.

Joe Gould was another, one whose ghost is still with us—a Greenwich Village self-proclaimed vagrant writer first brought to light by Joseph Mitchell's *New Yorker* profiles and a book. He returned in Stanley Tucci's movie *Joe Gould's Secret*, in 2000, and again in 2016 as the inspiration for Jill Lepore's book *Joe Gould's Teeth*. His notoriety rested on the mystery of his life and on his claim to being the unlikely author of what he declared would be the world's longest book, *The Oral History of Our Time*. He managed to convince a number of otherwise intelligent people—E. E. Cummings, Malcolm Cowley, Ezra Pound, Alice Neel, William Saroyan, and William Carlos Williams—that he could write, without any of them having seen his magnum opus, much less his minor opus. Gould's real secret was that Joseph Mitchell had kept some of his story hidden from his readers: there was no such work, only scribbled bits of conversation. Gould managed to survive as long as he did by entertaining Village people with his bizarre and antic behavior on the streets, in bars, and at parties that he crashed. When he died in a mental hospital, no one bothered to come to his funeral.

The weirdness of such characters was honored, their craziness tolerated, in the spirit of social rebellion. Ross Wetzsteon, a chronicler of Greenwich Village culture, once suggested that if it were true that Americans want tragedies with happy endings, the Village bohemians too often wanted farces with tragic endings.

Harry Smith is sometimes unjustly included among such colorful Village failures. But he, in contrast, succeeded at much of what he attempted, sometimes spectacularly, producing important work in several fields, and influencing many. He wrote proposals and received grants. He talked about his work and life in terms that at times could be a bit strange, but just as often could be highly enlightening and even well-documented. The enigma of Harry lies in the story of his life, the full range of the work he produced, how he managed to accomplish as much as he did with no money of his own, even during long periods of bad health, excessive use of drugs, and addiction to alcohol.

If Harry is not better known, part of the reason is that he lived much of his life as what most would call a bum, or a mendicant, panhandler, beggar, a schnorrer. Yet that seems unfair, too, as Harry was never lazy or a tramp, though he was indigent. He was an artist. Critics' and artists' perception of street artists, intellectual vagrants, and hobos (like the legendary musician Moondog or the tramp composer Harry Partch) is typically that of the naïve, raw outsider; the mad or half-mad; or, in more enlightened or Romantic terms, heroes of madness or victims of society. These are artists whose works are often obscured and undervalued by the superficial and lurid narratives of their lives. Smith was well aware of this prejudice, and never let it daunt him. In fact, he daringly tried to make it work for him, as when he revealed what drugs he had used during his film projects, or claimed madness when he applied for grants.

Harry could certainly appear to be performing the role of the bum, but could turn into an artist when he wished. John Cohen remembered he and Peggy Seeger bumping into Harry on Eighth Street in 1962: "Harry asked if I had a drink on me, and when I said 'no' he excused himself and rolled over on the sidewalk and into the gutter.

He was writhing with his legs in the air, and a crowd gathered around him. Then a Bowery derelict came along, pulled a flask from his belt, and gave Harry a drink, Harry then got up, the fellow left and the crowd dispersed. Harry said he wanted a drink and had seen the Bowery guy coming in our direction."

> Then the three of us went to Harlem to view twist dancing in a club called Smalls Paradise. The taxis and club entrance fee had used up most of my money, so we started looking for a subway late at night. Walking along the sidewalk, we were the only white people around. Harry dived headfirst into a basket and came out with a stack of discarded studio portrait photographs. He started to sort them out on the sidewalk according to size. A small crowd of people gathered around him, and he gave each of them a photograph from the sidewalk. They walked off, satisfied, and we took the subway back down to the Village.

Some saw Harry as an angry bum—not one of those sad ones who have accepted their fate, resigned to unstable dependency, but rather an ungrateful parasite who is dangerous to society, in his case, parasitic on the avant-garde and the bohemians. Harry could certainly appear to be angry, and his displays of rage were the stuff of local legend. Typically, they were accompanied by some form of destruction of his own property—films, recordings, books, reading glasses, whatever was at hand. Some found them funny, or frightening, yet to others it was a form of personal potlatch, an act of art renunciation, or the result of pain and loss.

"When someone had aroused Harry's rage, he would rip his glasses off his face and throw them down on the sidewalk and then proceed to jump up and down on them until they were shattered into tiny fragments," according to Marc Berger.

> His eyes had very deep and dark rings on them and he became almost blind in this state. He might have appeared pitiful, if it wasn't for his ire, which he was a genius at radiating out of waves of evil energy to an unbelievably intense level. Usually, the victim of his wrath would beat a hasty retreat and I was left in the tsunami's wake, to lead Mr. Smith to his room to sleep it off. Then, the next day we would visit his optician, who knew him oh so well and had his prescription on file and they would quickly produce another duplicate pair of spectacles . . . I was helpless to stop it and Harry rendered himself helpless in the act of self-destruction.

His response to those who tried to restrain his destructiveness? "It's my stuff."

Was it a performance? Stan Brakhage felt that "Harry's trick to stay out of the asylum was to dance it openly and be funny." Deborah Freeman saw him as having trouble relating to people in any way but some kind of fight or competition. "Intimacy was not something he felt too comfortable with . . . I think his compulsion to control things was overriding. But he was always very funny, and that's how he got away with a lot of things, and torture people, and still they would speak to him. Because it was always done in jest. But a lot of it was he just needed money and he wanted to get as much from people as he could. He felt his art came first, and therefore everything else was secondary."

Or was it drugs and alcohol? Charles Compo said he always thought it was kind of funny. "It felt like superb acting on his part. The pills definitely had an effect on his behavior. At one point he stopped taking Valium and it wasn't pretty." Jonas Mekas saw the other side of his anger: "I think he was one of the kindest, sweetest human beings

I have ever known . . . Because of his health and asthma, he had to take so many doses of cortisone and all kinds of drugs. After he took cortisone, he said 'Nobody should talk to me because I will go into fits for I don't know how many hours.'"

No question that Harry needed money like any bum, but he aimed higher. He would take handouts from those on the lower rungs of the ladder when necessary, but he mainly sought out the rich. And he did share with those not so fortunate when he could, almost recklessly at times. He was generous with his knowledge, and there were some who studied with him for years without paying. Those with means who sought to learn from him were often surprised when asked for money, as was Marty Balin, the singer with Jefferson Airplane, who was shocked when Harry gave him a bill for service.

He wanted to know the financial status of those who were drawn to him. Patti Smith met Harry when she and Robert Mapplethorpe were trying to get a room at the Chelsea. As they waited to see Stanley Bard, the manager, "Harry Smith suddenly materialized, as if he had disengaged from the wall."

> He had wild silver hair, a tangled beard, and peered at me with bright inquisitive eyes magnified by Buddy Holly glasses. He shot animated questions that overlapped my answers. "Who are you do you have money are you twins why are you wearing a ribbon around your wrist?" He was waiting for his friend Peggy Biderman, hoping she would stand him a meal . . . He stood before us, slightly hunchbacked in a shabby tweed jacket, chinos, and desert boots, with his head cocked like a highly intelligent hound. Although barely forty-five, he was like an old man with ceaseless childlike enthusiasm . . . he followed me around the lobby, saying "Are you sure you're not rich?" "We Smiths are never rich," I said. He seemed taken aback. "Are you sure your name is really Smith?" "Yes," I said, "and even surer that we're related."

When she recited a few lines of "Pirate Jenny" from Brecht and Weill's *The Threepenny Opera*, "[that] sealed things between us," she said.

"Early in his life," as Dr. Gross saw it, "Harry found that he could not bear to work at any job that did not allow him to explore new projects, new discoveries. He had no ambition to become a beggar or a bum . . . Harry had a funny karmic 'thing' for landlords, including of course that Great-Landlord-in-the-Sky. One day, later in life, Harry announced after scratching some figures on a pad, 'I just figured that God owes me $18,324 dollars and 60 cents!' (or some such amount). I was too dumbfounded and struck by a giggle fit (this one-liner was delivered with his usual semi-mock W. C. Fields nasal intonation) to inquire further, especially as Harry regarded the 'account closed.'"

After Harry's films were made available for rent at the Film-Makers' Cooperative, he stopped by weekly, thinking there would be a steady flow of cash. But they were rented largely by schools and museums that used them only occasionally. On days when there was none, he might explode in a rage and start throwing cans of film around. Jonas Mekas worked out tactics for dealing with him, sometimes advancing him money against rentals. More often it was a small ritual: he'd say, "Harry you're broke, so now I will take what I have in my pocket and I will put everything on the table and I will take yours from what I have and we'll split. I was the winner in many instances, but Harry usually had nothing left."

Mekas wrote in his diary on February 25, 1975, "Harry Smith calls. Could I lend him two or three hundred, whatever I can? Completely broke. His daily budget is 50 cents. Harry said he was due $400 from NYU." Mekas remembers there's $100 in the *Film Culture* magazine bank account. Harry agrees he'll pay it back when he gets the $400. "Can't leave the hotel for health reasons, he'll send someone to get it. He's only planning ahead, he still has $109 that he got from the Co-op, but wants to be sure that there is money somewhere after he spends the Co-op money." Mekas came up with the money for him the next day, though he only had $12 left in his own bank account.

The complexity of Harry's finances is shown in a note from the Film-Makers' Cooperative dated January 20, 1965: "There will be $300 from rental of Smith's films in his account (rental to Rhode Island School of Design) thus Moe Asch can advance money to Smith and will be reimbursed from his account with the [Film-Makers'] Coop."

On the other hand, "once he got money it was always burning a hole in his pocket and in his mind because he didn't want the stuff," according to Khem Caigan, a follower of Harry's. "It was such a burden to him. To him, it meant everything wrong and evil with the world. And yet in order to pursue his craft, there were certain financial needs. But once it was there, there was the responsibility of having it. That is why he was constantly doing things like giving a 50-dollar bill to a cab driver because he just had to get rid of it." Raymond Foye recalled that "[he] collected his mail at the Chelsea, took it out of the box and without looking put it in the trash, including checks, rental and financial statements."

Harry might beg for money but could not be bought. He would go hungry and be homeless in order to spend whatever he had to have for his work, his search for knowledge. Izzy Young told of a cold February night in 1973 when Harry invited him to visit. Izzy had dinner that night in Chinatown with a wealthy art dealer who asked if he could come along. Knowing that Harry could object to an uninvited guest, he got the dealer to agree that he would leave if Harry was unhappy with him being there. But after they were in his room at the Chelsea for a few minutes it was clear that Harry wanted him out and the dealer was not going to leave.

"Harry is sick," Young recalled, "spitting up blood four or five times a day, drinking vodka and water, a container of yogurt, and bicarbonate candy for his stomach . . . [The guest] tried to trade sarcasm with Harry, and even money, but he always lost . . . Hungry after Harry's collections, he offered to pay the $106 a month rent to store Harry's stuff in an apartment in Astoria. Harry said he'd take the money but he didn't need the apartment . . . He offered Harry $40 which Harry refused to take, but then said he just could leave the money on the table. Since that was not payment for or gratitude enough for the dealer, he took the money back. Later he offered $80 to Harry for one of his drawings."

Harry then went into an antique-store spiel: "This is a fine piece, a Franco-Greco shoelace, probably belonged to a count, $85. And you know, the tip of the shoelace is pure gold, and if I might say so you really know what you want." The dealer is losing. "He offers the $80 again. Harry says, 'Get the double triptych from Izzy—that's worth three or four thousand dollars.'" The dealer leaves.

"At times virtually homeless," Dr. Gross said, "living in a succession of Bowery flea-bag hotels, but forever energized by the vision of his masterpieces to come, eking a hand to mouth existence, fiercely uncompromising—the all-too-common lot of creative geniuses, difficult, even impossible to deal with . . . Harry was sure to bite the hand that tried to feed him."

Others had a quite different vision of Harry. Anne Waldman, for one:

> I visited Harry on occasion at the Chelsea in New York City, found him extraordinarily magnetizing, charming, scattered, distracted, but not by ordinary things but by constantly making the cognitive tentacular links all the time. He had a very rhizomic mind, elliptical . . . He was more the Keeper of the Archive, the Chief Magus, Docent & Shaman, he knew exactly where everything was and he has "seered" his own collections . . . magical stuff, hermetic, deep. He was always on the "left hand" path, so to speak, the exceptional, the weird, the visionary . . . the antithesis reality. I truly loved him.

David Amram:

> Harry had a kind of regal elegance, like a Russian emigre in Paris in a frayed tuxedo. He led a life of beauty, with little

regard for money. He took it and he gave it away. He felt no monetary obligation to others. Harry was not a willing member of any movement. He distrusted them. Fluxus, pop art, abstract expressionism, hard edge, minimalism, dada, even surrealism and the occult. He took the definition of field research and carried it to another level. He began like a college professor on a field trip and then became the field trip.

Rather than a bum, Harry might instead be thought of as the ultimate bohemian. By the time he surfaced publicly in the sixties, Village culture had come to respect the nonprofessional in the arts, even the artless, the ordinary, or artists whose work was modeled on pop or folk. It understood those who were in search of a community without the ties of a community. Harry had pushed the bohemian life to its extremes, and even some of those who found him annoying grudgingly admired him as pure a bohemian as could be imagined. Yet, at age forty-one in 1965, his drinking, chaotic drug use, poor health, and increasingly erratic and regressive behavior were now subtitled to his genius. He was arrested for drunkenness in Washington Square, and setting off false fire alarms ("for minor charges, you know") marked him for the hospital or prison.

Rose Feliu, a young, free spirit of the streets, renamed Rosebud by Allen Ginsberg, first encountered Harry at a poetry reading at the Café Metro, where Harry tried to grab an antique jade-green cape off her shoulders. Later, the two of them found their various encounters amusing enough that she moved into Harry's room at the Hotel Earle, where she stayed for several months, she sleeping on the floor, Harry in the bed. In the midst of Harry's long season of drink, Rosebud panhandled enough to keep them in two bottles of white port a day, added to whatever drugs he could scratch together. Their adventures ranged from meeting interesting drunks on the Bowery, to going to cheap movie houses on Forty-Second Street and poetry readings, where he enjoyed heckling mercilessly. Together they crashed the

Beatles concert at Shea Stadium in August 1965. Nights, they might mix with the folkniks at the Folklore Center, or watch street performers like Andrew "Harmonica Slim" Parsons, who Harry wanted to record, and talked Moe Asch into giving him a $100 advance for a record that was never released. Rosebud declared herself Harry's spiritual wife, a title that amused Harry, but she took more seriously, announcing it widely.

Sometimes Harry also explored the city in the company of another young woman, Wendy Clarke, the daughter of the filmmaker Shirley Clarke, who recalled that "One day on Eighth Street, we vandalized cars and broke off the radio antennas. It makes no sense, and we must have been really stoned or something because we thought it [was] just so funny."

Harry had his guardians—there's no other way to describe them, so devoted were they to protecting him from the destructive elements of Downtown New York and from himself. Two of his filmmaker friends, Barbara Rubin and Shirley Clarke, saw that, left to himself, Harry would soon end up in a single-room-occupancy hotel at best. SROs, as Lucy Sante describes them, were "tenanted by the luckless, the bereft, the unemployable, dipsomaniacs, junkies, released mental patients—exactly that portion of the population that would be otherwise turned out and left to conduct its existence in shelters or doorways or drainpipes or jails . . . those that could not blend into mainstream society." Rubin and Clarke knew that the Chelsea Hotel was the obvious place for him, a de facto artists' colony hidden in a Queen Anne Revival building on the city's West Side.

XANADU ON TWENTY-THIRD STREET

The Chelsea was built in the mid-1890s, when its looming twelve stories made it the tallest building in Manhattan. An early attempt at cooperative living inspired by Charles Fourier's utopian planning, its top floor was set aside as studios for artists. In 1905 it went bankrupt and was converted to a hotel that over the years drew writers like Mark Twain, O. Henry, and Thomas Wolfe to its dark iron balconies, winding staircase, and brick-red façade. When Harry moved there in 1965, it was a hothouse of creativity: Bob Dylan was working toward *Blonde on Blonde*, Arthur C. Clarke was writing *2001: A Space Odyssey*, Arthur Miller was finishing *After the Fall*, painters like Claes Oldenburg and Larry Rivers were at work, Warhol was shooting *Chelsea Girls*, Christo and Jeanne-Claude were wrapping the world, William Burroughs and Brion Gysin were cutting up magazines, poems, plays, and old song lyrics, and rearranging them to break away from the "word virus" that dominated them. There was tolerance and interest in even the most peculiar and quirky forms of creativity. Stanley Bard, manager-curator of residents, asked for no deposit, payments in advance, no leases, and favored artistes, oddballs, and the nondescript. Policies, few as they were, were lax. As Patti Smith said, "[You] weren't immediately kicked out if you got behind on the rent." Bard had no interest in the private lives of his residents, took pride in their artistic work, successful or not, and turned a blind eye to behavior that would have a tenant ejected from most hotels. Shirley Clarke had just moved into the Chelsea, and she urged Bard to take in Harry with the promise of her guaranteeing his rent. Harry would be able to move his collections, art and film works, books, and records into a small room, and would find care and sympathy for his idiosyncrasies.

Once settled in, Harry set up shop with a DO NOT DISTURB sign on a three-by-five card on the door (though it was open more often than not) and a DO NOT TOUCH sign inside. Despite his plea for seclusion, his room became a gathering place for helpers and fans in a half-dozen disciplines, a smoking lounge, a reference desk, a tourists' attraction, and sometimes a stop-off for junkies and thieves. Far from being a recluse, he would roam the halls (using the elevator so much at one point that the one near his room was turned off) and haunt the lobby, socializing and fundraising. He began to gather a modicum of local fame when Jonas Mekas's column began praising his art, and even though hardly anyone had seen his work, he became someone who was pointed out to Chelsea visitors.

A SELECT CHELSEA PERSONAE

Up on the Roof: Shirley Clarke

Clarke moved into the Chelsea in 1965 to escape her marriage and to retreat from Hollywood's interest in her after she won an Academy Award for one documentary film and was nominated for another. Her role in Harry's life at this point was far more than one of kindness; she was fascinated by his films, and saw a chance to work with him. She had already made twelve films, each of them taking a different direction. Among them were *Bridges-Go-Round*, which superimposed various Manhattan bridges and animated them by camera movement; *The Connection*, a cinema verité filming of a Jack Gelber play that had been banned for its use of obscenity, and was promptly banned again when her film appeared; and *The Cool World*, which followed a young Black man's life in Harlem. Jonas Mekas and Shirley had founded the Film-Makers' Cooperative for independent films in 1962, and she was one of the first to declare the New American Cinema movement of the sixties.

At the Chelsea in 1966, she was completing *Portrait of Jason*, an interview with a Black gay male prostitute, and finishing *Kaleido-scope* with Harry, which was an unlikely subject for either of them—a film funded by the Office of Economic Opportunity and made for the Women's Job Corps. In it a group of women fancied making a film together and tried out different genres, from documentary to musical, TV drama to advertisement, all in twenty-eight minutes. In a handwritten note about the project, Clarke declared "I 'gave' this film to Harry—and he shows it as part of his repertoire at the Anthology Film Archives. I helped him make the film in order to get him back on his feet creatively—it was conceived one nite when stoned at Tedlock's where Harry took me to show me a TV sculpture . . . I had brought along my Teleidescope to look at the images with and asked Harry why film could never give you what I was looking at. He said he could build a special lens and do it. So I said I'd help and I did and he did." Though *Kaleidoscope* seems to be lost, fragments of it were later used in Harry's *Film No. 16: The Tin Woodman's Dream.*

Clarke received a grant through the Museum of Modern Art in 1970 that enabled well-known artists to work in a different medium. Her plan was to develop new ways of film editing by using new video recording technology. But once she had bought all the gear used in videotaping, she realized it had possibilities that excited her more than film: video was cheaper, required no processing, and needed no darkened theater. It could be shown and transmitted instantly, without editing (she had learned that tape editing at the time was difficult if not nearly impossible); it was a highly interactive form, in which more than one camera could be used at the same time and the images from both combined on multiple monitors. Even members of the audience could join in the creation of new images by various means during projection. To her, video went beyond the limits of a solitary film camera or the painter's canvas to something close to the shared performance of a jazz band: "Mainly we need the skill to see our own images in our own monitors and at the same time see what everyone else is doing. We need to acquire the ability to see in much the same way that a jazz musician can hear what he is playing and at the same time hear what the other musicians are doing and together they make music."

She had a penthouse at the Chelsea that included a Mayan-like pyramid originally built to support a flagpole that she called the Tee-Pee Totem Pole. She centered her work there and gathered a collective she called the Tee Pee Video Space Troupe, which for five years experimented with video at nights, often all night, creating events and installations that stacked monitors in various configurations, perhaps as a human body or a Ferris wheel, mosaics of monitors, each monitor projecting a different image.

Soon, those nocturnal productions and Shirley's parties began to draw a long list of art, literary, and film figures whom Harry met, including Agnès Varda, Nam June Paik, Virgil Thomson, Louis Malle, Susan Sontag, Alan Watts, Viva, Peter Brook, Jean Rouch, Arthur C. Clarke, Shelley Winters, Nicholas Ray, Ornette Coleman, and Jean-Luc Godard, who asked to be introduced to Harry when he came to New York.

Harry and Shirley were now both working with multiple screens; they thought of natural sounds as part of their works (roof recording picked up pigeons gurgling, street sounds, and steam pipes) and not noises to be limited (Harry soon began making film and audio soundscapes that made extraneous sounds the focus of his films). Both thought of what they were doing as a performative rather than a recording art, and jazz was their model. Making a video or changing the way a film was being projected in front of an audience could be as risky as a jazz performance, where improvisors take chances and reject the "licks" and clichéd figures they have inherited and practiced.

The Hostess: Peggy Biderman

Biderman was close to Harry in age, and had moved into the Chelsea just before him. She had been active in the civil rights movement, worked in the Museum of Modern Art bookstore, and was now living in the tiniest of Chelsea rooms, with a shared bath, buying carefully chosen items from thrift shops and washing and ironing them to sell on the street. She and Patti Smith liked to joke that they were the only people in the hotel who were officially employed. Unofficially, she was the greeter of new residents to the Chelsea, the house photographer, the guide to shops and services, aid to the sick and the elderly, and she had made Robert Mapplethorpe, Gregory Corso, and Harry her boys to be watched over. Despite the teasing that Harry directed at her, she saw to his health, made sure he was eating, and kept him afloat with small gifts of money and encouragement.

Poor Little Rich Girl: Isabella Gardner

Isabella Gardner, the great-niece of the fabled doyenne of Boston society Isabella Stewart Gardner, after years of squandering her talent, beauty, and inheritance, moved into the Chelsea in 1966, another escapee from a failed marriage. She settled into large rooms on the seventh floor, where she entertained the Newark Museum of Art's curator Mildred Baker, the Romanian Count Roderick Gheka (a descendant of Prince Vlad the Impaler), the composer Virgil Thomson, the poet Stefan Brecht (the son of Bertolt Brecht), and the playwright Arnold Weinstein, Gardner's sometime lover. Down the hall in his crowded single room, Harry was playing Bob Dylan's new album, *Blonde on Blonde*, and Stefan's father's opera *Rise and Fall of the City of Mahagonny* in heavy rotation.

But Gardner was not happy at the Chelsea. In a letter to the artist and country music writer Jay Bolotin, she wrote:

> [Stanley Bard] is hated by the entire staff, and deplored by the more stable members of the cesspool cum lunatic asylum to which he has reduced the once noble Chelsea . . . The hotel has deteriorated terribly as far as the inhabitants are concerned. It is full of lonely hearts and the hotel is a comfort to them (all of us) . . . The owners of the restaurant (El Quijote) and the waiters are protective of me. Especially protective as far as the tragic gifted monster Harry Smith is concerned . . . Robberies are rife. Beatings, rapes, even homicides. The police appear to be paid by both the hotel and the restaurant . . .

Harry entered Gardner's life when her daughter, Rose Van Kirk, moved into the hotel. (Gardner was also supporting her stepdaughter, Anneke Van Kirk, Woody Guthrie's last wife, who, according to Harry, had given him some of Woody's song sheets.) Rose apprenticed with Harry in studies of Kabbalah, magic, and anthropology; Harry sometimes instructed her while he was in what she called a trance, from one to twelve hours a day "with very few breaks," as she described it. She and Harry apparently had some form of emotional relationship, though she was paying him large sums of her mother's money for the privilege.

Rose was in Spain in the spring of 1970 when she discovered she was pregnant (possibly by a waiter at El Quijote). The baby was born when she came back to New York in September, and she returned to Spain two months later with the child, leaving her mother instructions to tell Stanley Bard she'd pay him the rent when she got back, and she should see to Harry's health: "I know you are extremely ambivalent in regards to Harry especially in relation to me but I will never forgive you if you don't keep me posted on how he is—often . . . And try to impress on him that he means as much to me as anyone in the world."

When she told her mother that she was in Haiti, and that she had been made a voodoo princess, Gardner was livid, and wrote her that there could be "no possibility of a meeting of minds or spirits, as voodoo represents, forcibly, an aspect of the forces of evil . . ." Rose's response was that her stepmother needed to read Maya Deren and Alfred Métraux on Haiti, books recommended to her by Harry. Gardner replied that Harry was the sickest man she'd ever met. When Rose later committed herself to a psychiatric hospital in Connecticut, her mother blamed Harry for turning her into his slave and driving her mad with mysticism.

Dr. Herbert Krohn, singer, poet, and the Chelsea's default physician, supported Gardner's diagnosis of the "weasel weighing about ninety-five pounds of distilled ironical VENOM":

He collected Seminole with birds flying everywhere in this room, shitting. He would open his closet, and instead of his own clothes—I do not think he ever changed his clothes—he had a collection of seventy Seminole costumes that he has written a study on, an anthropological study . . . He was always trying to get people to kill themselves, suggesting suicide as a serious thing. He was a very destructive person.

Harry had been studying Cuban Santeria and Haitian vodun, and continued for years. From time to time he put that knowledge to the test. When William Moritz was traveling to Ottawa in 1976 with Elfriede Fischinger, the widow of Oskar Fischinger, to attend a retrospective of her husband's work, they stopped on the way in New York City to see Harry at the Chelsea:

His room was covered from floor to ceiling with boxes and stacks of books, artworks, periodicals, records, figurines, and many other things, so that one could hardly get around much. I had visited him twice before, so I knew what to expect, but Elfriede was flabbergasted, and then thrilled at the dozens of curious and priceless things that kept emerging from the seeming chaos (which Harry, however, seemed to know down to the last scrap, and could retrieve any particular item with relative ease). He spoke glowingly of how inspirational Oskar was to him, and said it must be nice for her to have his legacy so well preserved. Elfriede told him frankly how many things—films, paintings and papers—had not been properly preserved yet. "Well, something should be done about that!" Harry proclaimed, and disappeared for a moment into his "Archive." He emerged shortly with a few magic paraphernalia and a live chicken, and proceeded to perform a ritual, chanting, dancing around, and finally sacrificing the chicken to use its blood to mark symbols on various objects including Elfriede's hand. "Now," he said in conclusion, "you should not be having so much financial worry, and most of your precious things will be taken care of in the next few years."

Moritz confirmed that Harry's magic seemed to have worked, as the Frankfurt Filmmuseum and the National Endowment for the Arts began preserving and restoring Fischinger's films shortly after.

The Baron: Jacques Loup Stern

A new resident appeared in the Chelsea in 1970: Jacques Loup Stern, a rich Frenchman, crippled by polio, and a flamboyant poet and novelist given to wild stories of a heritage of nobility (he insisted on being addressed as Baron Jacques Stern de Rothschild). He was also prone to drug overdoses and violent outbursts of rage, smashing furniture and writing on the walls. The poet Gregory Corso had met him in Paris in 1958 and brought him to meet Kerouac and Burroughs in the "Beat Hotel," a seedy lodging house without a name in the Latin Quarter. Stern was generous with money and drugs to the then unknown Beats, and introduced them to Harry Phipps, equally wealthy and charitable with drugs and clothing.

Stern soon became a well-known personage at the Chelsea, noted for stories such as his days as a race car driver, his claims to noble birth, and the scripts he had written for Terry Southern. Patti Smith dedicated her book *Ha! Ha! Houdini* to him. William Burroughs was especially impressed. They both had studied anthropology at Harvard, and once traveled together to London to take a cure for heroin. He declared Stern the greatest writer of their generation, and wrote an introduction to Stern's self-published 1965 novel, *The Fluke*. The Baron in turn was free with cash and praise: he thought Harry and Burroughs were geniuses. He was working on a biography of Burroughs, and offered to produce a film of Burroughs's novel *Junkie*, with Terry Southern as screenwriter, Dennis Hopper directing, and Samuel Beckett and Bob Dylan as lead actors.

He often picked up his friends in his chauffeured limo. Andrew Noren recalled seeing his car pull up in front of a theater for a screening, and out popped Harry, followed by mysterious, wealthy-looking acolytes—no idea who they were. "I remember he was wearing shades and a rather snazzy summer suit, and he was looking good."

Harry and Stern dreamed up an idea for a book of poetry, paintings, and photographs, *Evensongs of Exstacy*. The poets were Harry, Jacques, Ginsberg, Corso, and Peter Orlovsky, "with selections by two previously unpublished poets, Conception Estramadura and Jonathan Robbins." The illustrations were by Malcolm McNeill, Rosita Dewez, Count Aymon de Roussy de Sales, and Jacques, who also designed the book. Harry's poems were filled with equal amounts of erudition and the usual words with fricatives and velars that he sometimes liked to blurt out to shock those new to him. The book was completed but never published.

The Morning of the Magicians by the French journalists Louis Pauwels and Jacques Bergier had become an occult favorite by 1970, bringing ufology, alchemy, alien invasions, spiritual philosophy, and conspiracy theories together by what they claimed was documentation that reinterpreted historical events as occult phenomena. From the time that Harry first became known in New York, he was often spoken of as a magician, which some meant literally, others metaphorically. Harry did nothing to discourage either perception. He, too, was lifting the cover off received wisdom and exposing another reality. The trouble was that other people in the Chelsea were also claiming that role. Stanley Amos, for instance, a British occultist who ran an art gallery in his rooms and was visited by curators from the Metropolitan Museum of Art and *Artforum* magazine. (Robert Mapplethorpe had his first showing in Amos's gallery.) Jacques Stern also announced his powers of magic, and when a rare fifteenth-century manuscript disappeared from his apartment, he and Harry were seen battling in the lobby with tarot cards and curses thrown at each other. "A battle of speed vs. alcohol," remarked Dr. Gross.

Surrealism and the Dogon: Mary Beach and Claude Pélieu

Beach and Pélieu were artists, writers, translators, and friends of Allen Ginsberg from San Francisco, where they had worked at City Lights bookstore, and Mary had published William Burroughs, Bob Kaufman, and others under her own imprint. She had recently become aware of the work of Marcel Griaule, a French ethnographer who had spent much of his life studying the Dogon people of current-day Mali, and she translated one of his later books, *Le renard pâle* (*The Pale Fox*), published in France in 1965. Griaule was one of France's first anthropologists, and concentrated on philosophy, art, and language at a time when most anthropologists in Europe were more focused on social organization. Though his research was admired for its creativity and infinite detail, some anthropologists who later followed up his work with the Dogon were never able to replicate much of his research, and many of his findings were questioned. The publication of *Le renard pâle* after his death by his colleague Germaine Dieterlen faced even closer critical reading. According to their research, the legends of the Dogon seemed to suggest that they had very advanced knowledge of astronomy, and knew about the existence of Sirius B (a second star orbiting around Sirius A) without the aid of technology. To ethnographers this was a doubtful finding, but for occultists it opened new doors of interest, and to some evangelical Christians it was a sign of God's footsteps. Harry and Shirley discussed the book at length under the stars on the roof of the Chelsea.

Harry gave a copy of the Dogon translation to Arthur Young in hopes that he might pay for its publication, but Young passed it on to his student Robert Temple in 1968, who claimed that the CIA later stole that copy from him, and that MI5 was interested in seeing it. Temple's popular 1976 book, *The Sirius Mystery*, claimed that the Dogon had either learned of such things from an advanced civilization such as Egypt's, or they had received it from aliens in ancient times.

Harry, still attempting to find a publisher for Beach's English translation in 1980, wrote Arthur Young that Beach had given him her copy "as my personal property to see or dispose of as I saw fit. Nonetheless I feel that part of any payment for the translation should go to her." Shortly after, Harry contacted the Theosophical University Press of California, asking if they would be interested in publishing it. They responded by asking him if he might ask Mary Beach to donate the book to them "as a labor of love." When Harry replied that he was now the owner of the English translation, he was offered $1,000 plus royalties, but no agreement followed. It was not published in English until 1986, when it was translated by Stephen C. Infantino of the Continuum Foundation of Chino Valley, Arizona.

Panna Grady: Doyenne of the Downtown

Though not a resident of the Chelsea, Panna Grady, an elegant American heiress, had the resources to bring the hotel to her home at her New York apartment in the Dakota (large enough that Andy Warhol shot some of his movies in it). It was a veritable arts salon where writers like Norman Mailer, Anthony Burgess, Peter Handke, Diane di Prima, Burroughs, and Ginsberg gathered. Harry, Herbert Huncke, and Gregory Corso drifted in and out, asking for money and sometimes receiving it. Her parties (and her appetites) were the stuff of legend—elaborate, large, with care to mix Uptown intellectuals with those of the Lower East Side.

There were others: Leonard Cohen was often around Harry, listening rather than talking. He sometimes asked Harry to dinner, even though Harry might show up with a small entourage that also had to be fed. Tennessee Williams recalled seeing Harry's films in the Village and talking theosophy with him. The painter and filmmaker Doris Totten Chase, like Harry, also from Anacortes, Washington, and the same age, lived on the same floor of the Chelsea, but wanted nothing to do with him.

FUG UNIVERSITY

Back in 1962, Ed Sanders, a poet, environmentalist, and student of the classics and Egyptology at New York University, met Harry at Stanley's bar on Avenue A and Twelfth Street. Ed was already known for his poetry and for having just founded the mimeo-zine *Fuck You / A Magazine of the Arts*. H. L. "Doc" Humes, a novelist and a founder of *The Paris Review*, introduced Harry to Ed as a magician and filmmaker. Harry bought rounds of drinks and boasted that he had just received a grant from the Rockefeller Foundation to make a film based on Gaston Maspero's translation of the *Egyptian Tale of Two Brothers*. He was clutching a first edition of Aleister Crowley's *Book of Lies*, and was declaring it a work of genius. Ed had his doubts, especially when later that evening he spotted the Crowley book in the bar's urinal. But once he and Harry had run into each other at Stanley's and various film screenings at the Charles Theater, Harry did some drawings for Ed's magazine and became his guide into film-making, encouraging him by showing him how cheaply a film could be made.

In late 1964, Sanders and the poet Tuli Kupferberg got the idea to form a band of poets and musicians after they had seen Robert Creeley and LeRoi Jones dancing to the Beatles on the jukebox at the Dom, the Polish club that was rented out for dances and other events. Beatlemania had seriously reached the Village. Ginsberg wrote a poem about their performance at the Portland Memorial Coliseum and celebrated them as helping white people rediscover their bodies.

But Tuli and Ed were not that impressed by those early Beatles lyrics and thought they could do something better. Musicians and poets might seem an odd mix for a band, but at that moment, both were being rousted by the police in the Village, one group for where they played, the other for both where they read and what they read. Coffee shops and small clubs like Cafe Wha?, Le Métro, Café Bizarre, and the Gaslight had been closed due to having bands performing in bars where no food was served, or for obscenity at poetry readings. New York's weird, draconian cabaret laws turned filmmakers, poets, and musicians into petty criminals, and the police into critics. As Lenny Bruce said of his stand-up routine, cops were doing his act before juries after each of his performances.

Their response was to relocate their performance sites, and it was in just such homegrown outlaw spaces that the band that Tuli and Ed named the Fugs would surprise even the hippest boho audience with songs that were profane, blasphemous, adolescent, elegiac, and rude commentaries on topics roiling and swirling through the culture of Greenwich Village. They drew on forms of music emerging at the moment: folk, blues, surf music, and the Beatles, but at the same time used lyrics borrowed from old country music and poetry from the English Romantics and Victorians. They were called the underground Rolling Stones, the first punk band, and celebrated as a group that merged pop sensibility with that of the literati. The Fugs surfaced at the same moment that Frank Zappa on the West Coast was rerouting rhythm and blues, free jazz, and Eurotrash avant-garde compositions into a new form of high vulgarity. Both groups could bring together teens in search of gross-outs, hippies laughing at the mix of political savvy and cheap sexual jokes, and older folks tired of folk-revival sanctimony.

Sanders, meanwhile, had opened Peace Eye Bookstore on Tenth Street in a former Kosher butcher shop, where he sold books and gathered together pamphlets and notices for civil rights, free drugs, free sex, and the anti–Vietnam War and ban-the-bomb movements. Soon, he was hosting poetry readings and underground comic book art exhibitions, and the store was becoming a gathering place for rock and folk fans and musicians. It was there that the Fugs practiced and first performed, framed by banners of hand-silk-screened flowers by Andy Warhol. Soon they moved to off-off-Broadway venues like the American Theater for Poets and did midnight shows in the Bridge at St. Marks Place. Though they had come together for fun, their audiences began to include reviewers from newspapers and literary magazines, the New York City Police, and the FBI, and some of the reviews made several of the Fugs the subjects of criminal files. Harry, as a nonperformer and enthusiastic supporter, escaped their wrath: no FBI record ever existed for him. But he attended those early performances, and loved their folk-song mockery, which reminded him of the Jack Spicer radio programs back in Berkeley. Later, he even recorded himself singing what he called "imitations of folksongs," parodies of classic ballads and folk songs with titles like "Something Is Wrong," "Sugar Cube," and "If I Should Die on a Railroad Train." Sanders often called out to Harry in the audience, and the Fugs also included his name in "Nothing," a song they used for apocalyptic freak-outs at the end of performances with strobe lights blinking and musicians rolling on the floor, ripping up Warhol's banners, and breaking things. It quintessentially caught the spirit of the moment—the hopelessness of the Vietnam war and rising fears over racial turmoil. The Fugs shouted out a virtual glossary of the Village's most hallowed and detested concerns—the arts, sex, *Sing Out!* magazine, Folkways Records, the names of leaders of both political parties and those of the gods of the New Left, the meaninglessness of the days of the week, the months, recent years, all dutifully recited in English, Yiddish, and Spanish, and each followed by a cry of "nothing."

Harry touted the Fugs to Moe Asch as a jug band (instead of using the group's own choices for names, the Yodeling Socialists or the

Freaks). Although he had never recorded anything aimed at a pop audience and the Fugs had only played publicly two or three times, Moe agreed to pay for a recording with Harry acting as unpaid producer. In April 1965, they arrived at a studio with more than twenty songs, including an Everly Brothers treatment of William Blake's "Ah, Sunflower Weary of Time" and "How Sweet I Roamed from Field to Field" that sounded like early bluegrass, a surf version of "Slum Goddess," and a country and western "Boobs a Lot." None of them had ever recorded, and they milled aimlessly around the studio until Harry yelled, "Just get started!" and later breaking a bottle of rum against the wall to spur them on. He also broke studio rules by letting the recording tape run, capturing everything that happened, including false starts, his suggestions for positioning the microphones, private conversations, and even the talk concerning the Folkways contract when it arrived during the session. Some of this ephemera wound up on their finished recordings, introducing an extreme form of vérité into the world.

Moe liked the results enough that he offered them a second recording session in June as part of a deal with Verve Records that sought a wider audience for Folkways artists like Pete Seeger, Lead Belly, and Dave Van Ronk, and for new artists such as the Blues Project and Laura Nyro. But the Fugs were too far out even for the company that had signed Frank Zappa, and Moe decided to introduce them on his own new subsidiary label, Broadside Records. Harry showed Ed how professionals edit and sequence songs from tape to records, and in the fall of 1965, they released *The Village Fugs Sing Ballads of Contemporary Protest, Point of Views, and General Dissatisfaction* (later rereleased as *The Fugs First Album* on ESP Disk). Not that Harry was always that disciplined. Shortly before the record went on sale in 1965, he came into Peace Eye hoping to ask for $2 from Ed. When he told him he didn't have it, Harry ripped up the three scholarly books he had with him—Frances Densmore's *Cheyenne and Arapaho Music*, Bruno Nettl's *North American Indian Musical Styles*, and N. J. Van Warmelo's *Place Names of the Kruger National Park*, then grabbed his own Tree of

Life print off the wall and tore it in half. Ed later framed the trashed books and put them up on the wall as art.

Even though Harry had ceased working on new films, he was now being taken seriously as a filmmaker. Films called "underground" had gained enough cachet by the mid-1960s to be screened at most major college towns, art schools, and museums. The French New Wave, Andy Warhol's turn to filmmaking, new technology that made film cheaper—all helped pull Harry into the New American Cinema group. He sometimes traveled along with his films to places like the Boston Tea Party concert venue or Queens Museum, and on those occasions, Harry was the whole show, sometimes quite literally, talking over the films or refusing to show them once he was there. When he was brought to Yale in the fall of 1965 by P. Adams Sitney, then still an undergraduate, to screen *Film No. 12* at a "Filmmakers Showcase" series, Harry showed up late and drunk, having stopped at every bar along the way from the railroad station. "He stumbled onto the stage and said 'Good evening, faggots,' then, noticing a woman in the front row he apologized, and said, 'Good evening faggots and dykes.'" He suddenly introduced *Heaven and Earth Magic* by saying, "This film ruined my life." He next stopped the film and demanded vodka. As it was too late to get liquor from a store, a faculty member went home to find a bottle. When a woman asked why they had to wait until he got the vodka to see the film, he warned, "Shut up, lady, and for that you're not going to get any." Sitney recalls that at that same performance Harry referred to Giordano Bruno as the inventor of cinema, since in his 1591 thesis, *De innumerabilibus, immenso, et infigurabili*, he wrote that "there are an infinite number of universes, each possessing a similar world with some slight differences—a hand raised in one, lowered in another"—so that the perception of motion is an act of the mind swiftly choosing a course among an infinite number of these "freeze-frames," and thereby animating them.

Once, when John Cohen asked Harry about the difference between his films and his *Anthology* records, Harry replied:

> Movies are a different thing. They're a technological thing, more than music is. Anybody who listens to music can buy a guitar for eight dollars and learn to play it and sing, at least as sufficiently to please themselves and a few friends, whereas to make movies of the same subject is ridiculous, nobody would do it. So naturally my movies are made as a kind of final gesture towards film. They've just about run their course. There's no reason to have movies anymore, life is much more horrible and adventurous and everything . . . I've never done much with them as far as elucidating what the subject matter is but they are like the basic rhythms that're in music. It's also a way of making money, more than Folkways anthologies, which are a total loss.

Harry's research into ancient astrology for Arthur Young was continuing in 1966, though Young was sorely tested by Harry, whose letters and reports always ended by requesting grants for various projects. Young's diaries and notebooks from that period contain jottings such as "Harry Smith descends on me and lives in Philadelphia," or Harry's name turns up in a list of "disturbances" in his life. But their lives remained intertwined for at least thirty years, and Young credited Harry's help publicly. In 1956, for example, Young was trying to integrate notions from mythology and astrology with mathematical concepts and was having trouble understanding the significance of the number seven, when Harry Smith "reminded me of the torus. The topology of the torus, or donut shape, requires seven hues in order to color a map on the surface with no two adjacent areas having the same color . . . Harry's reminder helped everything fall into place." When Young thanked him for his important contribution, Harry's response was odd, even for him: "Well, I knew I was supposed to give this to you, because of a dream I had. I was driving a car along a mountain road with my girl, and the car started to go off the road. I quickly grabbed the spare tire and saved it, instead of saving the girl." Young, always the straight man with Harry, dryly interpreted the dream: "The tire, of course, is a torus."

When the New York City police arrested Ed Sanders and closed down Peace Eye Bookstore in 1964, Allen Ginsberg created a Committee on Poetry to help defend poets and artists who were arrested or harassed. In 1966 he widened the role of the committee to be of greater help to writers and arts people. Their charter statement read:

> This group is formed to gather money from those who have it in amounts excess to their needs and disburse it among poets and philosophers who lack personal finance or wherewithal to accomplish small material projects in the society at large. The committee's money will be used to sustain artists and their projects in times of stress; promote freedom of expression where such expression is threatened by social prejudice or outside force; publish works of art which have no immediate commercial vehicles for publicity; aid sick, wounded or nervous creative souls who might otherwise be financially isolated; participate in projects for altering the consciousness of the nation toward a more humane spirit

of adhesiveness prophesied by Whitman; give joy to writers and artists who wish to escape unpleasant circumstances and travel or meditate; help unlucky poets and painters avoid confinement in jails and madhouses or ease their return to freedom; and otherwise aid in spiritual emergencies.

Allen Ginsberg,
March 26, 1966

Ginsberg was often the chief donor, and Harry, along with a few others, like Gregory Corso, Orlovsky, Huncke, and James Schuyler, were the principal beneficiaries of the committee's grants. Whenever he was able, Ginsberg was always supporting several people, and he would aid Harry for the rest of his life. Barry Miles once saw Ginsberg in San Francisco just after he had received royalties from City Lights. "He sat in a café and wrote out an entire checkbook to impoverished friends such as Corso and the artist-filmmaker Harry Smith, underground newspapers that had been busted, and political and sociological pressure groups. He kept hardly anything for himself." On another occasion, Allen sent a postdated check for $250 to Mekas in September 1971, asking that the money be given to Harry now, but to hold the check until November 1, 1972. "I'll give a few poetry readings in October end, so money should be in bank to cover it by then—I'm broke and in debt now so I can't do it smoother."

WE'LL NEED A COW

Though Harry usually steered clear of acting on political issues, and had missed early efforts to protest the Vietnam War while he was doing his research in Oklahoma and Florida, when he returned to Greenwich Village mass demonstrations were breaking out in New York City and across the country. The civil rights movement already had enormous effect on politics and culture. The Fugs were involved with the movement, inspired by the power of the religious songs of Black Americans to move an audience to action. Freedom marches and sit-ins gave shape to free speech, free sex, free drugs, free jazz, freedom riders, be-ins, teach-ins, fly-ins, and sweep-ins. A massive "Great Human-Be-In: A Gathering of the Tribes" in San Francisco in January 1967 drew together Beats, hippies, old and new political radicals, free-spirited teens, eco-activists, and Hells Angels. Poets like Ginsberg and Gary Snyder emceed the event, while the Grateful Dead and other San Francisco bands enlivened the crowd.

In New York, Happenings had, a few years earlier, been a small art movement of painters and a few musicians beginning in 1960. Though they lasted only until 1963, they were highly influential. More structured than they appeared, Happenings involved audiences in short-lived events that crossed the line from art to everyday life. These artists' performances in cramped, derelict spaces could make abstract expressionist paintings in art galleries suddenly seem stale, static, and boring. They were imagining ways to make visual art move, to go beyond the wall and make it more participatory for the spectator. Allan Kaprow, one of the initiators of Happenings, wrote a manifesto in 1958 after seeing Jackson Pollock's action paintings: "Not satisfied with the suggestion through paint of our other senses, we shall utilize the specific substances of sight, sound, movements, people, odors, touch." The artists behind Happenings felt they should be in the event to see what it was like and to be an example to the audience.

Even though Happenings might have scripts, the events were highly visual and improvised. (Kaprow said "a happening is something that just happens to happen.") Many of the small audiences at these events were likely to be other artists, and they attracted some of the most famous—Duchamp was a regular at many of them. Claes Oldenburg's were among the most interesting and dramatic, and since he and Harry were friends, Harry went to a number of them. Oldenburg's *Sports*, in early October 1962, at Green Gallery in New York, was the first of his shows uptown in a real gallery. The invited audience of twenty-five included Andy Warhol, the mathematician Samuel Wagstaff Jr., and the artists John Chamberlain, Martha Edelheit, and Harry Smith. Though he is never mentioned as an influence on Happenings, Harry's performances at his own film showings and his actions, which took the event beyond the projector and the screen, were well-known among artists in the Village.

Susan Sontag, in a 1966 essay, had already singled out Harry as a performative filmmaker:

> It is because the film is an object, a totality that is set, that movie roles are identical with the actors' performances; while in the theatre (in the West, an additive rather than an organic art?) only the written play is "fixed," an object and therefore existing apart from any staging of it. Yet this dichotomy is not beyond dispute. Just as movies needn't necessarily be designed to be shown in theatres at all (they can be intended for more continuous and casual looking), a movie *may* be altered from one projection to the next. Harry Smith, when he runs off his own films, makes each projection an unrepeatable performance. And, again, it is not true that all theatre is only about written plays which may be given a good or a bad production. In Happenings and other recent theatre-events, we are precisely being offered "plays" identical with their productions in the same sense as the screenplay is identical with the film.

When the anti–Vietnam War movement began to mobilize in 1967 for a gathering in Washington, some thought the Pentagon should be their focus. The five-sided polygon figure's long history and deep meaning for early Christians and Freemasons suggested to Ginsberg, Gary Snyder, Jerry Rubin, and Ed Sanders that the Department of

Defense's building should be the site at which an exorcism could be staged by joining hands, encircling the building, and chanting against the demons. Then someone proposed levitating the building: it could be the ultimate Happening, rather than a traditional orderly protest. After serious calculation it was decided to raise the building twenty-two feet into the air. During their negotiations with the military, the planners claimed that they agreed not to raise it more than three feet. But how to do it? Sanders was given the task of planning the ritual:

> For the actual Exorcism/Levitation of the Pentagon, I con-
> sulted with my authority on all things magic—Harry Smith.
> As long as we were ACTUALLY going to exorcise demons,
> I figured we might as well prepare a structure that, at least
> in the theories of actual Mageia, might do the job. Harry
> advised consecrating a circle around the Pentagon and using
> the alchemical symbols of Earth, Air, Fire, and Water. He
> also suggested adding the Egyptian elements to the Exor-
> cism, such as a cow, to represent the goddess Hathor. (We
> did have a cow prepared, painted with mythic symbols, but
> the police prevented it from getting near the Pentagon.)

A mini-demonstration was planned for the press at the Village Theater, and on October 13 a small model of the Pentagon with wires attached and a cornmeal circle drawn around it was lifted above the stage while the gatherers chanted. Then, on October 20, the Fugs flew to Washington for a performance at a local club. Shirley Clarke and Barbara Rubin filmed their arrival at the airport, and the next day they continued filming the exorcism ritual in the Pentagon parking lot from a flatbed truck. (Kenneth Anger, who disagreed with the plans for the lift, worked his own magic from under the truck.) Sanders said two hundred thousand marchers gathered as the chanting of "Out, Demons, Out" rang off the concrete walls ("Jericho" was the word of the day). Sanders told interviewers that they did elevate the building, but they forgot to rotate it and so the war would continue. Harry, the theorist, had stayed home.

THE COLLECTOR

Harry was a collector from childhood to his death. There were pop-up books, Scots tartans, Seminole dresses and patches, paper airplanes, Ukrainian painted eggs, American Indian artifacts, books and journals, phonograph and tape recordings, folk song and poetry texts, tarot and playing cards, gourds, images clipped from old newspapers and catalogs, antique door keys, Mennonite farm tools, string figures, quilts, blankets, artworks, toys, crushed cans, and, on the darker side, frozen dead birds, the recorded death coughs of bums, tattoo blood patches, and his own bodily fluids. Harry believed if he could collect enough examples of anything, he might make a discovery, find a connection, even if he had never known any of the artists who had created them. It was the mode of operation that drove all of his collecting. If he found a sample of every Seminole dressmaker's work, those designs might provide a road map to the heavens. A collection of every known version of the folk poem "Shine and the Titanic" could open the door to some part of Black American culture.

Ukrainian Easter eggs, for example: "What I've been interested in are unconscious developments of cosmographic notions that appear on the eggs, so I haven't had to know the people who made them." Ukrainian painted eggs (*pysanky*) are decorated with a variety of designs, many of them rural, such as rams' horns, stars, combs, rakes, radiating spokes, and the Tree of Life. One common motif is an endless line wrapping around the egg representing eternity. He saw in the eggs parallels to his own techniques in making his early films: they were often batiked, and intricately shaped into elaborate geometric patterns. Their delicacy and fragility seemed to interest him as well, and he was particularly careful in guarding the ones on display in his room, shouting at visitors not to move or they might explode. He may not have needed to know the name of the eggs' artists, but he was able to identify the work of anonymous painters by the repeated patterns of their work. Every Easter he would head for a shop on East Seventh Street across from the First Ukrainian Church of God to buy what he could. At one point he claimed to have spent $5,000 on eggs, and had made notes on twenty-nine thousand designs and spoke of donating the collection to the Göteborg Museum. But somehow all but a few disappeared. Some speculated that they were stolen by a junkie in the Chelsea.

His collections were not something he necessarily wanted to display, though in the confines of the small rooms he lived in they were nearly always visible. One collection not visible was his paper airplanes, something he seldom mentioned and kept folded flat in boxes. Some knew that it was one of his interests, but only a few had spoken to him about it, usually when they saw him finding them on the street. Remembering a trip he took with Harry to the Strand Bookstore, Bill Breeze said, "He found several planes and would immediately stop to fish out a pencil and make notes on it. As I recall he was interested in the changes in their morphology over the years, with some plane designs disappearing and then mysteriously reappearing years later." There are many ways to fold a paper airplane, to produce flying origami. He kept an array of examples of different folding methods and noted the ones he threw away as duplicates or less interesting. "He was always, always, always looking for them on the street any time he could find them," according to M. Henry Jones, an animator and 3-D photographer who worked with Harry. "He would run out in front of the cabs to get them, you know, before they got run over. I remember one time, we saw one in the air and he was just running everywhere trying to figure out where it was going to be." It might appear that paper airplanes are no longer being made, but at the time Harry collected them it was also believed that they had been forgotten. It was, and still is, a classic case of being hidden in plain sight.

Between 1961 and 1983, he filled several boxes with paper planes, of which only 251 still remain. Each was carefully noted as to the time and location of their finding, and a map of Manhattan was marked with each site. Harry was believed to have donated all his airplanes to the Smithsonian Institution's National Air and Space Museum, but when Rani Singh went to Washington to research the collection, they were found in the Smithsonian Center for Folklife and Cultural Heritage, where they had never been put on exhibit.

Whatever Harry's purpose in finding them, they are quite beautiful and varied in their design, color, and paper. They were made from restaurant menus, a page from a phone book, a scribbled note, a receipt for a mink coat, or a flyer for a Mothers of Invention performance. They may have been stepped on, driven over, or soaked by rain, but they were saved by Harry, the urban gleaner, and are truly examples of alchemy, of turning dross into gold, as Klacsmann and Lampert suggest in *Paper Airplanes: The Collections of Harry Smith, Catalogue Raisonné, Volume 1*. Hotels, flophouses, and friends' apartments served as make-do museums, much as that abandoned shed did in Anacortes, Washington, when he was a child.

Many of his films were made up from collections. He cut out figures of people, animals, and objects from magazines, categorized them, and put them in envelopes. Later he would plan a sequence of the cutouts, or just dump them together on the table and let chance determine their order. Harry also made lists of things—a modernist practice in itself—whether the things were in his collections or not. Sometimes they were indices, lists of names, or numbers (especially the numbers of folktales or page numbers in books and articles). Others appear to be mnemonic devices to recall something, a form of collage where seemingly unrelated things on a list can form their own patterns of relationships, or jar the reader into seeing how disparate items might create new meanings when seen together.

In later years he kept meticulous notes on where, when, and how much he paid for books. This may have had some scholarly value to him or others, but it was also his means of negotiating with bookstores, sometimes selling them back to the store, then later buying them back, much in the same way he used pawnshops. It's impossible to know how many books and journals he acquired in his lifetime, but at the time of his death he had 4,204, and the price he had paid and noted totaled $62,550 ($117,260 in current value).

When asked what he was going to do with his collections, or what they meant, he answered that was something others should do: "I'm leaving it to the future to figure out the exact purpose of having all these rotten eggs, the blankets, the Seminole patchwork I never look at, and the records that I never listen to. However, it's as justifiable as anything that can be done—as any other type of research, and is probably more justifiable than more violent types, like fighting with someone or becoming an export banker. It is a way of fooling away the time, harmlessly as possible."

9

Mahagonny
1967–1977

Harry appeared unfazed by the *Wizard of Oz* failure, and instead seemed energized by Warhol's recent success with film. Andy had re-defined what a film could be, much as he had expanded the definition of painting. *Chelsea Girls* had drawn a great deal of attention and was shown in theaters that would never have touched his earlier films like *Sleep* or *Empire*. Warhol was patient with Harry's drunken insults to him and anyone else he encountered on his visits to what Harry in-sisted on calling the "Faggotry," and ignored his efforts to outpunk the Velvet Underground's performances. The truth was, Harry liked Warhol, and called him the best filmmaker of their time. He admired his ability to pull together a checkered group of writers, actors, and film people and complete well over a hundred films in less than four years. And despite the differences in their films, he and Warhol both believed in documenting everything they could by film and tape, and in varying the methods and subjects of their films. Both were also well-known collectors and accumulators.

Harry lost interest in what he called small underground films. He approached Warhol, Jack Smith, and Robert Frank with the idea of making an omnibus film, "a really elaborate super-underground movie for showing in neighborhood theaters . . . It would be like a trip around the world. Various people would come in. It would be marvelous, for instance, if Andy were able to supervise maybe a twenty-minute color picture of Mt. Fuji, with a really good cameraman and technicians and everything so it would be really his beauty. Stan Vanderbeek was going to work on it. What he would do would be to go to northern Australia and animate bark paintings . . ." But with no backers, he returned to the idea of making a full-length movie by himself, and this one would be even more complex and time-consuming than *Oz*. He wanted to do something that would forever change how people thought about moviemaking. Yet from the beginning his plans were grandiose but vague.

When the film he would call *Mahagonny* premiered ten years later, the press release and the title card that opened the film both said it was "a mathematical analysis of Duchamp's La Mariée mise à nu par ses célibataires, même, expressed in terms of Kurt Weill's score for *Aufsteig und Fall der Stadt Mahagonny* with contrapuntal images (not necessarily in order) derived from Brecht's libretto for the latter work." It was a description that has yet to be fully understood by film scholars or his friends. Even his use of the original French and German titles of Duchamp's *The Bride Stripped Bare by Her Bachelors, Even* (also known as *The Large Glass*) and Brecht and Weill's *Rise and Fall of the City of Mahagonny* was puzzlingly un–Harry Smith. Jonas Mekas was aware of Harry's plans from the start, and was never sure of what he was getting at. But his explanation was as good as any: "Harry may have said there was a connection between these two works, but I can't see it. The only insight I could offer is that one shouldn't try to interpret Harry's *Mahagonny* by comparing it with the Brecht opera, because, as *The Large Glass* is shattered, Harry shattered Brecht's original. He didn't interpret Brecht's opera, he transformed it. He basically used that piece of music as a launching point into a work of his own." The most lucid description of the film as Harry had first imagined it appeared in his successful 1974 applications for grants from the American Film Institute Independent Filmmaker Program and the Committee on Poetry:

I selected "Mahagonny" as a vehicle for two reasons. First, because despite the complexity of repetition in the 21 songs in the opera, there are sections that approximate the sounds of other musical cultures that select melody as their fundamental trait and those which use rhythm as the point for development. Second, because the story is simple and widespread: the joyous gathering together of a great number of people, their breaking of the rules of liberty and love, and consequent fall into oblivion.

My photography has not been directed toward making a "realistic" version of the opera, but rather toward the translating, as nearly as I can, of images of the German text into universal, or near universal, symbols and synchronizing the appropriate images with music.

These images consist of about 250 categories such as eggs breaking, plants growing, rain falling, fire burning, parts of the human body and even scenes of the city. About half of the footage consists of animation of one sort or another. The animation is based mostly on the fundamental symbols found in all art such as the circle or dots. The emotional connotations of objects moving toward, past or away from the spectator, or things suddenly forming or dissolving, have also been utilized.

This method has been followed in order that the final film will be just as intelligible to the Zulu, the Eskimo, or the Australian Aborigine as to people of any other cultural background or age.

In its final form the film will be a series of scenes of varying lengths synchronized to the time of an entire song, and on occasion, synchronized to the length of a single line of the lyrics, but all designed to translate the opera into a universal script based on the similarities of life and aspiration in all humans. As far as I know, the attempt to make a film for all people, whether they be Papuans or New Yorkers, has not been so far made. It is by far the most complex of the 20

or so films I have made in the last 30 years; and my hope is
that it will not only be successful, but will introduce a new
theoretical basis for films and through the use of world-wide
symbols, help to bring all people of the earth closer together.

Throughout his discussions of both this film and *Heaven and
Earth Magic*, Harry continually stressed that as an anthropologist
he wanted to make films that would have universal meaning, that
could be understood by all peoples and cultures by using universal
symbols. It was an odd goal for an anthropologist, as it was generally
understood that symbols are grounded in shared experience, and such
experiences were not shared by people of disparate cultures. At least
once he hedged his claim for universality: "Because everybody knows
what it means when an egg breaks or when tears run out of the eyes or
when someone dies. They may view it in a different fashion; I mean,
it's not the same. Death among the Eskimos and the Zulus but, nonetheless, it is a death and there are certain minor qualities that appear
in both of them."

When asked to name his goals for this project in his grant applications, he simply wrote: "My long-range goal is to raise the general
level of film art by applying the concentrated energy of one person
working alone to the creative act in film."

His explanation for choosing the Brecht-Weill opera as a basis for
a new film doesn't fully address the appeal of the music of a forty-
year-old German work that broke with opera tradition. A few songs
from Brecht and Weill's *The Threepenny Opera* had recently drifted into
the jazz and pop repertoires through recordings by Louis Armstrong
and Bobby Darin, and "The Alabama Song" from the *Mahagonny*
opera had been made popular by the Doors. Arnold Weinstein, the
translator of *Rise and Fall of the City of Mahagonny* for the opera's first
American production that was briefly staged off-Broadway in 1970,
was living in the Chelsea, as was Brecht's son, Stefan. He had been
listening to the opera since it had been recorded in 1957, obsessively,

devotedly, sometimes as often as three or four times a day despite its two-hour-and-twenty-one-minute length. He was captivated by the peculiar mix of talking and song, stilted antique jazz rhythms, and deep cynicism that even a non-German-speaking listener could sense.

The opera's story is set in a perversely American utopia near Pensacola, Florida, founded by criminals. The city attracts wanderers and misfits to its ethos of pleasure without having to work, and ultimately collapses from boredom, insolvency, and corruption. A satire of Berlin in the 1920s? A critique of capitalism? At the time of its U.S. production, it was often seen as a thinly veiled comparison of Berlin in the twenties and New York City in the decline and chaos of the 1970s.

One of the principal places where Harry did his research for the film was Weiser Books on Broadway, the oldest occult bookstore in New York. It was a constant source of reference for Harry, who used it as a hangout, and its basement of occult materials as a library. His knowledge of the obscure and the rare was respected there, and he was treated like royalty by its employees. Weiser's also had its own publishing company, and Harry did the cover of Aleister Crowley's *The Holy Books of Thelema* for them.

Patti Smith and Robert Mapplethorpe often went to Weiser's with Harry, and she recalled that "One time, when I was sitting in the lobby reading *The Golden Bough*, Harry noticed I had a beat-up two-volume first edition."

He insisted we go on an expedition to Samuel Weiser's to bask in the proximity of the preferred and vastly expanded third edition. Weiser's harbored the greatest selection of books on esoteric matters in the city. I agreed to go if he and Robert didn't get stoned, as the combination of the three of us in the outside world, in an occult bookstore, was lethal enough.

Harry knew the Weiser brothers quite well, and I was

given the key to a glass case to examine the famous 1955 edition . . . Harry disappeared into some antechamber with Mr. Weiser, most likely to decipher some mystical manuscript. Robert was reading *Diary of a Drug Fiend*.

It seemed like we milled around in there for hours. Harry was gone for a long time, and we found him standing, as though transfixed, in the center of the main floor. We watched him for quite a while but he never moved. Finally, Robert, perplexed, went up to him and asked, "What are you doing?"

Harry gazed at him with the eyes of an enchanted goat. "I'm reading," he said.

It was also the place where Harry met Khem Caigan. Barely out of high school, Caigan was the perfect assistant for Harry at the time. He knew little about filmmaking, but he had studied the occult almost from childhood, described himself as a rogue scholar, artist, alchemist, Kabbalist, and daemonic astrologer, and could devour books at a rate that rivaled Harry's. Caigan began visiting Harry at the Hotel Breslin, sharing books and taking walks with him. He once described a typical conversation with Harry as ranging from the great chain of being to bioelectromagnetics and electrophysiology and the geomagnetic field, Silvanus Thompson and Max Knoll and the generation of phosphenes, musicology and molecular physics, parapsychology and poltergeist phenomena, Hélène Smith (a medium who claimed to have communicated with Martians), tarot cards, Harry's collections of Easter eggs and Seminole quilts, and alchemy, all in an effort to understand and communicate the underlying connectedness and interrelatedness of everything.

As Harry was beginning planning *Mahagonny*, he and Khem were reading Eric Havelock's *Preface to Plato*, and focusing on the relationship of orality to literature. They were toying with Duchamp's idea of the use of a fourth dimension in his *Large Glass* work, and reading the writers associated with the French Oulipo movement, who were reckoning with arguments concerning freedom vs. constraint in art and literature. (Harry leaned toward constraint as a means to great art, which might help explain his lack of interest in the rise of free jazz in the late 1950s through the 1970s.)

They were also studying the Enochian language, a means of communication with the angels in the sixteenth century. It was that language that Edward Kelley, a sixteenth-century alchemist and spirit medium, said he had learned from angels who communicated with him in a trance. He taught it to John Dee, the most accomplished mathematician and philosopher of his time in Britain. It was a language studied and elaborated on by the Hermetic Order of the Golden Dawn, Aleister Crowley, and the OTO. The seventeenth-century book *A True and Faithful Relation of What Passed for Many Yeers Between Dr. John Dee and Some Spirits* was their main source as they for several years compiled a concordance of Enochian or angelic language, filling shoeboxes of notes written on Hotel Chelsea stationery. Harry began to see a connection between Scots tartans and the angelic language: the crosshatched designs seemed to correspond to the crossed axes of Angelic names in Dee's Enochian word tables. According to Caigan, Harry was only half-serious while he was high on Desoxyn (similar to crystal meth, a street drug that produces euphoria and high energy). "It's only natural to link the two of them, especially when you've been wired for any length of time, because everything becomes significant and any sort of resemblance just challenges you to make it significant. So it's one of those things he had fun with." He was also interested in the ancient concept of the magic square, reckoning that anything so widespread over time and that had survived for so long was some form of a universal. He toyed with two nine-cell squares, writing the words "Manhattan" in one and "Mahagonny" in the other, and looked for ways to connect the two squares.

Out of these discussions of alternative realities, puzzles, squares, and alphabetic tables Harry began to imagine using several screens at once in his next film. The idea was not entirely original, as split screens are almost as old as motion pictures, having been used at least as early as 1902, and multiple screens were first used in 1927 for Abel Gance's *Napoleon*. Harry was well aware of Andy Warhol's experiments in multiscreens on the walls of the Exploding Plastic Inevitable dance hall and in his film *Chelsea Girls*. But Warhol's pairings of images on two screens was largely random, while Harry's idea was to use four or more screens with different images scrupulously planned, with each image for each projector mapped out on large scrolls beforehand. Once he settled on four screens, he planned to have twenty-four scenes in each of twelve reels, with as many as four images visible at a time. The images would sometimes be paired vertically, horizontally, or mirroring each other, and sometimes there would be only one, two, or none (when the screens went black). Beyond the images themselves, he intended the conjunction of colors to form a matrix, a quilt (or perhaps a tartan), and for the screens stacked together to change the shape of the standard movie screen. He explained that "Four screens are to be used and rhythmic patterns will occur between the length of the scenes, the general form of twenty-four interlocking shots is the same, backwards and forwards. Individuals in the audience will have their attention directed to one particular part of the counterpoint at each minute . . ." The multiple screens also formed a montage or collage or magic square. He hoped the opera soundtrack would help thread the images together, but feared that if the meaning of the words were known, it would distract from the film, and he resisted an offer to have it shown to a German-speaking audience in Europe. By tying the images to the musical elements, he aimed at making the music visual, much as he had with his paintings of jazz recordings.

There were to be four categories of imagery in all the four films: "P" for "portraits" (Harry's friends and neighbors from the Chelsea, such as Mekas, Ginsberg, Rosebud, and Patti Smith, all of them silently appearing), "A" for "animation" (of objects such as cigarettes and household items), "S" for "symbols" (signs and street scenes), and "N" for "nature" (mostly shot in Central Park). "Any one reel is a structure made up of twenty-four units in palindrome form: P.A.S.A.N.A.S.A.P., and so on . . . There are twenty-four shots in each of twelve reels, adding up to two gross or two hundred and eighty-eight shots." (Caigan, however, noted that the palindrome form was not used consistently.) The four screens would relate by mirrored scenes, contrasts, repetition, and visual counterpoint. Throughout there were surprises: black screen pauses, overexposed scenes, changes in film speeds, dancers, string figures, hands drawing figures in sand, objects in Robert Mapplethorpe's room, drugs and alcoholic drinks, caped figures, and silent talk.

"The original set of *Mahagonny* had a boxing ring with a pool table in the middle of it and some chairs. In our case," said Harry, "it was more expedient to put the boxing ring against the wall, and put the four pool tables under the boxing ring so they could all be lit independently. The boxing ring itself should be lit from behind." The films would be projected onto the tops of the pool tables.

By February 1971, Harry had been working on *Mahagonny* for a little over a year, and was struggling to find the money to complete the movie, shooting whenever he could find help and afford film stock and the costs of developing. Much of the filming had been done in Central Park, and now that winter had come, his new worry was how he could continue since the trees no longer had leaves on them and would clash with the footage of greenery already shot. As he so often did, he dropped by to see Jonas Mekas for a loan of $200, but also to ask him to spread the message that he needed money for the film. Mekas gave him the $200, and then devoted his June 13, 1971, *Village Voice* column (titled "God Helps Harry Smith, Because He Helps

Himself") to making public the discussion he had had with Harry
when he asked for the money:

> I think I'll have to shoot two-to-one. But there are important
> scenes that are missing. Because the reason for this process of
> like dividing a song maybe one picture for one word, or one
> line of the poem to one picture, or one song for one picture,
> is that I want to make the film intelligible for the Eskimos
> or the Australian aborigines, and so forth. I derived a great
> pleasure from Eskimo poetry, you know, that's my line. It's
> like anthropology. In a sense I want to give them something
> back. So, I took Brecht's poem "Mahagonny" and I tried to
> translate it to ideographs that are universally known. The film
> isn't going to be shown very much commercially, because I'm
> making a special screen for it, of torn-off newspapers, so that
> the whole thing looks like a collage, a two-and-a-quarter
> hour collage . . . I wouldn't bother you about this. Except that
> I think the world is in peril and I'm trying to do something
> now other than the mere artistic thing . . .

Mekas explained to readers that he wanted to show the seriousness
of Harry's work and his financial needs because he felt he was "one of
the four or five greatest living film-makers, plus, Harry is a genius."

Three years later, Mekas saw some of the film for the first time,
and once again pitched for more money from his readers to help
Harry complete it: "The experience of what we saw was so incredibly
beautiful, that later we walked, we sat, and we spoke, and we said 'genius,' and 'masterpiece,' and we were out of words. There was no doubt
in our minds that we were given a glimpse into one of the sublime
masterpieces of the Art of Cinema in progress . . ."

Harry's films had become well-known enough for him to have the
respect of a number of established filmmakers. If some were not completely impressed by his films, they at least appreciated the amount of

work and thought that went into them. Younger filmmakers sought him out for advice or to work with him. M. Henry Jones recalled that when Harry was staying with him as he was recovering from an illness, he carried him out on the steps to get some sun, and a line of young people would form to talk with him.

When Shirley Clarke decided to switch from film to video, she loaned her 16-millimeter camera to Harry to use for his film. At times she also helped out, shooting segments such as one in which Allen Gins-berg silently read from *Howl* while eating a banana. Peggy Biderman also helped in shooting film in Central Park. Some of those who assisted or supported Harry in his later films have given accounts of their work with him. One of them, Patrick Hulsey, in the fall of 1971 moved into the Chelsea, where his sister had an apartment. She told him that Harry Smith was looking for an assistant for a film he was making, and he was hired on to the production as the principal camera operator. Hulsey planned to write a book about it—*Harry Smith, Mahagonny, and the Fall of Western Civilization*. It was never finished, but the few pages he did write provide a rare view of how Harry worked and lived in the early 1970s.

> Every day I would go to room 731 and the ritual of prepar-ing to depart the room with all the film gear and supplies we would need for a day of shooting would begin. I would go to the deli for beer and cigarettes, Salem 100s and quart bottles of Ballantine Ale. Harry would try to ingest the per-fect combination of Dexedrine and Valium. Then we would turn on, usually smoking some good bud . . . I would check and recheck the camera bag, making sure the Bell & Howell Filmo 16mm camera was loaded and the 50mm Angenieaux

lens was clean. The Filmo is a metal cased camera accepting only 100 ft reels of film that must be wound for each one minute of shooting or about 3 times per 100 ft reel. It was developed as a newsreel camera during World War II. Harry said it could be dropped from an airplane and you could just pick it up and start shooting. Then I would make sure the Spectra light meter was in the bag along with a couple of quarts of beer. Harry would then start trying to catch his two parakeets, Bluey and Greeny and get them in their cage. This was hilarious because Harry would get them perched on his fingers and just as he got them to the cage they would fly off and land on the curtain rod. Harry would have to navigate through boxes of artifacts stacked all over the room and shoo the birds off the curtain rod. They would then land on the bathroom door where he would again get them to perch on his finger. And when he got them to the cage . . . off they would fly again. Finally after numerous attempts, he would get them into the cage.

I would grab the camera bag and the wooden tripod with a Miller Fluid Head (that Harry claimed had been to the North Pole with Admiral Byrd) and we would exit 731. Harry would lock the door with a key on a string that was tied to a belt loop in his jeans. About halfway to the elevators Harry would worry that he had left a cigarette burning and would go back to check. He would then come to the elevators where I would be patiently waiting. But then he would wonder if he had remembered to lock the door after checking for the burning cigarette. So he would have to go back and check the lock. As you can imagine, by the time we got out to the street to hail a cab, it was already afternoon.

We would arrive at the location—Central Park, Times Square, the NY Public Library, or whatever, and I would set up the tripod and camera. Harry would then take exposure readings, frame the composition and invariably instruct me to move the tripod while he took another exposure reading and framed another composition. We filmed as much as we could through the Fall, Winter, and Spring. Harry explained to me that this was to be his Magnum Opus. It was to be projected on 4 screens simultaneously. When we had a reel of film shot, we dropped it at the lab for processing and picked it up the next day.

We would take the dailies to the Anthology Film Archives and Jonas Mekas would project them. Jonas and P. Adams Sitney, an avant-garde film critic would watch the dailies with us and rave about the marvelous images Harry had captured. One day we came in with some film shots of cherry blossom trees in Central Park that we had somehow overexposed badly. They were really washed out and Harry just sat watching silently. Jonas and P. Adams were out and just overwhelmed with the beauty, the artistic comment that Harry had achieved. Harry, of course, accepted their praises dutifully, but when we got outside, he had to crack up. It was hilarious to him that our screw-up was interpreted as a triumph.

Back in room 731, Harry would play *Mahagonny* constantly. At first, I couldn't relate to it at all. But it grew on me. Harry would expound on Brecht and Weill and Lotte Lenya, explaining how controversial the opera was in Germany when it opened in 1931. How it caused riots and shut down and how Brecht and company had to flee Germany.

There was so much to learn and absorb from Harry and the scene at the Chelsea. Harry would relate tales from his life—life experience, stories that were at once ironic, comic, and tragic.

1. How his hair turned white on the Oz film.

2. How his mother was Anastasia.

3. How he had been arrested many times for pulling fire alarms, his last conscious act before passing out in a drunken stupor.

4. How he had never had sexual intercourse with another living thing. Harry told me that he was 71 years old (in 1971). Of course, I believed him. I was just 21. But by all accounts he was really only 50 or so.

Often he would be speaking about something like the fall of the Aztecs and suddenly be off on Thelonious Monk and segue into a particular string figure he had collected or the story of how Aleister Crowley came to found the Abbey of Thelema. The really odd thing was he would end up picking up the thread of each story hours or days later. After spending months listening to this stuff I would finally get the whole point. Sometimes.

For *Mahagonny* we filmed a lot of people acting out scenes from *Mahagonny* or in many cases, people doing their thing—dancing, or whatever. The "actors" were people who were part of the Chelsea scene—Allen Ginsberg, Patti Smith and Robert Mapplethorpe who were living together in a loft down the street from the Chelsea. Marty Balin from the Jefferson Airplane (Harry got him to slap his girlfriend and pull her hair for a scene in the film). Robert Mapplethorpe had all these sort of collage instructions that were very sacrilegious and dark, so we filmed his stuff at his loft.

Shirley Clarke, who lived in the penthouse and made the film *The Connection* and lived with actor Carl Lee, who was the co-star in *Superfly* . . . and then she lived with Ornette Coleman, the jazz horn player. Anyway, she loaned Harry a 16mm Beaulieu camera. It actually had a battery and took 200 ft. magazines, so we could do longer takes and she had one of the first Sony reel-to-reel decks and cameras, so we did something with her that turned out really cool—video feedback. Pointing the camera at the video monitor caused these swirls that turned into snowflake patterns. Very intricate ones and lots of variations. In black and white, of course, there were no color videos.

M. Henry Jones assisted Harry on several film projects in the early 1970s:

> I was always totally fixated on the film frames that were meant to be projected around his movies. Harry's varied descriptions of how the film frames could be used all related to his fundamental idea about the experience of seeing a movie: "You always feel like you are sitting in the middle of a shoebox looking in one end."
>
> This simple but profound observation led Harry to a unique innovation: the peripheral film frames he incorporated into his show stemmed directly from his intent to break down the edge of the movie and extend it outward. These film frames create an "animating surround" causing the movements of the eye to wander around all the projected imagery while still taking in the central image of the movie. This way of screening allows for unconscious selection to take over the viewing. The border images themselves are quintessential because they visually recycled Harry's eclectic Native American, folk, Buddhist, Egyptian and arcane hermetic influences . . . and this border imagery [juxtaposed] around the glowing dissolves a sublime super-imposition of form and color. The total effect has a distinctly kinetic wit and a unique hypnotic dimension . . .
>
> He was involved in unframing boundaries of vision to the point that his works took on a sculptural aspect.

Harry also pointed out that some people were really attentive and could stare into the middle of the screen without moving their eyes at all and this would have a different effect that was also good: the more the eye movement is focused the more over-saturated the retina becomes with after-images that could induce hallucinatory effects. He always said that at the end of the movie if some people in the audience are asleep it is OK because that means most people in the audience are half-asleep and therefore you've affected most of the people the way you wanted to.

Harry was fascinated with after-image effects because he saw them as movies unto themselves. This led us into some way-out experimentation. He had us staring into light bulbs through different netting and screens. Sometimes we held different objects in front of a 500-watt reflector light switching the light on and off as we slowly moved our eyes around in circles. The patterns we saw were "animating in color" by the action of the retina.

Robert Polidori:

> It was like a lot of work doing stuff for Harry because of his pot, beer and Dexedrine consumption habits. I would say that like every splice would mean one joint, one beer and one Dexedrine.

Deborah Freeman, a student at Barnard who lived at the Chelsea, had gone to Europe for a year after she first met Harry, and when she returned, he was starting to work on *Mahagonny*, and was filming people at the hotel:

> [He] was in quite a frenzy. He was drinking a lot of alcohol and taking more speed and more marijuana than before

and everything got crazier and crazier . . . He had a lot of people hanging out with him, and that was his sort of diabolical side. I mean he would have temper tantrums and throw goldfish down the toilet or break his glasses or something. And he talked about these tantrums more than they actually happened, but eventually the scene got even more destructive. So *Mahagonny* was made in some kind of diabolical frenzy—I mean Harry was very . . . evil at that point. I mean a lot of people really probably hated him, or if they didn't hate him they grew to hate him because he was very destructive and very, very manipulative. He knew how to tune into your weaknesses and then use them . . .

After working on the film for almost three years, Harry had completed eleven hours of footage by July 1972, and edited them down to six hours. His plan was to further cut it to two hours and twenty minutes—the length of the opera. "The shots will be edited according to certain mathematical permutations, in multiples of twelve, so that the emotional connotations of the various categories correspond to the natural emotional pulse of the observer. This is the most complex and critical step in the production and will take at least a year." It took another eight.

TATTOO MAGIC ON THE LOWER EAST SIDE

And this tattooing had been the work of a departed prophet and seer of his island, who, by those hieroglyphic marks, had written out on his body a complete theory of the heavens and the earth, and a mystical treatise on the art of attaining truth;

> so that Queequeg in his own proper person was a riddle to
> unfold; a wondrous work in one volume; but whose mysteries
> not even himself could read, though his own
> live heart beat against them.
>
> —Herman Melville, *Moby-Dick*

Despite the time he put in on the film and the number of people involved, hardly any of Harry's friends and helpers in the Chelsea knew about his interest in tattooing in the early 1970s. New York City banned tattooing in 1961, and for the next thirty-five years it was an art driven underground and kept alive by a small number of artists working out of basements and apartments across the city. On the Lower East Side, the most noted of these was the painter-turned-tattooist Thom DeVita, who began tattoo work the day after the city's ban went into effect. He thought of it as folk art, and his first clients were mostly laborers and hard cases. Nevertheless, his was an art also shaped in part by abstract expressionist painters like Willem de Kooning and Franz Kline, who he drank with in the Cedar Bar.

Harry first encountered DeVita in the Chelsea, where he was doing tattoo house calls. "Harry," he thought, "was the only man I know of, in forty years of tattooing, who collected bandages. A very unusual thing. The bandage has a mirror image of the tattoo. Sometimes, very rarely, the blood on the bandage was better than the tattoo. These were the bandages that Harry collected. He collected the best. You see, what people would do was, as soon as they left the parlor, they'd rip off the bandage. Throw it away." Harry began finding them in the halls of the hotel.

The few who knew of Harry's tattoo collection considered it an odd if not perverse hobby. But tattooing was a major interest of early anthropologists, and for many of those who were tattooed it was an introduction to the wide historical and ethnic forms of the art. For Harry, they were a parallel to string figures—universal, ancient, and seemingly infinite in meaning. Tattooing was something that Franz

Boas called attention to in his early writings, along with masking, and it was a major part of his student Margaret Mead's research in Samoa. Tattooing and face-painting was also central to Claude Lévi-Strauss's understanding of the people of the Mato Grosso region of Brazil.

Another Lower East Side practitioner in the art was Richard O. Tyler, a painter, astrologer, and follower of Charles Fourier, who came to New York from the Chicago Institute of Fine Art. His tattooing was derived from Tibetan Buddhist designs that were used to heal or magically guide the living. Tyler, along with Claes Oldenburg, Jim Dine, and others, created a gallery at Judson Memorial Church on Washington Square, where he sold his art and self-published books from a pushcart in front of the church. Under the name of Reverend Relytor, he founded the Uranian Phalanstery, Gnostic Lyceum Temple; the Uranian Press; Uranian Burial Society; Uranian Tattooage; and the Workshop Gallery and Mythological Museum on Fourth Street, which, altogether, were a center concerned with cosmology, arcane symbolism, and mind-altering drugs. Tyler, like De-Vita, was part of a circle that included Ziprin, Huncke, Harry, and also Bill Heine, a trained painter and musician, an early creator of tie-dye paintings, and a drummer who played with Charlie Parker at the Open Door in the Village. He was a member of Tyler's Phalanstery, where he learned about magic and the occult from Lionel and Harry, and developed a fearsome reputation for black magic.

When Allen Ginsberg met Bob Dylan in 1964, Ginsberg had just returned from India and had begun to introduce chanting into his poetry readings, accompanying himself with an Indian harmonium. Soon after, he was setting William Blake's poems to music. Dylan had been in New York for two years, playing in small clubs in Greenwich Village where folk, poetry, and jazz often appeared on the same stage. Dylan remembered meeting Thelonious Monk, who asked him what kind of music he played. When he said folk music, Monk replied, "We all play folk music." As if to prove the point, Dylan once joined the avant-garde jazz pianist Cecil Taylor in playing "The River Is Wide." At the time Dylan was drifting toward the poetry of the Beats, who he called "the Be Bop crowd." "My songs were influenced not so much by poetry on the page but by the poets who recited poems with jazz bands." Meanwhile, Ginsberg was meeting the Beatles and the Stones, and beginning to see a way of returning poetry to the ancient oral bardic tradition. When Dylan heard Ginsberg improvising a song at Ginsberg's apartment, he was amazed, and sat with him and played various blues and Latin rhythms as Ginsberg "tongued syllables and sentences as fast as I could to 'I'm Going Down to Puerto Rico.'" Dylan urged him to go into a studio and record his impromptu songs.

At the time, Harry was using Moe Asch's Wollensak tape recorder to record people in the Chelsea, piling up tapes of Gregory Corso's poetry or Peter Orlovsky's songs, and Ginsberg asked him to record his new song/poems. Several days a week for months in 1971, they recorded "CIA Dope Calypso," "Prayer Blues," "Put Down Your Cigarette Rag," and every song Ginsberg had written, until they had amassed sixteen reels of him singing solo or with harmonium. Several versions of each were recorded until they had ones that Harry liked. "One thing I remember," Ginsberg said,

> he kept saying, "It's all right." I was tapping my foot, and he said, "Do that heavier." I said, won't the tape pick it up? He said, "Yeah, that's what the old blues people used to do." Bang. Make little drum noises on the guitars or bang their feet on the floor, so that's part of the rhythm thing. I was amazed at his openness to whatever happened . . . Then Harry went into a funny kind of amphetamine tailspin . . . he wouldn't talk to anybody, wouldn't talk to me, maybe be-

cause I didn't supply him with money, because I was broke
at the time. I remember going down 13th Street in a taxicab
and seeing him pass by near University Place, and I called
out "Harry!" He looked at me and turned away—high, as if
he'd just seen the Devil.

The tapes sat around for years until Ginsberg gave them to Moe
Asch, who had Sam and Ann Charters put together the album *First
Blues: Rags, Ballads and Harmonium Songs* on Folkways in 1981.
Harry's comment on it was "they got all wrong takes of it." But Gins-
berg was happy with the results, and told Hal Willner that he wanted
to do something bigger, maybe make a hit record. Another record he
also called *First Blues* was the result, this time on John Hammond
Records in 1982 with some of the same songs from Harry's recording,
but now with arrangements by Arthur Russell, David Amram, and
Happy Traum, and accompanied by Bob Dylan, Amram, Russell,
Perry Robinson, and Steven Taylor.

Despite his connection to Dylan and Ginsberg, Harry was not
included in the Rolling Thunder Revue tour of 1975–1976, or in the
film *Renaldo and Clara* that followed. Nor could he be seen in Warhol's *Chelsea Girls*. After his death he was seen in Robert Frank's 1994
silent film, *Moving Pictures*, a tribute to those who inspired Frank's
work—Jean-Luc Godard, Ginsberg, and others. Harry is in his room.
Across the screen the text says, "Today is your birthday. How does it
feel?" Smith's response: "It sucks . . . it sucks," and he walks out of the
frame.

When Harry applied for an extension of the grant he had received
from the Creative Artists Public Service Program in New York in
1973, he jumped headfirst into a discussion of the stereotypical mad

genius, in what might be the most extraordinary application letter ever written—and one even more extraordinary in that the grant was again funded:

> I am writing to you this rather informal progress report for two reasons. First because though I have tried to convince you by word and deed that I was suffering from what my doctor enigmatically calls "severe psychic decompensation," you have been adamant in your refusal to accept the fact that I was perhaps loco. I now may prove it to you. Second, because even among the laity there is an ever-increasing interest in the literature of the mentally deranged in which genre I am always ready, nay, eager to be a Master. I am, alas, myself a maniac.
>
> There is admittedly a connection between art and madness whether it is a severe case of the latter, or a scarcely noticeable but telltale super-accuracy of the brush or pen. I have always used my God-given gift of mental disease as perhaps the most valuable component of my work. In point of fact, the whole film on the merits of which I was awarded the CAPS [Creative Artists Public Service] grant was made during a period of particularly severe derangement.
>
> When I drunkenly told you when I accepted the first check how unlikely it was that I would follow the budget, I little suspected just how far my barque would drift from its appointed mooring. How the money was actually spent can be learnt from the bills, etc. that accompany this report. As the sort of film I make is "improvised" according to the dictates of a diseased brain I can never tell which direction it's going to jump any more than I can tell what I am going to dream of a week from next Thursday.
>
> *Mahagonny* is particularly difficult. You have to live *Mahagonny*, in fact be *Mahagonny* in order to work on it. Thus

it is that it became more convenient and cheaper to set up a cutting [table] where I live rather than to rent one. I can also change things in the room like the city of Mahagonny itself. Money that was allocated to raw stock, etc., for achieving certain effects by the use of filters, was used to study more about movement and personality in relation to emotion in so far as they affected the rhythmic technique I am using. As to the tedious task of analyzing the sound track and translating the several thousand curls into "universal" symbols proceded [*sic*] it was necessary to make an extensive study of [Weill's] achievements before and after *Mahagonny* and especially to increase available information on non-European religion and art. Thus a number of books and records had to be obtained and people rewarded to obtain information. This on top of paying the Hotel, a psychiatrist, etc.

As to the film itself, it is proceeding very nicely. The problems involved in turning the opera into "One" Big Ceremony (for that is what it is), and at the same time preserving the meaning and flavor of Brecht's libretto is not easy. The sound track has been analyzed, to almost its final form, a premium cutting of the film made and the final one charted.

The completion of the film will undoubtably be later than the deadline originally agreed upon. I was drunk and sick most of the time before I went to the hospital in August and September and am still weak. Nonetheless I will, thanks to CAPS, soon finish a film that has taken all of my resources for the last seven years.

He was asking for $8,500 to complete the film, and attempted to justify the expenses:

This is slightly above the budget, but where there's a will there's a way, I guess. You must remember that I spend all my income on one thing or another directly connected with making *Mahagonny* by living through the birth and death of *Mahagonny* myself (more detailed information concerning the general method of approach to and theoretical background of the film [can] be found in the original application).

I enclose a letter from my psychiatrist and general advisor to things medical to attest that I no longer drink and am Good, etc., etc. The doctor himself is a little balmy. Dating the letter January 3, 1976, and in a spasm of garbled syntax, seemingly makes CAPS responsible for my drunkenness "of 20 years standing." There is no doubt that the CAPS grant precipitated an eating and drinking frenzy unparallel in my recent history; a frenzy that was terminated only when I was strapped in a bed with a twenty % chance of living, a raving maniac raving for two weeks from hallucinatory dolours that rivaled those Senate-president Schreber delineates so skillfully in his "Memoirs of My Nervous Illness." So that if CAPS did nothing else it saved my life by frightening me so thoroughly that I no longer have the bad, bad desire for fire water.

Now I can proceed serenely, but sternly, on with *Mahagonny* producing a film that will make CAPS and all the millions of people who see it during 1976 and the next few hundred years, thoughtful, edified, and pleased.

The application included a letter from Dr. Gross certifying Harry's ability to complete the project. Such a public declaration of one's mental instability was very unusual in the arts, but not unparalleled. Ten years earlier, the jazz musician Charles Mingus had his psychoanalyst, Edmund Pollock, write part of the liner notes to Mingus's 1963 *The Black Saint and the Sinner Lady*. When Harry was asked to list his expenses that were covered by one grant, he was incensed, and wrote several pages of drugs and intoxicants and their prices, but listed only one very small item relating to the filming.

Harry once again asked Arthur Young for money to help make *Mahagonny*, but Young instead bought a copy of *Film No. 12*. A year later Harry tried him again. "I was in a voluntary trance when working on it and the character and objects took on a life of their own to such a degree that every time I look at the film I see things I didn't know were there . . . You realize that my cinematic work is scarcely tailored for mass distribution at this time. For a long period, *No. 12* was shown only once or twice a year or so, but since the 'occult revival' it has become a little more popular."

> The film I am working on now is of much greater elegance, longer, in color, and had the advantage of 15 more years of studies of the ancient teachings. It will no doubt be much more popular than Number 12, but like the latter was designed to be shown over a 500-year period, or so, and consequently will scarcely be a box office smash during my life time: but will continually grow in popularity and be there for the increasingly large number of people who have the consciousness to unravel its cryptograms. All my films, with the exception of one (the worst) have been financed by contributions rather than investments and you must understand that the number of people willing to part with cash to finance esoteric alchemical works are still much less than in the 17th century . . . I know that our respective approaches to those necessary science[s] that the nations of this world abandon or suppress in their quest for power differ, but I also realize

that unless those of us who have been conscious of the secret course of history must cooperate or be agents to the destruction of all. Albion is more than just a word, it is a way of life that will lead us on our "deaths" to those wonders of other planets and galaxies where our work can still go on.

Mahagonny was supported, directly or indirectly, by the New York City Department of Cultural Affairs, the Creative Artists Public Service Program, the American Film Institute, and the Institute for the Study of Consciousness.

New York City's decline in the early seventies—threats of the city's bankruptcy, a surge in drug use, power blackouts, police corruption, a general deterioration in urban maintenance—was echoed in the Chelsea. Suicides, fires, overdoses, robberies, bulletproof shields up at the desk, the lobby a gathering place for lost teens. As Dr. Krohn assessed the situation, "In the Chelsea there were welfare families there, there were ambulatory schizophrenics living in rooms that were scarcely more than a closet, there were whores and their pimps set up in extended apartments . . . There were clusters of apartments in which rock bands and their managers would all camp."

Life in the Chelsea had become especially hellish for Harry in the late 1970s. There were bullet holes in the walls of his room, the door had been broken open several times, a thief had threatened to shoot his birds, Gregory Corso had chopped his way into Harry's room and set a fire in front of his door. There was also a continuing problem with Jacques Stern, with Harry making frantic calls to Jim Wasserman, Moe Asch, or anyone who would listen and could maybe help him find a lawyer to get a restraining order against Stern, who he claimed was accusing him of practicing black magic, which Harry fervently denied—"I don't even know how to do it!" Stern was black-mailing him, he charged, and having people beaten up. He had struck Harry with his cane.

Harry was using cocaine and methamphetamine and was sick, coughing up blood and hallucinating. Hotel maids found him in a coma, and had him sent to St. Vincent's Hospital. When he later regained consciousness, he was raging, reciting Aleister Crowley's poetry, and ripped out his feeding tubes, damaging his throat and esophagus, making normal eating even more difficult than it had been.

Stanley Bard began to pressure Harry to leave, perhaps not so much for the rent money he owed, but because he felt that his room was the source of many of the hotel's troubles and feared for Harry's life. Harry agreed to nothing, but he saw that what he had enjoyed and benefited from in the Chelsea was coming to a nasty ending. Somehow, he managed to move all of his collections and art materials quietly out of the hotel without being seen, leaving behind a $7,000 bill and disappearing into the New York night at the beginning of the new year, 1977. As Raymond Foye put it, "After three fires in his room, arrests and incarceration in prisons and mental institutions of numerous friends, the casting of numerous black magic curses and spells, and an armed robbery in which he was tied to a chair, slashed, and pistol-whipped by a former assistant, Smith decided it was time to move on."

When Raymond ran into Bard in the hotel a few days later, Bard asked him into his office. "All Stanley wanted to know was how do we get him back?"

10

Lost and Found

1977–1990

The greatest public service I could have pulled at the time was
to disappear, and I did it! . . . I moved out of Chelsea Hotel to
a secret location on the Lower East Side, or some side.

—Harry Smith

Harry had burned down a lot of bridges. When you disappear
in New York, you really disappear.

—Allen Ginsberg

A few days later, Harry was found in the Breslin, a welfare hotel, an
SRO, and was living in room 714 (the number that Harry would dryly
note was the street name for quaaludes). Now, at age fifty-four, he
was cut off from the artists and the hotel manager in the Chelsea,
where he'd had the freedom and support he needed to pursue his
many projects for over a decade. Gone were the dinners with friends
at El Quijote, gatherings in the lobby or on the roof, the flow of artists' traffic to his room . . . but also gone was the craziness of the
Chelsea. "The Breslin years were very quiet," Raymond Foye recalls.
"He was not seeing a lot of people, just working hard on his projects
and paintings—the edit of *Mahagonny*, the shape note project." Asked
if he never saw any of the people from the old days at the Chelsea,
Harry answered that he had just "pulled the stilts out from under a

bunch of people and we wouldn't be seeing too much of them." Ed
Sanders once said that someone could write a six-hundred-page book
on Harry's complex interconnection with hotel managers and tenants. He might have added flophouses and friends' apartments to that
book. There were times throughout his life in which no one knew
where Harry was or what he was doing. Secrets and contradictions
were not unusual for Harry, but his peripatetic life in New York increased the need for gaps and asterisks in his story.

It was true that he had cut off a number of his older acquaintances,
but he had added a few new and talented ones who were anxious to
learn from him and become his followers, assistants, those he liked
to ironically call his "staff." With the help of Khem Caigan and Jim
Wasserman, a young occult acolyte he met browsing at Weiser Books,
he unpacked and reorganized his library and his collections, and returned to completing *Mahagonny* with new energy. In his new hotel
room, there were a few folding card tables for work, metal shelves for
books, artifacts, and his films of things, places, and people shot for
Mahagonny over the last five years. He now had to find some sequence
for them, not just a single narrative or visual line but a complex pattern for four films interacting, all of them set to music running for
over two hours, but it had to be done without the money and the
daily excitement of the early camerawork. "*Mahagonny* has required
all my energy, many hundred thousand dollars. At this point, it is
running about two thousand a month just to keep going, with no food
or clothing allowed out of these two thousand dollars . . . And the
rent is always behind. It's funny what it gets spent on."

In a draft of a proposal he wrote explaining why it was taking so
long to finish and why he needed more money, Harry wrote: "I never
made the slightest effort to advertise or promote my films (it not being
generally known 'till the mid-sixties that I made films at all). During
the last fifteen years they have become quite well-known, however,
and have been shown at most of the major art museums of the world."

For the last eight years I have been working on a cinematic translation of Weill and Brecht's opera *Mahagonny*, a film that in its final form will require four main screens and a number of coincident projections. All of my income during this period has been used directly or indirectly toward the realization of this project.

The photography took over 3 years (more than half of it being in specialized animation techniques that I had developed) [and] about two years were then spent in preliminary editing and classification of the more than 60 hours of film shot. A grant from CAPS of $20,000 in 1975 made possible this analysis of the footage finally selected and an elaborate analysis of the soundtrack requiring more than 1800 subliminal cues.

My obligations to CAPS were extended to April 1977 due to impossible working conditions at the Hotel Chelsea, my residence for 12 years. In February of that year Mr. Patrick Hulsey, who had worked with me on about half of the photography some years ago having in the meantime organized a film company of his own for the production of "commercial" film suggested he invest $25,000 to underwrite the final design and construction of the projection equipment required in the light of the most recent studies in relation to brain function and differential response in the various parts of the world in which the film would eventually be shown (my object from the beginning to translate the libretto of the opera into specialized images and color sequences on the subsidiary projectors appropriate to the audience of any particular local performance, hereby avoiding the distracting influence by their very nature increasing as time passes, and are not at all affected by the here-today-and-gone-tomorrow gamble of production designed for mass distribution). Eileen Bowser,

curator of the Museum of Modern Art [remarked] that I was
probably unique in that not a single one of my films had been
a failure within the limits that I set upon it.

P. Adams Sitney interviewed Harry about *Mahagonny* on his
monthly *Arts Forum* program on WNYC-FM on June 3, 1977. They
arrived late for the broadcast, and opened with Harry saying that
he assumed that their listeners would be familiar with Claude Lévi-
Strauss's *The Raw and the Cooked*, Noam Chomsky's doctoral dissertation, and "a little bit about Ludwig Wittgenstein." But most of the
program was taken up with his comments on the writings of John
Dee, the calypsonian Mighty Sparrow, Jung, Goethe, *Eye Movements
and Psychological Processes* by Richard A. Monty and John W. Senders,
the anthropologists Gladys Reichard and Edward Sapir, Plato, Ploti-
nus, and J. J. Boissard's 1506 book, *Theatrum Vitae Humanae*. He
ended the show by saying that he wasn't going to allow anyone to see
Mahagonny who he knew, he had ever seen, or was likely to meet,
after the way they had treated him, were treating him, or were going
to treat him. Instead, he was saving it for things like *Playboy* magazine, no-good tin kings of Bolivia, and the millionairess Barbara
Hutton, if she was still alive. It was to be the first of three interviews
with Smith, but the show was terminated by the station when listeners
complained that they had been broadcasting stoned.

Though he was spending more time alone in his new room, and
working on yet another film, *No. 17*, a revision of *Film No. 11*, Harry
was still going to art gallery openings of friends' work that was often well beneath the quality of his own, still seeing live music in clubs
and concerts. When he had the money, he'd take his friends and assistants with him. But he also had a reputation for finding his way into
events without paying, by sneaking in, bum-rushing, threatening, and
outright lying. Once, on a visit to the Museum of Natural History
with his young friend Scott Feero, Scott put a penny in the "Suggested Donation" ticket booth and stepped aside to let Harry get his

own ticket, but Harry told the attendant that he didn't need a ticket, and that he should just be admitted:

> He gets into the "I don't think you seem to know who I am." Stuff like that. This goes on for a few rounds and somewhat modified I say, "Harry I'll pay for your ticket—no big deal it's only a penny." The ticket attendant looks at me longingly, but Harry steps in saying, with great anger, "No, I do not need a ticket to get in this museum." Now roaring, "My family made extremely important contributions to this museum . . . You people don't seem to realize who I am!"
>
> The guard edges in, and now I'm thinking this has all the elements of a "developing situation." Harry is so incredibly angry I am getting scared, and start pleading for him to let me buy him a ticket. But this just makes him incredulous, and he flies off the handle demanding to be let in. I believe the thing that saved the day is Harry's acting ability. I mean another person pulling this stunt would have gotten arrested. It's an act, but it is not entirely an act, he's pissed at me because of some sort of comment he made to me about some certain Northwest Coast (Haida & Kwakiutl) artifacts being donated to the museum by his family, and I didn't see any Donated by the Smiths plaque anywhere.
>
> So, standing there, affecting the supreme outrage of all consuming indignation, Harry demands that the attendant get so and so on the phone—repeating the name for emphasis . . . The poor attendant stands there frozen like a deer in headlights until the guard steps in asking her for the phone. The guard calls upstairs and hearing the connection made, Harry steps in snatching the receiver, "Hello, Mr. _____ this is Harry Smith and these people down here won't let me into your museum. Could you please tell them to let me in . . ."

And so on. After which Harry passes the receiver back to the guard, who snaps to attention at the words coming from up- stairs, "Yes sir. Yes sir. Yes, I understand." At that he hangs up the phone and ushers us in.

The guard seemed amused, but my face was about as red as fresh blood, and I'm as speechless as the ticket attendant. I'm thinking, What the hell was that . . . Harry's face was painted with a low watt smirk, and we didn't do anything but walk straight past the Northwest Coast Amerindian ex- hibition and land in the book store . . . where he pointed out a couple of books that I ought to buy. Harry was flush that day and he bought a pile of books.

It wasn't until sometime later that I was able to laugh about the incident. It was hilarious. It was always that way, in the midst of these scenes I had no time to enjoy the humor in what Harry was doing—partly because I was involved, playing a part—bodyguard, foil, lookout, straight man—and partly because I was disoriented and had no idea what ex- actly was going on.

Harry was not part of Timothy Leary's circle, nor was he ever invited to the gatherings at the Millbrook estate, but Leary admired his films because he thought they produced some of the same effects as LSD. Leary had presented public LSD events in the mid-1960s, and in the seventies was staging a series of fundraisers for his Castalia Founda- tion in the New Theater on East Fifty-Fourth Street in New York. The multimedia artist Gerd Stern's USCO (Company of US) joined him on some of these events, with light sculptures, multiscreen film projections, strobes, and other experimental light show effects as an introduction to other performers and lectures by Leary. "It was a great success," recalled Stern. "The auditorium was always full; everybody paid except Harry Smith":

> Harry came to one of the Psychedelic Theater pieces, and he started screaming about he was whatever he was, that he wasn't going to pay, these were old friends of his. Timothy and Richard Alpert had said there were nothing but spongers and people who didn't have any money in this world of ours, and they all wanted to get in free, and they were all friends of ours. We had set a definite policy. No one was going to get in free. Well, Harry got in free because he told Timothy that if [he] didn't get in free there wasn't going to be a show and there'd be a riot.

There were times when he spoke seriously, professorially, publicly lecturing a larger group, even on the street. On one occasion he approached a basketball court in the Village where a number of Black men regularly played and called through the wire fence to get their attention by calling them with the n-word. He proceeded to offer a history of the word, beginning with Latin roots and following its shifting meanings over time, then concluded by urging them to reclaim the word for their own proud use. (In a similar vein, around the same time period, Sun Ra lectured a downtown New York nightclub audience on the same word, though he derived it from a Hebrew word meaning "stranger" or "foreigner," and ended by claiming that word should be applied to every American—even Native Americans—America was a veritable land of n-worders.)

To those who had felt the sting of Harry's insults, it was always mystifying to see his behavior around children and women. He was patient and amusing to the young, entertaining them with music or games, teaching them, enjoying their presence. With women he could be respectful, admiring, protective, even courtly. When he was introduced. to Mireille Leterrier, a principal dancer with the Milwaukee

Ballet and the Pittsburgh Ballet Theatre, he went to see her dance, complimented her, found a place for her to stay in New York, stored some of her things, recorded her singing French folk songs, and warned her off people he thought were dangerous. Rani Singh, Anne Waldman, Rosebud Feliu, Peggy Biderman, Miriam Sanders, Rose Van Kirk, Barbara Rubin, and Shirley Clarke were among his friends and protectors.

Reggae had been thriving in Jamaica for some time before Harry first heard the music in the 1972 film *The Harder They Come*, with its pre-Rasta songs and its hints of spaghetti westerns. He was overjoyed by it, recommended it to everyone he knew, and began visiting West Indian festivals in Brooklyn, buying some folk instruments, and attempting to play them. When Patrick Hulsey became the producer of *Rockers*, a reggae-based film cloaked as a docudrama of the life of musicians in Jamaica, Harry was made an adviser. Hulsey, the director Ted Bafaloukos, and Harry had agreed that the star of the film should be the reggae drummer Leroy "Horsemouth" Wallace, and following some planning at dinner, the four of them went to Harry's room at the Chelsea, where, according to Bafaloukos, Wallace and Harry were:

> going at each other the whole time, two showmen trying to wear each other down. About six hours of non-stop talking. This time Horsey was playing straight man. A genuinely surreal performance. The topics? The Queen's racehorse getting a hard-on at the Ascot races, Fidel Castro's inability to move freely within Cuba, the Colonial system and its actual nonexistence, real estate in Rhodesia, whether Jamaica belongs to the Third World or the Turd World, Pliny the Elder's discovery of opium in the roots of lettuce, the Ninth

Cycle which represents the end of the world, the unbuttoned military fatigue jacket and air-brushed nipples on the cover of the Wailers' *Soul [Rebels]* album, on and on . . .

"The Friday and Saturday midnight screenings of *Rockers* and *The Harder They Come* were a ritual for Harry," Bafaloukos said. "The theater would be packed and Harry was thrilled to be with all the young people and the West Indian community. As soon as the lights would go down the entire theater would fill up with marijuana smoke."

Harry's turn to reggae was not merely another case of a taste for the exotic and unusual that had driven his choices in putting together his *Anthology*. He clearly enjoyed highly rhythmic music, as he also took to disco in the same time period, buying records and recommending that people should see Donna Summer in the film *Thank God It's Friday*.

His interest in different music was not always shared with his friends. If he went to jazz clubs, it was with Charles Compo, a young musician who was working in funk bands and touring with oldies acts like the Ink Spots and the Platters; for punk clubs he went with Raymond Foye. "He especially liked the punk scene, the youthful energy, where he could act out (and out-punk the punks) and not get in trouble. Rosebud's son, Harley, was in a band called the Cro-Mags, and Harry followed them club to club."

As he neared the completion of *Mahagonny*, Harry also finished *Film No. 17*, a new version of 1957's *Film No. 11* that he expanded slightly and synchronized to Thelonious Monk's *Misterioso* in *Film No. 11, Mirror Animations*. Harry described this third version, *Mirror Animations Extended*, as "a collage animation" and had it printed forward, backward, and then forward again. The soundtrack was once more Monk's *Misterioso*, and it, too, was run forward, backward, and forward. In a lecture, he talked about *No. 17* as "the film that The-lonious Monk, Nellie Monk, and Percy Heath were paying for" and explained the film:

> If (as many suppose), the unseen world is the real world and the world of our senses but the transient symbols of the eternal unseen, and limiting ourselves to the aesthetic experience's well-known predilection for the eyes and ears, we could logically propose that any one projection of a film is variant from any other. This is particularly true of *Mirror Animations*. Although studies for this film were made in the early 1960s, the non-existence of suitable printing equipment until recently, my inability to locate the original camera footage until 1979, and particularity, the lack of an audience ready to evaluate L. Wittgenstein's "Ethics and Aesthetics are One and the Same," in the light of H. C. Agrippa's earlier, "there is no form of madness more dangerous than that arrived at by rational means" have all contributed to delaying until now the availability of a print in the full mirror-reverse form originally envisioned. I hope you like it.

The planning, filming, and editing of *Mahagonny* had taken almost ten years, and Harry was again asking for money to finish it, this time from the New York Film Awards, and, again, he was given money, $10,000, with the backing of the judges, Robert Frank and Henry Geldzahler. But this time Geldzahler insisted that the film be finished and screened within six months. To everyone's surprise, Harry met the deadline, though he would never say he had finished it.

The premiere of *Film No. 18* (as Harry initially titled it) was at Anthology Film Archives on March 13, 1980, and scheduled for nine more evenings over two weeks. The press release said (or warned) that it would be a 241-minute, four-projector presentation, "a highly structured mathematical analysis of the emotional connotations of Weill and Brecht's Mahagonny, the film will be a 'live' presentation with Smith restructuring the film at each performance. No two screenings will be absolutely identical because of this reorganization . . . (Smith hopes to eventually expand the film to more than four screens) . . . No. 18 is more of an event than a film . . . In Smith's art the opera of Brecht and Weill has been transformed into a numerological system and a primordial symbol system."

In the projection booth, there were four Elmo 16 CL 16mm projectors with gels attached to them to change the films' color, and hand-painted glass slides. Originally, he had intended to fit each projector lens with the glass slides so that on-screen images would appear framed in Moorish or Greek borders, baroque theater prosceniums, or comedy and tragedy masks. Two projectionists handled twelve twenty-minute rolls of film, and Harry operated a tape recording of the opera records and a spotlight with red, green, and yellow filters. He was in the booth at all times, following his notes but making changes nightly, though all four films always ended exactly at the same moment. The four screens were stacked in twos, in effect changing the shape of a motion picture screen from a rectangle to a square.

At the premiere of the film, Harry walked to the front, looked around, and said, "Some of you are friends, some of you are in this film, and then there are all these other people who I've never seen before." Susan Sontag, sitting next to Raymond Foye, whispered, "That's called audience." He next thanked several people including Robert Mapplethorpe for the footage he shot in Robert's studio, and then paraphrased the closing paragraph of Claude Lévi-Strauss's *The Origin of Table Manners: Introduction to a Science of Mythology, Vol. 3*:

In the present century, when man is actively destroying countless living forms, after wiping out so many societies whose wealth and diversity had, from time immemorial, constituted the better part of his inheritance, it has probably been never more necessary to proclaim, as do the myths, that sound humanism does not begin with oneself, but puts the world before life, life before man, and respect for others before self-interest; and that no species, not even our own, can take the fact that of having been on this earth for one or even two million years—since, in any case, man's stay here will one day come to an end—as an excuse for appropriating the world as if it were a thing and behaving on it with neither decency nor discretion.

The film opens at dusk in Manhattan. Some of what follows takes place in the Chelsea, but most of it is in Central Park and the streets of the city. A woman is seen knitting, Allen Ginsberg eats a banana, Rosebud and Patti Smith make appearances, string figures are performed by Kathy Elbaum, lovers kiss and quarrel; there is origami, dancers, Hindu deities, stop-action animation of cigarettes and household items; cars, bicycles, and people kaleidoscopically crash together and then disappear; throughout there are candles, marbles, shells, and colored sand—things that might also be found in a young boy's homemade museum. A Times Square sign repeatedly appears, reading, YOU'VE GOT A GREAT FUTURE BEHIND YOU. An animated tearing up of real money draws some of the strongest reactions from the audience. In the first hour the images are often paired in different ways, some reversed so they face one another, part Rorschach, part hallucination. For most of the second hour, the images are not often paired; in the third portion, roughly the last thirty-five minutes, images are paired again, though slightly out of sync and so might seem to be moving.

In addition to Harry's plan to reach audiences across the globe, he also intended *Mahagonny* to be a totally new film experience. The

opera soundtrack was played at high volume at each of its performances, and could at times seem detached from the film. In some
of the animated sequences involving colored pills and joints, Peggy
Biderman's fingers appear in the frame when she was not able to get
them out of the way before Harry clicked the image. (He was delighted with the effect, according to Foye.) Out-of-sync sequences,
overexposure, reversed images, speed changes, repetition of images,
reframing and reshaping the screen from rectangle to square, and verbal disruptions of the performances—all would appear to be an effort
to expose and demystify the techniques of conventional narrative motion pictures. He again said that the best response to the film would
be for the audience to fall asleep.

True or not, stories about Harry's presentations on different nights
quickly became local legends. Depending on his mood or drug intake,
they said, he played tricks on the audience, set off fireworks in the theater, or verbally insulted the audience. As Mekas put it, he was "very
temperamental . . . Harry could behave badly, but we respected him
because he was a very erudite, complex person." The house was full each
night, made up of Smith fans, devotees of the new cinema, and a larger-
than-usual number of young people. Dr. Gross came on opening night
and other nights, but after an argument the day before the sixth performance, Harry told him to stay away. At the next screening, Harry,
again high on amphetamines, began shouting at the projectionists and
throwing things. The audience could hear the noise, and was staring
back at the booth; some of those already familiar with Harry's performances were amused, while others were left wondering what was
wrong. As the films started, Dr. Gross walked into the theater, and
when Harry saw him, he stopped the projectors, ran into the audience,
grabbed Gross, shoved him out the door, then returned to grab the
painted glass slides and threw them into the street. The film series could
have been continued as planned, since most of the broken slides were
not being used, but Mekas canceled the remaining four screenings.

"I think everyone had the sense that they were seeing something completely different from anything that had ever been seen before in film," Foye recalled. "It was autobiographical, symbolic, anthropological, hermetic . . . it had no boundaries . . . [Afterward] you left the theater with a lot of questions, very puzzled, and slightly uneasy. Harry always operated between the extremes of creativity and destructiveness. [*Mahagonny*] presented that tension, but also happily resolved it with a work that was clearly a masterpiece."

Mahagonny was seen by only a few hundred people, and received just two reviews at the time, both favorable, then faded quietly into film studies history. It was restored in 2002 by Rani Singh, with Michael Friend, Simon Lund, and Balázs Nyari in a single screen 35mm print divided into four parts. (Their work was helped by Harry having had 35mm slides shot by Robert Haller during one live performance, anticipating a restoration.) J. Hoberman's review of the new version in *The Village Voice* showed that it was still a film to be reckoned with, and remained difficult to explain and describe: "Smith's *Mahagonny* is essentially an object of contemplation, like an altarpiece or a 19th-century philosophical toy . . . [It] works far more as a composition than a narrative . . . The movie is a magic assemblage—subject to its own recognizable but baffling laws. The uncanniest thing about this ceremonial projection is the sense that the screen is literally casting a spell, gesticulating back at you." Since 2002 it has been publicly screened only a few times.

If *Mahagonny* was in any way a disappointment to Harry, it wasn't reflected in his work plans. He was hoping that it might create renewed interest in the *Oz* film, and in the next twelve months he completed five new films. *No. 19*, now lost, was in 35-millimeter, color, and wide-screen, and used excerpts from *Oz*. Shortly after, he set to work on *Film No. 20: Fragments of a Faith Restored*, a color and wide-screen 35mm compilation of films *No. 16* and *19*, a film that was to be shown at Alice Tully Hall on June 29, 1981, as part of a fundraiser for Anthology Film Archives. Harry worked hard preparing posters for it, styled like Plains Indian beadwork, joking that when he was finished with them, he would stencil CANCELED across them. Then the show was canceled. Little is known about *Film No. 21* (also known as *Raoul* or *Rose/Raoul*), and *No. 22* is now lost. *Film No. 23* consists of two rolls of film, superimposed on each other, with a single soundtrack, made up of samples from Kurt Weill's 1934 *Johnny Johnson* musical, but adding Burgess Meredith reading various World War II–related statements over the music, along with bird noises, phone calls, and Harry talking. Portraits of Robert Mapplethorpe and Patti Smith shot in the early seventies during the filming of *Mahagonny* are superimposed over string figures, storefronts, and sand animation. Harry's plan was to distribute the film with a booklet that would contain a series of papers Kathy Elbaum had written for her dissertation on string figures, along with instructions on how to make those seen in the film. "All in all, the film, together with the booklet will give a species of cross-cultural comparison between Rankin Inlet and Manhattan and thus correct some of those ills that affect destinies."

James Litaker, a painter and a member of the Chelsea staff, introduced Harry to Charles Compo. "The first time I ever met Harry was at Litaker's loft on thirtieth street and Broadway a couple of blocks from the Breslin in 1978."

> I had just turned twenty and was very interested in Aleister Crowley and the whole Golden Dawn thing. James told me that I should really meet this guy he knew from the Chelsea Hotel and invited me over one time while he was there at his loft. Harry didn't say a word, just sat there and seemed to take in the freewheeling, weed induced conversation that the rest of us were having ranging from art to sports to the occult to money to girls. As we were all heading on our way, he

came up to me and told me that I should drop by the Breslin sometime to say hello.

I dropped by a week or so later and was amazed by the collection of art, books and records that he managed to fit into the tiny room. He had stacks of his India ink drawings, some of them on the wall. I asked him about the one that was most central just above his record player and he told me that it was [*The Fall of the Rebel Angels*]. He had constructed really intricate frames for the paintings out of cardboard. It turned out that he had only recently moved in and over the next couple of years he managed to accumulate at least twice that amount. He set a chair in the middle of the room and told me to take a seat, like it was an interview. He asked me what I had been reading and I told him about the occult stuff, Crowley, MacGregor Mathers and the others and he dismissed them as a waste of time, stating that Crowley was nothing more than a Victorian parlor poet. Once when my girlfriend and I were making out in front of the [Magickal] Childe where an [OTO] ritual was being performed, Harry saw us and said, "What you're doing out here, they should be doing in there." His focus was anthropology, not esotericism. Over the next five years I spent at least four days a week with him, many times leaving at two or three in the morning to catch the train back to Williamsburg.

Harry was looking for someone to help him with music projects. Music was more important to him than most of his friends seemed to know. Though he had moved on from the days of the *Anthology of American Folk Music*, he could sing American Indian songs and was up-to-date on the latest jazz styles. Harry liked to dance, and when he was asked about some of the older forms of dance, he and Peggy Biderman would perform them in his tiny room.

He wanted to know more about music theory, and Compo was

teaching him, so Harry hired him as his music assistant and paid him in money, food, and gifts. Harry was still working on the "forty-nine" songs and wanted to produce another Kiowa album. Moe Asch had recently found the misplaced master tapes for the shape note singing record set that had been missing for twenty-five years, and gave Harry an advance of $100 for the notes. At the same time, Harry was searching for all the recordings he could find of the ballad "Barbara Allen" and the African American folk poem "Shine and the *Titanic*," and making tapes of the different versions. He had chosen two examples of folk forms that were truly iconic: a classic British and American ballad and an oral poem, one believed to have originated among Black prisoners in the United States who called such heroic epics "toasts."

"Barbara Allen" tells the story of a dying man who asked for his beloved to visit him before he died, but she refused. Harry had recorded it with "a lady in a flowered hat," Litha Chesney, who came into the hotel in Oklahoma where he was staying and asked to be recorded, and she told Harry she knew Barbara Allen and hated her. "Oh! I could tell you some things about her!" "She then proceeded to sing a pretty good version of the song. And never realizing that Samuel Pepys had mentioned it in his diary for 1666." "Shine and the *Titanic*" is the story of a Black seaman who repeatedly warns the captain of the *Titanic* that they are sinking, only to be ignored. As the ship sinks, the captain calls for his help, but Shine has already jumped in the water and begun to swim. Some versions have the seaman calling back to the captain, "Get your ass in the water and swim like me," and end with him safe in a bar by the time the news arrives of the disaster: "When all them white folks went to heaven / Shine was in Sugar Ray's in Harlem drinking Seagram's Seven."

This search for songs and oral poetry were part of a self-study of American folklore that Harry was pursuing in depth. He read all the important books on the subject, his favorite being Stith Thompson's *The Folktale*, which attempted to find all the written versions of the folktales in the world, describing and classifying them by their motifs, showing how widespread and yet similar they were. It was the kind of thing that Harry aspired to, and occasionally tried himself, making lists of new versions of tales that appeared in print after Thompson's book was published in 1946, and noting similarities.

Compo accompanied Harry almost daily to the Strand Bookstore and Barnes & Noble to buy books. Together they often went to the Sidney Janis Gallery, which was then shifting from the promotion of pop art to graffiti. "Part of our daily routine during the years I was apprenticed to him," Compo said, "[was that] we would head directly to the Anthology Film Archives and pick up about twenty dollars from Jonas, then head directly to Strand to buy some books (often $1 each), and then he would allocate the balance to Salem 100s and beer. When we were particularly flush, we would go to Cedars of Lebanon or A Taste of India to eat. He usually ordered a Black Russian (vodka and coffee) and soup."

Charles was a multi-instrumentalist and a composer, and Harry had him play solo flute for some of the films he showed at the Film-Makers' Cooperative and Anthology Film Archives. When he introduced Charles to Moe Asch in 1983, Compo became one of the last to be signed to Folkways Records. His album was *Seven Flute Solos*, a title that doesn't reveal that by using a four-track machine, Harry overdubbed the flute, shifted tape speeds, and used reverberation and echoes to create a series of flute quartets with Compo playing each part. It was an avant-garde recording of its time, using ethnic sources, jazz improvisation, as well as improvised recording techniques. Asch asked Compo who was writing the liner notes for the album, and when he said Harry, Asch exclaimed, "Are you crazy? We'll all be dead before he finishes them!" He was almost right. Harry had written hundreds of pages about the flute in different cultures, but without mentioning Compo or the record. Asch died shortly after it was finished, Harry a few years later. The record was not available until 2004, when the Smithsonian acquired Folkways.

"For Harry the world was a magical universe filled with nefarious forces," according to Compo.

> He only really seemed to care about two things, the plight of the underdog and the great work of the artist. I spent hundreds of days with him during my early twenties and we never ever discussed anything to do with current affairs or politics. The time was divided between making art, talking about ideas, listening to music, looking at books or just laughing. We talked a lot about Max Müller, the Upanishads, and the discovery of the first Mesopotamian law collection, the Hammurabi Code. Lots of times he would ramble on telling story after story and I would have no idea about who or what he was talking about . . .
>
> When he was at work on something, he would not say what it meant. Or how he was doing it, if asked. But you could learn from his free-associated talk. He had little interest in the outcome of his work; the doing of it was most important, and he often dropped the projects before finishing them. He was one of the few people I've known completely committed to art. He was only interested in the thing itself, not the idea of art or worthwhile activities that would lead to fame and fortune.

In 1982 the Anthology Film Archives created a portfolio of contemporary artists' prints to sell in aid of renovating and moving into a permanent home on Second Avenue. The project was supported by praise from Henry Geldzahler, Edward Koch, Elia Kazan, Martin

Scorsese, Leo Castelli, and others. *A Portfolio of Thirteen Prints to Commemorate the Conversion of New York City's Second Avenue Courthouse Building into the New Home of Anthology Film Archives, the First Museum Dedicated to Avantgarde Film and Video, 1981–82* was set in a burgundy portfolio case, each print signed, numbered, and dated by the artist, and limited to seventy-five editions at $8,000 each. The artists were Raimund Abraham, Rudolf Baranik, Joseph Beuys, Alice Neel, Claes Oldenburg, Robert Rauschenberg, James Rosenquist, Richard Serra, Harry Smith, May Stevens, Andy Warhol, and William Wegman. Harry's contribution was *Untitled*, embossing with Chine-collé on kozo (mulberry) and Arches cover, 22 x 30, 1982. His own copy of the portfolio was later destroyed when he ripped it to pieces in anger.

Despite the work he was accomplishing, he was weak and suffering from stomach ulcers in early spring of 1983, and not seeing many people. He once locked himself in over Thanksgiving in protest over a "hypocritical holiday," and disappeared over Christmas and New Year's.

An exception was Harvey Bialy. Near the Breslin was the office of *Bio/Technology*, and Harry came to know one of its editors, Bialy, a molecular biologist who was also a poet and artist with deep interest in the occult. Harry was fascinated by genetic engineering and was keeping up with its early results. "I could bring Harry as many back issues of *Nature* as he wanted, as well as review copies of expensive, unreadable (by anybody but him and the copy editors) scientific tomes on astrophysics, seismic activities, aboriginal weaving patterns, etc. . . . In return for these arcanic journals and books, which I would deliver once a week, Harry would play a 90-minute cassette he had recorded especially to educate me about the astounding varieties of music in the world from his really big library. He would command me to sit and not move and not say anything and would proceed to put the tape in his quality deck. After we would smoke and talk, and before I left he would give me the cassette." Bialy later devoted much of a web-site to some of those DJ cassettes: One included music from Togo and Cameroon, Rabbi Abulafia singing a Seder song, Shel Silverstein's "The Ballad of the Dying Beatnik" and "I Know She's Going to Get Around to Me," and a hare-and-tortoise children's song/tale from the Shona of Zimbabwe. Another had nineteen versions of "Barbara Al-len." Bialy also put up several of Harry's Naropa lectures, but with annotations, such as Harry singing part of a Silverstein song in the middle of a lecture, and another where Gregory Corso interrupted the talk with comments about the students in the class.

After nine years at the Hotel Breslin, Harry, now sixty-one, was given notice in August 1984 that he would have to move to another room in the hotel because of renovations. But he refused their offer ("because I was stubborn"), and it took four months of packing with the help of friends to get ready to move out of the hotel. Robert Frank thought it was important enough that he filmed one of the days when he was packing. Many of his books and records were moved into storage in the basement of the Anthology Film Archives. His paintings were taken to Jonas Mekas's loft.

Allen Ginsberg invited him to stay with him for a couple of weeks until he found a new place, but during the second week, Harry suf-fered a compression fracture of the knee when he stepped between two cars, and one moved and pinned his leg between the bumpers. "Two weeks turned into eight months," Ginsberg lamented, "eight stormy and amazing months," with Harry's agenda clashing with Ginsberg's, while his host cooked for him and saw to his health problems. Harry, however, did some book covers for him. Ginsberg had planned to ask de Kooning to do the artwork for *Collected Poems 1947–1980*, but gave the job to Harry as he did for *White Shroud* and *The Annotated Howl*. He also did a drawing for "Journal Night Thoughts," a poem Ginsberg said had been influenced by Harry's presence. Four years later, Ginsberg, perhaps in the spirit of Harry's drug notes on his film productions, added a list of the drugs he used in the writing of the poem (yage, psilocybin, LSD, nitrous oxide, and mescaline). He identified Harry as the magician mentioned in the poem and as the source of one part of it which he marked with a note saying "Smith's Anthropological Gossip" (recalling T. S. Eliot's "The Waste Land," in which there were included what Eliot called "anthropological footnotes"). In 1984, Ginsberg asked Harry for some artwork to accompany the 1961 poem, for which he produced an ink, pencil, and charcoal sketch titled *Southern Cult Composite: The Staten Island Massacre*, with some of the figures in it drawn from an *American Anthropologist* article by A. J. Waring and Preston Holder, "A Prehistoric Ceremonial Complex in the Southeastern United States," and the second part of the title possibly referring to the Dutch massacre of a Raritan village on Long Island in 1654.

THE NIGHT THAT BOB DYLAN ALMOST MET HARRY SMITH

One spring night in 1985, Harry, Ginsberg, and Raymond Foye were going over photographs in Ginsberg's apartment that he intended to turn into a book. Harry went to bed around eleven. Shortly afterward, Bob Dylan called and asked if Ginsberg would listen to a tape of what was to be his new album, *Empire Burlesque*. A few minutes later Dylan arrived with his tape and a six-pack of beer, and as they started listening, Allen complained that he couldn't hear the words, so Dylan had to recite them to him as the record played. "Suddenly," Foye said, "Harry Smith was yelling from his room off the kitchen: 'Turn down that music! Don't you understand I'm trying to sleep!'" Allen turned off the speakers in the kitchen but they continued listening.

"'So, Harry Smith is living with me,' Ginsberg proudly announced. Dylan looked genuinely amazed at this fact. 'Harry Smith,' he repeated the name slowly. 'Now that's somebody I've always wanted to meet,' Dylan said with enthusiasm. 'I'll go get him,' Allen said, hurrying out of the room. But Harry, having retired, simply refused to get out of bed. He began yelling for them to turn down the music, as the speakers were right next to his room. When Ginsberg came back and reported that Harry was not getting out of bed, Dylan looked disappointed but impressed." (During the evening Ginsberg and Dylan ran out of cigarettes, so Ginsberg went back into Harry's room and took some of his, with more yelling from Harry.)

The next day Raymond phoned the apartment: "Harry Smith answered. I asked why he hadn't got up the previous night and he mumbled some excuse, and I got the sense he was actually afraid to meet him." But Harry did remark that Dylan's speaking voice was much higher-pitched than he'd imagined. He also noted how humane he sounded. That same day, Harry called Scott Feero, saying, "You should have been here last night, Bob Dylan was here." He then invited Feero to come over to Ginsberg's, and "at some point started talking about Dylan, talking of this and that, and without giving me any context says, 'The man doesn't understand why I refuse to meet him.'" Scott believed that Harry thought of Dylan as his own creation, the product of the *Anthology*, and that he didn't want to upset the spiritual relationship between them.

Eight months in an apartment already crowded with Ginsberg's office employees and constant visitors, and he had still been unable to talk Harry into finding his own place. Then, early in September 1985, he arranged for Harry to move to Cooperstown, New York, to live with Mary Beach and Claude Pélieu, who had offered to take Harry in and care for him. Ginsberg thought life in the country would help him reduce his drinking and improve his health, and he gave him $5,000 to help sustain him upstate for months, all of which he spent as soon as he arrived on the train, buying old farm tools, locks, and keys at a local shop. He soon became involved with the town's residents and its history, and made a four-by-five-foot city out of paper towel and toilet paper tubes and blown-out eggs, something similar to what he had also created at Ginsberg's and when he was a child. But he was still too weak to easily get from his upstairs bedroom to the bathroom below, and filled bottles and paper bags with excreta (as Harry would say), which led to him being asked to leave by his hosts. When asked about his move, he said he was asked by the town's health officials for "growing certain kinds of mushrooms out of season, and it was giving off a terrible smell."

By early spring 1986, he was back in New York, where Bill Breeze met him at the train and helped him check into the Washington Square Hotel, the former Hotel Earle. But when he was unable to pay, Dr. Gross took him into his Upper West Side apartment, and quickly found that he would not be able to keep him. Once again, Harry disappeared.

Gross located him in the Andrews House on the Bowery (a "Franciscan flophouse," Harry called it) in December, malnourished and bedridden by flu, so he asked Bill Breeze if Harry could stay in one of three apartments Breeze was renting in a brownstone building at 345 Twelfth Street in Brooklyn that was to be unoccupied for a few months. There he remained for the winter of 1986–1987, mostly sleeping, living on little more than milk and aspirin, and seeing few visitors other than Dr. Gross. When the new tenants arrived, he had to move again. "They kind of shuffle me around like a valuable antique," Harry said. "It's been terrible."

Once again, he returned to Andrews House, but then moved in with Charles and Susan Compo on Fourteenth Street in Park Slope,

Brooklyn. He lasted there for a few months until the lice he had picked up in the Bowery became too much for them. There was next a brief stay with the photographer Jean-Loup Dumortier and Kat Le Beau on Tenth Street, on the Lower East Side.

During this strange New York odyssey, Harry was still visiting Ginsberg. Sometimes it was because he had a check that needed cashing and having no bank account, Ginsberg's assistant, Bob Rosenthal, would run the checks through Ginsberg's account and give him cash. He'd stay for tea and leave. Then he stopped coming.

Someone heard that he was again back in the Andrews House, and Ginsberg found him there, in his tiny cubicle.

> In order to get in and out he had to move books aside and so I couldn't get in the room with him, I had to talk to him from the half-opened door. And it turned out that he had gotten so weak from malnutrition that he couldn't very easily get out to go get food and he had no money anyway and he was starving . . . So I told him that he'd better come back and stay with me for a while and he recovered some . . . But one problem was that his mouth was full of decayed, abscessed teeth, and his friend Dr. Gross was trying to arrange a mouth operation, but Harry was adamant . . . So all he could eat was certain kinds of pea soup and mashed bananas. And eating at the table with him he gurgled up all the saliva. It was horrifying . . .

It was clear to Ginsberg that Harry could not survive living alone, and that he would be the only one willing to put up with his idiosyncratic behavior, now all the more aggravating since Harry's health meant he would be in the apartment more than ever. Harry did keep busy, however, doing some of the things he did when he was more mobile—artwork and recording.

EAVESDROPPING ON THE WORLD

> That summer I would ride my bike over the bridge, lock it
> up in front of one of the bars on Orchard Street and drift
> through the city on foot, recording. Sidewalk smokers, lovers'
> quarrels, drug deals. I wanted to store the world and play it
> back just as I'd found it, without change or addition. I collected
> thunderstorms, music coming out of cars, the subway trains
> rumbling underfoot . . .
>
> —Hari Kunzru, *White Tears* (in interviews, Kunzru credits Smith's
> recording activities with inspiring his novel)

Harry carried a camera with him everywhere he went during high
school and in his years in California. When small tape recorders first
appeared, they became his instrument of choice, his constant com-
panion on the streets when his health allowed. Some of his recordings were simply a record of his wandering. At other times, his street
recordings were of the type that folklorists, ethnomusicologists, and
bird-watchers make. He recorded children's game songs and birds
heard during his walks. Later, when he was again living alone in a
Bowery shelter, too weak and sick to leave the building, he recorded
the prayers and dying sounds of the sick in the cubicles near his own.
He wanted to match the dying with the sounds of children being born.

With Bob Dylan's encouragement, Ginsberg began using Sony
portable recorders to document his poems and songs during his travels, some of which were worked into *The Fall of America* and other
poems over the years. When Harry first moved into Ginsberg's apartment, he began soundscaping the ambient sounds of New York City:

> I had this kind of machine [Sony D6], and he exhausted
> two of them—or over-used them. If he'd see a machine of
> mine he'd grab it for his studies, so I gave him one, but he
> got the other one off me too. He put the microphone out

the window, wrapped in a towel, and just sucked in all the sounds of the city for miles around with the microphone● Sort of like Cageian music. And it climaxed on July 4th when you get all the fireworks. That's mostly what he was doing. He did it hour after hour, day after day. Also he'd take the machine to Brooklyn and taped Haitian street fairs, or Hispanic celebrations, concerts in open parks.

Peter O. Whitmer, an author visiting Ginsberg, got his first view of Harry in the midst of what seemed to be his effort to record the entire island of Manhattan from the Lower East Side:

> He was excited about his latest project, which involved a new way of "listening to the world." One microphone is stuck out onto the street side of the apartment and another is stuck out onto the more peaceful courtyard side in a sort of urban stereo. "That's what I do . . . is take all the sounds and speed them up so I can edit them. I have found surges in sound, punctuated by a single bird call or dog bark, that are pure beauty. These surges—these waves of energy—are really fascinating. So far I have recorded two full moons and a summer solstice—about one hundred hours in all."
>
> I asked Harry what was the best way to listen to it, meaning should you use earphones, or maybe it should be heard in a large indoor auditorium or . . . "I'd say with heroin," he replied. "That's probably the best. After all, it is one hundred twenty hours."

These soundscape recordings were similar to those being made by Tony Schwartz, then the most important sound documentarian in the country. Harry knew his work, since Moe Asch had begun issuing Schwartz's recordings on Folkways in 1956. The first was a recording of a radio program Schwartz had done for WNYC called *Sounds of My City*, which included rain, street musicians, subways, conversations, and an abbreviated version of a twenty-four-hour recording made from the window of his mid-Manhattan apartment. Schwartz's fascination with the sounds of the city was largely limited to an area around his west Midtown Manhattan apartment, as he was agoraphobic (one of his Folkways records was titled *New York 19*, an early postal zone in which he lived). He had also been blinded for a time during his childhood, and was conscious of what Harry called "the universal rhythm that pulses through the city."

Harry sometimes explained the hundreds of hours he put into these recordings as part of a project he called *Materials for the Study of the Religion and Culture of the Lower East Side*. Or he would say that projects such as the recording of the sounds of hammers, fans, or everyday objects and activities could be used for education of the blind, and that he planned to donate them to the Helen Keller Services for the Blind. But neither was ever followed through on.

Harry's constant presence had again become unbearable to Ginsberg. He was appropriating Ginsberg's space and possessions, constantly recording activities both inside the apartment and out the window, expecting Ginsberg to schedule his days around him, and pay his bills. (Once asked if he had any aspirin, Harry replied, "I don't have any, but here's some of Allen's. The way I see it, what's mine is mine, but what's Ginsberg's is the world's.") He was an unreliable host when Ginsberg wasn't there, sending some visitors quickly out the door, or complaining about Ginsberg not liking him. Ginsberg's analyst had warned that Harry was driving up Ginsberg's blood pressure and that he should make him leave. He admitted that he had once hit Harry in exasperation.

Pleas to several people to accept Harry as a roommate failed, so when Allen was invited to the University of Mississippi by the folklorist William Ferris for a poetry reading in the spring of 1987, he brought his stepmother, Edith, and Harry along with him. "At one point," Ferris recalled, "Allen took me aside and said that Harry had broken his leg the previous fall and moved into Allen's apartment to recover. Harry's leg had healed, but he refused to move out. Allen asked if I could find a way to keep him in Oxford, and I said that was probably not a solution."

The guests stayed longer than was planned, wandering across Faulkner country, with Harry recording a number of songs by various singers. One was a man who worked with the blues singer Furry Lewis, and had learned some songs that Lewis had never recorded. When Harry heard of a Black barbershop owned by the barber and blues singer Wade Walton, they traveled to Clarksdale, where Ginsberg had his hair cut while Harry recorded scissor rhythms and the slaps of a straight razor against a leather sharpening strop.

That spring Harry said he had a seizure. Dr. Gross doubted it was a seizure, and thought it was a tantrum, but it was also possible that it was a bad result of freebasing cocaine. Whatever it was, Gross said Harry wound up in Beth Israel Hospital, where a doctor told him that if he kept drinking, he would die. He did cut his alcohol intake, and struggled to quit Valium altogether. For a brief spell, he lived in the Jane Hotel in the West Village, a former sailor's inn that had become a favorite of downtown theater and music performers. He had a desk at nearby Mystical Fire Video, a company cofounded by Bill Breeze, and was doing covers for them. Breeze by then had become patriarch of Ecclesia Gnostica Catholica, the liturgical part of OTO, and he in turn made Harry a bishop. (Harry delighted in referring to his office as the bishopric.)

But bishop or not, when Harry returned to Ginsberg's apartment, Allen in desperation turned to Jonas Mekas to ask if he could help set up some kind of fund to ensure Harry's survival during the next twelve months or so. Instead, Mekas made him artist in residence at Anthology Film Archives for 1987 to 1988, where "he used to come early and work all day in the little room I had given him." By summer he had regained his strength in part, but was nowhere near recovered when Ginsberg, Steve Taylor, and Peter Orlovsky were scheduled to go to Naropa Institute in Boulder, Colorado. Naropa, the first Buddhist-inspired institution of higher learning in the United States, had been founded in 1974 by Ginsberg's guru, the Tibetan Buddhist Chögyam Trungpa, an advocate of "crazy wisdom." He had asked Ginsberg to create a summer writing program for the school, and Ginsberg, Anne Waldman, John Cage, and Diane di Prima formed the Jack Kerouac School of Disembodied Poetics. When summer arrived in 1988, Allen saw no other option but to take Harry with them to Boulder.

SHAMAN-IN-RESIDENCE

To introduce Harry to the Boulder community, Ginsberg made plans with the University of Colorado film department to sponsor a mini-festival of his works. Stan Brakhage was teaching there, and in every course made a point of stressing his debt as a filmmaker to Harry. But when Harry failed to respond to letters from the university about what he would be screening or the date they had in mind, Ginsberg answered for him, and set a date for late June. Harry did appear at the festival and introduced *Heaven and Earth Magic* with what had become his standard opening, "I hope you enjoy the films. They made me gray." Then he left while it was still showing, declaring it as "too damn long."

At first, he stayed with Ginsberg in one of the apartments where the summer faculty was housed when they arrived in late June. Harry was not yet aware that Ginsberg was planning to have him remain at Naropa, and he was not told until the end of the summer session in July, when Ginsberg was leaving for New York. He had arranged for Harry to move into one of the cottages on campus that usually housed groundskeepers. Harry was surprised, but accepted it. After years of uncertainty and transience, he would now have his own house. Though it had only two rooms, it would be paid for. Someone would be assigned to make sure he had enough food and medicine. He even found a way to have his weed delivered to him through the campus mail room. With the climate and the comfort of not having to hustle someone for food and housing, Harry slipped quietly into campus life as a sixty-five-year-old, bearded, ninety-pound curiosity dressed in a blue-and-white seersucker jacket and sneakers.

Anne Waldman, professor and administrator of the summer program, had the weight of his presence dropped on her, but she said she was "totally supportive of bringing Harry to Naropa from New York City and to live on the campus, which was highly unusual/irregular. I had to argue for that to Naropa authorities on occasion and there was concern about him having marijuana constantly in the cottage, etc. Sometimes I waylaid visitors from the Administration who wanted to 'check-up' on him. But he was warmly respected by most of the community."

He was given the title of Shaman-in-Residence in the Jack Kerouac School, an unpaid position that had no duties except to give several lectures during the Summer Writing Program each year. But he took his role seriously, spending a great deal of time preparing for these lectures, making copies of academic publications for distribution to students, organizing films and recordings. The piles of books he was buying and adding to his cottage library were worked into the lectures and his discussions with students.

As part of his introduction to the campus, Harry submitted a handwritten "Life of Harry Smith," titled "And the Sins of the Children Shall be Visited Upon the Parents."

Born 1923 in Portland, Oregon to parents whose folly regarding their gender led to cyclical social and religious mania forcing Smith to accept his own duality with generous enthusiasm, and espouse the dualistic dictum of "make a person think they think and they love you; make them think, and they hate you."

Naturally the grandeur of this never-ending unhappiness, combined with his well-known greed, have provided many a private or corporate Maecenas to finance his excursions into that blunted hunger on the boundary of voice and vision.

He has made about 1500 recordings for restricted scientific use, and some 120 cuts commercially released, and has produced 23 films, about half of these being easily available.

His reason for coming to Boulder is to find out why he's such a damn fool, and he has heard that Naropa is the best place to find out such things.

Harry's insatiable curiosity was familiar to everyone who knew him, but what he wanted to know was often surprising. To learn about the Boulder area, he had three requests: a Presbyterian hymnal from a local church and visits to a bald eagle's nest and to the large weather station—the aeronautical weather station that's outside of Boulder (the National Center for Atmospheric Research).

His first appearance in public in Boulder was at Naropa's annual Fourth of July picnic. Rani Singh, a student at the University of Colorado and an assistant to Ginsberg in the summer program, said, "He showed up wearing a trench coat in ninety-degree heat, and strolled elegantly across the great lawn holding a Sony Walkman Professional cassette recorder (the second one he had borrowed from Ginsberg) in one gloved hand and a microphone in the other. He spent the entire day making audiotape recordings of the sounds at the party, which culminated in the fireworks display at evening's end."

The campus soon accepted that there was nothing he would not

be willing to document. Within a few weeks of his arrival, he had recorded hundreds of hours of ambient sounds, "pointing to the correla-
tion between auto horns, and birdcalls, and the inter-communication
between the machines and the animate world." He could record the
sounds of Boulder with a mike out the window, including crickets, ci-
cadas, and squirrels at different times of the day. He told Beth Borrus,
his assistant for his summer lectures, that he was looking for patterns:
"It was a long time before I realized that the squirrels were carrying
on intelligent communication between each other, which reached a
peak in the day when they were able to stop the birds from singing
when the sun came up, which is why I was recording the thing anyhow. They evidently had some prior agreement, the Dawn Chorale."

Naropa students wondered about the length of the recordings he
was making: "Harry will sometimes make continuous eight-hour
tapes of driving in cars, going to nightclubs, going to restaurants, . . .
being driven home. He will remain silent the whole time. An archive
of the night's events, he calls it. Then he gets home and listens with
his headphones, over and over. 'The interesting thing to do,' Harry
said, 'would be to record different sunrises at the same time, considering certain whistling noises that have been heard by thousands,
probably millions of people at this point. When the sun comes up. It
gives out definite squeals . . . And I'm sure there are periods also when
major and minor surges occur—during conversations in a nightclub.'"

A concert of some of his tapes was once given at Naropa, run
through a large sound system. "It was absorbing, it is music," Steven
Taylor told him. "Harry you're actually a great composer." "I know,"
he said, "'but don't tell anybody."

He could show up in classes and record them as field documents
of social gatherings, as he once did in Anne Waldman's class: "One
day I was teaching a Dharma class in an upstairs room in the main
building with a sizeable audience. And Harry was recording and later
commented on the way people were seated—how many women on
the right side, or men on the left. How many people were sneezing or

coughing or fidgeting? Also my phrasing. The actual content was less of an issue."

Visitors to his cottage treated him as an elder guru, and once again, as in Berkeley forty years before, there were students walking past Harry's tiny quarters, drawn by the stories they'd heard about its occupant. He was fascinated and amused by the Buddhist focus of the campus, and wandered through the city's parks and stores, quickly becoming a Boulder personage. He took his role seriously—the sonic documents, building his own library, working on various projects such as a film that he began with Nina Paul, a student of Stan Brakhage. It was to be called *Keys*, an animation of keys he had collected and copied from books.

Rani said, "Harry could turn the mundane, everyday things into magic":

> Harry's phone was a treasure trove to be explored as we became enthralled in the capacities of the phone and its services provided by US West. Harry subscribed to the Voice Messaging Service in which 175 three-minute messages could be stored and retrieved at whim. Harry then invited people to call up and leave creative messages on the recording, dream interpretations, songs, imitations, horrific stories, anything: as long as it was creative. I remember that Harry used to ask everyday: "Have you been creative today?" . . . I was amazed at the scope and depth of the recordings that were made. Harry was forever transcribing the times, dates, the who, what, where, and whys of the calls, and upon packing up his possessions I found pages of these lovingly, meticulous transcriptions.

He often received letters from prisoners whom he knew from his days at the Breslin or in one of the Lower East Side facilities. Somehow, they located him in his Rockies hideaway and reminisced about their days together in a bar on the Bowery, enclosing songs or poetry or crediting his *Anthology* for its influence. One talked of signaling to outer space from his cell, another about his successful robbery of a bank in Rockefeller Center, and wrote him on that bank's stationery. A drug dealer told him he was writing a book on Jack Kerouac.

Ginsberg left money to carry him for a few weeks, after which Harry would receive $10 a day for food, with necessary expenses such as his rent and his assistant's pay. When the student aides he hired didn't work out, the job was given to Jacqueline Gens, a poet and director of marketing and publications for Naropa. Harry was still weak and in bad health, and needed many visits to a doctor and a dentist, yet resisted their efforts for help and refused to apply for Social Security, Medicare, Medicaid, or Colorado State benefits. Rani Singh befriended Harry, and volunteered to drive him to stores and around Boulder. Gens happily passed her job on to Singh, who became "his assistant, secretary, chauffeur, valet, laundress, personal trainer, and dietician," as she put it.

Harry's house was furnished with little more than shelves, a card table, and a log and a rock to sit on. For outdoor furniture he arranged several tree stumps. He was sleeping on a pile of blankets until Singh urged him to buy a futon (child-sized, Harry's choice). Though he loudly complained to the administration that he didn't need a "manager," Singh became his ally, his champion on campus and off, and the main protector of his legacy after his death.

Shortly after Ginsberg returned to New York, Harry's unpaid bills were forwarded to him, and he was appalled to see that Harry had spent all the money he'd given him in local bookstores, but had failed to pay for medical care, rent, or food. "When Harry would get into his mind that he needed a particular book, completely necessary to his path of thought at that moment," Singh explained, "nothing could stand in his way. Every possible way to cash an invisible check, along with creative bartering would be used until we'd arrive at the bookstore, money or scheme in hand . . . He often bought second and third copies of critical books that he'd already had in New York, surreptitiously packed."

John Feins, a graduate student in writing at Naropa, sometimes accompanied Harry on his buying trips. "Harry was the only being who could ever outlast me in a bookstore":

I had best friends who would simply abandon me, leave and take the wheels rather than continue to wait for me to respond at long last to their pleas to leave after hours of browsing. Yet I would drive Harry to a store and after about half a day I might be ready for the next phase, if only to recaffeinate or eat—but not Harry. He searched and searched and searched and searched and searched, no matter how recently he might have done the very same.

We'd go to a massive, packed, half a city-block long two-story affair and you could actually experience a customer come in, ask the proprietor something, and then hear him holler out to Harry, "Hey Harry, have we got any Leo Frobenius?"

"Yes," Harry would answer in his signature sly, drawn out throaty and nasally way, "there's a second edition of *Kulturgeschichte Afrikas* misfiled in Travel, behind the double stack on the second shelf from the bottom."

We'd leave with a stack of mostly complex and scholarly/ historic titles that only a polymath's polymath would gather together, near half as tall as Harry. He'd hustled the dough for the books of course, often from his slightly exasperated but ever-accommodating main patron Allen Ginsberg—and repair to his cabin for nutritional smoke and conversation.

Ginsberg had his own peculiar attitude toward money. He hated accumulating it, and had no savings account. When he needed money, he knew how to get it. For a long time, he wouldn't accept money for poetry readings, and when he finally did, he put the earnings into the Committee on Poetry fund or gave it away. Between the personal expenses that he wrote off on his taxes and the money he spent on his staff or others he was supporting, he had very little money of his own. So when Harry began making large purchases in Boulder and charging them to him, Ginsberg realized that if this continued, he would not be able to support him.

He wrote Harry, and included a list of what his expenses had been since late June to early September, all of which had already been paid for by Ginsberg, or were new bills suddenly come due. Harry had left New York without paying for storage of his books, or for the repairs on his sound equipment. When he developed pneumonia in Boulder, he still had not applied for benefits, and was unable to pay for anything, and was down to his last can of soup.

> Well, Harry I can't afford this subsidy of all your book buy-
> ing habits. This may seem religious or noble behavior to you,
> but the fact is at my expense, and others, financially. Small
> amounts of money in the past have been OK, but such sub-
> sidy as $3887 [$8,000 in current dollars] for ten weeks is
> impossible for me to maintain, and even you must recog-
> nize this unless you are so imperceptive and habituated that
> I would be advised to kick our relationship cold turkey as far
> as money. If you force me to, I will do that. You have other
> sources of money: grants (Guggenheim, NEA or Smithso-
> nian, whatever) or sale of your archives and collections or
> pictures, or getting SSI [Supplemental Security Income].

Ginsberg offered his help in finding ways of support, as did Singh, with no success. Ginsberg then laid out a new set of terms:

Henceforth I will send half of your $140.00 food money to
Rani or whomever you designate to buy you food, shopping
for 5 hours a week and send you the other 70 or whatever's
left . . . I'll continue some minimum subsidy till SSI comes
through. If SSI and Guggenheim and NEA grants are not
applied for and paperwork completed, I'll stop paying any
money at all even for rent, and you can take care of yourself
after November 1 . . . Your similarity to Alan [Ginsberg's
nephew] is that you both try to evade looking directly at your
dependency, and indulge in magical thinking and evasive
yak to keep the dependency going and a little muddled, in a
state of continuing crisis. When I asked you yesterday about
SSI on the phone you said you were already having something done about it in Boulder when that was a fib. That's
why I got so mad, you were obscuring the situation and de-
laying action making a muddle confusing the facts evading
the issue thus continuing to drain me of money as long as
I would put up with it. Harry I've tried to be friendly and
somewhat helpful, but can't do it, on your terms any more,
and we will either work with your problems gracefully with
your cooperation or I won't help at all.

His benefits were finally arranged, but Ginsberg was still plagued
by the debts that Harry was accumulating, knowing that no one else
was going to help. Someone suggested that maybe the Rex Foundation set up by the Grateful Dead could be of assistance. When the
Dead were appearing in New York, Ginsberg asked their manager if
he could come to their performance at Madison Square Garden. He
arrived before the show, and while they were setting up onstage, he
told Jerry Garcia that he couldn't manage to bear the burden of Harry
anymore, and asked if Rex could help. "I owe a lot to Harry Smith for
that six LP collection," Garcia said, and on the spot offered a grant

of $5,000 a year. Ginsberg said he would need more, and Garcia increased it to $10,000.

"Over his last years," Diane di Prima said, "he became quite a figure on the Naropa campus. He was many persons' confidante, inspiration, father figure, sage, whatever, and also something of a touchstone for people to see where they were at." Stan Brakhage told his film classes that "Harry was receptive in those years at Naropa to everybody's most far-out stuff: any of the students there, especially in the Poetry or the Dance Departments. The most far-out idea or your wildest rebellions or quarrels or whatever, were not very far-out to Harry, so it was really a kind of ballast to have him there. He had ironically a steadying effect on everybody else." Anne Waldman felt that "[he] inspired many to more exploratory pursuits outside academia. They were drawn to the folk music. The *Anthology of American Folk Music* has been taught at Naropa for decades." (He was also a trusted babysitter for her son, Ambrose.)

Chuck Pirtle, a graduate student in writing and poetics, asked Harry about the *Anthology of American Folk Music*, and "he mentioned he hadn't heard the *Anthology* in 30 years, so I made him cassette copies of the LPs and dropped them off one day."

> I returned later to find him intently listening on headphones and weeping at hearing his creation again. He complained about some slight wobble at the beginning of the tape that distorted the first few seconds of "Henry Lee," and told me I should have made sure the tape was wound tightly, but he was moved and delighted to hear those old records again . . .

> He was relatively comfortable in those years. Although his

health was failing, he still had the energy to do his work . . .
He could be both cantankerous and charming, even at the
same time. He had given up drinking, but smoked a lot of
both grass and Salem menthols and took pills that he said
kept him from feeling "too translucent."

Between 1988 and 1990, Harry gave a series of eight summer lectures under a tent on campus: "The Rationality of Namelessness," "Is
Self-Reference Possible?," "Old Age and the New Age," "Untitled"
(on music and film), "The Native American Cosmos" (I and II), "On
Creation Myths," and "Cosmographies." He said he picked the titles of his lectures "because they sounded scientific," but he put performer before scholarly lecturer. There were always celebrities and
Beat scholars in the audience: Ginsberg, Marianne Faithfull, Gregory
Corso, Peter Lamborn Wilson, some of them asking questions, Harry
responding, if not answering. His lectures can be a challenge to read,
as they must have been to hear over thirty years ago. Sentences are
often incomplete, self-disparaging asides are mixed with exaggerated
claims, sarcasm with casually identified character references, serious
ethnographic information undercut by jokes and interruptions as he
searched for some reference. Heard live, it was part Dada, part stand-up
comedy, the absentminded professor shuffling papers, speaking lines
from songs, playing to the audience, and then ignoring it. He would
sometimes say, "I simply can't answer all of your questions," when no
questions had been asked. "The Native American Cosmos," on July 8,
1990, was one of his more straightforward talks:

One thing that was customary in the so-called Old World
was the domestication of animals. Whereas the New World
sexualizing the domestication and the developments of new
species of plants—plants like corn and beans and so forth.
Most of them have the property of also being herbal in nature. We seldom think of food as having, you know, being

good for us, or as one author calls it "food that cures." And, of course in 1480 . . . the, I don't know what to call them, the Natives I guess—Because America is just another Italian—America is just a . . . Anyhow whoever lived here was extremely healthy. They had a life expectancy much longer than the Europeans at the time.

On his second voyage in 1494, Columbus brought 1200 specimens of things: men, seeds, cuttings for planting, wheat, chickpeas, melons, onions, radishes, salad greens, grapevines, sugarcane, and fruit stones for planting orchards. As far as disease is concerned, scholarly debate still goes on regarding the origins of syphilis. It is however the only ambiguous case of mysterious diseases. All diseases transmitted from one continent to another went westward: smallpox, measles, typhoid fever, tuberculosis, plague, diphtheria, etc.

Now, what causes tuberculosis? Is it the tuberculosis bacilli that causes it? Or is it poverty and malnutrition? It doesn't take much thinking to decide that it's not the germs really. To give you some idea of how serious these epidemics were. You may have seen George Catlin's paintings. At the beginning of 1837 there were 1600 people. In July only about 31 were left.

Let's see, the Europeans also had other bad habits, such as associating physical labor with status. It was hard for them, you must remember that Cortez was a contemporary of Henry VIII; it gives you one idea of why the Europeans were so unhealthy, 'cause they had so much clothing on. This was supposed to be somehow connected with the above, but I forget how.

In one famous formulation of this idea, this kind of view, the amoeba and Einstein used the same method, which is trial and error. If truth were created with that which increases the probability of survival, then science would certainly be untrue, because it increases the possibility of non-survival through, they say, various types of human or natural disaster. But the Europeans have always been willing to exchange good health for cultural complexity. They would rather see a clock tick than . . . live ten years longer.

The fascination with machinery is very strange. Another thing that is typical of the Western hemisphere are the child training practices, that lead to the theories in age aggression, that Lorenz and Thunberg and Morris, et cetera . . . consider aggression, they consider it to be universal, but this simply happens to be untrue. Actually, Montague made an analysis of a great number of cultures and it usually revolves around people who are emotionally deprived. I don't have to go into this 'cause you already know it.

I was going to conclude this by describing—Oh, someone asked me the question, "How did you get into these things?" Some cousins of mine had a book on string figures, and in learning them, I realized that—this is happening north of Seattle, Washington—children from the reservation of course went to school with me, and I would ride out on the bus to school with them to see if their parents knew any string figures.

I don't think it's going to work; I can't stand up and draw. But I was going—And rather than give generalized thoughts regarding the way that certain methods of thinking—One peculiar thing that happens is that very often light is stolen and released in the Northern hemisphere, whereas in the valley of the Amazon, it is usually darkness that is stolen and sent into the eternal light. So, there was, near where I was visiting, what was called the spirit dance . . .

The lectures were far from dull. His examples, whether musical, visual, or spoken, were invariably aimed to surprise, amuse, or shock an audience. The poet Charles Stein wrote that "[at] practically every point in his lectures Harry is concerned to unsettle (or reveal the unsettled nature of) conventionally 'settled' things. For Harry, the ethnographic approach to reality encourages the relativization and disruption of conventionally held views of what is real and the displaying of patterns and possibilities conventionally unnoticed, disregarded or denied. Consider this list of topics culled almost at random from the lectures:"

> Epileptic auras; ecological reasons for human sacrifice; cannibalism; the tonal pitches of car horns at different epochs of modernity; Paleolithic plate-tectonic collisions; floods and "The Flood"; voodoo possession; untoward information about ethnogastronomy; the untoward implications of certain scientific findings; contact with the dead; life at the edge of hazard, chance, danger, and indeed over the edge, for the sake of energies accessible only by means of such adventures; an invocation of the very principles of truth he is at the same time undermining and yet a conscientious concern for lost and repressed realities and the truth-realms embodied in suppressed and embodied vanquished peoples; ritual wounding; scarification; ritual role reversals; boundary crossings; cruelty and self-cruelty; obscenity, ritual and otherwise; extreme physical states (hunger, sleep deprivation, ecstatic dance, hallucinogens, concentration); instances of extreme order (ceremonies, categorical, taxonomical); the uncanny nature of children's games; the termination of the human species; demonology; Native American smoke signals; whistles as signals in city slums; tribal warfare as tribal games; initiation through horror; the power of sticks . . .

By 1990 his health seemed to have improved. He gained forty pounds, and was able to walk into downtown Boulder on his own. He approached the last lecture professorially by preparing two packets of readings for the students, fifty-two pages in each, one pink the other blue (for gender, he joked). The lecture was focused on comparative myth and cosmology, and drew upon his own fieldwork and extensive reading in Amerindian culture and history.

That winter, Harry traveled to New York with Steven Taylor with the intention of having his upper teeth operated on in a hospital. "His teeth were so bad that there was a risk of brain infection. There was a dentist in Boulder who was part of the Buddhist community, and he told Allen that Harry needed to have his teeth out, but it should be done in a hospital." But once in New York, Harry dropped the idea. He avoided doctors and dentists until pain or incapacity drove him to them, and could expound on his reasons to any willing audience. Medical doctors, he claimed, had a long history of difficulty in deciding what to do with blood—let some out or put more in—from bloodletting to transfusions, leeches to blood tests, barbershops to doctors' offices. He could rattle off tales of debunked theories and the bad practices of the medical arts through history, illustrating them verbally with dentist scenes from Charlie Chaplin's *Laughing Gas* and Erich von Stroheim's *Greed*. Once he was in New York, he refused to see a dentist.

11

A New York Ending
1991

He was barely back at Naropa when Harry learned that he was to be awarded a Grammy. Bill Ivey, the chairman of the National Academy of Recording Arts and Sciences, picked three people for the Grammy Chairman's Special Merit Awards in 1991: Harry Belafonte, Alan Lomax, and Harry Smith. Belafonte never replied to the award, and Lomax asked that his be sent to him. Harry agreed to accept his award in person. But to get to Radio City Music Hall in New York on February 20, he had to find someone who could help him and pay his way. After a few calls, Nick Amster, a musician friend from Ohio, said he could do it, and bought them both airline tickets and covered Harry's expenses. They flew in the day before the awards and checked into the New York Hilton Midtown, Harry smuggling in five kittens that had traveled with him. They were both measured for rented tuxes, and settled in for room service. The next night, Ivey met them back-stage before the telecast, where Harry was fretting because he couldn't light up anywhere in the hall. He had asked Dr. Michaeleen Maher, a parapsychologist he'd met on his last trip, to be his guest at the cere-mony, and when she arrived, he handed her a few of his cats and asked her to keep them from running up and down the aisles. He thought if he was to be honored, the cats should experience it.

When he was called to the stage he missed a step, and had to be helped up. Amster said that after he received the award,

[he] mentioned his arthritis, me, and his flight from Colorado, and said, "So, thank you. I'm glad to say that all my dreams came true. That I saw America changed through music . . . and all that stuff that the rest of you are talking about. Thank you." Bob Dylan was receiving a lifetime award of his own from Jack Nicholson, and someone said that Bob wanted to see him and I had hoped that Harry might want to say hello, but, alas, he really wanted to get back to the hotel; so we walked back. We remained at the hotel for two more days listening to a lot of music and eating room service, and I offered to stake him to a couple more nights, but he didn't want to stay there alone. I gave him some money and got him in a taxi.

Harry had decided not to return to Boulder.

Once again Dr. Gross took him to his uptown apartment in what Gross said turned into a "tragi-comedy sojourn with a passel of kittens." Scott Feero visited him there a few times, and saw that "he appeared to be living on Skittles; later on, Jell-O, capers and pickled herring; still later on yogurt." Bill Breeze agreed to take him in again, this time in one of his apartments in the Greenpoint section of Brooklyn. On the day that Gross dropped him off, Breeze was being visited by Michaeleen Maher, and he warned her that Harry was in fragile shape. Seeing little furniture in his room, she bought bedding for him and he immediately went to sleep. "The next morning when he came upstairs for breakfast, he told me a frightening story":

> He had been taking a walk in Manhattan a few days before when suddenly he didn't know where he was. He couldn't remember how he got there or what he was doing there or where he had been before or how to return to the place he had started out from. The streets all looked completely unfamiliar and hostile to him, though he knew Manhattan very well

and had lived there for many years. He was so frightened, he said, that he fell into a great panic and had a total meltdown, feeling helpless and weeping profusely on the street, and not knowing what to do next . . . the whole experience had made him believe that his death was imminent, and he had been obsessing about that ever since. He was afraid that this sudden, inexplicable disorientation was a premonition that he had come to the end of his life and was about to die.

Harry's panic in Brooklyn drove him back to Manhattan. Raymond Foye got a call from the switchboard operator at the Chelsea, who said Harry was in the hotel and was coming up to see him. Raymond then assumed the responsibility to get him a room there, backed by the Rex Foundation's grant for his rent, as well as money from the sale of an artwork by Philip Taaffe, another hotel resident. On May 9, 1991, Harry was back in the Chelsea. He tried to reestablish some old friendships and found that some were avoiding him. He discovered that Jacqueline Gens had also left Naropa and was in New York working for Ginsberg and Anne Waldman's father, and she recalls Harry coming by for dinner many times, and asking her out "on several 'dates' to see his films at Film Forum, picking me up in a taxi and delivering me home—an unusual departure from his previous neediness. In retrospect, I think he might have wanted to show me that out there in the world he was respected and not just the wreck I had experienced in doctor's offices . . . It was amazing how he cleaned himself up for these excursions wearing a snazzy new trench coat."

Harry stayed at the Chelsea for nine months, a period in which he was increasingly weakening and suffering hallucinations and paranoid fantasies. "Those last months at the Chelsea Hotel were probably the poorest and most dire of his life," Raymond remembered. "He'd burnt down everyone, and he didn't have the physical strength to get around and make new connections. I recall walking out on 23rd Street one afternoon and seeing Harry at the pay phone on the corner.

His pants, which were covered in pee stains, were held up by a rope. His glasses were taped together with scotch tape. He had a stack of index cards with names and telephone numbers on them and he was shuffling through them trying to figure out who he could call to borrow a few dollars. He asked me if I had two dollars so that he could go to the deli on the corner and buy a box of instant mashed potatoes."

Rani Singh was in town for a publisher's conference, and had made plans to fly back to Boulder with Harry. She visited him in his Chelsea room the day before Thanksgiving, and was shocked to see blood on his clothes, his sheets, everywhere in the room. He was so weak he could hardly open the door. He'd been surviving on NyQuil, Alka-Seltzer, flu medicine, Zand Insure Herbal Immune Support, instant mashed potatoes, ginger ale, coffee, and cigarettes. When she tried to call for an ambulance, he insisted they stay and talk. She sat with him as he told her of his hallucinations and thumbed through tarot cards, imagining what they would be wearing when they were dead and if they would recognize each other, until finally he agreed that if she drove him to the hospital he'd go. As she left to get the car, she called Raymond's office upstairs to tell him that Harry was in very bad shape. When he came downstairs, he saw that "Harry was bleeding profusely on the bed and he was saying over and over, 'I'm dying, I'm dying' . . . He repeated those words six or seven times, like a chant, and then he was dead, slumped over on the bed." Foye's assistant telephoned Paola Igliori, an Italian poet, photographer, and publisher, who soon arrived; an ambulance was called. EMTs were unable to revive him, and he was taken to St. Vincent's Hospital and declared dead on arrival from bleeding ulcers and cardiac arrest.

Stories spread about his death, including one in which Ginsberg had his body kept at the hospital for more than forty days in accord with some Tibetan Buddhist tradition. But Ginsberg had arrived at the hospital that night and was allowed to visit Harry in the morgue, where he did a Tibetan liturgy and spent an hour meditating. "How strange I took Harry on Earth for granted, now he'll be gone forever, and myself later on, but for now, no more Harry living so unique, so painfully suffering, so self-abrogating, so devious, so saintly."

"It's strange," Raymond said, "how only when a person dies does one finally see their life in its entirety":

> After Harry's passing the chaos passed too, and what remained was a remarkable sensibility that took many forms, both material and spirit. In the ensuing months, two meetings were convened in my Chelsea Hotel room #814. Attendees included Jonas Mekas, Allen Ginsberg, John Cohen, Rani Singh, Rosebud, Joe Gross, Deborah Freeman, Bill Breeze, and others. We first gathered simply to mourn a dear friend, and that evolved into a discussion of how best to preserve his legacy. It was Allen who was pragmatic in asking how we were going to use the remaining Rex Foundation money, and what we were going to do with his physical belongings.
>
> It is easy from today's perspective to see how all the various aspects of Harry's work and interests fit together, but at the time there were just a lot of questions. There were also crazy personal agendas, like the person who wanted to build a full-size pyramid to house his ashes, for the cult that was sure to follow. It felt like we were his apostles, ready to carry his message out into the world. Something or someone was directing us. There was a messianic feel to the gatherings. Looking back, we were not wrong. To paraphrase Harry's

remark about seeing America changed by the music he loved,
I have come to see how this strange little man somehow managed to shift the world in his direction, just a tiny bit.

It was decided that the remaining funds in the Rex grant would
be used to gather and organize Harry's materials, and Rani and Bill
Morgan, Ginsberg's archivist, were to be in charge of it. Lionel Ziprin
suggested to Igliori that she should interview those who knew Harry,
and her interviews, her photographs, and Harry's art appeared in her
book *American Magus Harry Smith: A Modern Alchemist*, published by
Inanout Press, a company she created in New York in 1996. In 1998,
Mekas attempted to build an extension to the Anthology building at
32 Second Avenue that would be called the Heaven and Earth Library
in honor of Harry, and would house his music, paintings, and books,
as well as all of the Anthology's paper collection. "Not many people
support libraries, but many supported Harry Smith," he said, "so we
decided to use Harry for the publicity." Rani Singh edited *Think of
the Self Speaking: Harry Smith—Selected Interviews* in 1999, and created
the Harry Smith Archives to enable his followers to apply for funding
and to give Smith's works a public platform. The James Cohan gallery
published *The Heavenly Tree Grows Downward*, edited by Raymond
Foye, which accompanied an exhibition of the works of Harry Smith,
Philip Taaffe, and Fred Tomaselli in New York in 2002.

> Perfection may be perfect, but the hell with it.
>
> —Harry Smith

Though I never read all of those books of Harry Smith's or listened to
his records that were boxed up in Red Hook, there were many times
when I wished I had. (Now, by a simple twist of fate, they are in the

Bob Dylan Archive at the University of Tulsa.) I did visit libraries, museums, reservations, the upstates and downtowns and the east and west of America tracking his life. I began this book by raising the problems that beset writers of biography, well aware that a life such as Harry's makes them all the trickier. What should I leave in and leave out? Even the longest biographies still ignore some things. But Harry had already left a lot out in what he had said about himself, and the documentation of his life was scanty.

His intentional and unintentional moments of bizarre and darkly humorous behavior, his recklessness with his own work and health, the uncertainty and improbabilities of his autobiographical accounts, the disjunctions of his speech—all of it can make it difficult to connect him to his life's work. During an interview with Harry for his book *Making People's Music: Moe Asch and Folkways Records*, Peter Goldsmith jotted down notes on his impressions: "It also must be said that Harry is prone to digress from the topic at hand, sometimes changing subjects several times in the course of a single sentence. Unless you are very sharp, very interested, or both, it is not difficult to lose track of what he is talking about. As he gets older in years, this tendency will no doubt be taken by some casual observers for a sign of senility. It is no such thing. It is merely the result of the fact that Harry's mind works much too fast for his mouth to handle the output."

Harry did indeed often speak in cut-up form, and complained that no language was yet invented that could convey his thoughts. He was well regarded or at least tolerated because of his knowledge of so many things, and for his eternal quest as a cosmic scholar. It was a very special kind of knowledge, though he could scatter it through rambling exegeses, joking interviews, and annoying nonanswers to questions.

Doubtlessly, there are psychiatrists who could tell us what his problems were and what Harry's works meant, but who wants a psychiatrist to explain a work of art, much less biographers writing as if they were trained to evaluate an artist/patient? As Paul Valéry said about the poetry of Racine, you could collect all the facts that could be collected about his life and you will never learn from them the art of his verse.

Whatever the difficulties of understanding Harry, it is the scope, innovation, and influence of his work that counts. His life was a series of moves from the coastal islands and small towns of the North Puget Sound, where the oldest Americans are still a visible and defining presence, to the Black neighborhoods and arts colonies of the Bay Area, across the country to the Bowery and the art byways of Greenwich Village, out to the mythic Indian territories that Ralph Ellison and Huck Finn only imagined, south to the Everglades and then further west to Boulder, and finally back to the Hotel Chelsea, if only to say that he was still alive, and then could die. It was a life lived not so much along a biographer's timeline, but as a disorienting zigzag of choices and contingencies.

Harry was a witness and a player in the period that began in the forties, unfolded in the fifties, and exploded in the sixties, bringing about major revolutions in the arts, in the social sciences, in society itself. He closely observed and then ignored the lines between the low and high arts, the folk and the fine, the commonplace and the esoteric, and by consistently moving across these artistic registers in his work he was able to see not just the cultural but the aesthetic value of otherwise ignored arts, suspecting or knowing, all the while, that everything in the world is connected.

In all of his work he was looking for patterns in culture, things that required decoding, but he was also interested in continuities between those patterns that might suggest something larger, something pan-human. He was excited by the idea that there might be a correspondence between colors, sounds, movements, and images. Perhaps there was a link between Appalachian quilting patterns and folk songs, or between language and Seminole dress designs, or string figures and myths? The collecting came first, always with the hope that he would find examples of every style of artful efforts of a people. The patterns could be as small as repeated or clashing figures in a quilt, or as large as the breathing of an entire city late at night.

But as a collector, too, he anticipated if not actually helped affect radical changes that are only now being grasped. The concept of the collector has changed from the domain of the very rich to those whose personal obsessions or predilections are now recognized, regardless of monetary value. Anyone can now be a curator; anything can be collected. For Harry, collecting was a means of finding universal patterns that might illuminate a unified theory of culture. M. Henry Jones recalled that "[the] one thing that he said to me that I particularly remember was the most important thing about reality is the relationship of objects . . . [What] makes everything real is the fact that things are ordered in the present status. In other words, things are set beside themselves and that is what makes reality. Reality is made up of just the placement of objects." In the last thirty years, downloading and streaming have turned the work of the connoisseur into freeloading and hoarding, a change Harry's work anticipated.

Despite the loss of most of Harry's paintings, those that remain are so full of information, so completely realized and disciplined, that he escaped the disparaging terms "primitive" or "outsider." Though he always insisted that his primary interest was anthropology, he also acknowledged that his painting was more important than his films. He worked on stencils, canvas, scratchboard, wood, paper, Mylar, tile, film, cardboard, and walls, using pen and ink, brush and paint or watercolor, producing paintings, book covers, typewriter art, sand portraits, murals, greeting cards, tarot cards, and more. None of his artworks are collected in any institution where they can be viewed, though Anthology Film Archives has a number of his paintings in storage. (When Mekas was considering buying some of Harry's paintings, Harry asked Henry Geldzahler to appraise them. Geldzahler told him that if he were dead his paintings would be worth a lot more. Harry's response was, "I'm half-dead, so they should be worth half more.")

A bit of fame in the small art-film world did not lead to his making a living. Even the greater attention to his role as a curator and collector of recordings didn't translate into a sustainable life. He might have followed Alan Lomax's practice of transcribing the words of folk and old-time records into songbooks, something he wanted to do, since he considered many songbooks poorly done. In his interview with John Cohen, Harry complained that there was no money for improving songbooks, really no money for any of his efforts. He knew all too well what the cost of the life he was living would be:

SMITH: Everybody has to eat. We're all trapped in a social system where you have to do something to provide food and shelter. I thought for a while that drinking got me out of food and shelter, but it's a way of living that is pushed underground. Thousands and thousands of derelicts.

COHEN: I've heard people accuse you of living off others—trying to disregard that whole concept of doing things that would earn your living. You've bothered me, my friends, and others in the sense that you don't accept the whole concept of doing things that would earn money to be a fruitful part of society. Now that's a hard thing for me to say.

SMITH: Certainly, I said it just before you did. Naturally, that situation exists. There are certain ways you can evade that responsibility, but it's like, the wages of sin are death. I try not to do that. I've reformed, but the strain on the poor fevered brain of adjusting to capitalism after years of being a sort of Robin Hood type.

COHEN: I'm trying to translate your analogy now in terms of your own work. What value is your work to society, Harry?

SMITH: [It's] provided tunes that people made things off of. Now at this point, there is a whole school of filmmakers that imitate some of my double-exposure films. They want to thank me. That type of film is a good idea—so you don't care what happens really, you just shoot anything on top of anything—that solves problems. I haven't wanted to do anything that would be injurious. It's very difficult working out a personal philosophy in relation to the environment. Consistently I have tried different methods to give out the maximum. Some Czechoslovakians who visited recently looked on my films as outstanding, while nobody here thinks very much of them. Or what's his name, [Jean-Luc] Godard, asked especially for me when he visited here, et cetera. So one of the things I've done is films, and I believe I added pleasure to people's lives through that. When I was interested in music, the simple fact of collecting new copies of a lot of records that will be important in the future is as valuable as anything. After I assembled the *Anthology* and sold the remaining records to the Public Library in 1951 that was the end of that project. Then I devoted a great deal of time to painting, but through mischance I destroyed all my paintings, and I abandoned my films somewhere in a theater because I didn't want to see them again. Somebody got hold of them and made copies—and when I wanted better copies I got interested again. I try to bring people together.

COHEN: Are you supported to do what you do?

SMITH: Pretty much. People keep giving me money. Foundations would, but they don't give enough. They are always dissatisfied with me for not doing enough. That with the amount of labor to get a few thousand dollars from a foundation, it's simpler to get it from somebody who will deduct it from their income tax.

In a conversation with the folklorist Nick Spitzer twenty years later:

> I'd seen myself sort of turning into a derelict, and I didn't
> know what to do. Every move I made seemed to be wrong.
> I have a certain number of physical difficulties, all of my
> friends thinking I'd be cured if I have all my teeth pulled . . .
> But the reason, as I say, is that I try to fill all the moments
> that God, whatever that is, that . . . infinitely small im-
> mensity that draws all things together by thrusting them
> apart . . . like at this point I'm in a heavily recording mood
> because there's been nothing else to do. I pay twenty dol-
> lars a week for a room that has no window, it's pitch dark at
> noon, and no lock on the door, but in complete honesty, I
> feel, among the people there.

There were those who were put off by Harry's behavior. Irascibil-
ity is a gambit of the old, but he played it far too young, beginning
as early as his late twenties in the Bay Area. His biographical claims
could be seen as self-aggrandizing, but they were at least sometimes
self-mocking. If Jack Kerouac thought of Harry as one of those Village "unselfconfident egomaniacs" that he described in his novel *The
Subterraneans*, he would have been wrong: Harry was confident that
he had knowledge and abilities others lacked, and felt free to forcefully
demonstrate that sense of self if the occasion arose.

He is often called a polymath, a person with encyclopedic knowledge.
"Genius" is another term used for Harry, similar to polymath, though
it implies the ability and a position of power to apply knowledge ef-
fectively to a number of enterprises. "Tortured" is the cliché used to

modify "genius" if mental disorders are suspected to have held back a genius. Harry's persistent overreach, his disregard for the human and monetary cost of his projects, the destruction of his works and his own health, all point toward tragedy. But I would prefer to think of Harry as an eccentric, not in the usual meaning of one who acts in strange or unusual ways but in the sense that Virginia Woolf meant it in her essay "Impassioned Prose" to describe a certain type of writer when she says, "[Happily] there are in every age some writers who puzzle the critics, who refuse to go along with the herd. They stand obstinately across the boundary lines, and do a greater service by enlarging and fertilizing and influencing than by their actual achievement, which, indeed, is often too eccentric to be satisfactory." In another essay, "The Eccentrics," she expands her definition:

> The quality which marks all true eccentrics is that never for a moment do they believe themselves to be eccentric. They are persuaded—and who shall say that they are wrong?—that it is the rest of the world who are cramped and malformed and spiritually decrepit, while they alone have lived their lives according to the dictates of nature. It must be owned that in the battle of life, the triumph of civilization, or whatever we choose to call it, they have invariably been worsted . . . For such reasons as these it is extremely rare to find a full and satisfactory biography of an eccentric.

That last sentence hurts, but I take her point that there are, in the arts especially, a few who operate on the edge of society (the Latin origin of the word "eccentric" is "out of center"), who renounce or fail to seek fame while expanding and redrawing the lines of the possible.

There are undoubtedly other ways to write a biography of a person like Smith whose life and work suggest an infinity of interpretations, but none are ever likely to be as succinct and all-embracing as this elegiac song by Peter Stampfel:

"His Tapes Roll On"

Harry recorded with a wire recorder back in World War II
Harry recorded with a reel-to-reel when the reel-to-reel was new
Harry recorded cassettes by the hundreds as the century rolled on
He even used a telephone answering machine, but Harry Smith
    is gone.
Speed-rapping killers and jump-rope rhymes, fireworks on the
    fourth of July
Complete early canon of Gregory Corso, kittens, snowstorms
    and airplane trips
What is the sound of one hand clapping, where's tomorrow gone?
Most of his tapes are missing in action, and Harry Smith is gone
But his tapes roll on and they'll never stop 'till they roll all over
    the world,
to the north and south, east and west
. . .
Amphetamine babble, junky mumbles, concerts in the park
Banging pans, banging pots, squeaky hinges, dead bolt locks,
Singing birds at sunset, singing bird at dawn,
Once upon a time, he got 'em all, but Harry Smith is gone
Deathbed prayers of Bowery bums, their death rattles, too
Ambient sounds of the Rocky Mountains, tea kettles by the slew
Squealing brakes, honking horns, on and on and on
He worked his magic with a microphone, but Harry Smith is
    gone
But his tapes roll on, and they'll never stop, 'till they roll all over
    the world
Over the mountain, across the sea
. . .

Peyote songs of the Kiowa, the Fugs' first record, too

The songs of Orlovsky and Ginsberg, roosters cock-a-doodle-doo

Church bells ringin' and children's singin', he kept on keeping on

Rolling his tapes 'till they rolled him up, and Harry Smith was
gone

Rodeos, carnivals, games of basketball, dogs and cats and squirrels and cows,

creatures great and small

. . .

He hustled many hustles, he conned a couple cons

He lived the life he wanted to, but Harry Smith is gone

And his tapes roll on and they'll never stop, 'till they roll all over
the world

They'll roll to the moon and the sun and the stars

He tried to tape the whole wide world and shove it up his ears

He heard it all as one great song, the music of the spheres

He planned to tape a series called movies for the blind

But time and fate had other plans, fate's not always kind

Sonic sociology, audio vérité, a kind of meditation, God's own
guest DJ

Genius, shaman, pain in the ass, peerless paragon

We'll never see his like again, Harry Smith is gone

And his tapes roll on and they'll never, never stop 'till they roll all
over the world

Over, under, sideways, down

NOTES

HARRY SMITH: AN INTRODUCTION

11 *He told me about the relationship*: Andrew Noren unpublished writings on Harry Smith, courtesy of Risé Hall-Noren.

16 *Now if you would like to ask*: Rani Singh, *Think of the Self Speaking* (Seattle: Elbow/Cityful Press, 1999), 143.

1. A BOY'S LIFE

19 *As Harry Everett Smith told it*: This chapter has benefited greatly from the research and generosity of Bret Lunsford, especially his *Sounding for Harry Smith: Early Pacific Northwest Influences* (Anacortes, WA: P. W. Elverum & Sun, 2020).

19 *His father, he said*: Harry Smith, unpublished lecture on "The Rationality of Nothingness," July 2, 1988, Naropa University, Getty Library.

20 *But then he also said*: Singh, 112.

20 *On yet another hand, he said*: Scott Feero email to John Szwed, September 21, 2021.

20 *The general had also revived*: Frater Lux Ad Mundi, *Behutet*, no. 6, 2000, 26.

21 *superintendent for the People's Party*: Lunsford, 62.

21 *running a hardware store*: Lunsford, 89.

22 *Harry recalled that he "insisted"*: Singh, 114.

22 *first grade at the Campus School*: Lunsford, 95.

23 *"I had built"*: Singh, 60.

23 *bouts of illness*: Lunsford, 123.

24 *fundamentals such as color*: Lunsford, 158.

24 *junior high school newspaper*, Searchlight: Lunsford, 129.

25 *When his father built*: Harry Smith interviewed by Nick Spitzer, unpublished, December 7, 1987.

26 *tours for the occasional child*: Lunsford, 134.

26 *As one scholar put it*: Isaiah Lorado Wilner, "Raven Cried for Me: Narratives of Transformation on the Northwest Coast of America" (PhD dissertation, Yale University, 2016).

28 *The Smiths kept alive*: Though it is usually said that Harry Smith's mother taught on the Lummi reservation, there are no records of her ever working there.

28 *"When I was a child"*: Singh, 56.

29 *After the mid-1940s*: Bill Holm letter to Darrin Daniel, January 22, 2001, Getty Library; Tom Wooten, "Messages from Your Samish Council Members," *Samish News*, March 2004, 3.

33 *essay he wrote*: Bret Lunsford, "Teenage Harry Smith 1941 Opinion Piece on Civic Duty Comes to Light," *Resounding*, May 19, 2022, https://resounding harrysmith.substack.com/p/teenage-harry-smith-1941-opinion.

34 *Jack and Harry really shared*: Lunsford, 141–42.

35 *"Spirits," Holm said*: Bill Holm, lecture at the Northwest Film Forum, 2006, in Lunsford, 151.

36 *"Toward the end"*: Bill Holm, lecture at Northwest Film Forum.

36 *With more than two hundred people*: Bill Holm letter to John Szwed, 2020.

36 *"Harry made all the contacts"*: Bill Holm letter to Darrin Daniel, January 22, 2001, Getty Library.

37 *came to Anacortes*: Lunsford, 178–79.

37 *Some of what he gave*: "Notice of Inventory Completion: Department of Anthropology at Indiana University, Bloomington," *The Federal Register*, FIND81.004, January 7, 2016.

37 *"He was way ahead"*: Darrin Daniel, "Hypnotist Collector: The Alchemy of Harry Smith," The Harry Smith Archives, https://harrysmitharchives.com /events/hypnotist-collector-the-alchemy-of-harry-smith-by-darrin-daniel.

38 *Its meaning was rather unclear*: Karl J. Davis, "Objects of Desire: Surrealist Collecting and the Art of the Pacific Northwest Coast" (master's thesis, University of Alberta, 2014), https://era.library.ualberta.ca/items/850c06a0-b88a-4571 -ba18-392ae4541c95.

40 *"Even removed from the atmosphere"*: André Breton, "Phenix du Masque," in *Oeuvres complètes* (Paris: Gallimard, tome IV, 2008), 993.

40 *On the other hand*: Claude Lévi-Strauss and Didier Eribon, *Conversations with Claude Lévi-Strauss* (Chicago: The University of Chicago Press, 1991), 34–35.

41 *He also discovered*: Emmanuelle Loyer, *Lévi-Strauss* (Medford, MA: Polity Books, 2018), 205–27.

42 *Despite a relatively small number of people*: Claude Lévi-Strauss, *The Way of the Masks* (Seattle: University of Washington Press, 1982), 4–5.

42 *To describe the painted*: Claude Lévi-Strauss, "The Art of the Northwest Coast at the American Museum of Natural History," *Gazette des Beaux-Arts*, 1943, 175–82, reprinted in part with a new translation by the author in his *The Way of the Masks*, 5–7; Charles Baudelaire's "Correspondances" is reprinted on p. 5.

42 *"Dandyism is the last flicker"*: Charles Baudelaire, "The Painter of Modern Life," https://www.writing.upenn.edu/library/Baudelaire_Painter-of-Modern-Life _1863.pdf.

43 *A lecture he called "Native American Cosmos"*: Harry was not alone in protecting the secrets of the Lummi. June Burn, a journalist who spent most of her adult life traveling across the country, homesteading from place to place, in her book *Living High* vividly described a night she spent with the Lummi during the winter spirit dances in the 1920s. Her description of the events of that night is detailed, but when a group of "scientists" from the University of Washington left and the restricted portion of the event began, she stayed hidden behind some Indian women friends, but says she fell asleep and never saw it. June Burn, *Living High* (Friday Harbor, WA: Griffin Bay Book Store, 1992 [1941]), 219–22.

43 *"I really can't describe it"*: Harry Smith, unpublished lecture on "Native American Cosmos," July 8, 1990, Getty Library. What Harry had seen is similar to a ritual described by Franz Boas in *The Social Organization and the Secret Societies of the*

Kwakiutl Indians, although Boas said that he only had a slight knowledge of such events, suggesting that he had been told about it and hadn't witnessed it. Franz Boas, *The Social Organization and the Secret Societies of the Kwakiutl Indians*, Reports of the United States National Museum (Washington, DC: 1895), 645–46.

45 *In Berkeley, at the university*: Andrew Schelling, *Tracks along the Left Coast: Jaime de Angulo & Pacific Coast Culture* (Berkeley, CA: Counterpoint, 2017), 78–79.

47 *Once, on a visit*: Kathleen Haddon, *String Games for Beginners* (Cambridge, UK: Heffer, 1934).

47 *What he found*: Smith, "Native American Cosmos."

47 *He thought they looked like patterns*: This may have been suggested to him by the introduction to Kathleen Haddon's book where she remarks on the cinematic qualities of string figure storytelling.

48 *His library research revealed*: Franz Boas, "Nouvelles et Correspondance—Kleine Notizen und Correspondez," *International Archiv für Ethnographie* 1, 1888, 229–30.

49 *Nor would he fall*: Leslie Fiedler, *Waiting for the End* (New York: Stein and Day, 1964), 134.

49 *He said of such cosmetic*: Paola Igliori, *American Magus Harry Smith: A Modern Alchemist*, Paola Igliori, ed. (New York: Inandout Press, 1996), 144.

50 *Some of his classmates recalled years later that he had a sense of humor*: Rani Singh video interview in Getty Library.

51 *Harry had given talks*: Bret Lunsford, "Early Collaborators," *Resounding*, May 28, 2022, https://resoundingharrysmith.substack.com/p/early-collaborators.

51 *He also was acknowledged nationally*: "Injuneer," *American Magazine* CXXXV, no. 3, March 1943, 118.

51 *Despite the leaders' ritual dress*: Bill Holm email to Rani Singh, April 21, 2001, Getty Library.

51 *"He is undoubtedly a lad"*: Melville Jacobs letter to Vance Packard, October 30, 1942, Melville Jacobs Collection, University of Washington Library.

52 *He begged his parents*: John Szwed interview with M. Henry Jones.

53 *It was* Drums of Fu Manchu: Singh, 64.

53 *They were the means*: Philip Lamantia, "Radio Voices: A Child's Bed of Sirens," in Philip Lamantia, *Preserving Fire: Selected Prose* (Seattle and New York: Wave Books, 2018), 104–29.

53 *Harry had been experimenting*: Bill Holm letter to Darrin Daniel, January 22, 2001, Getty Library; Frater Lux Ad Mundi, 28.

53 *"I had thousands of those"*: Singh, 49.

53 *"I went to cowboy movies"*: Singh, 134.

56 *"It's easy to think of hunters"*: Amanda Petrusich, *Do Not Sell at Any Price: The Wild, Obsessive Hunt for the World's Rarest 78 rpm Records* (New York: Scribner, 2014).

56 *One of the most fervent collectors*: His collection of 78-rpm single records was solid enough that years later R. Crumb would eagerly acquire some of them in exchange for drawings of Lomax and Jelly Roll Morton.

58 *"The labels, the record jackets"*: Luis Kemnitzer, "West Coast Record Collector," in *A Booklet of Essays, Appreciations, and Annotations Pertaining to the Anthology of American Folk Music*, Harry Smith, ed. (Washington, DC: Smithsonian Folkways Recordings, 1997), 29–30.

58 *But that led to problems*: Singh, 46.
59 *Jacobs had just written*: Melville Jacobs and Bernhard J. Stern, *Outline of Anthropology* (New York: Barnes & Noble, 1947); Bernhard J. Stern, *The Lummi Indians of Northwest Washington* (New York: Columbia University Press, 1934).
60 *Japanese resettlement was opposed*: Singh, 51; Jennifer Speidel, "After Internment: Seattle's Debate Over Japanese Americans' Right to Return Home," Seattle Civil Rights & Labor History Project, depts.washington.edu/civilr/after _internment.htm.
60 *Though little more is known*: Harry Smith interviewed by Nick Spitzer.
60 *"Someone had taken me to see [Woody]"*: Singh, 71.
61 *It was there that Smith*: Phil Elwood quoted in Richie Unterberger, *Eight Miles High: Folk-Rock's Flight from Haight-Ashbury to Woodstock* (San Francisco: Backbeat Books, 2003), 12.
61 *But I didn't like [Guthrie's] singing*: Singh, 71.

2. DARK THEY WERE, WITH GOLDEN EYES

64 *In 1947,* Harper's Magazine *published*: Mildred Edie Brady, "The New Cult of Sex and Anarchy," *Harper's Magazine*, April 1949, 312–22.
65 *Guests took turns*: Oral history of Warren d'Azevedo, 220, http://www.onlinenevada.org/articles/warren-dazevedo-oral-history.
66 *A people who may not have invented*: Jerome Rothenberg, *Technicians of the Sacred: A Range of Poetries from Africa, America, Asia & Oceania*, quoted by Schelling, *Tracks along the Left Coast*, 153.
66 *"He converted God to himself"*: Paul Radin, foreword to *God Struck Me Dead: Religious Conversion Experiences and Autobiographies of Ex-Slaves* (Nashville, TN: Department of Social Sciences, Fisk University, 1945); Schelling, 74–77.
67 *"He was so odd and strange"*: "Jordan Belson," in Igliori, 19.
67 *Belson recalled*: Igliori, 19.
68 *In a lecture he gave at Naropa*: Harry Smith, "The Rationality of Namelessness," July 2, 1988.
68 *When he was with those he knew well*: Igliori, 21.
68 *"Harry Smith was the first person"*: Unpublished interview with Jordan Belson by Scott MacDonald, Raymond Foye Archive.
69 *Harry, in turn, shared with him*: Philip Lamantia, *The Collected Poems of Philip Lamantia* (Los Angeles: The University of California Press, 2015), xxxii.
70 *"Harry was passionate"*: Interview with Lamantia by Rani Singh, Getty Library.
70 *"He was surprisingly social"*: Interview with Belson by Rani Singh, Getty Library.
71 *Just as he was arriving*: Interview with Belson by Rani Singh, Getty Library.
72 *If she didn't have a name*: John Cohen, "John Cohen's Corner," *The Little Sandy Review*, no. 20, 1964, 33.
72 *"She didn't understand me"*: Singh, 85.
72 *In one of the first articles written*: "John Cohen's Corner," 36.
73 *When Harry asked her*: Singh, 144.
73 *The American affinity for jazz and painting*: Diane Kelder, ed., *Stuart Davis* (New York: Praeger, 1971), 23–24.
74 *It was noticed that*: René Guilleré, "Il n'y a plus de perspective," *Le Cahier bleu*, no. 4, 1933, 174.

74 *The Museum of Modern Art*: Blesh's lectures were privately published as *This Is Jazz* in San Francisco in 1943.

74 *While Clement Greenberg was holding forth*: When Clement Greenberg encountered Piet Mondrian's *Broadway Boogie Woogie* and was obliged to say something about it in the review he was writing, one would have thought he would have to say something about jazz and painting. But when he failed to do so, he not only missed the point of the painting, he got the colors wrong.

74 *"The films are minor accessories"*: Singh, 53.

75 *"He always had a rather scornful attitude"*: Unpublished interview with Jordan Belson by Scott MacDonald.

75 *It would be important to know*: Raymond Foye, ed., *The Heavenly Tree Grows Downward: Selected Works by Harry Smith, Philip Taaffe, and Fred Tomaselli* (New York: James Cohan Gallery, 2002), 13–14.

75 *Once, in a burst of profanity*: Genevieve Yue, "Festival Reports. Observation in Progress: The 11th Views from the Avant-Garde," *Sense of Cinema*, issue 45, November 2007.

76 *Philip Lamantia remembered some of Harry's paintings*: It's said that the Gillespie performances were taken from a live recording that Hy Hirsh reportedly taped at a Gillespie concert, and was later bootlegged as *Dizzy Gillespie Live in Sweden*. But there appears to be no recording from that period from Sweden that includes all these compositions. It's more likely that they were taken from the 78-rpm records made in the late 1940s that were reissued some fifty years later as *Dizzy Gillespie: The Complete RCA Victor Recordings*.

77 *Harry first worked out his record paintings*: Raymond Foye, "Delineators: Jordan Belson and Harry Smith," *Gagosian Quarterly*, Spring 2021, 95.

77 *Luis Kemnitzer had seen the same thing*: Kemnitzer, 31.

77 *"Each stroke in that painting"*: Singh, 55.

78 *He told Sitney that "the most complex one"*: Singh, 55.

78 *"one of Charlie Parker's records"*: See the end title from *Film No. 3* on page 287 of *American Magus*.

78 *Dizzy Gillespie's 1948 "Algo Bueno" and "Ool-Ya-Koo"*: See Paola Igliori's film *American Magus Harry Smith*, https://www.youtube.com/watch?v=s2XqGTn_8Xs on YouTube, or the inside of the back cover of *American Magus*.

79 *"We hope that this series will"*: Scott MacDonald, *A Critical Cinema 3: Interviews with Independent Filmmakers* (Los Angeles: University of California Press, 1998), 37.

80 *Disney's cartoons*: Kerry Brougher, "Visual-Music Culture," Kerry Brougher and Judith Zilcer, eds. *Visual Music: Synaesthesia in Art and Music Since 1900* (New York: Thames & Hudson, 2005).

80 *"The audience was the best part"*: Barbara Stauffacher Solomon, unpublished autobiography in Brecht Andersch, "Art & Cinema 1," April 16, 2010, https://openspace.sfmoma.org/2010/04/art-cinema-1/.

82 *But to some, music was already*: William Moritz, "Absolute Film, Center for Visual Music," http://www.centerforvisualmusic.org/library/WMAbsoluteFilm.htm.

83 *But he had doubts about art films*: Fischinger insisted that great film art could be done only by those who worked outside of the film industry. Oskar Fischinger, "My Statements Are in My Work," *Art in Cinema Catalog* (San Francisco: The San Francisco Museum of Art and the Art in Cinema Society, 1947), 38–40.

83 *"Your films have excited many people"*: Richard Foster letter to Oskar Fischinger, June 8, 1947, in *Art in Cinema: Documents Toward a History of the Film Society* (Philadelphia: Temple University Press, 2006), 159.

83 *"I am writing you, first of all"*: Letter to Oskar Fischinger from Harry Smith, July 25, 1947, in *Art in Cinema*, 163.

84 *He returned to Los Angeles*: Raymond Foye email to John Szwed.

84 *"I learned concentration from him"*: William Moritz, "Harry Smith, Mythologist," Center for Visual Music, 2008–2009, http://www.centerforvisualmusic.org /MoritzHarrySmith.htm.

84 *He had just made* Fireworks: "America Year Zero," *Artforum*, January 2017, 190–241.

85 *It was a film that stunned*: Singh, 45.

86 *Methods and processes of production*: Margo Miller, "Animation," csmt.uchicago .edu/glossary2004/animation.htm.

87 *"He would have the clear film"*: Igliori, 23.

88 *"He got paint all over"*: Igliori, 23.

88 *The complexity (or disorder)*: Daniel Spoerri, *An Anecdoted Topography of Chance* (London: Atlas Press, 1995).

88 *Philip Lamantia said that throughout Harry's life*: Philip Lamantia interviewed by Rani Singh, Getty Library.

89 *As Belson put it*: MacDonald, *A Critical Cinema 3*, 67.

89 *Harry once advised a group*: P. Adams Sitney, *Visionary Film: The American Avant-Garde 1943–2000* (New York: Oxford University Press, 2002), 257.

89 *"The titles . . . were added"*: Harry Smith letter to Hilla Rebay, June 17, 1950, Guggenheim Museum Archives.

90 *"All those so-called abstract films"*: Robert Russett and Cecile Starr, eds., *Experimental Animation: An Illustrated Anthology* (New York: Van Nostrand Reinhold, 1976), 139.

90 *"My cinematic excreta"*: Harry Smith, *Film-Makers' Cooperative Catalogue* 3 (New York, 1965), 57–58.

90 *"They were first meant to be silent"*: Steven Taylor and Ariella Ruth, "Remembering Harry Smith," *Bombay Gin* 37, no. 1, 2001, 66.

91 *The film was silent*: The underlying riff of "Manteca" was the inspiration for Bobby Parker's 1961 "Watch Your Step," which in turn inspired the Beatles' "I Feel Fine" and "Day Tripper" and a dozen or so other rock recordings.

91 *P. Adams Sitney, in* Visionary Film: Sitney, 239.

91 *Harry seemed to confirm*: Sitney, 239.

91 *But sometimes "dirty" can just mean "dirty"*: Judith A. Switzer, "The Animated Abstractions of Harry Smith," *Millennium Film Journal* 6 (Spring 1980): 75.

93 *He credited the Whitney brothers*: Sitney, 243.

93 *"The colors were based"*: Singh, 115.

93 *He also said that*: Harry Smith letter to Hilla Rebay, June 17, 1950, Getty Library.

93 *"[He] put cutout forms"*: MacDonald, *A Critical Cinema 3*, 68.

94 *"For those who are interested"*: William Moritz, "Non-Objective Film: The Second Generation," Center for Visual Music, no date.

94 *He had seen several people die*: Singh, 240.

95 *He immediately replied*: Either Belson's memory was off, or Harry was not completely correct, for Buñuel, acting as his own DJ, alternated excerpts from

Wagner with two Argentinian tangos, "Tango Argentino" and "Recuerdos" by the Vicente Alvarez, Carlos Otero Et Son Orchestre Tropical.

95 *His experience with different forms*: Burroughs, who disliked Harry, was none-theless impressed by his films. Barry Miles, *Call Me Burroughs* (New York: Twelve Books, 2014), 434.

95 *In Harry's view there were no*: This discussion of Smith's use of sound benefited greatly from David Chapman's "Chance Encounters: Serendipity and the Use of Music in the Films of Jean Cocteau and Harry Smith," *The Soundtrack* 2, no. 1 (2009): 5–18.

95 *"After I met Griff"*: Singh, 56.

96 *"They were, really, listening"*: Jonas Mekas, "Music Journal: On Music and Cinema," *The Village Voice*, June 29, 1967.

97 *At Naropa University in 1989*: Rani Singh, "Harry Smith," *Film Culture*, no. 76 (June 1992): 14.

97 *"He also kept interrupting himself"*: Fred Camper, "Harry Smith—Other Material," http://people.wcsu.edu/mccarneyh/fva/S/HSmith_Other.html.

98 *In 1963*: Mel Brooks, Ernest Pintoff, "The Critic," https://www.youtube.com/watch?v=v3GMSQrzNbk.

3. HARRY THE HIPSTER

100 *"I habitually wore, for example"*: Singh, 240.

100 *Harry knew some of these musicians*: Phil Elwood, "A Profoundly Influential Folk Anthology," *SF Gate*, September 12, 1997, https://www.sfgate.com/news/article/A-profoundly-influential-folk-anthology-3101071.php.

101 *"It was simply the most radical thing"*: Raymond Foye and Jordan Belson, "'It's a Glorious Thing If You Don't Expect an Explanation': Jordan Belson on his Art," *Brooklyn Rail*, December 18, 2014.

103 *"Smith looked like most"*: Elwood, "A Profoundly Influential Folk Anthology."

105 *"Important contacts with genius Harry Smith"*: Lamantia, *Collected Poems*, lxi.

105 *For two years Harry lived there*: Rani Singh interview with Philip Lamantia, Getty Library.

106 *"Black musicians were imitating"*: Allen Ginsberg, *The Best Minds of My Generation: A Literary History of the Beats* (New York: Grove Press, 2017), 8.

106 *In the recording*: Jack Kerouac, "History of Bebop," *Readings by Jack Kerouac on the Beat Generation*, Verve Records 314 537574–2, recorded 1958–1959.

108 *How much Harry joined in*: Robin Blaser, ed., *The Collected Books of Jack Spicer* (Santa Rosa, CA: Black Sparrow Press, 1999), 375. The tape is FW-ASCH-7RR-1774 in the Smithsonian Center for Folklife and Cultural Heritage Archive.

109 *"One Bubble"*: Lunsford, 24.

109 *gave the Whatcom Museum*: Bret Lunsford, "Harry Smith Donated Artifacts at the Whatcom Museum in the 1940s Now on Display," *Resounding*, May 13, 2022, https://resoundingharrysmith.substack.com/p/harry-smith-donated-artifacts-at.

110 *"Harry walked out"*: Lunsford, 24.

110 *Harry answered by sending him*: Singh, 46.

110 *"He was kept in food"*: Rani Singh interview with Philip Lamantia, Getty Library.

111 *Running beneath the mural*: Carol P. Chamberland, "The House That Bop Built," *California History* 75, no. 3 (Fall 1996), 272–83; John Ross, "When Jazz

Was the Thing," *Datebook*, May 23, 1993, 20–21; Carol Chamberland, "Jimbo Edwards," http://users.rcn.com/jazzinfo/v10n01May00/FinJimbo.html; Elizabeth Pepen and Lewis Watts, *Harlem of the West: The San Francisco Fillmore Jazz Era* (San Francisco: Chronicle Books, 2006), 158–62; Jordan Belson letter to Rani Singh, April 17, 1992, Getty Library.

111 *"Since he was there every night"*: *Harry Smith: Selected Films*, DVD, Harry Smith Archive, 2013.

111 *In one, an interview*: Singh, 156–57.

112 *"I first met Harry"*: "Gerd Stern–3 (Gerd Stern Remembers Harry Smith)," The Allen Ginsberg Project, October 21, 2014, https://allenginsberg.org/2014/10 /gerd-stern-3-gerd-stern-remembers-harry-smith/.

112 *She had convinced Solomon*: Rebay later commissioned Frank Lloyd Wright to design the current Guggenheim Museum with its unorthodox shape and hallways for a different form of viewing.

113 *"The film has always"*: Joan M. Lukach, *Hilla Rebay: In Search of the Spirit in Art* (New York: George Braziller, 1983), 221.

113 *When they entered Belson's studio*: MacDonald, *A Critical Cinema 3*, 68.

114 *Belson said that Harry*: Scott MacDonald, *Cinema 16* (Philadelphia: Temple University Press, 2002),70.

114 *Harry had told Baroness*: Harry Smith letter to Rebay, April 4, 1950, Guggenheim Museum Archives.

115 *Film No. 3 was something*: Some sources credit the San Francisco State College art professor Seymour Locks with light shows in 1952, a year or two after Smith's work. But for the record, Oskar Fischinger did light shows in Berlin in the 1920s with music played with projected abstract objects.

115 *Jordan Belson and Henry Jacobs*: A hint of such events can be seen in the DVD *Space Is the Place* with the Sun Ra Arkestra playing in a similar light show in the same planetarium some years later. Louise Sandhaus, *Earthquakes, Mudslides, Fires & Riots: California & Graphic Design 1936–1986* (Los Angeles: Metropolis Books, 2014).

115 *The evening's program notes described it*: The San Francisco Museum of Art, Art in Cinema, Sixth Series, program, Getty Library.

116 *"SAN FRANCISCO—Atlee Chapman's band"*: "Bop Band Accompanies Non-Objective Films," *DownBeat*, June 30, 1950, 3.

117 *"Each frame itself"*: The San Francisco Museum of Art, Art in Cinema, Sixth Series, program, Getty Library.

117 *He also created a light show*: Robert Robertson, *Cinema and the Audiovisual Imagination: Music, Image, Sound* (London: I. B. Tauris, 2015), 63; "All Souls Carnival: A Lecture by Roger Horrocks," https://www.circuit.org.nz/film/all -souls-carnival-a-lecture-by-roger-horrocks.

118 *"Since I showed my films"*: Harry Smith letter to Hilla Rebay, June 17, 1950, Guggenheim Museum Archives.

120 *To show that he had been*: Harry Smith letter to Hilla Rebay, January 26, 1951, Guggenheim Museum Archives.

120 *The baroness granted him*: Hilla Rebay letter to Harry Smith, February 12, 1951, Guggenheim Museum Archives.

120 *But once she saw*: Hilla Rebay letter to Harry Smith, April 6, 1951, Guggenheim Museum Archives.

120 *"Three Dimensional Films"*: Hilla Rebay letter to Harry Smith, April, 6, 1951, Guggenheim Museum Archives.

121 *She was accustomed*: Scott MacDonald, *Art in Cinema: Documents Toward a History of the Film Society* (Philadelphia: Temple University Press, 2006), 328–29.

121 *He wrote Rebay that*: Harry Smith letter to Hilla Rebay, May 9, 1951, Guggenheim Museum Archives.

4. HARRY SMITH IN NEW YORK

123 *Andrews would move to London*: Kerry Colonna email to John Szwed, 2021.

124 *A knock on the door*: Igliori, 37.

124 *Lionel was annoyed*: Igliori, 37.

125 *"I didn't mean to indicate"*: Harry Smith letter to Hilla Rebay, November 11, 1951, Guggenheim Museum Archives.

126 *Rebay told her assistant*: Undated note from Rebay to Margaret Russell, and a letter from Russell to Smith, November 20, 1951, Guggenheim Museum Archives.

126 *An office note*: Harry Smith letter to Hilla Rebay, December 20, 1951; office memo from Mary McC. to Peg, December 22, 1951, Getty Library.

127 *His grandparents*: John Strausbaugh, "The Rabbi's Basement Tapes," *New York Press* 1, no. 40, October 1, 1997, 1; John Strausbaugh, "The Angel and R. J. Reynolds," *New York Press* 8, no. 47, November 20–28, 1988, 44.

128 *Lionel recalled that*: Igliori, 41.

128 *"Any damn subject"*: Igliori, 41. Other sources for this section are Rani Singh's video interviews with Lionel Ziprin in the Getty Library.

130 *"It is pure escapism"*: Hal Boyle, "'Devil Dealer' Cites Magic as a Form of Escape," *The Portsmouth (OH) Times*, April 29, 1947.

131 *"I smoked a lot"*: "Gerrit Lansing Interviewed by Patrick Dowd," *Let the Bucket Down*, issue 3, 2015, 2–4; John Szwed conversations with Bill Breeze, 2020–21.

131 *Dr. Joe Gross, a psychiatrist*: Program for *A Night of Art, Film, and Ultraperception*, September 14, 2006, New York, 38.

131 *"If my memory serves me"*: Herbert Huncke, "Thanksgiving, 1991: Harry Smith," in *The Herbert Huncke Reader*, Benjamin G. Schafer, ed. (New York: William Morrow and Company, 1997), 344–45.

132 *"I met the real Harry"*: "A Tribute to Harry from Izzy Young," notes to *The Harry Smith Project*, Shout Records 826663–10041, 2006, 18.

132 *Jonas Mekas encountered him*: Igliori, 79.

133 *"Harry came for a visit"*: Diane di Prima letter to Rani Singh, August 13, 1996, Getty Library.

133 *The company would be called*: Inkweed letter to potential investors, 1953, Getty Library.

135 *"It's no big thing"*: David Katz, "'Angels Are Just One More Species," *Jewish Quarterly*, no. 204 (Winter 2006–2007).

136 *"But children do that"*: Katz, 51.

137 *"I said, 'Listen Harry'"*: John Strausbaugh, "The Rabbi's Basement Tapes," *New York Press* 1, no. 40, October 1, 1997, 1.

137 *The rabbi's house*: Jon Kalish, "High on Kabbala," *Jerusalem Post*, June 11, 1999, 9.

138 *The recordings piled up*: Song categories provided in a lecture by Naomi Cohn Zentner.

138 *"You see anthropologists are whites"*: Igliori, 49.

5. THE ANTHOLOGIST

143 *"Woody would come to the studio"*: Moses Asch interviewed by Gary Kenton, Moses Asch folder, Folkways Collection, Smithsonian Center for Folklife and Cultural Heritage Archive.

143 *He understood the content*: Moses Asch, *The Birth and Growth of the Anthology of American Folk Music: A Booklet of Essays, Appreciations, and Annotations Pertaining to the Anthology of American Folk*, 33.

143 *Harry offered to sell*: Robert Palmer, "How a Recording Pioneer Created a Treasury of Folk Music," *The New York Times*, May 1983.

143 *"I began selling off"*: Harry Smith interviewed by Nick Spitzer.

144 *If Cleanth Brooks and*: Cleanth Brooks and Robert Penn Warren, *Understanding Poetry: An Anthology for College Students* (New York: Holt & Company, 1938); Florence Dore, *Novel Sounds: Southern Fiction in the Age of Rock and Roll* (New York: Columbia University Press, 2018), 42.

144 *"Harry Smith is an authority"*: Moses Asch interviewed by Gary Kenton.

144 *Rinzler doubted that Asch*: Peter Goldsmith interview with Ralph Rinzler, in the Ralph Rinzler folder of the Moses and Frances Asch Collection, the Smithsonian Center for Folklife and Cultural Heritage Archive.

145 *Another of Harry's sources*: Alan Lomax, *List of American Folk Songs on Commercial Records* (Washington, DC: United States Government Printing Office, 1940).

146 *Smith said he had chosen*: Singh, 70.

146 *"Intuition is employed in determining"*: Singh, 82–83.

147 *"The choices have been"*: Lomax, *List of American Folk Music*. See also Rory Crutchfield, "I Saw America Changed Through Music: An Examination of the American Collecting Tradition" (PhD dissertation, University of Glasgow, 2012).

147 *This was the only recording*: Ross Hair and Thomas Ruys Smith, eds., *Harry Smith's Anthology of American Folk Music: America Changed Through Music* (London and New York: Routledge, 2017), 144–71.

148 *"You didn't see"*: Mike McGonigal, "Old Folk," *Metro Pulse Online*, 1997.

150 *In 1952, they would have been*: Ralph Peer, the pioneer of country recording, found much of it distasteful. Years later, the reaction to the considerable success of the soundtrack to the Coen brothers' film *O Brother, Where Art Thou?* was generally negative among country music recording companies.

150 *It seems odd*: See Christina Ruth Hastie, "'This Murder Done': Misogyny, Femicide and Modernity in 19th Century Appalachian Murder Ballads" (master's thesis, University of Tennessee, 2011).

152 *He went further into detail*: These examples are drawn from a fine and provocative dissertation by Richard Daniel Blim, "Patchwork Nation: Collage, Music, and American Identity" (PhD dissertation, University of Michigan, 2013), 216–28.

153 *"There is a provision in the copyright law"*: Gary Kenton interview with Moses Asch, July 1990.

154 *In Harry's essay*: Elwood, "A Profoundly Influential Folk Anthology."

154 *he was the first*: Gary Kenton, "Moses Asch of Folkways," *Audio*, July 1990, 45.

155 *"Harry talked in our"*: Mike McGonigal. "Old Folk," *Metro Pulse Online*, 1997.

155 *"This inspired collection"*: Paul Oliver, "String Ticklers and Skillet Licker," *Jazz Monthly*, February 1963.

155 *"Smith was acutely aware"*: John Fahey, "April 1997," in *A Booklet of Essays, Appreciations, and Annotations Pertaining to the Anthology of American Folk Music*, 9.

156 *"Only through recordings"*: Harry Smith, ed., "American Folk Music," booklet included with the *Anthology of American Folk Music*, Folkways Records, 1952, 251–53.

156 *European set dances*: Erin Blakemore, "The Slave Roots of Square Dancing," JSTOR Daily, June 16, 2017, https://daily.jstor.org/the-slave-roots-of-square -dancing/; Terry Zwigoff, "Louie Bluie: The Life and Music of William Howard Armstrong," *78 Quarterly* 1, no. 5, 48.

157 *"The thing that amazed me"*: Harry Smith interviewed by Nick Spitzer.

158 *"All the transcriptions"*: Kenton.

158 *In its first year*: Moses and Frances Asch Collection, the Smithsonian Center for Folklife and Cultural Heritage Archive.

158 *The next review*: Philip L. Miller, "Recorded Americana," *Music Library Association Notes*, September 1952, 1; Oliver, "String Ticklers and Skillet Licker."

158 *This pattern continued*: Folkways file, Smithsonian Center for Folklife and Cultural Heritage Archive.

159 *Lomax himself strongly approved*: John Szwed interview with Anna Lomax Wood.

159 *Dylan would later record*: "The House Carpenter" (Clarence Ashley); "The Cuckoo" ("The Coo Bird," Clarence Ashley); "The Butcher's Boy" ("Railroad Boy," Buell Kazee); "The Wagoner's Lad" ("Loving Nancy," Buell Kazee); "Omie Wise" (G. B. Grayson); "My Name Is John Johannah" (Kelly Harrell); "John Hardy Was a Desperate Little Man" (Carter Family); "Stackalee" (Frank Hutchison); "Little Moses" (Carter Family); "James Alley Blues" (Richard "Rabbit" Brown); "See That My Grave Is Kept Clean" (Blind Lemon Jefferson); "K. C. Moan" (The Memphis Jug Band); "Fishing Blues" (Henry "Ragtime Texas" Thomas); "Frankie" (Mississippi John Hurt), "Influential Folkways Albums—Roots of Bob Dylan," http://bobdylanroots.com/folkways.html.

159 *Mike Seeger found Dock Boggs*: Petrusich, *Do Not Sell at Any Price*, 148–51.

159 *When they were told*: Roger Abrahams email to John Szwed, 2017.

160 *"He was not interested"*: John Cohen email to John Szwed, 2018.

161 *The music Smith's* Anthology: Greil Marcus, *The Old, Weird America: The World of Bob Dylan's Basement Tapes* (New York: Picador, 2011).

161 *"The whole anthology was a collage"*: Singh, 81.

161 *"like something or other"*: Singh, 81.

162 *"This is Smithville"*: Greil Marcus, "The Old, Weird America," in *A Booklet of Essays, Appreciations, and Annotations Pertaining to the Anthology of American Folk Music*, 5–25, 37.

162 *"With its three volumes"*: Robert Cantwell, "Smith's Memory Theater: The Folkways Anthology of American Folk Music," *New England Review*—Middlebury Series 13, no. 3–4 (Spring–Summer 1991): 375.

163 *"Let us make a body"*: "John Fahey on The Nature of Reality," http://www .johnfahey.com/reality.htm.

164 *Lomax had long acknowledged*: John Szwed interviews with Anna Lomax Wood and Charles Compo.

164 *If at first*: Michael J. Kramer, "Alan Lomax, Harry Smith, and the Proto-Digital Study of Folk Music," http://www.michaeljkramer.net/nudhl-6-fri-38 -12-2pm-research-presentation-michael-j-kramer-alan-lomax-harry-smith-and -the-proto-digital-study-of-folk-music/.

165 *"Harry's aesthetic was very complex"*: Kemnitzer, 31.

165 *"We learned everything we knew"*: Unpublished Dave Van Ronk interview by David Hadju for *Positively 4th Street: The Lives and Times of Joan Baez, Bob Dylan, Mimi Baez Fariña, and Richard Fariña* (New York: Picador, 2001).

166 *"Here's what it was about"*: Unpublished John Sebastian interview by David Hajdu for *Positively 4th Street.*

167 *Peter Stampfel of the Holy Modal Rounders*: Jason Gross, "Peter Stampfel Interview, Part 1," *Perfect Sound Forever*, 1996, https://www.furious.com/perfect /stampfel.html.

167 *Harry quarreled with Marian Distler*: Interview conducted by Gary Kenton at the Breslin Hotel, NYC, 1983, quoted in the liner notes to *Harry Smith's Anthology of American Folk Music, Volume 4*, Revenant RVM 211, 2000, 42.

168 *Ralph Rinzler, Mike Seeger*: Several other lists of songs for Volume 4 are in the Moses and Frances Asch Collection in the Smithsonian Center for Folklife and Cultural Heritage Archive, one of which has sixty selections.

168 *Harry seemed to have disappeared*: Liner notes included with *Harry Smith's Anthology of American Folk Music, Volume 4*, 33.

168 *"I wanted to make more of a content analysis"*: Singh, 84.

169 *"The evidence is in the shakedown"*: John Fahey in liner notes to *Harry Smith's Anthology of American Folk Music, Volume 4*, 90.

169 *Four different-shaped notes*: There is also a seven-note version from the early nineteenth century.

170 *He studied a series of methods*: For examples of visible music, see Patrick Feaster, *Pictures of Sound: One Thousand Years of Educed Audio: 980–1980* (Atlanta: Dust-to-Digital, 2012).

171 *In his notes*: Some of these recordings can be heard on YouTube, though the size of the recorded groups is sometimes much smaller than those of the live performances.

171 *new set of recordings*: The records on Smith's list of projected albums in order are:

DISC 1

Middle Georgia Singing Convention No. 1: "The Song of Love," Okeh 8903 404656

Middle Georgia Singing Convention No. 1: "I Am Going Home," Okeh 8903 404657

Fa Sol La Singers: "Happy on the Way," Columbia 14636-D 15192

Fa Sol La Singers: "I'll Stay on the Right Road Now," Columbia 14636-D 151915

Fa Sol La Singers: "Rejoicing on the Way," Columbia 14656-D 151913

Fa Sol La Singers: "Jesus Walks with Me," Columbia 14656-D 151914

Alabama Sacred Heart Singers: "Rocky Road," Columbia 15274-D 146091

Alabama Sacred Heart Singers: "Present Joys," Columbia 15274-D 1146092

Alabama Sacred Heart Singers: "Religion Is a Freedom," Columbia Black 1915359-D 147329

DISC 2

The Denson Quartet: "Christian Soldier," Columbia 15526-D 147331

The Denson Quartet: "I'm on My Journey Home," Columbia 15526-D 147332

Denson's Sacred Harp Singers of Arley, Alabama: "Nighty-Fifth," Brunswick 287

Denson's Sacred Harp Singers of Arley, Alabama: "The Christian's Hope," Brunswick 287

Denson's Sacred Harp Singers of Arley, Alabama: "The Happy Sailor," Brunswick 302

Denson's Sacred Harp Singers of Arley, Alabama: "Protection," Brunswick 302

Denson-Parris Sacred Harp Singers: "Blooming Youth," Bluebird B-5599A

Denson-Parris Sacred Harp Singers: "The Good Old Way," Bluebird B-5599B

DISC 3

Denson-Parris Sacred Harp Singers: "Resurrected," Bluebird B-5979A

Denson-Parris Sacred Harp Singers: "Reverential Anthem," B-5979B

Denson-Parris Sacred Harp Singers: "Passing Away," Bluebird B-5980-A

Denson-Parris Sacred Harp Singers: "Exhortation," Bluebird B-5980-B

Daniels-Deason Sacred Heart Singers: "Primrose Hall," Columbia Black 15323-D 147280

Daniels-Deason Sacred Heart Singers: "Coronation," Columbia Black 15323-D 147281

L. V. Jones and his Virginia Singing Class: "In That Crowning Day," Okeh (Red) 45187 81627

L. V. Jones and his Virginia Singing Class: "Will My Mother Know Me There?" Okeh (Red) 45187 81627

T. K. Browne: "Iya-Mamumi," Gramophone (English) E.Z. 64 X-5–42259

T. K. Browne: "Omo To Mo Iya Re Losu," Gramophone (English) E.Z. 64 X-5–42259

Kwabima Mensa: "Furansa Ayemi," HMV J.Z. 194194 OAB 486

Kwabima Mensa: "Onipa Beye Yie," HMV J.Z. 194 OAB 503

Kwesi Menu: "High Life," HMV J-Z.185 OAB 479

171 *"This essay is an attempt"*: The notes for a shape note anthology are in the Anthology Film Archives library.

172 *As Harry put it*: Notes for a shape note anthology.

172 *He was calling attention*: There is still little interest in African American shape note singing, but for one early attempt to draw attention to it, see John W. Work, "Plantation Meistersinger," *The Musical Quarterly* 27, no. 1 (January 1, 1941), 97–106. For more recent efforts, there is Joe Dan Boyd, *Judge Jackson and the Colored Sacred Harp* (Montgomery, AL: Alabama Folklife Association), 2002, and Jesse P. Karlsberg, "Folklore's Filter: Race, Place, and Sacred Harp Singing" (PhD dissertation, Emory University, 2015), https://etd.library.emory.edu /concern/etds/n009w256n.

173 *Though it took*: With the folk music revival in full bloom in the 1960s, Folkways introduced a repackaged set of Smith's albums retitled *Anthology of American Folk Music*, and, over Smith's objections, replaced the original covers with a Ben Shahn photograph of a Depression-era farmer in order to heighten the

political content of the records and take advantage of the New Left's embrace of folk music. Then, in 1973, Josh Dunson and Ethel Raim published a new book with Moses Asch's Oak Publications also titled *Anthology of American Folk Music*, with words and sheet music of forty-three of the eighty-four songs on the records in Smith's collection, plus five songs that were planned for volume four of the *Anthology*. Some of the introductions to these songs were from Smith's record notes, but most were reprinted from others' books, now with the words and music added.

The first of a series of tributes to the *Anthology* was broadcast in that same year, April 21, 1973, on "The Free Music Store," a WBAI radio program in New York City, where the Village folk stars Phil Ochs, Dave Van Ronk, and Patrick Sky sang their favorite songs from the albums. But for the next two decades, there was little public mention of the *Anthology*.

The Smithsonian Institution acquired Folkways Records in 1987, and in 1997 reissued the Smith collection on six compact discs, each disc corresponding to each album of the original set of LPs, including replicas of Smith's original artwork and booklet of notes. At first there was some doubt about reissuing the *Anthology* because so many of the songs had already become available on CDs by 1990. But the success of Greil Marcus's book *The Old, Weird America* (then titled *Invisible Republic*) helped persuade Smithsonian Folkways that Smith's unique sequencing, art, and notes justified reissuing in a new edition. A new booklet was added that expanded track information for each song and included essays and appreciations by Greil Marcus, Moses Asch, John Fahey, John Cohen, Elvis Costello, Lucy Sante, Dave Van Ronk, Allen Ginsberg, and others. It received Grammy awards for Best Historical Album and Best Album Notes, and in 2021 it was selected for the Grammy Hall of Fame.

Following the reissue of the *Anthology* in 1997, a two-day conference, "Revelations of Tradition: Harry Smith's *Anthology of American Folk Music* and Its Legacy" was held in October at the Smithsonian and sponsored by the Rock and Roll Hall of Fame, the Smithsonian Institution's National Museum of American History, and Smithsonian Folkways Records. Two concerts at the Barns of Wolf Trap in Virginia accompanied the conference, with performances by folk and pop singers such as the Fugs, Jeff Tweedy, John Jackson, Ella Jenkins, and John Sebastian. A CD recording of those concerts, *The Harry Smith Connection: A Live Tribute to the Anthology of American Folk Music*, was issued in 1998 by Smithsonian Folkways.

Nick Cave approached the producer Hal Willner about organizing the Meltdown Festival in London in 1999, and they came up with the idea of the *Harry Smith Project: Anthology of American Folk Music Revisited*, another series of performances of the songs on Smith's original *Anthology* performed by a broader range of contemporary classical, folk, and pop artists in London, but also in Brooklyn and Los Angeles, from 1999 to 2001. The concerts ran for over five hours, and featured a shifting lineup including Marianne Faithfull, Elvis Costello, Richard Thompson, Philip Glass, Beth Orton, Beck, Van Dyke Parks, David Johansen, Lou Reed, Sonic Youth, DJ Spooky, Rufus Wainwright, Wilco, Todd Rundgren, and dozens more. Shout Records in 2006 issued the *Project* as a boxed set of two CDs, a DVD of live performances and three of Smith's films accompanied by new live music performances, plus another DVD of Rani Singh's documentary film, *The Old Weird America: Harry Smith's Anthology of American Folk Music*. In April 2001, Rani Singh and Andrew Perchuk organized a two-day seminar, "Harry Smith: The Avant-Garde in the American Vernacular," at the Getty Foundation in Los Angeles. A second seminar, "Investigating *Mahagonny*," followed in May 2002. A Getty publication covering the two seminars was edited by Singh and Perchuk and published as *Harry Smith: The Avant-Garde in the American Vernacular* in 2010.

Smith's volume four of the *Anthology* was finally issued in 2005 by Revenant Records, and in the same year, the National Recording Registry at the Library of Congress added the *Anthology* to its list of records that best represent art and life in the United States. It now sits alongside recordings such as Stravinsky's *The Rite of Spring* and *The Freewheelin' Bob Dylan*.

The *Anthology* continues to inspire and spin off new formats, versions, and publications. It was again reissued on LP by Mississippi Records in 2014. Dust-to-Digital assembled *The Harry Smith B-Sides* in 2020, a collection of the flip side of each 78-rpm record on the Smith set (minus three that were considered offensive); *The Other Anthology of Folk Music* is a collection of different songs by many of the same artists and others, on Sheep Shaggers Records; *Tribute to the Anthology of American Folk Music by Harry Smith* is a 2016 online collection of modern versions from France's Hinah Records; and *Playhead: The Parallel Anthology* is a British online collection of different versions of the same songs done by other singers on early recordings.

In 2017 a flood of video and sound recordings again gave new life to the Smith collection. *American Epic*, a 2017 TV documentary that was also released on DVD featured many of the *Anthology*'s recordings and others of the same era, visually documented with period films and texts, and with brilliant sonic restoration that made them sound as if they had been recorded twenty years later. *American Epic* (Columbia Legacy, 88875129012) was a five-CD collection of one hundred recordings made between 1920 and 1930, including those used in the TV film, all remastered. *American Epic: The Sessions* is the soundtrack of the film on CD.

Numerous music festivals have honored Harry's work, and some, like the Harry Smith Frolic in Massachusetts and the Harry Smith Festival in Pennsylvania, have long histories. *Harry Smith's Anthology of American Folk Music: America Changed Through Music*, edited by Ross Hair and Thomas Ruys Smith, is a 2017 book on the *Anthology* and its influence.

173 *Though he was shocked*: Marc Silber Museum Music Newsletter, December 1991.

174 *"At the present time"*: Peter Goldsmith in the Moses and Frances Asch Collection, Smithsonian Center for Folklife and Cultural Heritage Archive.

6. THE PARAPSYCHOLOGIST

176 *Puharich's aim*: Aldous Huxley, *Moksha: Aldous Huxley's Classic Writings on Psychedelics and the Visionary* (Rochester, VT: Park Street Press, 1999), chapter 14.

177 *Harry wrote Arthur*: Harry Smith letter to Arthur Young, June 3, 1955, Anodos Foundation Archive.

177 *Harry said his interest in Wither*: Harry Smith letter to Arthur Young, June 3, 1955.

177   *Among them were*: Harry Smith letter to Arthur Young, August 20, 1955, Anodos Foundation Archive.

177   *"Francis [sic], Elinor, and the Stumps"*: Harry Smith letter to Arthur Young, August 20, 1955.

178   *While he was at work on these projects*: Elinor Bond letter to Arthur Young, June 16, 1955, Anodos Foundation Archive.

179   *He was still engaged with Young's*: Arthur M. Young, *Nested Time: An Astrological Autobiography* (Cambria, CA: The Anodos Publications, 2004), 180; Harry Smith letter to Arthur Young, July 30, 1956, Anodos Foundation Archives.

179   *He was so upset*: Harry Smith letter to Arthur Young, September 10, 1957, Anodos Foundation Archives.

180   *"To make this film"*: Sitney, 240.

180   *Once again, audiences*: Moritz, "Non-Objective Film."

180   *Films No. 8 and No. 9 were both lost*: Film-Makers' Cooperative Catalogue 3, 57–58.

181   *He had been cutting up magazines*: Singh, 57–58.

181   *There is also the likely possibility*: Maya Deren and Marcel Duchamp, *Witch's Cradle*, https://www.youtube.com/watch?v=RuA9TPlwA7M.7.

181   *At the front of the catalog*: "Sixteen Miles of String," https://www.wikiart.org/en/marcel-duchamp/sixteen-miles-of-string-installation-for-the-first-papers-of-surrealism-exhibition-1942.

182   *"I'd been able to hear"*: Singh, 57.

182   *It's said that Mondrian and Monk*: Geoff Winston, "Mondrian and Jazz," *London Jazz News*, March 3, 2012. https://londonjazznews.com/2012/03/21/mondrian-and-jazz/; "Nelly van Doesburg," *Wikipedia*, https://en.wikipedia.org/wiki/Nelly_van_Doesburg.

183   *Lewis H. Lapham was often there*: Lewis H. Lapham, "'Round Midnight," *Lapham's Quarterly* X, no. 4 (Fall 2017), 18.

183   *The filmmaker Andrew Noren once saw Harry*: Andrew Noren unpublished writings on Harry Smith, courtesy of Risé Hall-Noren, June 23, 2016.

184   *"I noticed an old guy"*: Bill Morgan, *I Celebrate Myself* (New York: Viking, 2006), 278; "Allen Ginsberg," in Igliori, 107. The "old guy" was thirty-eight. Ginsberg remembered this meeting as taking place in 1959, but it would have been 1958, since Monk did not play at the Five Spot the next year.

184   *The system that Ginsberg spoke of*: Singh, 3.

185   *"When I came to New York"*: Singh, 57.

185   *"When we asked him"*: Percy Heath in conversation with Rani Singh, *Harry Smith Selected Films*, DVD, Harry Smith Archives, 2001.

185   *We went to see some cat name Harry Smith's*: Amiri Baraka and Edward Dorn, *The Collected Letters*, Claudia Moreno Pisano, ed. (Albuquerque: University of New Mexico Press, 2013), 17.

185   *"A commentary on and exposition"*: Film-Makers' Cooperative Catalogue 3.

186   *P. Adams Sitney rightly says*: Sitney, 246–49.

186   *No. 12 was Harry's first long work*: Allen Ginsberg, *Journals Early Fifties, Early Sixties*, Gordon Ball, ed. (New York: Grove Press, 1977), 185–86; *Heaven and Earth Magic*, https://www.youtube.com/watch?v=zbjSSyAo9WA.

186   *"A much-expanded version of No. 8"*: Film-Makers' Cooperative Catalogue 3, 57–58.

187   *When Harry showed the film at Queens Museum*: "Queens Museum of Art Talk, November 11, 1978," *Harry Smith: The Avant-Garde in the American Vernacular*, Andrew Perchuk and Rani Singh, eds. (Los Angeles: Getty Research Institute, 2010), 118.

187   *"I must say that I'm amazed"*: Sitney, 249–50.

187   *"What I want to do"*: Singh, 139–140.

188   *A film of this complexity*: Annette Michelson, "The Mummy's Return: A Kleinian Film Scenario," in *Harry Smith: The Avant-Garde in the American Vernacular*, 85–102.

188   *Noël Carroll said*: Noël Carroll, "Mind, Medium and Metaphor in Harry Smith's *Heaven and Earth Magic*," *Film Quarterly* 31, no. 2 (Winter 1977–78): 37–44.

188   *Sitney understood it*: P. Adams Sitney, "Harry Smith, Bibliophile, and the Origins of Cinema," *Harry Smith: The Avant-Garde in the American Vernacular*, 103–14.

188   *When he spoke to Harry*: Allen S. Weiss email to John Szwed, September 12, 2020.

188   *"When a woman in the audience"*: Allen S. Weiss email to John Szwed, September 12, 2020.

189   *"So he screened from '62–'63"*: Igliori, 80.

189   *When the poet Carol Bergé went to Le Metro*: Carol Bergé, "The Work of Harry Smith," *Film Culture*, no. 37 (Summer 1965), 3–4.

190   *"I have shown the film"*: Harry Smith letter to Arthur M. Young, August 30, 1960, Anodos Foundation Archives.

190   *As unlikely as it sounds*: Goldsmith in the Moses and Frances Asch Collection, the Smithsonian Center for Folklife and Cultural Heritage Archive.

190   *Percy Heath visited him*: Percy Heath in conversation with Rani Singh, *Harry Smith Selected Films*, DVD, Harry Smith Archives, 2001.

190   *"He was paranoid"*: Percy Heath in conversation with Rani Singh.

191   *"Sort of like the idea"*: Singh, 3.

191   *"The only person I met"*: Nicholas Davidoff, "Hidden America," *The New York Times Magazine*, July 5, 2015, 48.

193   *Leary wrote Burroughs*: Timothy Leary letter to Burroughs, February 28, 1961, File C-27, BP, New York Public Library.

193   *Burroughs was impressed by Smith's animations*: Miles, *Call Me Burroughs*, 434.

194   *"Lucien and Harry Smith called"*: Jack Kerouac in a letter to Allen Ginsberg, April 14, 1961, *Jack Kerouac, Selected Letters 1957–1969*, Ann Charters, ed. (New York: Penguin, 1999), 325.

195   *On one such occasion Carr*: Marc Berger email to John Szwed, January 21, 2019.

195   *For a few, like Harry*: Salman Rushdie, "Out of Kansas," *The New Yorker*, May 11, 1992.

196   *"Number 13 had all the characters"*: Singh, 59–60.

198   *"What I was really trying to do"*: Singh, 60–61.

199   *"Fragments and tests of Shamanism"*: *Film-Makers' Cooperative Catalogue 3*, 57–58.

199   *Harry noted that*: *Film-Makers' Cooperative Catalogue 3*, 57–58.

199   *"I was trying to help Harry"*: Igliori, 150–51.

200   *They were filmed in 1968 and added to the earlier Tinman footage*: "No. 16: Oz: The Tin Woodman's Dream," https://letterboxd.com/film/no-16-oz-the-tin-woodmans-dream/.

201   *The Land of Oz in the form*: Igliori, 218.

201 *"Those who have been especially lucky"*: Jonas Mekas, "Movie Journal: Spiritualization of the Image," *The Village Voice*, June 25, 1964.

202 *"Harry Smith's films"*: Jonas Mekas, "Movie Journal: The Year 1964," *The Village Voice*, January 7, 1965.

202 *"For thirty years"*: Jonas Mekas, "Movie Journal: The Magic Cinema of Harry Smith," *The Village Voice*, March 16, 1965, 89–90.

202 *High praise indeed*: Mekas, "Movie Journal: The Year 1964," 89.

203 *Yet he wrote in his diary*: Jonas Mekas, *I Seem to Live. The New York Diaries, Vol. 1 1950–1969* (New York: Spector Books, 2020), 462.

203 *A year later*: Jonas Mekas, "On the Tactile Interactions in Cinema, or Creation with Your Total Body," *The Village Voice*, June 23, 1966, 254–57.

203 *"Really, what's happening"*: Jonas Mekas, *Scrapbooks of the Sixties: Writings 1954–2010* (Leipzig: Spector Books, 2015), 140.

204 *It was an idea that could be extended*: Harold Rosenberg, "American Action Painters," *ARTnews* 51, no. 8, 1952.

204 *"When I met him"*: Carl Abrahamsson, "Conrad Rooks and Chappaqua," https:// carlabrahamsson.blogspot.com/2012/06/conrad-rooks-chappaqua-and -beyond.html.

206 *"Rooks rented a studio"*: Igliori, 119–20.

206 *"Sand was everywhere"*: Lawrence Shainberg, "Notes from the Underground," *Evergreen Review*, no. 50, December 1967, 106.

7. THE ANTHROPOLOGIST

209 *Harry was to be his on-site guide*: Bill Breeze email to John Szwed, 2021.

209 *"[Harry] received around $5,000"*: *Harry Smith: The Avant-Garde in the American Vernacular*, 59, footnote 46.

209 *Rooks failed to mention*: Bill Breeze email to John Szwed, 2021.

209 *An ad appeared in the* Daily Oklahoman: Philip Smith email to John Szwed, 2019.

210 *These artistic uses of the drug*: The San Francisco artist Lee Mullican's 1951 *Peyote Candle* was one of the first psychedelic paintings. *Peyote Candle* is in the Huntington Museum in Pasadena. My thanks to Kerry Colonna for information about San Francisco and Berkeley arts and drug history.

210 *"They differed from other Plains tribes"*: Harry Smith, Liner notes to *The Kiowa Peyote Meeting: Songs and Narratives by Members of a Tribe That Was Fundamental in Popularizing the Native American Church*, Ethnic Folkways Records FE460, 1973, https://folkways.si.edu/kiowa-peyote-meeting/american-indian /music/album/smithsonian.

211 *"Before I had been there"*: Smith, *Kiowa Peyote Meeting*.

212 *"Except for the police, white people"*: Smith, *Kiowa Peyote Meeting*.

212 *"When I awoke"*: Smith, *Kiowa Peyote Meeting*.

213 *"I would like to make it clear"*: Smith, *Kiowa Peyote Meeting*.

215 *"There is no doubt"*: Smith, *Kiowa Peyote Meeting*.

216 *During his recording*: Singh, 84.

217 *In good folklorist fashion*: Harry Smith collection, Smithsonian Center for Folklife and Cultural Heritage.

218 *He boasted that it was he*: Conrad Rooks email to Rani Singh, November 5, 1997, Getty Library.

218 *"One of the reasons I made this film"*: Lawrence Shainberg, "Notes from the Underground," *Evergreen Review*, no. 50, December 1968, 22.

219 *"I've usually just borrowed"*: Singh, 57.

219 *He described it*: Film-Makers' Cooperative Catalog 3, 57–58.

219 *Asked if the synchrony*: Singh, 129.

220 *"At the beginning"*: P. Adams Sitney, notes for the Avant Garde Tuesdays series at the Jewish Museum, New York City, November 19, 1968, Getty Library.

220 *"All of my paintings, all of my films"*: *Harry Smith: The Avant-Garde in the American Vernacular*, 139.

221 *For "collateral," he wrote*: Goldsmith, in the Moses and Frances Asch Collection at the Smithsonian Center for Folklife and Cultural Heritage Archive.

221 *"As I financed Harry Smith's OKLA trip"*: Postcard from Rooks to Asch, Paris, August 23, 1965, in the Moses and Frances Asch Collection at the Smithsonian Center for Folklife and Cultural Heritage Archive.

223 *When Harry asked their spiritual leader*: Marc Berger email to John Szwed, 2020; James W. Covington, *The Seminoles of Florida* (Gainesville, FL: University of Florida Press, 1993).

224 *"I went to Florida"*: Harry Smith's notes for a research proposal to the Newport Folk Festival, 1965, Smithsonian Center for Folklife and Cultural Heritage Archive.

224 *While Harry was searching*: Izzy Young, "A Tribute to Harry," The American Folklife Center at the Library of Congress.

225 *"There was great difficulty"*: Marc Berger email to John Szwed, 2020.

226 *"If we got cash"*: Berger email to Szwed, 2020.

227 *"When I was in Oklahoma"*: Singh, 85.

228 *"Harry told me that he showed up"*: Bill Breeze email to John Szwed, November 20, 2020.

229 *"on a state holiday"*: Marc Berger email to John Szwed, 2021.

229 *Harry didn't appreciate*: Berger email to Szwed, 2021.

230 *"We visited Ralph Rinzler"*: Berger email to Szwed, 2021.

230 *"About 1300 examples"*: Harry Smith letter to Newport Folk Festival 1965, Smithsonian Center for Folklife and Cultural Heritage Archive.

231 *"Mr. Smith constructed"*: Berger email to Szwed, 2021.

231 *"I thought it was totally astonishing"*: Berger email to Szwed, 2021.

232 *He said that the film*: Harry Smith, Report to Newport Folk Festival, 1966, Smithsonian Center for Folklife and Cultural Heritage Archive.

232 *He had planned a soundtrack*: Harry Smith interviewed by Nick Spitzer.

232 *"What made the . . . Harry Smith fabric movie work"*: Jonas Mekas, "Movie Journal: On Tactile Senses and Television," *The Village Voice*, December 7, 1967.

232 *In his rough draft he began*: Harry Smith, draft of article for the 1966 Newport Program, Smithsonian Center for Folklife and Cultural Heritage Archive.

8. NIGHTS IN BOHEMIA

235 *"Downtown was where it was all happening"*: "That's the Cathedral of Cinema, Don't You Know It?": Jonas Mekas on the Wonders of Downtown New York, *ARTnews*, January 23, 2019, https://www.artnews.com/art-news/artists/thats-cathedral-cinema-dont-know-jonas-mekas-wonders-downtown-new-york-11749/#!.

236 *Ross Wetzsteon*: Russ Wetzsteon, *Republic of Dreams: Greenwich Village: The American Bohemia, 1910–1960* (New York: Simon & Schuster, 2002), 394.

237 *John Cohen remembered*: John Cohen, untitled essay in *Harry Smith's Anthology of American Folk Music, Volume Four*, Revenant Records, RVN 211, 2005, 33–34.

238 *"When someone had aroused"*: Marc Berger email to John Szwed, 2020.

239 *Stan Brakhage felt*: Philip Taaffe, "With Stan Brakhage," https://philiptaaffe .info/statements-interviews-2/a-conversation-with-stan-brakhage/.

239 *Deborah Freeman saw him*: Igliori, 66.

239 *Charles Compo said he always thought it was kind of funny*: Charles Compo email to John Szwed, 2020.

240 *"Harry Smith suddenly materialized"*: Patti Smith, *Just Kids* (New York: Harper-Collins, 2010), 93–94.

241 *"Early in his life"*: Dr. Joe Gross, "Thinking of Harry," Program for *A Night of Art*, 39.

241 *More often it was*: Jonas Mekas, *A Dance with Fred Astaire* (Brooklyn: Anthology Editions, 2017), 145.

241 *"Harry Smith calls"*: Amy Taubin interviews with Jonas Mekas, "Web of Stories," https://webofstories.com/play/jonas.mekas/76.

242 *"There will be $300"*: Moses and Frances Asch Collection at the Smithsonian Center for Folklife and Cultural Heritage Archive.

242 *On the other hand*: John Szwed interview with Caigan, New York, July 21, 2017.

242 *Raymond Foye*: Raymond Foye email to John Szwed, 2021.

242 *Izzy Young told of a cold*: Untitled notes by Israel Young, dated February 25, 1973, Israel Young Collection, The American Folklife Center at the Library of Congress.

243 *"At times virtually homeless"*: Dr. Joe Gross, "Thinking of Harry," 38.

243 *"I visited Harry"*: Anne Waldman email to John Szwed, March 7, 2021.

243 *"Harry had a kind of regal"*: David Amram letter to John Szwed, 2018.

245 *Sometimes Harry also explored*: Kembrew McLeod, *The Downtown Pop Underground* (New York: Abrams Press, 2018), 201, and phone interview with Wendy Clarke, 2020.

245 *SROs, as Lucy Sante*: Luc Sante, "My Lost City," *The New York Review of Books*, November 6, 2003.

247 *In a handwritten note*: Rebecca Kanost, "Off the Hip: A Thermodynamics of the Cool" (PhD dissertation, University of Rhode Island, 2015), 140–42; Shirley Clarke Papers, 1936–1983, Wisconsin Center for Film and Theater Research, Wisconsin Historical Society, Madison, Wisconsin.

248 *Though* Kaleidoscope *seems*: John Klacsmann email to John Szwed, November 1, 2021.

248 *To her, video went beyond*: "Shirley Clarke: An Interview," *Radical Software* ii, no. 4 (1973), 27.

249 *Making a video*: Clarke's later film *Ornette in America* was conceived and edited following the saxophonist Ornette Coleman's melodic lines and phrasing. Ginsberg was also influenced by Ornette's playing—continuing a musical line until he ran out of breath. He translated that into writing lines of poetry until they reached the end of the page.

250 *Down the hall*: Sherill Tippins, *Inside the Dream Palace: The Life and Times of New York's Legendary Chelsea Hotel* (New York: First Mariner Books, 2014), 216–17.

250 *"[Stanley Bard] is hated"*: Marian Janssen, *Not at All What One Is Used To: The Life and Times of Isabella Gardner* (Columbia, MO: University of Missouri Press, 2010), 290.

251 *"I know you are extremely"*: Janssen, 272–73.

251 *When she told her mother*: Janssen, 276.

251 *Dr. Herbert Krohn, singer, poet*: Janssen, 273.

252 *"His room was covered"*: William Moritz, "Harry Smith, Mythologist," Center for Visual Music, 2001, 1–2, http://www.centerforvisualmusic.org /MoritzHarrySmith.htm.

253 *Stern was generous with money*: Barry Miles, *The Beat Hotel* (New York: Grove Press, 2000).

254 *Andrew Noren recalled*: Andrew Noren, unpublished writings on Harry Smith.

256 *Harry, still attempting*: Harry Smith letter to Arthur M. Young, 1980, Getty Library.

256 *They responded by asking*: Blair A. Moffett letters to Harry Smith on February 1, 1980, and March 2, 1980, Getty Library.

256 *There were others*: James Grissom quoted by Anne Richardson, https:// harrysmithpdx.wordpress.com/2013/05/07/genius-in-the-village-tennessee -williams-on-harry-smith/.

257 *Back in 1962, Ed Sanders*: Ed Sanders, Liner notes to *Harry Smith's Anthology of American Folk Song, Volume Four*, 9–10; Ed Sanders, *Fug You* (Boston: Da Capo Press, 2012), 34–35.

259 *Later, he even recorded himself*: "Harry Smith Sings Folksongs of the South," Tape FW-SASCH-7RR-1774, Moses and Frances Asch Collection, Smithsonian Center for Folklife and Cultural Heritage Archive.

260 *Shortly before the record*: "Ed Sanders on Harry Smith," https://allenginsberg .org/2014/08/ed-sanders-on-harry-smith/.

261 *"He stumbled onto the stage"*: Telephone interview with Sitney, 2017; Sitney, 237–38.

261 *Sitney recalls*: Sitney, 237–38.

262 *"Movies are a different thing"*: Igliori, 96–97.

262 *Young's diaries and notebooks*: Arthur M. Young journal, 70; Joan Schleicher email to John Szwed, June 8, 2019.

262 *In 1956, for example*: Arthur M. Young, *Nested Time: An Astrological Autobiography* (Cambria, CA: Anodos Publications, 2004), 180; Joan Schleicher email to John Szwed, June 8, 2019.

264 *"He sat in a café"*: Barry Miles, "The Beat Goes On: A Century of Lawrence Ferlinghetti," http://www.poetryfoundation.org/articles/149462/the-beat-goes-on.

264 *On another occasion*: Mekas, *A Dance with Fred Astaire*, 152, 154.

265 *"Not satisfied with the suggestion"*: Allan Kaprow, "The Legacy of Jackson Pollock," in *Reading Abstract Expressionism: Context and Critique*, Ellen Landau, ed. (New York: Columbia University Press, 2005), 187 (originally published in *ARTnews*, 1958).

266 *"It is because the film is an object"*: Susan Sontag, "Film and Theater," *The Tulane Drama Review* 11, no. 1 (Autumn 1966), 31.

267 *"For the actual Exorcism/Levitation"*: Sanders, *Fug You*, 99, 277–78.

268 *Ukranian Easter eggs*: "What I've been interested in": Singh, 95.

269 *Every Easter he would*: Barry Miles, *In the Sixties* (London: Pimlico, 2002), 272.

269 *Remembering a trip*: John Klacsmann and Andrew Lampert, eds., *Paper Airplanes: The Collections of Harry Smith, Catalog Raisonné, Volume 1* (New York: J and L Books and Anthology Film Archives, 1994), 16.

269 *"He was always, always"*: Klacsmann and Lampert, 17.

271 *"I'm leaving it to the future"*: Igliori, 230.

9. MAHAGONNY

273 *Harry appeared unfazed*: I'm indebted to a close reading and edit of this chapter by Bill Breeze. Any errors are mine.

273 *He approached Warhol*: Singh, 62–63.

274 *When the film he would call* Mahagonny: Harry Smith, *Film No. 18* (New York: Anthology Film Archives, 2002).

274 *It was a description*: The most serious and important of the studies of *Mahagonny* (and one I am indebted to) is Rose Marcus, "Appropriation of the Highest Order: A Study of Harry Smith's Master Work, Film No. 18 Mahagonny in Relation to the Brecht-Weill Opera *Rise and Fall of the City of Mahagonny* and Duchamp's *The Large Glass*" (master's thesis, Hunter College, The City University of New York, 2021).

274 *"Harry may have said"*: Kristine McKenna, "Last Stop, Mahagonny," *LA Weekly*, May 22, 2002.

274 *I selected "Mahagonny" as a vehicle*: Harry Smith grant applications to the American Film Institute Independent Filmmaker Program, 1974, and the Committee on Poetry, 1974, Anthology Film Archives.

276 *At least once*: Singh, 173; William S. Lewis, "Harry Smith's Filmwork and the Possibility of a Universal Symbology," *The American Journal of Semiotics* 17, no. 3 (Fall 2001), 220.

277 *He was captivated*: In his description of his *Film No. 14*, he had suggested that if the sound bulb failed, the projectionist should play Brecht's "Mahagonny."

277 *"One time, when I was sitting"*: Patti Smith, *Just Kids* (New York: Ecco, 2010), 115.

278 *He once described*: "Harry Smith" on the *Experimental Cinema* website, https://expcinema.org/site/en/wiki/artist/harry-smith.

279 *"It's only natural to link"*: Igliori, 175, 182; Barry Williams Hale makes a serious case for Harry's thoughts in Hale's "The Clans of Enok" (no longer on the internet).

280 *Beyond the images themselves*: Anne Friedberg, *The Virtual Window from Alberti to Microsoft* (Cambridge, MA: MIT Press, 2006), 212–13.

281 *"Any one reel is a structure"*: Singh, 106–107.

281 *Caigan, however, noted*: Khem Caigan interviewed by John Szwed, July 21, 2017.

281 *"The original set of* Mahagonny": Singh, 106.

282 *Mekas explained to readers*: Jonas Mekas, "God Helps Harry Smith, Because He Helps Himself," *The Village Voice*, June 13, 1971.

282 *"The experience of what"*: Jonas Mekas, "Movie Journal," *The Village Voice*, May 23, 1974.

283 *At times she also helped out*: Barry Miles, *In the Sixties* (London: Vintage UK, 2003), 178–79.

283 *"Every day I would go"*: Patrick Hulsey, untitled draft, Getty Library. Most accounts of Smith's use of Shirley Clarke's camera say that it was a Bolex, but from Hulsey's description, it was a Beaulieu.

287 *"I was always totally fixated"*: M. Henry Jones, "Henry on Harry," Program for *A Night of Art Film and Ultraperception*, September 14, 2006, The Angel Orensanz Foundation, New York, 32–33.

287 *"He was involved in unframing boundaries"*: Ray Jadwick, "M. Henry Jones & Snake Monkey Studio," in *Captured: A Film/Video History of the Lower East Side* (New York: Seven Stories Press, 2005), 347.

288 *"Harry also pointed out"*: M. Henry Jones, "Henry on Harry," Program for *A Night of Art*, 32–33.

288 *Robert Polidori*: "Robert Polidori," *Bomb*, April 1, 2007, https://bombmagazine.org/articles/robert-polidori/.

288 *Deborah Freeman, a student at Barnard*: Igliori, 59.

289 *"The shots will be edited"*: Harry Smith, draft of grant applications, 1974, Getty Library.

290 *"Harry," he thought*: Clayton Caps (Patterson), "Tattooing on the East Coast," *Tattoo Gazette* 1, no. 2, 1988.

291 *He was a member of Tyler's Phalanstery*: V. Vale, "Uranian Tattoo Magician: Richard O. Tyler," *Tattoo Time* (Tattoo Magic Issue), 1988, 52–60.

292 *When he said folk music*: Bob Dylan, *Chronicles, Volume One* (New York: Simon & Schuster, 2004), 7.

292 *"One thing I remember"*: Singh, 6–7.

294 *"I am writing to you"*: Application from Harry Smith to Andy Berler, Creative Artists Public Service Program, December 12, 1973, in Perchuk and Singh, "Selected Documents," *Harry Smith: The Avant-Garde in the American Vernacular*, 274–75.

297 *"I was in a voluntary trance"*: Harry Smith letter to Arthur M. Young, 1974, Getty Library.

298 *in the Chelsea there were welfare families*: Janssen, 250.

298 *There was also a continuing problem*: Harry Smith taped phone messages, Getty Library.

299 *As Raymond Foye put it*: *The Heavenly Tree Grows Downward*, 39.

10. LOST AND FOUND

301 *"The Breslin years were very quiet"*: Raymond Foye email to John Szwed, 2021.

301 *Asked if he never saw*: Charles Compo email to John Szwed, 2021.

302 *"Mahagonny has required"*: Singh, 108.

302 *"I never made the slightest effort"*: Untitled draft of application for financial support of *Mahagonny*, June 4, 1978, Getty Library.

304 *He ended the show*: John Szwed interview of P. Adams Sitney, 2019.

305 *"He gets into the"*: Scott Feero email to John Szwed, February 2021.

306 *"It was a great success"*: "Gerd Stern—3," The Allen Ginsberg Project, https://allenginsberg.org/2014/10/gerd-stern-3-gerd-stern-remembers-harry-smith/.

307 *When he was introduced*: Mireille Leterrier email to Scott Feero, 2021.

308 *"going at each other the whole time"*: Ted Bafaloukos, *Rockers* (Berkeley, CA: Gingko Press, 2020), 164.

309 *"The Friday and Saturday midnight"*: Raymond Foye email to John Szwed, October 2021.

309 *He clearly enjoyed*: Steven Taylor email to John Szwed, 2021; "Harry Smith," *Cinemanews*, 1978 and 1979, 4.

309 *"He especially liked the punk scene"*: Raymond Foye email to John Szwed, October 2021.

310 *"If (as many suppose), the unseen world"*: Harry Smith's lecture No. 4, "Music + Film," at Naropa University, July 23, 1989.

311 *The press release*: Harry Smith, "Film No. 18" (New York: Anthology Film Archives, 2002).

311 *Originally, he had intended*: Tippins, *Inside the Dream Palace*, 336.

312 *"In the present century"*: Claude Lévi-Strauss, *The Origin of Table Manners: Introduction to a Science of Mythology*, vol. 3 (New York: Harper & Row, 1978 [1968]), 508.

312 *An animated tearing up of real money*: Scott Feero email to John Szwed, December 20, 2020.

313 *As Mekas put it*: Jonas Mekas interview, Getty Library; Tippins, 226–40; Raymond Foye email to John Szwed, 2021.

313 *"I think everyone had the sense"*: Raymond Foye, in Tippins, 337–38.

314 *Their work was helped*: Raymond Foye email to John Szwed, November 1, 2021.

314 *"Smith's* Mahagonny *is essentially an object"*: J. Hoberman, "Mirror Men," *The Village Voice*, September 10, 2002.

315 Film No. 23 *consists of two rolls*: "Excerpts from Harry Smith's Film 23," https://vimeo.com/90566734.

315 *"All in all, the film"*: Harry Smith letter to Marc Silber and Marc Berger, undated, Getty Library. Marc Berger was of great help to the author in clarifying the importance of these figures.

315 *"The first time I ever met Harry"*: Charles Compo email to John Szwed, 2021.

317 *"Oh! I could tell you"*: Harry Smith interviewed by Nick Spitzer.

318 *Thompson's book*: Stith Thompson, *The Folktale* (New York: The Dryden Press, 1946).

319 *The record was not available*: Charles Compo, *Seven Flute Solos*, Smithsonian Folkways 37463.

320 *An exception was Harvey Bialy*: The Harvey Bialy website is no longer available on the web.

321 *Robert Frank thought*: Harry Smith at the Breslin Hotel, 1984, an eleven-minute color film showing him boxing up his books, films, and artworks was not completed until 2017.

322 *In 1984, Ginsberg asked Harry*: A. J. Waring and Preston Holder, "A Prehistoric Ceremonial Complex in the Southeastern United States," *American Anthropologist* 47, no. 1, January–March 1945.

322 *"Suddenly," Foye said*: Raymond Foye, "The Night Bob Came Around," March 22, 2019, https://raymondfoye.info/2019/03/22/on-bob-dylans-birthday/.

323 *During the evening Ginsberg and Dylan*: Raymond Foye email to John Szwed, October 2021.

323 *That same day, Harry called Scott Feero*: Feero email to John Szwed, 2021.

324 *When asked about his move*: *American Magus*, 2002 film by Paola Igliori, https://www.youtube.com/watch?v=s2XqGTn_8Xs.

324 *When the new tenants arrived*: Igliori, *American Magus*.

325 *"In order to get in and out"*: Interview between Allen Ginsberg and Hal Willner recorded at Ginsberg's apartment in New York City in June 1993 for the liner notes of Ginsberg's CD release on Rhino Records, Getty Library.

326 *"That summer I would ride"*: Hari Kunzru, *White Tears* (New York: Knopf, 2017), 3.

326 *Later, when he was again living*: Steven Taylor, *Reality Sandwich* (no longer on the web).

326 *"I had this kind of machine"*: Allen Ginsberg interview, *Harry Smith, American Magus*, 113–14.

327 *"He was excited"*: Peter O. Whitmer with Bruce Van Wyngarden, *Aquarius Revisited: Seven Who Created the Sixties Counterculture That Changed America* (New York: Citadel Press Books, 2007), 141.

328 *Once asked if he had*: Whitmer, *Aquarius Revisited*, 147.

329 *"At one point," Ferris recalled*: Bill Ferris email to John Szwed, October 5, 2020.

330 *Instead, Mekas made him artist*: Mekas, *A Dance with Fred Astaire*, 152, 154.

330 *"I hope you enjoy the films"*: Steven Taylor email to John Szwed, 2021.

331 *Harry submitted a handwritten*: "Life of Harry Smith," Getty Library.

332 *To learn about the Boulder area*: Diane di Prima, "Diane di Prima on Filmmaker Harry Smith," lecture at the Art Institute of San Francisco, undated, Getty Library.

332 *Rani Singh, a student*: Rani Singh, "Harry Smith: An Ethnographic Modernist," in Perchuk and Singh, *Harry Smith: The Avant-Garde in the American Vernacular*, 52.

333 *Within a few weeks*: Interview between Allen Ginsberg and Hal Willner.

333 *He told Beth Borrus*: Beth Borrus, "A Conversation with Harry Smith," *Bombay Gin* 1, no. 4 (Summer 1989), 7, 69–74.

333 *"Harry will sometimes make"*: Warren Karlenzig, Tim Hulihan, and Eileen O'Halloran, "The Art of Alchemy," *As Is* (Boulder, CO: Naropa University, 1989; reprinted in Igliori, 89).

333 *"It was absorbing"*: Taylor, "Remembering Harry," in *Reality Sandwich*.

333 *"One day I was teaching"*: Anne Waldman email to John Szwed, July 7, 2021.

334 *Rani said, "Harry could turn"*: Singh, "Harry Smith," *Film Culture*, 15.

335 *"When Harry would get into"*: Singh, "Harry Smith," 14–15.

336 *"Harry was the only being"*: John Feins email to John Szwed, July 26, 2021.

337 *Ginsberg had his own peculiar attitude*: Bob Rosenthal, "Allen Ginsberg Revisited by his Right-Hand Man," *Local East Village Blog*, 2012, http://www.poetspath.com/Scholarship_Project/bob.html.

337 *"Well, Harry I can't afford"*: Allen Ginsberg letter to Harry Smith, September 8, 1988, in *The Letters of Allen Ginsberg*, Bill Morgan, ed. (Boston, MA: Da Capo Press, 2008), 423–25.

338 *"I owe a lot to Harry"*: Dennis McNally email to John Szwed, October 4, 2021.

339 *"Over his last years"*: Di Prima, "Diane di Prima on Filmmaker Harry Smith."

339 *Stan Brakhage told his film classes*: Stan Brakhage, class lecture, March 3, 1993, Getty Library.

339 *Anne Waldman felt that*: Anne Waldman email to John Szwed, October 2, 2020.

339 *Chuck Pirtle, a graduate student*: Chuck Pirtle email to John Szwed, June 22, 2018.

342 *The poet Charles Stein wrote that*: Charles Stein, "Some Notes on Harry Smith's Alchemy and Magic," unpublished essay, 2020.

343 *preparing two packets of readings*: The articles and excerpts included George Devereaux on "Mohave Ethnopsychiatry and Suicide," a selection of Rube Goldberg cartoons, Christopher Vecsey on the Ojibwa Creation Myth, and Sergai

Kan's writing about the Tlingit Potlatch. For a complete list of readings, see Singh, "Harry Smith," 19. Smith's discussion of the handouts can be found on pages 16–19 of the same article. The last lecture can be heard in the Harry Smith Archive.

344 *"His teeth were so bad"*: Steven Taylor email to John Szwed, March 2021.

11. A NEW YORK ENDING

346 *"[he] mentioned his arthritis"*: Nick Amster email to John Szwed, December 13, 2015.

346 *Scott Feero visited him*: Scott Feero email to John Szwed, 2021.

346 *"The next morning"*: Michaeleen Maher email to John Szwed, April 4, 2021.

347 *He discovered that Jacqueline Gens*: Jacqueline Gens, *Poetrymind*, https://tsetso .blogspot.com/search/label/Harry%20Smith.

347 *"Those last months"*: Raymond Foye email to John Szwed, November 21, 2021.

348 *She visited him*: Rani Singh, "The Last Day in the Life of Harry Smith," *Film Culture*, no. 76 (June 1992), 20–22.

348 *"Harry was bleeding profusely"*: Raymond Foye email to John Szwed, 2022.

349 *"It's strange"*: Raymond Foye email to John Szwed, March 18, 2021.

351 *"It also must be said"*: Goldsmith in the Moses and Frances Asch Collection at the Smithsonian Center for Folklife and Cultural Heritage Archive.

352 *Harry was a witness*: I'm indebted to Ana Cara, who helped me reckon with Smith's influence and importance.

353 *"[the] one thing that he said"*: Igliori, 209.

354 *"Everybody has to eat"*: Singh, 80–81.

355 *"Are you supported"*: Singh, 89.

356 *"I'd seen myself"*: Harry Smith interviewed by Nick Spitzer.

357 *Virginia Woolf*: Virginia Woolf, "Impassioned Prose," *Times Literary Supplement*, September 16, 1926.

357 *In another essay*: Virginia Woolf, "The Eccentrics," *The Athenaeum*, April 25, 1919.

357 *That last sentence*: Eliza Haughton-Shaw, "The Eccentricity of Lydia Davis's Essays," *The London Magazine*, August 18, 2020.

358 *"His Tapes Roll On"*: Peter Stampfel, "His Tapes Roll On." This song can be heard as sung by Stampfel on YouTube.

ACKNOWLEDGMENTS

One of the pleasures of writing a biography is meeting new people while doing research. In the case of Harry Smith, it was an extraordinary group, a diverse body of people who were willing to share their very different memories of Harry and his encyclopedic interests. How fortunate I was to learn from them, for with Harry the traditional sources for a biography were lacking. The facts of his life were hard to locate, but even when they were discovered and added up, it could sometimes seem more like a novel than a biography, though a peculiar kind of novel, like Charlie Kaufman's recent sprawling *Antkind*. In fact, Kaufman's book seems at times to be about someone quite similar to Harry; in it, a filmmaker has spent so many years making a stop-animation film "about everything" that it is so long that it takes three months to view. But when a film critic is transporting the only existing cans of the film to New York City in a U-Haul truck, it catches fire and the film burns up. In an attempt to reconstruct the film frame by frame, the critic, with the help of a hypnotist . . .

Harry's people, those who knew him and were generous with their knowledge, are Rani Singh, Wendy Clarke, Marc Berger, Bill Holm, Dr. Joe Gross, John Cohen, Deborah Freeman, P. Adams Sitney, John Feins, Anne Waldman, Nick Amster, Brian Graham, Terese Coe, Peter Hale, Gerd Stern, Scott Feero, Betzalel Fleischman, Raymond Foye, Peter Lamborn Wilson, Eliot Greenspan, Zia Ziprin, Nick Spitzer, Ann Charters, Anna Lomax Wood, Hal Willner, Khem Caigan, M. Henry Jones, William Breeze, David Amram, William Ferris, Alan Weiss, Charles Stein, Charles Pirtle, Beth Borrus, Peter Stampfel, Rebecca Pirtle, Clayton Patterson, Charles Compo, Steven Taylor, and Marc Silber.

I'm also indebted to those who had already written about Harry: Rani Singh, Raymond Foye, Andrew Perchuk, John Cohen, Darrin Daniel, Steven Taylor, Paola Igliori, Philip Smith, Rose Marcus, Bret Lunsford,

John Klacsmann, Andrew Lampert, Alexander Provan, Ed Sanders, Greil Marcus, Robert Cantwell, Sherill Tippins, and the authors who contributed to Ross Hair and Thomas Ruys Smith's book, *Harry Smith's Anthology of American Folk Music.*

For their help with so many things, I am grateful to Catherine Heinrich, Risé Hall-Norem, George Quasha, Andrew Schelling, Joanna Pawlik, Kerry Colonna, Scott Barretta, Carol Bove, Jay Reed, David Hajdu, Hank O'Neal, and Scott MacDonald. My thanks especially for a Getty Scholar grant and the help of Rebecca Man and Rani Singh, which enabled me to study the Harry Smith collection at the Getty.

My people (if I may be so bold), those whom I often count on for advice and criticism, are Dan Rose, Grey Gundaker, Ana Cara, Valerie Bystrom, Nick Spitzer, Susan Stewart, Sid Sachs, Mary Dearborn, Henry Glassie, Roger Abrahams, Dan Ben-Amos, Robert O'Meally, Steve Feld, Ben Ratliff, Marilyn Szwed, and Matt Szwed.

For this book all praises are due to my longtime agent, Sarah Lazin, and her ace associate, Catharine Strong. At Farrar, Straus and Giroux, my thanks to Jeremy M. Davies, who dared to accept my idea for this book when many publishers had never heard of Harry (or had and didn't want to hear any more). Jackson Howard, my editor, put up with a fair amount of quirkiness from Harry and from me, but with kindness and grace helped steer me through the writing. My thanks also to the much-appreciated work of FSG's Brianna Fairman, Nancy Elgin, June Park, Janet Rosenberg, Debra Helfand, and Steve Weil.

The librarians and archivists—gods for writers and researchers—who aided me are Steven Weiss and Aaron Smithers at the Wilson Library, University of North Carolina at Chapel Hill; Sarah Sherman and Tracey Schuster, the Getty Library; James Stack, the University of Washington Libraries; John Klacsmann, John Mhiripiri, and Robert Haller, Anthology Film Archives; Marian Luntz, the Museum of Fine Arts in Houston; Christina Favretto, the G. Richter Library, University of Miami; Joan Schleicher, the Anodos Foundation Archives; Todd Harvey, the American Folklife Center at the Library of Congress; and Jeff Place, Smithsonian Folkways.

For help with corrections in this edition, my thanks to Grey Gundaker, Andrew Lampert, Rani Singh, Scott Feero, and Bret Lunsford.

INDEX